THE ANTHROPOLOGY
OF ANCIENT GREECE

LOUIS GERNET

THE ANTHROPOLOGY OF ANCIENT GREECE

Translated by
John Hamilton, S.J.
and Blaise Nagy

THE JOHNS HOPKINS UNIVERSITY PRESS
Baltimore and London

This book has been brought to publication with the generous assistance of the David M. Robinson Publication Fund.

Originally published in Paris in 1968 as *Anthopologie de la grèce antique*
Copyright © 1968 by François Maspero

English translation copyright © 1981 by The Johns Hopkins University Press

The Johns Hopkins University Press, Baltimore, Maryland 21218
The Johns Hopkins Press Ltd., London

Library of Congress Cataloging in Publication Data

Gernet, Louis, 1882–1962
    The anthropology of ancient Greece.

    Translation of: *Anthropologie de la grèce antique*.
    Includes bibliographical references and index.
    1. Civilization, Greek—Addresses, essays, lectures.   I. Title.
DF78.G5313   938   81–47598
ISBN 0–8018–2112–6   AACR2

Contents

v

Preface

Not long before his death, Louis Gernet conceived the project of bringing together in a single volume a series of his articles that had appeared in a number of different journals. To determine his choice of articles, he had to take into account not only the relative importance he assigned to his writings but other factors that were beyond his control: the very limited dimension of the work he had in mind, the difficulty or even impossibility of obtaining the original texts, and the more or less specialized character of the periodicals in which they had been published. Some of these periodicals, especially those concerned with the disciplines of sociology and psychology, were unknown to the general public or to Hellenists. Finally, Louis Gernet settled on the following eight contributions that he himself had reviewed, corrected, and brought up to date: "L'Anthropologie dans la religion grecque," "La Notion mythique de la valeur en Grèce," "Dolon le loup," "Droit et prédroit en Grèce ancienne," "Le Temps dans les formes archaïques du droit," "Horoi hypothécaires," "Sur le symbolisme politique: Le Foyer commun," and "Les Origines de la philosophie."

In addition to these eight articles, which appear in the present volume together with the author's revisions, we thought that nine others should be added; they are published here in their original form.

Why, then, this expansion of a project we had so often discussed with our mentor, but that after his death seemed, like Gernet himself, too modest? The reason is this: a whole aspect of Gernet's work—a dimension that might well be called the most important one were it not for the fundamental unity of all his work—has been, and still remains, virtually unrecognized.

Like his friend Henri Jeanmaire, who in the manner of Gernet had contributed to the renewal of Greek studies in France, Gernet did not establish as a goal for himself a career as a Hellenist. This man, who had so many things to transmit and who could have formed so many pupils, passed most of his life as a teacher of Greek prose composition on the Faculté des

vii

Lettres d'Alger. He was over sixty-five when he was able to come to the Ecole Pratique des Hautes Etudes to speak about a subject dear to his heart, one about which he alone could speak. We were a handful who followed his seminars, and most of us were non-Hellenists. During these years, each Thursday morning was a festive day for us, a day of grand intellectual feasting. We saw him arrive with rapid and lively pace, this old man still full of youth; he was tall, with a fine face framed by a well-trimmed beard, and it seemed as if the great Poseidon, such as the figure seen in the Museum at Athens, were coming to us. As a sign of his nonconformism, he wore a black, round hat in the style of Blum, and the cravat of Lavalliere. He carried not a single lecture note; only a few references jotted down on a single sheet of paper. Penal law, testament, property, war, legends and cults of heroes, family and marriage, Orphism and religious sects, tragedy—it did not matter what the question was. Whatever it was, Gernet was at home in his subject, because he was at home in ancient Greece. Like an ethnologist who, beginning with the dawn of civilization, sets out to a distant land, he would never abandon his quest, and would understand the people from within and from without, with the twofold perspective of native and foreigner. Louis Gernet had read everything; in all the areas of Hellenism, his knowledge was faultless. This knowledge went far beyond ours, but it never crushed or paralyzed us. There was not a shadow of pedantry in this learned man, who considered erudition only a means, a tool with which to pose the problems correctly and to discover each time answers that were better nuanced than before. We used to debate every subject freely in his presence, and I cannot think of a better eulogy for him than this: none of us ever feared to lose face because of some error or silly mistake. He rescued us from our own mistakes, gave us direction, and informed us. Our shortcomings were mere trifles in his eyes. The research he pursued continually looked far beyond.

In the course of his precise and fine analysis of institutions, secondary sources, and original documents, the question that was constantly posed by Gernet concerned us directly—it put us at the very heart of things: why and how were these forms of social life constituted, these modes of thought where the West has its origins, where it believes it can recognize itself, and that today still serve as a reference point and justification for European civilization? From this perspective, what one traditionally calls "humanism" finds its proper place, its correct historical context, and becomes something relative. Despoiled of its pretension to incarnate absolute Spirit/eternal Reason, the Greek experience recovers its color and full shape. It finds its full meaning only when confronted with great civilizations as different as those of the Near East, India, China, Africa, and pre-Columbian America; it appears as only one way among others in which human history has developed.

Louis Gernet was better armed than anyone to take his inquiry in this direction. As a philosopher, sociologist, and Hellenist, he belonged to the generation of Herz, Mauss, and Granet. They were all his friends and he shared their intellectual scope. If one rereads his first article of 1909 on the supply of grain for Athens in the fifth and fourth centuries B.C.; or his doctoral thesis on the development of juridical and moral thought in Greece, which was so strongly influenced by Durkheim; and if one compares them to the study that near the end of his life he published in the *Journal de psychologie*, one discovers a twofold and constant concern: to take the sum total of human realities at every level as the starting point, to extract the core of this dense form, to measure the social import, but never to separate the realities from psychological attitudes or from the mental processes without which the first appearance and the eventual progress and changes of institutions would not be intelligible.[1]

To carry out this task effectively in the study of the ancient world, there had to be in one and the same man the perspective proper to the specialist, as well as an even larger view with which to situate a research project within the totality of the social and spiritual life of the Greeks and to integrate it with the complex that forms civilization. Gernet was a specialist in each area: philology, the science of law, social and economic history—he was a master of all these, as well as one of those individuals who had penetrated with accuracy and profundity the forms of Greek religiosity. Familiar with the philosophical debates and with those of the law courts, well versed in the poets, historians, and medical writers, Gernet could on every occasion contemplate the Greek in his entirety, while always respecting the specific nature of different areas of human experience, their own logic and language. Thus, the correlations that he established between the different factors of civilization are never presented only in terms of influences or parallels; they are also studied in terms of the dissonances, contradictions, and diversions that are present within the same system, giving it movement and life.

Marcel Detienne has helped in the publication of this volume. In the same spirit of loyal admiration for Louis Gernet, he has helped us in the choice of texts and has read over the entire volume in proof form. And we believe that this volume appears at just the right time. After publication of the new edition of *Droit et société en Grèce ancienne*—where the juridical studies of the author are collected—another facet of his work will be accessible to the public. But there is a more profound reason. At a time when one can envisage the elimination of human nature as the object of science, when someone can write, "in our times we can no longer think except in terms of the void left by the disappearance of man,"[2] the research of Louis Gernet is in our eyes something of great worth. What interests this sociologist, who is also a historian, is not so much the foundations of systems as the manner in which they were successively established, modified, and destroyed: the periods of crisis, the changes, the ruptures, the innovations in all areas of social life. These facts of change, abrupt and profound, whether technological, religious, scientific, or aesthetic in nature, always have a dimension that is properly human. It is possible to understand their dynamism only if one asks oneself questions not about man but about the particular mentality of the men and human groups that have put all these things in motion, and only if one attempts to penetrate their modes of thought, their intellectual tools, their forms of action and feeling, and their psychological categories, in the sense Mauss gives to this term. Louis Gernet demonstrates this point of view decisively when he examines a whole series of "turning points" in ancient Greece, where intellectual and social changes appear in dialectical relationship: the emergence of law from prelaw, the creation of coinage and the development of an economic system from modes that imply a mythical notion of value, the birth of the city and political thought, the origin of philosophy.

In the France of May 1968, where so many things have changed so rapidly, where so many new phenomena have appeared that could never have been anticipated, the work of Louis Gernet, though it deals with a very distant past, is nonetheless, because of its scope and anthropological dimension, a book that is truly alive.

JEAN-PIERRE VERNANT

NOTES

1.   In the review in *Année sociologique* that is dedicated to Gernet's work on the provisioning of grain, Simiand underlines the interest of a research that is not content with a simple description of facts but keeps as an integral part of the economic service studied "a certain sum of collective psychological states, a certain grouping of complex and special ideas that the Athenians had concerning the role of their city and the provisioning of grain."

In a report written between 1907 and 1910 for the Fondation Thiers, in which he summarized the orientation of the work that would conclude with his dissertation, Louis Gernet wrote: "I conceive of this work as a study of philology and law. The texts are sufficiently abundant, and sufficiently limited. Attic law is sufficiently original that one can arrive at some truly interesting and general conclusions. What connection is there between terminology and content? How can we explain the indetermination so often observed in the juridical terminology of the Greeks, and so often contrasted with the rigorous preciseness of the Latin terminology? How does juridical terminology develop, and eventually take its established form? How do the words of common language take on specialized form in the juridical context? How do changes in meaning and changes of vocabulary operate? And in what measure do they both correspond to the transformation, abandonment, or genesis of certain juridical and moral ideas? Finally, if there is, to be sure, a history of concepts connoted by words, what profit can we draw from the study of vocabulary for an understanding of the juridical psychology of the Athenians from the sixth to fourth centuries B.C.? For example, of contemporary 'prejuridical' notions of private vengeance and family sovereignty? What remains—if we are to scrutinize the use of words—that is conscious or implicit in the collective ideas that the Athenians of the classical epoch make of laws? These are the principal questions that I have in mind. Convinced of the interest that a comparative study would offer for my work, I will study certain suggestive elements in the terminology of law codes closest to Greek law. I have begun the study of Sanskrit: the direct knowledge of Hindu codes would be invaluable to me." (These lines are cited by George Davy in *Hommage à Louis Gernet* [1966].)

  2. Michel Foucault, *Les Mots et les choses* (1966), p. 353.

Translators'
Acknowledgment

Our special gratitude goes to Robert Healey, S.J., and Gregory Nagy, whose collaboration and many suggestions have been very helpful; and to Pearl Jolicoeur, for her expert work with the manuscript. We also wish to thank Edward Benson, Paul Perrot, and William Weeks, S.J. Finally, thanks are due to the College of the Holy Cross for its partial support of this project through a grant from the Charles and Rosanna Batchelor (Ford) Foundation.

JOHN HAMILTON
BLAISE NAGY

PART I

RELIGION
AND SOCIETY

CHAPTER 1

Anthropology in Greek Religion

Although in recent years the word "anthropology" has been subjected to different interpretations, its specific meaning is clear. Basic to an accurate reading of this study is an understanding of anthropology as the description and characterization of human activity in its religious dimension and the role that is assigned to the human within a world whose economy is religious. What is of particular interest in an anthropological study is the question about the barrier between human and divine reality: what separates the human from the divine, and, conversely, what brings them together?

This question is multifaceted, but its very complexity is in some way its uniting principle. It is our starting point. One of the first questions, of course, is how one can even speak of *Greek* religion. A reality of this order is extraordinarily complex. Our purpose in dealing with it will be as follows: (1) to define those religious concepts and trends for which we have more direct and accessible evidence from Greek anthropology; (2) to uncover the structure of this diverse body of evidence, granted that there is one for its different sectors; (3) to understand how this complex of religious concepts and trends eventually disintegrated. Our study is admittedly limited in perspective, since it deals with the history of the Greek polis, "city-state," a period stretching from the seventh or sixth century B.C. to the time of Alexander.

We intentionally begin our study by describing certain fundamental attitudes about life which prevailed in that period. The testimony concerning human nature, its range of activities and its potentialities, is often contradictory. For example, the famous choral passage from Sophocles'

This article originally appeared in *Anthropologie religieuse* (supplements to *Numen*), II (1955), pp. 49–59.

Antigone, although extolling man as the possessor, even the creator, of seemingly limitless skills, identifies two forces that make him absolutely limited: death, an invincible barrier, and the gods, who are man's source of justice. In Sophocles' words, man is a "marvelous thing" but he is radically limited and cannot act as an autonomous person.

The Prometheus myth, although articulated differently, carries the same kind of contradictory message. Although Prometheus is a symbol of human enterprise and its technological products, he is an immortal creature, a superior being to whom mortal men are indebted for their very means of activity and livelihood. But even these skills, the gifts of Prometheus, are not sufficient for man's survival. As even Protagoras, although a Sophist, admits, Prometheus ultimately fails, for he does not give man the quality absolutely necessary for human existence in an organized world: justice. It is Zeus alone who bestows justice on man. In other words, Zeus actually completes the work begun by Prometheus.

Justice, although it is coextensive with the city-state, is not coextensive with its citizens. For the polis is a transcendent reality, as the gods are transcendent over men. Condemnations of *hubris*, of excess, of prolonged dizzying success, as well as the appeals for moderation and self-knowledge, which is an awareness of one's limitations—all of these take on profound *religious* significance within the context of the polis. Such attitudes do not mean, as Philo of Alexandria later claimed, that man is nothing; but they do contain elements of restriction, limitation, and submission. These attitudes are part of the message of Delphi, the sanctuary of Apollo, where man seeks the source of ultimate wisdom. Apollo, its master, an exalted god, can be accommodating to his pious devotees; but his actions are often capricious. He is ultimately an unapproachable deity with whom communion is virtually impossible. As an oracular god, he can only portion out to men a fate in which he cannot allow anything but the most limited sort of freedom.

Such attitudes, if qualified, could still be termed optimistic. After all, within this religious view of the human and the divine, the universe is thought of as an ordered one. The concept of a *kosmos*, "structured world," can develop, particularly in certain speculations; however, in poetry it finds its spontaneous expression in a kind of popular philosophy where concepts of law and justice have a more or less cosmic application. It is especially in the perception of an ordered universe that human thought makes contact with the divine. Here "Zeus" becomes merely a symbol of what is perceived as an impersonal structure. When the Greeks speak of divine causality, they deliberately make use of a collective or neutral expression such as "the divinity" or "the gods." This contrasts strikingly with the very individualistic description of deities when they are not particularly active, that is, outside the realm of divine causality.

Outside of cult, which establishes (but under conditions established by the *mos maiorum*) contact and in some manner communication between the world of men and the world of gods, the general conception is that of two worlds, two races mutually inaccessible. This distance between men and gods is a major theme of the poetry of Pindar, the faithful interpreter of Delphic wisdom.

There are, of course, all sorts of other things also in the most obvious religious thought from this same period. Much has been made, for example, of the opposition between Apollo and Dionysus. These two deities are in fact antithetical. The religion of Dionysus, or to be more exact, certain aspects of it, signifies a liberation or exaltation of the human spirit through *ekstasis*, "escape from the here and now," and *enthousiasmos*, "divine possession." But do these experiences really bridge the gap between man and gods? Is the Dionysiac experience the same as communion? Even for his devotees, Dionysus is an elusive deity. Though one can recognize a momentary fusion between man and god in this cult, the union is not strictly a personal one. The historical evidence makes it clear that the religion of Dionysus had to be integrated into the religious life of the city-state, where it not only adjusted to the polis but found definite limits as well. There is great significance and symbolism in the fact that Dionysus was received, more or less early, at the shrine of Apollo at Delphi. Once this god was incorporated into the civic cult of Apollo, the potentials for a religion of individuality, inherent in the service of Dionysus, could not really develop.

Another important religious phenomenon for our consideration is the religion of the Mysteries, specifically the Mysteries of Eleusis. They contain a concept of religious experience different from that found in the cults of Apollo or Dionysus. Overt in Eleusinian ritual is an idea of communion; its raison d'être is the promise of immortality. Meeting man's needs in a more specific way than the religion of Dionysus, the cult of Eleusis allows no barriers. Even so, to a certain degree, and not unlike the cult of Dionysus, the religion of Eleusis was also integrated into the polis. Its patronage was part of the Athenian ancestral religion, and is practiced through the laws of the polis.

The Eleusinian religion, then, is not the equivalent of an independent, churchlike structure, even though its originality lies in its possession of a single tenet. But this doctrine remains localized, and cannot be termed representative of Hellenic religious thought.

It is within the framework of this thought that the Greek concepts of the soul must be examined. At first it is quite noteworthy that even in Dionysiac religion, and in the Eleusinian as well,[1] the concept of the soul has no part. It is true that the idea of the soul has an important place in mystic speculation and in the Pythagorean and Platonic teachings; but such a view has no intrinsic connection with the current conception. Plato recognizes this from the very moment he begins to discuss immortality. Moreover, it is not surprising that the idea of the soul in contemporary thought is of a nature that we would coarsely call positive. Its objectification scarcely goes beyond the giving of a name: *psukhē* designated either the complex of conscious activities of the person or a vaguely perceived principle from which these activities flow on the plane of present life. From a most ancient period, and even today in certain philosophical traditions, the term "soul" covers totally different notions. Homer, as we shall see, uses *psukhē* in a radically different way that is almost opposite from our usual understanding of the term. But in texts that still belong to the archaic period we meet a change of meaning—it is not excessive to call it a mutation and it is extraordinarily revealing.

This does not, of course, exhaust our survey. We have to mention "superstitions" or "survivals."

In a discussion of the soul, scholars have mentioned two related subjects: (1) the wandering souls of the dead, that is, ghosts and the like; (2) the kingdom of Hades, that is, as a kind of Hebrew Sheol. There are other concepts, more specific in nature and more consistent in their conceptual development: for example, the concept of a personal *génie*, analogous to the Latin *genius*, though the *génie* was never an object of cult before the Hellenistic period. At the other end of the spectrum are the cults of the dead, which are essentially familial in nature. Even these, though they imply a vague idea of survival after death, offer no concrete representation of immortality or even, at the outside, any real relief. Moreover, poetry can use images rather freely. For it, death is represented in terms of a separation of the "body" from the "soul." The "body" returns to the earth, and the "soul" is received into the ether. These are the terms that not only appear in an epitaph for fallen warriors from 432 B.C., but can also be found in the poetry of Euripides. In all this material there appears no expression of a firm belief in the soul's immortality or the kind of pathetic concern that would sustain such a belief.

There is, however, one idea that is integral to the structure of the Greek religious universe under discussion: the concept of the hero. Because of its great significance, it merits special attention.

Heroes are members of a separate race that lies halfway between gods and men. Although originally human, they acquired after death a superhuman condition or status. There is no simple answer to the question concerning the origins of heroes. The variety of heroes is large, and one can see in it several stages of historical and social development.

The notion is nourished first of all in a very ancient background: the hero is often associated with the earth and fertility. No matter who he is, the hero always retains his connection with these elements. Under the title of *arkhēgetēs*, "founding leader," he perpetuates the memory of the divine king who dispenses prosperity to his people. On yet another level, the hero is perceived as the warrior, one of those men from Hesiod's Fourth Age. He is also the ancestor of members of the nobility, who must cultivate him especially. All these views converge in the historic period when the hero finally becomes the protector of the polis. The ranks of heroes remain open, and some eminent or outstanding men can still enter them *after* death.

The heroic idea is closely connected with the pattern of religious thought which we have been discussing and which is that of classical Greece. Although the heroic condition elevates humanity since it involves humanity, it still emphasizes, even in the conception of an intermediary reality, the fact that man is in a congenital state of subordination and restriction. For the heroic condition is, by definition, an exception to the rule. The majority of heroes belong to a lost past, an unhistorical period. Although there are later additions to the heroic ranks, rules of admission are, at least in theory, extraordinarily rigid. One notes an interesting example from Delphi, which had the last word in naming later heroes: at the end of the fifth century B.C., the oracle proclaimed that one of its canonizations was its very last.

A very specific quality of the heroic condition is its gratuitous nature. The achievement of heroic status, even in the distant past, did not necessarily require merit or extraordinary exploits, and some late entrants into the heroic ranks seem especially surprising. What decides who is to be a hero is, above all, a "sign" (such as a disappearance), revealing for the space of a moment a sudden break in the barrier that separates men from gods. Finally, the hero's historical personality tends to evanesce within the framework of cult. His power is a functional one situated on an intermediate level, without the hero's normally penetrating into the divine realm and becoming an intercessor between it and the world of men.

At the time when the "serenity of the Greek soul" was a commonplace, one could simply stop there. Indeed, it must be said that this concept, along with its nuanced variants, has been the view of the great Hellenists; and it corresponds with a historical reality, that is, with the existence of a certain system of thoughts and attitudes. It matters little that this system includes elements that are diverse or even heterogeneous. Even opposition forms a part; Dionysus balances Apollo. But in fact one can sense certain tensions. It is not easy, for example, to accept the view that man, as such, can in no way attain a divine condition.

There could be something revealing in the very insistence with which Pindar repeats the lesson of Delphi: "Do not attempt to be god." Could this be a temptation Pindar is condemning? In reality, the lesson can be expressly contradicted. We are not, for the moment, thinking of "Orphic" teachings, since they can be regarded, strictly speaking, as only marginal. But when Aristotle maintains that the sage can become immortal in some fashion, he denies the truth of a traditional saying that he does not fear to cite: it is the saying of Pindar word for word. In an entirely different realm, there is a striking episode that we know of almost by chance: Lysander, the conquerer of Athens and the liberator of the cities it had subjugated, becomes the object of a cult in Asia Minor. He is not made into a hero after his death; he is deified while alive, just as the kings in the Hellenistic period will be. Slavish adulation, we might say; but why did it take this aberrant form?

These facts are all of a different sort, but they have this in common: they contradict a form of what might be called "normal" Hellenic thought. They also raise one or two historical problems: one about the origins of the philosophical tradition; and another about the "resurgences" revealed in the worship of rulers or kings. Some heritages weigh heavily on all human thought; and they sometimes destroy equilibrium.

It is a rather striking fact that what seemed to us a leading and particularly significant concept in a Hellenic view of the world—that is, the idea of the hero—did not really survive the demise of the polis. From the Hellenistic period onward, new values are introduced; and if the cult of heroes remains faithful to tradition, the category of hero as such is no longer recognizable in the final forms it has reached. On the one hand, the title of hero is generalized and is eventually applied to all the dead. On the other hand, the ambiguity between the heroic and the divine condition is accentuated, at least for the type of heroes who represent social functions: the military chief, the lawmaker, the founder of a colony, the restorer of the city. It is possible to speculate that the idea of the "divine man" did survive beneath the surface; already the Delphic oracle itself— or so it seems—vacillated between calling Lycurgus a man or a god. In the period of the city, the tendency is severely restricted; one is tempted to say that it is almost suppressed. The case of Lysander, then, is exceptional and striking. But we observe that, even while acknowledging the role of "oriental influences," one can recognize the culmination of a Hellenic tendency in the cult of monarchs in the Alexandrian period. This can also be seen in the post-mortem divinizations that alternate almost arbitrarily with heroizations.

As remarkable as this group of facts is, there is one in particular of much larger significance. In the more or less predominant representation of the "soul," the religious mentality is, at the least, uniquely dormant; this is a contradictory feature found in a group of beliefs that go far back and have important historical consequences.

Although this is an important item, we can barely find its origins; and its raison d'être in the most ancient literary testimony, a sure source of authority for the Greek, completely escapes us. The Homeric concept is far removed from what we might call the "mystical" one. Under the designation *psukhē*, insofar as it refers to a being, Homer preserves only the meaning of a "double," that which appears or is realized only at the moment of death in order to be consigned as an ephemeral phantom to an inaccessible and shadowy afterlife. As for the functions that are specifically psychological (especially the *thumos:* will and consciousness), these are linked to the living body and disappear at death. The prejudice is obvious. Still, one can assume that the Homeric view masks some profundities.

It is difficult to examine these; and this is not really our purpose. Let us merely say that we have the witness of a very ancient thought wherein the dead, directly attached to the world of man and nature (and in particular to the Earth Mother), are integrated into the life of an essentially local group—a life represented as cyclic. In this complex, which gave rise to many images, the image of "breath" (suggested by the etymology of the word *psukhē*) has to be important. (The *Tritopatores*, patrons of births, are both "winds" and "ancestors.") None of this ancient background appears any longer in Homer. In this psychological representation of the living, there is the same stylization and transcendence: in his handling of a traditional vocabulary, which gradually takes on what we would call an abstract force, and in his anatomical descriptions (the *phrenes*, for example, are a part of the body, but which part is not exactly clear; and they are the "spirit" or the "intelligence"), we recognize the heritage and the wear and tear of a formulaic style. But we know from the Greeks themselves (excluding Homer) that behind this Homeric mentality, which the *phusiologoi* will only prolong, there exists a very archaic representation that makes certain organs of the body privileged ones or gives them religious value. These organs include not only the head and the heart but the diaphragm, the lungs, the liver, and certain "humors" with which the imaginative thinking about the "soul" is narrowly associated in a kind of participationist mentality. The poet is unaware of these or chooses to ignore them.

One could say, therefore, that in spite of archaic expressions, Homer is moving in the direction of a "classical" mode of thought. He is, in a way, a prelude to it; but perhaps at the very time when the Homeric poems were being formulated an entirely different mode of thought was asserting itself in a world that we know only through a more or less mythological tradition. But it is still possible to identify this world with some certainty, since from one figure of mythology to another its traits are recovered or at least they complement one another. We are thinking of those marvelous figures who are called, in succession, sages or prophets: the Pythagoras of legend represents an outstanding example or offshoot, already suggestive by himself alone. Purifiers, healers, magicians, thaumaturges on occasion, and especially prophets, or rather seers—their legends allow us to recognize two essential elements: a systematic practice of asceticism (with clear traces of a yogalike discipline); and a fundamental theme, with aspects sometimes shamanistic, of the wandering soul, and of reincarnations as well.

If we see here nothing more than an accident in the history of Greek thought, then this would be the place to stop our inquiry. But this movement must be significant; it reveals in the archaic period, when it occurs, distinctive aspirations and a mentality that moves in a direction opposed to the spirit prevailing in the most obvious type of Hellenism. We can see this movement's extension; it is no stranger to the beginnings of philosophy (in the fifth century B.C., Empedocles strikingly recreated a kind of *magus*). It spread teachings that bore fruit both in the philosophical schools and in the religious sects. If the Platonic doctrine of the soul is far from being a carbon copy, it still owes its inspiration to the teachings of this movement; and these are recognizable in Plato. One finds them in a "mystery" religion that we designate by the somewhat conventional epithet "Orphic," but a religion whose tenets are of the same type and tone. In this same context, it is worth considering a form of religious speculation that puts the human soul in direct relationship with a divine world soul. Though quite marginal in the classical period, this speculation will have an illustrious future. Nothing in all this allows us to formulate a body of doctrines; but there are common tendencies, and they are equally aberrant.

There is first a common aspiration: a desire to enter into immediate and substantial contact with the divine. At its extreme, there is the ambition to become a god. Empedocles himself claims to be one. The so-called Orphic *lamellae*, which were deposited in tombs and have been compared to a "Book of the Dead," contain an explicit profession of faith: the dead person becomes a "hero" or a "god" (and we know that henceforth each is the equivalent of the other). Nevertheless, divine character cannot be inborn; to put it more precisely, it must be regained. The soul, having fallen, must be saved; for it now has a history that is unfolded outside the visible world and that goes back to a prior existence. The superiority of "spiritual" existence as a reality apart, a cycle of successive lives, and the possibility of redemption—all these ideas, which were the starting points of the tradition, have remained its essentials.

Apart from this belief of "sects," whose development was unique in the Platonic transformation, but whose extension was restrained, it is worth insisting on certain ideas that emerged from the same attitude of mind. They interest us on two levels. On the one hand, we find the extension of a prehistoric mentality, which we have seen flourish here and there, but which takes on a truly new sense in this instance because of the pathos it carries with it. On the other hand, though these notions are localized and occasional, it is possible to recognize in them preludes to a form of religious mentality that will develop in the following age.

One of these concepts is that of the individual *daimōn*. It has several aspects, but a common inspiration. First, it is the genius we alluded to earlier; but it is also the general title of divine beings. The idea of *daimōn* gravitates toward a very distinctive concept of divinity: the divinity dwelling in man which is revealed after his death and sometimes even during his lifetime. Empedocles is a *daimōn;* the famous dead are *daimones.* Plato ascribes a statute concerning them to the "guardians" of his city in the cult he instituted in honor of their *manes.* This is very different from the traditional view of the hero; it is a sign of a new kind of mentality which holds out for man unprecedented possibilities.

But the idea that nature itself is *demonic* (a formula of Aristotle) conflicts with this new view in a representation that is merely indicated. The spiritual being of the individual is not solitary (as that of the Greek man normally is). In the thought of Plato, man's spiritual being is reunited with the world soul; but outside philosophy—or parallel to it— there appears an analogous concept, and in unique forms. This is the place to mention everything involving "breath," "inspiration," "chance" (strangely associated altogether with a physical representation and the idea of a divine grace), and even the famous theory of the purification of passions, which, according to Aristotle, includes elements that are indivisibly physiological, psychological, and metaphysical.[2] The divine pneuma with which the individual can be in immediate communication appears at the center of a doctrine that has a conspicuous form; through some of its themes, it re-creates, in a strange way, a type of "primitive" mentality. And it leads to a religious representation of the universe, either Stoic or mystic, in which the place and worth of the human person are raised as questions. In other words, it poses the problem of man's personal means of access to the divine.

There is another characteristic element: in the graphic portrayal of man and the world, there is a change in orientation. One form of traditional thought, a heritage of groups living in symbiosis with the soil they occupy, has as its dominant image the land as the source of life and receptacle of the dead. An opposite polarization shows up immediately in the form of star worship, which is a striking new phenomenon of Platonism's last period. But this mutation is not only attested in Plato. This is a new religious attitude taking shape; it is an affirmation of the divine nature of the stars and the affinity between their existence and that of the soul. Here we discover the origin of an imaginative thought whose ultimate fortune in the Greco-Roman world needs no mention.

In comparison to the vision of the world that we qualify summarily as Hellenic, we clearly recognize the singularity of diverse and yet converging mentalities. There is an inversion of perspective: the "divine" is no longer a reality for "contemplation" only; in its own way, it is a being that turns toward man. And correspondingly, it is the concept of the soul and its future which recaptures with new content the religious stability that had been all but lost; this occurs by means of an integration of what is most remote in human memory.

We have already alluded to derivations. It is possible to recognize as such—at whatever level they are located, and in terms of whatever Oriental factors influenced them—certain striking phenomena of the postclassical period: the cult of monarchs, salvation religions, the doctrine of the cosmic God, and so forth. There is a startling and sudden emergence; a new type of humanity is proclaimed. But as we have seen, this new humanity has here and there its antecedents.

Perhaps Hellenic humanism concealed its own distinctive contradiction. The mental universe, which corresponds to a "political" society wherein the unifying principle is that of the abstract and interchangeable "citizen," is in fact that cosmos in which "man" find his place, but in which "men" do not as readily. This universe is ordered in a compelling way, but its equilibrium is unstable. From this universe it is impossible to abstract the past that survives in it and lends itself to striking transformations, or the future that is being readied in it, or the kind of dialectic that, once the age of the city-state had passed, led to its breakup.

NOTES

1. See U. von Wilamowitz-Moellendorff, *Der Glaube der Hellenen*, II, p. 59.
2. Concerning this entire aggregate, see P. Boyancé, *Le Culte des Muses*, pp. 185–99.

CHAPTER 2
Ancient Feasts

IIere and there within the religion of Greece elements of folk origin are still easily recognized. This is an observation so common that it does not need restating. There is, however, in this general area a subject that merits consideration on its own. But first I ask that these notes be regarded as just notes. This is not going to be a systematic study of the folk religion of Greece; such a study, I suppose, is not even recommended. Nor is this going to be an attempt to track down the "primitive," if primitive is defined beforehand as a group of concepts that have been made familiar to us by ethnographic studies. Such an undertaking, though useful in its time, has become a project that is hardly worthwhile, and one suspects it is no longer relevant. The present project is much more modest. We will consider in their concrete forms a certain number of ancient customs that belong to folk practices and at the center of which are feasts or revelries as they are understood in a religious sense. We are dealing with, or hope to deal with, an attempt to describe the emotional life of a society and the equally ancient pulse or rhythm[1] that these feasts reveal. We will also try to uncover, in the actual thinking that forms their background, the nucleus of certain religious and legal concepts and their course of development.

This twofold plan seems legitimate. Surely, primitive customs and concepts as a rule have undergone a great deal of elaboration, and the primitive layer is seldom obvious. In many places—and these are the ones we know best—the peasant has suffered a forceful urban encroachment. This intrusion by the city favored a cultural development characterized by free abstraction and stylization, elements that make the Greek so difficult to define. Even so, we do have direct testimony bearing on the persistent features of a more or less independent rural culture that lasted far into the full historical period. And the method of recognizing some of

This article originally appeared in *REG*, XLI (1928), pp. 313–59.

these cultural transformations does not necessarily involve a circular argument.

In the religion of the city, communal meals had an important place,[2] and in rites[3] and myths,[4] food is an important feature. A convenient formula can be used to explain the religious importance of the sacrificial meal, but it is an abstract one. There were antecedents to the relatively recent *hestiasis*, and some continuity with a very ancient past does exist. In the historical period, for example, women distributed food at feasts;[5] in such a role one can see clear evidence of an archaism,[6] and immediately it is possible to realize that a very ancient religious feature was taken over very early. The nobleman, according to Pindar, does not forget the origin of his special prestige, namely those "banquets of the gods," none of which he misses, since it is his function to provide them at his own expense.[7] But what were they before the appearance of leaders, a social hierarchy, an Olympus?

I

If any of these festivals are to be defined even partially, the most specific and concrete ones must be studied first.

Rural festivities are most evident in those banquets that are held over beds of leaves (*stibades*) and under tents (*skēnai*). Such customs, which bear the marks of their origins, remain singularly alive. In some relatively late texts, the verb *skēnoun* is still used as a synonym for "to sacrifice."[8] The sacrifices in question are the occasions for banquets, and in one case it is prescribed that they take place in the sanctuary itself.[9] Although we are not forced to conclude, as the verb indicates, that they always take place under tents, the semantics reveal a long-lived association of ideas, and in fact the tradition of using tents is often maintained for important celebrations. One need not ask if Euripides is archaizing when he describes in clearly significant terms[10] the banquet prepared at Delphi by Ion on his supposed father's orders. It is given under a huge tent; the only difference in this case is that the setting is a town, and we are dealing with the town's citizens as well as a king who entertains. The custom's close connection with its origins can be seen more clearly in a series of examples of Laconian festivals of a basically pre-Dorian type. They appear in the Karneia,[11] in the Hyakinthia during the ceremony called *kopis*, and in the Tithenidia.[12] There are also examples in the Mysteries of Andania[13] and in the cult instituted by Xenophon to honor the rustic Artemis.[14]

The *stibades* offer even more irrefutable evidence of archaism. They belong to a long-lived tradition; Herodes Atticus, with his religious snobbism, takes special delight in their archaic quality.[15] What is more illuminating is the discovery that the *stibades* in the Lacedaemonian *kopis* exist side by side with the custom of using tents.[16] Of even greater interest is the fact that one can catch a neat glimpse of the *stibades* in a distinctly archaic rite of Ephesus, whose etiological tale gives us a taste of its original freshness: one day the king's daughter led a group of boys and girls off to carouse in a field of wild celery,[17] and this became the origin of an annual feast.

All of this already suggests that the most ancient festivals are not narrowly localized within the town or village. They are generally celebrated in the middle of the countryside, in the fields. Practices such as the *aiōra*,[18] as well as the cults of rural heroes who represent avatars of peasant religion, attest to the importance of forests. The importance of springs, lakes, and rivers[19] will appear most appropriate to sexual rites, where there is an element of essentially the same origin. The importance of high places is apparent in some archaic ceremonies, such as the annual processions to the summits of Pelion and Cyllene.[20] This importance of heights is one of the clearest features of ancient festivals,[21] and it accounts for expressions of "ascents" and "descents" which, applied to festivals before being applied to the gods, had a direct and concrete meaning.[22] The sea, on the other hand, appears to play only a minor role.[23] Finally, to complete the picture, we should not forget the *sēmeia*, the strange "marks" in the soil. Legends must have been attached to these very early on; but at times, even without legends, they determined the places for festivities[24] before they became *thesmia*,[25] that is, marks of property and power among leaders of the *genē* and mythical themes surrounding the early "kingships."

Within this scheme must be represented the large festival, like the ones in Arcadia, a land of the lost past, where "everyone, even the slaves, takes part in festivals."[26] Here a brief reference we happen to have about the Thargelia of Miletus takes on considerable importance: "Much wine is brought here as a contribution, and precious belongings are distributed."[27] The "theme of consumption" should be noted right away. Virgil supplies us with a legitimate parallel when he says of his rustics,

Frigoribus parto agricolae plerumque fruuntur,
mutuaque inter se laeti convivia curant.
                              Georg., I.300

Plenty of food and plenty of drink. It is not without reason that in a popular song accompanying rural merrymaking, Dionysus, or rather "the

god," is described as *esphudōmenos*, the "stuffed one."[28] There is also reason why the same Dionysus, a god of vegetation in general, has been kept
in the winter festivals as an authentic patron of wine and the vine. The
large peasant cups remain an essential accessory to certain Theoxenia, or
divine receptions for the Dioscuri, festivals that maintain their popular
character.[29] In addition, it can be suspected that the expression *oinos xeni-
kos*, whose meaning in an inscription from Thera is difficult to determine,[30]
dates from a very early period, one earlier than the nobility's custom of
the "cup of hospitality."[31]

It would be of some interest to know what is eaten at festivals; but
we lack precise details on this subject. It would be important to know if
large animals are eaten. I would tend to think—but without supporting
evidence—that the sacrifice of cattle represents a stage later than the customs we are talking about. It is true that it is an ancient practice; witness
the sarcophagus of Hagia Triada. Still, the problem is to know if the sacrifice of cattle, since it remained the sacrifice par excellence of the polis,[32]
was not, in principle, a "royal" sacrifice.[33] The persistent traditions of respect for work animals,[34] traditions that specifically oppose ritual practices, might indicate a prehistoric taboo against animal sacrifice. There is
also something to be learned from those legends or traditions which suggest the great antiquity of bloodless sacrifices.[35] But these traditions do not
always exclude the use, even the religious use, of all animal food. The Pythagoreans did not always despise it, and even Pythagoras sometimes ate
pig and goat.[36] In an archaic ceremony of the Hyakinthia,[37] or in a no less
archaic festival of the Argolid, goats ("and no other animal") are sacrificed to be eaten.[38] As far as meat and vegetables are concerned, their religious importance seems to indicate their ancient status. In this connection,
one must keep in mind the boiling of seeds in the Pyanepsia and the *khu-
troi* of the Anthesteria.[39] Moreover, in the popular festivals, loaves of
bread are used which at times have special shapes and names unique to
the locale.[40]

❀

Our task is to understand a little better the social dimensions of festivals rather than to pinpoint their occasions.

Virgil gives us a picture of his rustics carousing in the winter, making good use of the stores they had been able to accumulate; he uses a
phrase rich in meaning, *genialis hiems*.[41] In a fragment of a poem, Alcman
speaks of spring as the season "in which there is growth—everywhere, but
not much to eat."[42] We can well believe him; the good eating has taken
place before spring. In the life of the farmer, there is an alternation of fru-
gality with prodigality; one almost requires the other. In fact, it suddenly

becomes clear that winter is the season of festivals. In spite of some accretions, systematizations, and inevitable displacements, the plan of city festivals—in Attica, at least, where we know it best—retains a good deal of archaism. Here one is inclined to add that in a simplified way, the events of ancient religious life parallel the cycle of nature, although this really is an overstatement, or rather is true only in the majority of instances. In considering the Attic calendar—and we recall that since Pisistratus it had been embellished with a system of festivals—one discovers a certain opposition or contrast between two parts of the year: one is an expanded form of winter; the other is summer. The winter period is rich in ancient festivals, the genuine kind, which not only have links with community life but also contain striking archaisms. In contrast, the summer is poor. From the end of the archaic period, the City Dionysia reveal their modern aspect. The Panathenaia are essentially a city festival, a political institution in the proper sense of the word, which reveal almost nothing of the past. We do have here and there some agrarian rites that are evidently of a very ancient type, but they are not characterized as festivals, and nothing about them suggests that they contain remnants of festivals. At the end of this same period, the Eleusinian Mysteries presuppose a religion too advanced to base any argument on. In short, what we get is the impression of a rhythm that belongs to the social dimension. Can we define it a little better?

It is a rare stroke of luck that Aristotle's *Nicomachean Ethics* allows us to discover the basic facts from which a theory of morality is constructed. There (VIII.11, 1160a), one finds an observation that, though certainly banal, Aristotle with his special genius connected to the study of the conditions of community life in Greece. After observing that the "political association" looks to the common advantage of the whole life, and that this goal is achieved through "sacrifices"[43] and "through assemblies[44] for the purpose of sacrifices, when men are together to honor the gods and provide themselves with delightful periods of leisure," Aristotle adds: "The most ancient sacrifices and assemblies are evidently those that take place after the gathering in of the harvest, for this is when there is the most leisure time." A timely remark; and these periods of "leisure" will most interest us. It is not the harvest's end that brings such a time; for attention must be given at least to the vintage; and the "fruits of the earth" have to be understood in a larger sense. In fact it is only the period of sowing which marks the end of the farmers' work. Significantly, this may not be a period of crisis, and the life of the community is not so tightly bound up with the natural cycle. The beginning of sufficient "leisure time" is, in the Attic calendar, characterized by rural festivals such as the Pyanepsia and Oskhophoria. This is the time when, in a new period of abundance and in the promise of abundance, there opens up, above all, a new period for men.[45] Moreover, it ends the way it begins; the final moment is marked by festivals, and in particular by festivals honoring the dead which fluctuate between the adjoining months of Anthesterion and Elaphebolion.[46] Even now we easily see that the beginning and end of this period may have had singular importance.

❈

What was the essential idea behind these seasonal "gatherings"? We know that they were characterized by some consumption. For what purpose?

There is a notion that persists throughout in the festivals, namely, the idea of hospitality: a *hestiasis* is a *xenismos*.[47] A theme that appears frequently in religious life, even in the later periods, is generosity; it is more or less spontaneous and yet almost obligatory. In particular, it is the generosity of the magistrate or the priest who gives the sacrificial banquet. It is also a mythical theme; in the legends about founders of cities, generosity is a common motif. But there is often question of a very extended hospitality; it is universal and addressed to "strangers" as well as "citizens." It is a remarkable phenomenon, since city cults, from the most ancient times, were exclusive. The question can be asked, then, Is this notion of hospitality a relic of a very ancient period when it had a very distinct significance?

It is precisely those festivals whose rural aspect is most accented that are characterized by generous hospitality. At the Laconian Hyakinthia, "not only one's own countrymen are hosted, but strangers who happen to be there as well."[48] During the festivals established by Xenophon in honor of a completely rural Artemis, the goddess treats all who wish to come.[49] The Thessalians, with their rustic customs, treat strangers in the same way during their celebrations.[50] And in popular custom there is a psychological trait that is as persistent as these reciprocal and periodic expressions of generosity. When inhabitants of Cyrene sacrifice to Kronos—and in Kronos' case there is always some vague relic of the Golden Age—they send one another gifts. And these gifts are noteworthy: cakes made of flour and, so it seems, gifts of fruit and honey as well.[51]

All this is significant, but naturally there is not a great deal of evidence in the historical period. The testimony concerning the concept and consciousness of rural hospitality is much more indirect; still, there is enough to indicate how highly valued it was in the lives of individuals. Some concrete images from ancient festivals persist in myths; and one of these—an entirely authentic one—is the practice of the *stibas*.[52] There are good reasons for this.

The use of *stibades* is mentioned in the regulations governing the

Athenian *thiasos* of the Iobakkhoi, regulations rich in curiosities pertaining to the history of religion. It is in connection with this text that the religious import of the *stibades* is raised. It seems certain that the term *stibas* is applied to the banquet of the Iobakkhoi themselves. But perhaps we are too quick to accept the view of Maass, who wanted to see in the *stibades* evidence of Theoxenia,[53] when we consider that at question here is a custom completely natural to open-air festivals, in fact too natural to merit any special comment. One might even say that "the gods" have nothing to do with it. Still, the persistence of the practice itself and the persistence of a term both consecrated and yet equivocal[54] give the impression that the practice, natural though it may be, might still have had a quasi-liturgical significance from the time of its origin. If it is in this context that one thinks of the Theoxenia, then Maass' insight was correct. What we must keep in mind is this: whether in the special case of the Iobakkhoi there are or are not Theoxenia makes little difference, even though the argument that there are remains plausible. For it is equally clear that the *agapai*, or "love feasts," of the gods are connected in some way with the archaic practice of the *stibades*. It can be demonstrated that the *xenia* of gods represents on a larger scale the practice of the hospitality found in rural festivals.

There is little doubt that during the historical epoch the Theoxenia are, properly speaking, *lectisternia*, or "couch feasts";[55] but, in contrast, the *klisis* in the ceremony of Daitis is of a simple type. The goddess's bed is made of wild celery grown in the meadow, and she reclines in the same fashion as the faithful. The welcomings given to gods are modeled on those given to men. There are couches for the gods, and this practice dates from an earlier time than the custom of the banquet bed,[56] since the former was also used in the *stibades*. The *xenismoi* for gods remain naturally associated with the *xenismoi* for men.[57] The two are persistently confused in the primitive conception, where the divinity is at times undifferentiated[58] and the roles of the entertainer and the entertained respectively alternate between the gods, heroes, and men.[59]

The mythical theme that Pindar recalls in a paean composed for the Delphic Theoxenia[60] is informative. It is precisely of the same type as the "ambrosial banquet" (recently studied by Dumézil), itself a seasonal banquet and one that is transformed into a banquet of gods, and it has all the earmarks of having been instituted following a famine.[61] Surely, given their seasonal recurrence and such rites as the offering of leeks at Delphi,[62] the classical Theoxenia, addressed as they are more naturally to *numina* closer to the world of man and nature than to the Olympian gods,[63] represent the heritage of a very ancient past. The very word Theoxenia, like Theodaisia (possibly a variant of it),[64] translates the collective and spontaneous sentiment of the rural *agapai*, or "love feasts." One can see a *kataklisis* of the gods in the large-scale *stibades*. In effect this is the same feeling that underpins a belief in the regular appearances of deities; and to the Theoxenia and Theodaisia, the Theophania must be added.[65] Each year at Delphi, Apollo returns from the country of the Hyperboreans, a land of legend from which offerings arrived at the seasonal gatherings of his devotees.[66] When Alcaeus refers to that epiphany in the midst of nature festivals, a bit of the primitive soul sings again in his poem.[67]

But how and among whom does hospitality, an essential ingredient of feasts, function?

The very nature of our *testimonia* calls for a hypothesis involving hospitality *among groups*.[68] We have already observed that festivals were held in the middle of the countryside. This is really to say that they are situated at rallying points already sacred in nature. They not only unite the inhabitants of one village but bring several villages together in common ceremonies and reunions. But such a hypothesis can be pushed further.

The *dēmoi* are not isolated, but are naturally organized into a "system of demes."[69] They exist as groups side by side, and it is again a festival that attests to this fact in classical Athens: the *Metageitnia*.[70] What we know of the Rural Dionysia gives the impression that there were comings and goings from one deme to the other. From a very early period, it was possible in a number of places in Attica to have centers of regional religious activity, antecedents of the Amphictiony.[71] People extend a welcome and are welcomed along the roads; Deipnias, the "Banquet Place," is one stop along the sacred way from Thessaly to Delphi.

Two types of historical facts illustrate and confirm these initial points.

First, there are certain details about the organization and quasi-articulation of historically recent festivals. We cannot really extrapolate an argument from the structure of Athenian festivals, where the tribes are simultaneously associated and compete with one another. Nonetheless, in their case there is perhaps evidence of a fundamental idea that is independent of the polis. The transposition is obvious in the case of the two tribes of Cos that, to the exclusion of the third, "participate in the cult of Apollo and Herakles at Halasarna."[72] The Lacedaemonian phratries are equally but separately represented in the celebration of the Karneia.[73] And in the archaic ceremonies presided over by the "Olympian Sixteen," the *duality* of the *choruses*, each of the same sex, is perhaps something even more suggestive.[74] On the other hand, the religious organization of Athens does at times admit of a system of relationships between the festivals and the *genē* presiding over them. These relationships, once they have been made part of the official state etiquette, translate themselves into invitations to banquets.[75]

Second, there are those facts that can be discovered in the organization of relationships between cities. Here the concept of hospitality is basic. It is not simply metaphorical, and it finds its most concrete expression in regions that remain the most backward. In Crete there is a custom that at public meals two tables be reserved for strangers who are to be served before the magistrates.[76] At a more advanced stage, there are features parallel to the Cretan custom which we are certain survived a long time. For example, the people of Delphi have the privilege of being seated at the sacred banquets of the Magnesians.[77]

Finally, in order to understand the nature of this relationship among groups in terms of its prehistoric origin, it is possible to draw on an analogy from another but parallel civilization. The Iguvine Tablets[78] present us with an organization that is at once archaic and yet already systematized—in a way, even fixed. Each year the Clavernii must supply the *fratres Atiedii* four pounds of flour—and flour from a specific locale—in addition to a meal for the two men who go to seek it. Every year the *fratres Atiedii* must supply the Clavernii ten portions of pork and give them a meal. And the same occurs for another group; one could go on.

So it is that when the legend of the Argonauts represents them or their descendants as hosted by the Lemnians, by the Kabeiroi, and by the Lacedaemonians[79]—in the context of festivals, as the tales indicate[80]—we get some idea of the remote realities echoed in the legend.

❦

We are catching some glimpse of human societies. What must still be discovered in the very institution of festivals is the social force that gives them their raison d'être.

In the historical period, there exist names of festivals that emphasize one basic concept: the Agrionia, whose name seems to be derived from *ageirō*;[81] the Agoreia, which contains the same root;[82] and the Apellai, which owe their designation to certain "assemblies" whose strictly "political" character is certainly not their most ancient feature.[83] In these "gatherings" of homogeneous groups, the periodic expression of reciprocal hospitality and the communal merrymaking expand and uplift the minds of the participants. What precisely are the purposes of these gatherings?

They do not only include the living; the Agrionia at Argos, for example, are a festival of the dead.[84] The dead play a major role in the most ancient religious sources, and they are more or less involved in all the festivals, especially at specific periods. One of these seems to be the beginning of winter, as is indicated by the offering of the *hōraia*, the fruits of the land, the kind of offering which characterizes certain festivals honoring the dead.[85] These remind us, moreover, of the period of the year marked by festivals like the Pyanepsia[86] and the Oskhophoria. However, the dead are above all associated with the festivals that occur at the end of winter. There appears in this context some near-perfect corroborative evidence.[87] In Attica, at the Anthesteria, the dead are welcomed and then dismissed.[88] The traditional rites in honor of the dead which represent them as collaborating with the powers of life correspond to an undifferentiated or ill-defined aspect of the social world. It is only in a much later period that the dead are individualized and become ancestors in the strict sense.[89]

Side by side with ancient festivals are the more recent arrivals. One of the characteristic rites of the *Apellai* remains the offering of the *apellaia*, the "victims of maturity."[90] The Attic festival of the Apatouria also contains as an essential element the sacrifices of the *koureia*, performed by youths upon their emergence from childhood.[91] *Apellaia* and *koureia* are known to us mainly from the regulations of the phratries. The Apatouria represent a festival of the phratries, and one of the festival's three days is called the *koureōtis hēmera*. Enrollment in the phratry (a modern form of which survives in a custom of the historical period, but has no juridical import) is perforce linked with the *koureia*. All this points to a direct line between the rites reserved for young men, or *kouroi*, and their admittance to a social group of the most ancient kind. Whatever the future of the phratry could be under the control of the city, we know that it experienced toleration more than incorporation. What was the nature of the primitive phratry of prehistoric groups so labeled perhaps from a relatively late date?[92] This is an obscure question, one I would not know how to begin answering here. Some observations of an ancient historian[93] may permit us to suppose that the phratry brought several groups together, groups connected by a *conubium*; this will become clearer later. Even if one has to see a unity that is strictly homogeneous, the festivals we have discussed have at the very least in common all the unities of the same kind.[94] And just as initiation ceremonies are normally tribal, we conclude that the admission of young men occurs, by definition, within the "assemblies" that the very name *Apellai* designates. The *kouroi* are received into a society that is neither feudal nor political in type; it is, in contrast, quite simple.

The title of the *kouroi* deserves some attention. The etymology that connects it with *keirō*, "cut," by alluding to the custom of the cutting of hair, is not only possible for the linguist;[95] it is compelling for the historian. We are dealing with a very old practice that has more or less survived as a rite surrounding the emergence from childhood.[96] Its significance is immediately apparent. Two observations allow us to understand it in terms of the primitive milieu it presupposes. (1) The offering of locks of hair is normally made not so much to gods as to heroes.[97] Still, this stage is itself a derivative one. There is evidence of a more ancient context in which the lock of hair is offered to *rivers*,[98] the functions of which we have seen and will see again. (2) The cutting of hair takes place often, even in the historical era, on the eve of marriage.[99] (One might add that in Homer a young married man is a *kouridios*.) What it is now possible to show is that these two observations are closely connected.

꧁

Rural festivals, or at least some of them, are marked by marriages.

In popular custom, even of late, marriages continue to take place by preference during a particular time of the year.[100] It has already been possible to presume the existence of genuine group marriages from a very early date;[101] and this practice has been directly attested in one region, Crete.[102] Even so, there is need here for more data.

We have only a relic, but again it is a relic from the historical period: formerly, marriages occurred at festivals.[103] The rites of popular festivals, which survive in the modern Thracian carnival,[104] are so spontaneously accompanied by symbolic representations of marriage that they also deserve our attention. The offering of the *gamēlia* at the Attic Apatouria bears accurate witness to this past.[105] Some attempt can be made to localize these festivals, and Aristotle indicates that "winter" is the preferable season for marriages. There is some evidence[106] that it is toward the end of autumn that one might be disposed to situate them, since the festivals of the dead occur most often at winter's end.

What concerns us more directly in these marriages is their social and religious significance.

But a preliminary observation is necessary: sexual union is itself a collective rite.

Myths of sacred marriages, etiological legends, and ordinary customs that still survive are so many clues that fall into the same category Not only the myths,[107] but marriage customs[108] as well, sometimes imply the idea of preliminary unions whose significance is easily recognized. These *proteleia* retain the relic of a *coniugium* more ancient than marriage in the strict sense. Artemis is not a goddess of marriage;[109] but there is an Artemis Hymnia,[110] just as there is, of course, an Artemis *parthenos*. It is remarkable that the idea of virginity is not directly expressed in the words *korē*, *numphē*, even *parthenos*, all of which refer to the young maiden or young wife; the terms oscillate between the two and their meaning is really fixed in an intermediate concept.[111] Pausanias recounts a legend that is instructive (V.3.2): "Since Elis was suffering from a dearth of people, the women of the country, it is said, asked Athena that they become pregnant every time they slept with a man.[112] Their prayers were answered and they consecrated a sanctuary to Athena under the title Mother. Men and women were so pleased with their sexual union that the place where it first took place was called by them 'Delights,'[113] the same name given in local parlance to the river there." The institution of a sanctuary, as well as the tenor of the legend, points to a festival associated with the memory of collective marriages. All of the sexual unions, the "preliminary unions," occur at the same time. They take place in the countryside by a river. We have already seen that this is the characteristic setting of rural festivals; and it is found elsewhere. A Cretan sacred marriage[114] takes place near the Theren River.[115] But it is the nuptial custom of Ilium, as reported to us by pseudo-Aeschines (*Ep.* X.3), which one thinks of before anything else: "In the Troad, it is the custom for girls who are getting married to go to the Scamander and bathe there. Then they intone the following ritual formula: 'Scamander, take my virginity.' " Here is a text as clear as one could wish for. The words addressed to the river—*labe mou, Skamandre, tēn parthenian*—clearly refer to the consummation of marriage. In fact, in the historical period, four days after the bathing rite, there is a procession of "newly married" women (ibid., 6). If legends frequently associate virginity with a river or spring,[116] and if Hera Parthenos, after losing her virginity in a *hieros gamos*,[117] periodically recovers it in a river, then the legend of Elis and the rite of the Troad give us the reason. In addition, the very ancient practices that these legends evoke[118] seem to have been widespread in the Mediterranean world. The well-known festival of Anna Perenna[119] reveals a practice of the same type. The tradition that affirmed a primitive state of promiscuity, while open to interpretation, has a specific meaning.[120]

In mythical and ritual survivals from the historical era, these *proteleia* naturally begin to have a mysterious attraction, and for the best of reasons. But certain legends give us an entirely different idea of the primitive *telos*. And even later, the idea of marriage is still evoked by the *paraklisis* of the popular Theoxenia.[121] The strewing of leaves was used not only for feasts; the powers attributed to such a practice are relics of equally spontaneous primitive customs.[122] According to Herodotus, the union of sexes could so easily appear to be a collective liturgy that it was not always necessary to prohibit it in sanctuaries.[123] In a certain religious regulation, it had to be expressly forbidden.[124]

But above all, marriages are accompanied by play. Here, the gathering of flowers, seemingly a ritual custom, should be mentioned. It is surely in this context that one must point to the use of fruits, the symbols of love and marriage,[125] which the young of both sexes give or throw at each other. Marriage is, moreover, an opportune time for *agōnes*. We know of heroines like Atalanta or Hippodameia, who must be won in a race. Pindar, reporting a Cyrenean legend that is a variation on this traditional theme, knows well the precedent from which a prudent father-in-law draws his inspiration. When Danaos found himself with forty-eight daughters to marry off, he stationed all of them together at the end of a race course and "stipulated that a foot race would determine which girl each of the suitors would obtain."[126] Pindar uses a significant term: the Danaids formed a *chorus*. It is important to pay special attention to this image. Active and lively choruses are an archaism as significant as the races of young girls in later festivals. It is in this connection that the very structure of face-to-face choruses emerges; and in that structure is adumbrated the opposition and competition between the sexes. The legend of the daughters of Proitos[127] tells of their being chased by Melampus and a crowd of young men, all of whom know the dance that must be performed in order to cure the girls. While we are not interested in identifying the specific dances and chants, we are at least justified in affirming their existence.[128]

Kouroi and *korai*, then, play an important role in every category of festivals. In its basic design, the *aition* of the Ephesian festival of Daitis presents us with *kouroi* and *korai* exclusively. The latter especially leave their imprint on religious depictions in art, and they are—as we well know—associated with familiar landscapes. The words *numphai*, *korai*, and *parthenoi* are applied to divinities of streams, fountains, forests, mountains, etc.[129]

But in the concrete—in the living organism of festivals—what is the significance of young men acting in unison? Evidently they reinforce the social bond; and their preliminary opposition followed by a rapprochement is symbolic of all the *agōnes* that point to a distant past and yet must have their raison d'être in a rural milieu. On this subject one would like to be more precise, but what we are dealing with here, as always, is a social prehistory that allows us only to conjecture. No positive datum, it must be said, allows us to prove any explicit rule of exogamy for the "deme" and endogamy within the "system of demes." But by its clearly exclusive character, the tradition that denied *conubium*[130] to two Attic demes attests indirectly to a marital routine in which each of the associated groups found wives for themselves in one or another of the groups. The legends referring to the ancient festivals are equally instructive. The legend of the Lemnians depicts the women of the island receiving the newly arrived Argonauts and having sexual intercourse with them. The tale of the Spartan Lemnians is even clearer: the descendants of the Argonauts arrive in Lacedaemonia, where they appeal to kinship. The Lacedaemonians agree to their settling among them and "immediately they intermarried, and they [the descendants of the Argonauts from Lemnos] gave in marriage to others the women they had brought with them from Lemnos."[131] It is futile in this case to introduce the hypothesis of "annual marriages."[132] What happens quite simply in this legend is an exchange of women for marriage between two social groups during periodical festivals.

II

In dealing with these primitive foundations of society, ethical behavior, and religion, it is not our intention to examine every detail;[133] this would amount to redoing prehistory, a process that would be abstract and conjectural. But in limiting the scope of our study, and "by squeezing the text more tightly," it is possible to recapture, in one or another term connected with the festivals,[134] the expression of a process of thought which is persistent and uniquely ancient.

Whether one conceives of them as gatherings at public expense or as receptions of one group by another—both aspects appear with equal frequency and complement each other—the rural *agapai* presuppose and require the gift, which is above all a "contribution." The verb *pherō*, along with its derivatives and compounds, has a direct relation to this custom[135] and is a specific term in the religious vocabulary, where it is applied to offerings in the form of cereals, wine, oil, etc.[136] Occasionally it connotes a ritual gesture.[137]

In an isolated example, yet one that still testifies to a technical and apparently traditional usage, it is curious to find the substantive *pherna*, a correlative of the verb, used to designate precisely that offering.[138] For we are aware of the special significance this term takes on elsewhere: namely, a "dowry" or, to be more specific, the "offering" of clothing and jewelry by the wife's family. Can we say, then, that the abstract notion of "to carry" is the common root of both meanings? This would be ignoring the fact that terms that refer to moral concepts are first of all attached to the concrete depiction of social activities, notably obligatory gestures. Such an explanation would also ignore the proper value of marriage dowries, which are meant to guarantee "alliances" through an exchange of gifts.[139] Moreover, there is an express connection between the dowry and the religious offering.[140] And this does not happen only in marriages; the *diaphora*, which came to mean "payments of interest," reveal an intermediate stage of development in which homage is given as acknowledgment of religious lordship.[141] From this concept there arises the notion of the census, a notion we shall see again, but one that we can also identify in the antecedents of *phoros*. The root or basic idea kept alive in *pherō-pherna* (of the religious vocabulary) is that of an obligatory payment or offering that in its primitive form is expressed in the contribution to the *agapai*. From this there emerged notions of offerings that were ritual, feudal, dictated by protocol, or associated with marriage[142]—like so many variations on the same established theme, but in a new context.

An examination of the most general term—but we do not call it the most abstract—already provides suggestive leads, for it prepares us to recognize the transformations that occurred in primitive thinking. In this context there appears a rather specific term, but one that is no less rich in significance: *eranos*. I recall that the word has two main uses. (1) It is applied to a loan made out of friendship, a loan that has two essential characteristics; it is gratuitous and it involves the mutual consent of several individuals. (2) It is also applied to a certain form of religious society that we know of mostly from epigraphical sources from the third century B.C. on. But its precise meaning, in the language of the religious associations,[143] is the *contributions* brought by the members of a society. Of course, this fee, for which the more general term is *phora*, is normally in the form of money.[144] But one can go further back in time to the use of *eranos* in Homer, where it designates a meal at the community's expense. It is easy to conjecture that the classical *eranos* is derived from a contribution in kind. The same word—and it appears in ancient examples—has an interesting meaning: an *eranos* is a festival; and one realizes that its meaning "picnic" results from a kind of fall from grace that social history might explain.[145] In any case, in Pindar, *eranos* keeps its religious dignity.[146] It is possible to determine its etymology with some precision. The connection *eranos-heortē* is called for and almost required by linguistics.[147] But there is more: the word *ēra*, fossilized in the Homeric expression *ēra pherein*, ought to have some connection with the two terms *eranos-heortē*. The Homeric expression does not have merely an abstract meaning. The verb lends to the noun—a noun that is very ancient and almost forgotten—the primitive and concrete sense of an offering or payment.[148] Thus we can reconstruct the history of this whole word group. The twofold idea of a festival and a contribution or offering is present. The banquet, as we have already pointed out in an example from Pindar,[149] is of an archaic type; the offering or contribution, the basic idea associated with the terms, makes the identification complete. *Eranos* brings us back to the rural *agapai*.[150]

The term has had a checkered career, conforming to different situations where primitive thought is refracted. *Eranos* itself is applied to offerings exacted by the feudal chief; it is in some way associated with the legend of Perseus,[151] where Polydektes[152] demands an *eranos* of his followers.[153] But the word develops in another context: namely, in those religious associations where the old traditions survive, and in the confraternities that toward the end of the third century B.C. are dedicated principally to the cults of foreign deities, but that are in fact considerably more ancient and have their origins in family or quasi-familial groups whose designations are sometimes homonyms of the associations.[154] In these societies, of which an essential function continues to be the organization of communal meals,[155] we discern some ideas and terms (*sunagein, phora, eispherein,* etc.)[156] that (as the use of *eranos* already indicates) preserve the past without break. This is an important point if it allows us to determine precisely the origins of a type of organization which must have played an important role in religious history.

It is in the process of rendering an account of other kinds of organizations—which are perhaps not without their parallels to the ones we are discussing—that we can understand the career of a more familiar and more obviously religious term: *telos*. There is hardly a concept that appears in more forms and at the same time has such a unity of meaning. Its unity, however, is intelligible only if one goes back to its roots. In the historical period, the diversity of meanings of *telos* is such that linguists feel obliged to distinguish several words within it.[157] They distinguish *telos* = "goal, terminus," from *telos* = "payment, tax." What is the connection between the two? Merely that the first is only an abstraction, while the second is a derived meaning that would have been an anachronism in a primitive milieu. In reality, however, *telein* means both "to pay"—that is, "to supply"—and "to perform a rite." The unity of meaning remains obvious in the religious vocabulary.[158] This unity played no more lively a role than in the ancient festivals, where the entire community provided resources and feasted, and where the very feasting itself was, and remained, an essentially religious act.[159] The later, quite divergent uses of the term are not so much due to the capriciousness of semantics. Payment in kind, demanded by the possession, or *precarium*, of a *terra sacra*,[160] is connected with the primitive "gift." A late document offers us a curious and yet unquestionable survival, namely, the use of *dōtinē* to designate the rent of goods that belong to the gods.[161] With the concentration of authority, the religious tithe evolved into a nonreligious tax; in the realm of Homeric kingship, the terms *dōtinai* and *themistes* reflect precisely this development.[162] It is from this point that the most ordinary uses of the terms *telos* and *telein* emerge, and it is here that one can easily overlook their ancient affinities.

But it is within a completely different domain that we wish to continue examining the semantic evidence. *Telein*, as we well know, is one of the terms that characterize mystery religions; the verb and its cognates refer to initiation. It is not our purpose to examine the intermediate stages between the primitive forms of religious life and the mystery religions of the historical period, but we readily admit that a continuity existed. It would be interesting to deal with this subject in more detail.[163]

In the collective religious activity of festivals, where the idea of *telein* is basic, the new classes of young men, as we have already seen, play an important role. Whether it is possible, as Jane Harrison maintains, to recover the relic of special initiation rites in Greece is not what we are attempting to decide. However, at the very least, there exists in folk festivals a form of initiation which is primary and of the greatest social value: sexual initiation. If we recall that the institution of collective marriages is precisely what most characterizes folk custom, then we see the importance of the frequent observation that *telos* and its cognates are freely associated with marriage.[164] And it is here that we find ourselves pointed toward mystery religions; for the groups of *kouroi* and *korai*, on the basis of their very names, admission into society and marriage are related notions. And one of the most characteristic (perhaps even cardinal) ideas employed by the mystery religions is that of sexual union as a symbol and even a direct expression of the union between the initiate and the god.[165] Defined as it is, such a concept is no arbitrary invention; at the least, it requires some antecedents, and we can discover them. In this context, a small detail takes on great importance: the rite of cutting hair is attested in the initiatory rites of the mystery religions.[166]

In the profane sphere as well, one can count on the fact that the elementary form of payment in country festivals had extensions. The word *eranos* assures us of this fact, and it is to this word that we now return.

It is no longer necessary, as was formerly thought, to look for the connection between the two ordinary meanings of this term in the historical period—namely, a loan based on friendship or fellowship—in the entirely hypothetical existence of a type of society that would have practiced loans of assistance. This is not to say that the connection between the two meanings was only logical.[167] Apart from the fact that the societies of *eranistai* occasionally practice the *eranos* loan, the psychological continuity between the custom of religious bodies and the practice of friendship loans reveals itself in the similarity of vocabulary and expressions that are applied to both.[168] One must admit that at a very early date the organizations of *thiasoi* and *orgeōnes*, heirs to a folk tradition, furnished the conditions that favored the development of a contractual form.[169]

Another term that is equally applicable to the language of religious associations is *sumballesthai*.[170] When applied to the contribution of the *eranistai*, it too perpetuates the primitive concept. But this primitive concept has evolved in a somewhat larger milieu, and has an entirely different scope. From the *sumbolē*, which applied on a wider level and under more or less varied aspects, there emerged the idea of a contract. But in an aristocratic milieu, the term *sumbolon* applies to the token of hospitality and is rich in meaning. Elsewhere, the deviation is less conspicuous, and so its expansion of meaning is more obvious. The *sumbolai* are the agreements between groups in which there persists, even if somewhat obscurely,[171] a sense of primitive hospitality. The verb *sumballesthai* and the substantive *sumbolaia* refer to a concept of contract which is opposed to the type implied in *nexum*. More or less implying a juridical concept of society, this concept of contract has finally found the terrain where it can develop in commercial law.

※

We would not be too disturbed if these comments caused some confusion. The gap between one subject and the other has been great, and the transitions abrupt. And given the extent to which things in process of evolution can be isolated, there is no clear continuity; at best we find a continuity of words. In religious thought, neither the *telos* of classical piety nor that of the mystery religions seems to have any dimension commensurate with the "primitive condition." What is left in juridical thought is the essential element, a sense of obligation, and above all its correlative, the feeling of expectation—the certainty of law. Nevertheless there are some verbal agreements. What lies behind them?

In reality, a single idea is implied in the practice of rural festivals—in the relationship of individuals and the groups in the festivals, in the exchanges involved in communal eating and drinking, in the union of marriages, and in the union with the dead. It is the idea of commerce, but it takes a form so simple and yet so rich as to resist analysis.

Let us examine a useful text. Although its date is unknown, it describes a belief that still survives, and it evokes some age-old customs. It is a precious text, because in its naïve liveliness it preserves for us a long-lost way of thinking. "Near the river Olynthiakos (in Chalcidice), there is a tomb of Olynthus, the son of Herakles and Bolbe. The people of the district say that, toward the months of Anthesterion and Elaphebolion, Bolbe sends the *apopuris* (a small, fried fish) to Olynthus and that, at that moment, there appears a great abundance of fish which leave the lake in order to swim up the Olynthiakos river" (Hegesander in Ath. 4.334E). We know for certain that a festival was held there. It is the end of the winter celebration, as the text itself indicates. And as is normal during that period, it resembles among other things a festival of the dead.[172] Its essential element is a banquet; the word *apopuris* alone is key since it does not designate the fish that swims up river but rather the dish of fried fish. In addition, the term is associated with a ritual usage, attested elsewhere, in the cult of heroes;[173] the article (*tēn apopurin*) underlines this. Fish is eaten in abundance; it is a popular meal, but one that the Achaeans disdained; Greece will eventually return to it. Now, behind this type of homage to Bolbe[174] there has to be a mythical transposition, one that is immediate and spontaneous. The festival presupposes those communal processions to which we have already referred. As for the expression *pempei hē Bolbē*, we know that the antecedents of the classical *pompē* are the rural folk processions. In the historical period, groups express the religious relationships between them by sending envoys and gifts; these are acts of homage and the verb *pempein* applies to both. But our text suggests a less polished form of the practice; we have to remind ourselves that the groups visit and welcome one another. Finally, and what we regard as the essential in our passage—something which in this shape could not have been invented by a mythographer, and given its simplicity, could not have been conceived of in the historical period—is the belief in nature's cooperation. At the moment when the *agapai* are to take place, the world of nature joins with the people, and the lakes provide fish in abundance.

This passage might have served as our epigraph; in it, themes from ritual and myth converge, themes that are basic and yet rich in meaning.

The idea of nature participating in the religious activities of men survives as one of the most vital and obvious themes in agrarian cults. These cults reveal a heritage of thought which is kept alive by the periodic celebration of rural festivals. Their objects were as yet impersonal forces. Sometimes this process of thought, too dependent on these festivals, has left behind only traces in folklore: for example, the legend of Bolbe, and the transformation of water into wine at Andros.[175] At other times it has retained its links with some isolated rites: for example, the offering of hair to the youth-nourishing rivers. Still again, it has sometimes been able to develop along the lines of later cults.

Let us point out briefly some of the essential elements of religious thought which are closely connected with the most ancient festivals. There is no need today to emphasize the role allotted to the dead, who, though nameless, give assurance of life and the earth's fertility.[176] At autumn's end and winter's beginning, the rites in their honor, linking them with festivities of the living, manifest by their important function the efficacy of seasonal gatherings.[177] But their connection with the living is even more direct; at the root of old customs there lies in an obscure fashion the idea of reincarnation;[178] and it reveals itself in the fact that sexual rites and rites honoring the dead are not rigorously separated in the festivals. On the subject of sexual rites, it would be superfluous to point out the belief that they respond to: a deep sympathy between earth, animals, and man. The creative power of man imitates and advances the reproduction and multiplication of beings throughout the whole of nature.[179] Such a belief is rooted in the ancient festivals; and we have been able to conjecture that if Demeter sexually unites with Iasion on the thrice-tilled soil, it is because the time for sowing was near the privileged moment when the rhythm of rural folk life brought about communal marriages.[180]

Vegetal offerings were given the dead; and marriage festivals also involve offerings, as do matrimonial rites, which are characterized by obligatory acts of generosity. Men continue to offer earth divinities their appropriate gifts: the edible products of the earth. In reality, communal expense, the gift, the offering, homage, retribution—all these elements, both human and divine, have been extricated from the sources with which they were previously enmeshed. The *telos* was the contribution to the common stock, the communal consummation, and the realization of natural processes—the "fulfillment."[181] Fundamentally, the idea of *do ut des* is not the recent and artificial product of an "Olympian intellectualism"; nor can one define a "primitive stage" by recourse to a "magical" and entirely pragmatic use of nature. If in the most ancient rites divine forces collaborate with man's desires, it is because they are drawn into an arena of commerce and exchange which at certain periods creates a type of communism. The name *Pyanepsia* suggests that nourishment was taken in common. In organized ritual, it also designates offerings of grain which, as products of the earth restored to the earth, project an image of obligatory remuneration and an assurance of nature's renewal. The Agrionia are, in part, a festival of the dead, who are guests at the "reunion" their name designates. But essentially they are a reunion of the living, an idea whose implications we are now going to see.

The verb *ageirō* has had a life of its own, which is of some interest. It has become a term associated with confraternities, and in the fifth century B.C., it is applied to the offerings made to mendicant priests of foreign gods, especially the Magna Mater.[182] But it is not in this context that the idea had its origins; elsewhere *ageirō* is associated with a religious vocabulary one might call national.[183] But even in the language of religious associations the term is connected with the idea of *pompē*.[184] In addition, we can always see in this language the remote antecedents still evoked by the term. The great event for the associations in question, as well as for the mystery religions (*ageirō* is used in both),[185] is initiation. If, when the priestess makes her rounds, the future initiate makes an offering generously, he does so in order to share in the god's benefits. There is a necessary link, if not an identity, between the *agermos* and the ritual payment of initiation. This cost sometimes has the characteristic name *pelanos*.[186] In this instance the *pelanos* is paid in money,[187] but originally it meant an offering of porridge. Prior to a *pelanos* of money in the mystery religions, there must have existed a *pelanos* of natural products,[188] one that points to very archaic customs.

But there is more. In a passage from Alcman (fr. 17, Page) *ageirō* designates the collection of grain during a rite; this makes one think immediately of the Pyanepsia and the Khytroi. If it is legitimate to say, as we have, that "reunion" on the one hand, and "offering"—"gift"—on the other, are reciprocal, then there is something valid to be learned from the synthesis contained in one and the same term. The strong tradition of seasonal festivals allows us perhaps to grasp this synthesis at its very origin, in its concrete and vital form. One of Dieterich's most successful works is devoted to the practice of *Sommertag*, a custom that still exists in some parts of Europe.[189] The *Sommertagen* belong to a whole religious complex that has been known for a long time. But the twofold merit and (for us) twofold interest of Dieterich's study is that it extracts the religious and human value of certain customs from a specific experience and establishes with some precision the connection between them and other customs that are attested in rural Greece until quite late.

The custom we wish to focus on here is the collection of fruits and cakes.[190] The person requesting these offerings brings spring and its blessings with him. While these offerings were formerly eaten in common, they nevertheless guaranteed prosperity to homes of generous individuals. It is of some interest to recall that in the ceremonies of the modern Thracian "carnival," offerings also serve as a community meal.[191] In any case, it is easy to see how the primitive *agapai* lend themselves to a natural and lively symbolism. The product of the *agermos*—under this symbolic form, which seems to have been an ancestral custom in Greece—guarantees the return of the fruits of the earth, which were the source of the *agermos*. It is also possible to see the future of this kind of thinking; it evolves, as is natural, along two divergent paths. The *sumbolon*, the individual's contribution, is the sign and guarantee of divine reciprocity; *sumbolon* is a term that belongs both to the confraternities and to the mystery religions. On the other hand, the certainty that one will be periodically rewarded with the earth's fruits gives rise to the early idea of the *tokos* ("interest"); the word itself preserves a relic of its true origins.[192]

And there are other perspectives. There is a religious structure that has survived until a late date and should be interpreted as a stylized adaptation of this same kind of thought. Piganiol discovers this essential rite in the ceremonial of the *ludi saeculares* at Rome:[193] the *quindecemviri* distribute to the people the instruments for purifying homes, but they also distribute *fruges* (wheat, barley, and beans).[194] The *fruges* are given out after the *quindecemviri* have received them as offerings and blessed them.[195] In explaining this "difficult" rite, Piganiol does not hesitate to find an analogy in the most ancient ritual of the Christian mass, as he sees it, in which offertory, consecration, and communion follow one another. It is a very bold theory, and we might as well make use of it.

The terms *dōra* and *antidōron* are applied to the first and third parts of the mass respectively. Now, the role of the fifteen, who distributed the *fruges* while seated on an elevated bench, immediately reminds us of the rite of the Delphic Kharila, in which "the king presides and distributes the farina and pods to all present, foreigners and citizens alike."[196] We are not suggesting that this distribution is a *re*distribution, nor is it legitimate to postulate such a view. The function of the king as giver of nourishment is characteristic of a very ancient period in the history of society. But we can see which practices, even more ancient, led to this conception of the king; and the analogy remains valuable. In addition, the distribution of food—and I do not mean public banquets—remains a persistent symbol in the rituals of Greek festivals. The theme of consecration should be mentioned; it is typical to find that in agrarian rites it is sometimes ipso facto the theme. In the Thesmophoria, the "bringing of the *thesmoi*"—most festivals involve the *"bringing"* of something—gives us a glimpse of a distribution rite, that is, the distribution of the former year's *thesmoi*,[197] which have automatically acquired powers of fertility. But a primitive form of thought has left us an even more easily recognizable bit of posterity. After they have been brought forward by attendants,[198] the loaves of bread that are so often elements in certain festivals tend to take on the quality of blessed or consecrated elements.[199]

The three moments we discern in this very late ritual, a ritual that nevertheless contains some long-lived survivals, are treated as distinct for purposes of analysis; the concepts corresponding to each of them, though they have developed on their own, are still essentially interrelated. The food and drink are offerings and at the same time sources of blessings. The symbolism is parallel and its very content reflects remote origins.

The idea of banquets held at community expense can no longer appear vapid and empty, as it may have at first. In the explosion of thought that the "assemblies" inspired, the dominant feeling in the hearts of a still-childlike people is that they are engaged in a magnificent exchange, a barter involving nature herself and the gods. This atmosphere supports the emergence of symbols through which the power of actual moral experiences continues to survive. The *do ut des* is no longer an abstract principle, and is valid for both worlds. Human commerce finds its reflection and guarantee in a religious form of commerce where the obligation to give and the expectation of reciprocation are direct and essential elements.

※

All this material of the past has been so eroded, so overworked, that we are no longer able to restore it within a specific period of history. We can, however, restore it across a span of history. Greece required a number of intermediate stages to arrive at a hard-and-fast idea of contractual commerce. Still, if the elementary life of rural communities is of any interest, it is not simply because they were the starting points of some unique developments. Greek societies, as we know them, were the product of much intermingling; the rural folk element ought to have preserved some of its original ingredients. In religious history we find symbolic evidence of this. As we have pointed out, at least in part, the cults of the heroes belong to the cults of the countryside. Heroes ought to have flourished especially within the "system of demes," a system of primary interest to us because demes are primitive organizational forms.[200]

In addition, it is in this category of cults that the tradition of folk festivals sometimes continues to survive. It is a tradition that is already modified and complicated. There is reason to assume that many hero cults represent a late synthesis[201] between the element furnished by rural society and that imposed by the dominant feudal *genē*.[202] Is this not the secret of Greece: that it allowed the least number of its legacies to die, and fused the largest possible number of its ancient values? In any case, one of its most authentic successes was to conceive as one an ideal of heroism and an ideal of wisdom. The two easily cohere in figures in whom a benevolent and organizing activity dominates, or in those vaguer ghosts of the founders of the sanctuaries and cities who were the welcoming hosts of men and gods. In the obscure regions where ideals are fashioned, the experiences of a thousand years count for something. A vivid feeling flourished in the past, a sense of joyous participation in a commerce with humanity and nature according to accepted rhythms of life. In contrast to the brutalities of daily life, the myth of the Hyperboreans[203] could, at a very early date, evoke from the distant past the image of a tranquil, just people engaged in the delightful hospitality of the *agapai*.

NOTES

1.   In matters of chronology, we can speak only in relative terms. Still, we are justified in affirming the primitive nature of certain customs: first of all, when their survivals are characterized both by a rustic flavor and by the undifferentiated aspect of a participating society; and second, when practices belonging to a later period involve acts or symbols that are not directly understood in that very period, but that presuppose a more ancient basis or substratum, one that is furnished by ancient feasts. In order to clarify these ideas (while at the same time acknowledging other points of view, and especially those of A. Piganiol's *Essai sur les origins de Rome*), we should affirm that these primitive customs as a whole seem to be "Mediterranean." The Indo-Europeans would have brought with them concepts of an already more advanced sort, concepts connected with the concrete notion of the potlatch (G. Dumézil, *Le Festin d'immortalité*), which consequently presupposes a society of tribal chiefs.

2.   Let us mention at random some aspects that are of more direct interest. In a religious vocabulary, the idea of sacrifice immediately calls to mind the notion of a communal

feast. Thus we have expressions such as *dainusthai* in the calendar of Mykonos (Michel, no. 714. 25 ff.) and *thoinasthai, thoinē*, in religious regulations (ibid., no. 695.11 ff.; no. 721)—expressions that are tied to the interdiction of the *apophora*, that is, to the obligation to consume on the spot and in the sanctuary (see J. de Prott and L. Ziehen, *Leges Sacrae*, II, pp. 238 ff.). The organization of a sacrifice is designated as that of a *hestiasis* (Michel, no. 402.6). References to *hestiatoreia* within the sanctuary are common (Hdt., IV.35; Michel, no. 594.114; Prott and Ziehen, *Leges Sacrae*, II, no. 146; Paus., V.15.2; Plut., *Conv. sept. sap.*, 2). Of particular interest is a passage in Strabo, X, p. 487, where the large *hestiatoreia* of Tenos are regarded as a sign of *tou sunerkhesthai plēthos hikanon tōn sunthuontōn autois astugeitonōn* (see Prott and Ziehen, *Leges Sacrae*, II, p. 259; P. Roussel, *Délos, col. athén.*, pp. 219, 223 [at Kynthion: that is, at a place of an extremely ancient cult], 237; C. Picard, *Ephèse et Claros*, p. 54).

3.   For the meaning of *drān* when it is applied to the Kerykes of Eleusis, see Cleidemus, *ap.* Ath., XIV.640A; concerning the *Kentriadai* and the *Daitroi*, and the ancestral rule of the Kerykes, see Phot., s.v.; J. Toepffer, *Attische Genealogie*, 149 ff.

4.   For the heroes Mattōn and Keraōn, see S. Wide, *Lakonische Kulte*, p. 278 (for the connection with the *mageiroi* of the Spartan *sussitia*, see Polemon, *ap.* Ath., II.39C; Demetrius of Skepsis, *ap.* Ath., IV.173F). In another line of thought, we need merely mention some myths, such as the banquet of Tantalus. Also, we should remark that in Lesbos, where there is a Mount Tantalus, we have both a Thyestes and a Daito (F. M. Cornford, in J. E. Harrison, *Themis*, p. 246). It is interesting that Tantalus' banquet, although retaining totally primitive aspects (Cornford, ibid.), is at the same time and from all evidence a kind of potlatch.

5.   The *Deipnophoroi* of the Oskhophoria at Athens (Harp., s.v.; Plut., *Thes.*, 23); the *Kitharistēs* of the Daitis at Ephesus (according to a fragment of Menander); see Michel, no. 993.36. We should recall here the position of the *Thoinarmostriai* (M. P. Nilsson, *Griech. Feste*, pp. 335, 339), who have to organize meals for the gods and the mortals in the cult of Demeter/Kore at Laconia and Messenia (cf. Prott and Ziehen, *Leges Sacrae*, I, p. 37; II, pp. 182, 186). In the Laconian feast of the Tithenidia (Polemon, *ap.* Ath., IV.139A), the women who celebrate it (the nurses) *thuousi . . . kai tous galathēnous orthagoriskous kai paratitheasin en tēi thoinēi tous ipnitas artous*.

6.   See Dumézil, *Festin*, p. 130. Compare the role of the Roman Vestals during the feasts concerned with the feeding of the community (W. Warde Fowler, *The Roman Festivals*, p. 114). In an admittedly late inscription from Sparta (*CIG*, no. 1239), a woman bears the title *Hestian tēs poleōs kai thoinarmostrian;* another woman is called *Hestian tēs poleōs kai thugatera* (ibid., no. 1442).

7.   Pind., *Isthm.*, II. 39: *theōn daitas proseptukto pasas*.

8.   Prott and Ziehen, *Leges Sacrae*, II, pp. 238 f.; it is used to mean *thoinasthai*. See Michel, no. 720.1, 3 f.

9.   An inscription from Elateia (Michel, no. 703); see Prott and Ziehen, *Leges Sacrae*, ad no. 79.

10.   Eur., *Ion*, 804 f. (*skēnas es hieras . . . koinēn xunapsōn daita paidi tōi neōi*), 1122 ff. (*deipna* [1125] have a highly religious nature, but are to be distinguished from the sacrifice *ant' optēriōn*, which is peculiar to Xouthos; *hōs panta Delphōn laon es thoinēn kalōn* [1140]; cf. the ritual formula intoned by the herald [1166 ff.]; the room is called a *sussition* [1165]. There are several recurring themes in this passage).

11.   Demetrius of Skepsis, *ap.* Ath., IV. 141E (*skiades*): the text indicates that for the Spartans the arrangement of a feast is *mimēma stratiōtikēs agōgēs*. This is a curious example of the change, one that is to be expected, that primitive institutions underwent in Sparta. We know that it is older than the *agogē*, since the division by tents corresponds to the division by phratries, the latter being very archaic and all but obliterated from historical Sparta.

12.   Polemon, *ap. Ath.*, IV. 138F: *skēnas poiountai...euōkhousin.*

13.   Regulation of the Mysteries, Michel, no. 694.34 ff. One entire article is titled *skanan.*

14.   Xen., *Anab.*, V.3.9. Although the Artemision of Skillous was supposed to be a branch of the Ephesian one (see Picard, op. cit., especially p. 59), we do not have to regard it as an import from the East. The cult at Skillous has a very simple nature, one suited for rural populations.

15.   Philostr., *VS*, II.3: at the time of the City Dionysia, *en Kerameikōi potizōn autous homoiōs kai xenous katakeimenous epi stibadōn kissou.*

16.   Polemon, loc. cit.: *en de tautais* [i. e., *skēnais*] *stibadas ex hulēs, epi toutōn de dapidas hupostrōnnuousin, eph' hais tous kataklithentas euōkhousin.*

17.   *Etym. Magn.*, s.v. *Daitis*, pp. 252 f. Strictly speaking the *aition* does not comprise "feasting." Still, a reading of the text suffices to show that its addition is not arbitrary. Groups of young people indulge in amusements and offer a meal to the goddess. Moreover, in regard to the rite instituted to commemorate the event, the *Etym. Magn.* mentions a feast; elsewhere (n. 5 above) we hear of *Deipnophoroi.*

18.   For tales of the Rural Dionysia, see *Etym. Magn.*, 42.3. This practice is at the base of the very widespread mythical theme of the *apankhomenē* goddess (see L. R. Farnell, *Cults of the Greek States*, II, pp. 427 ff.). Note that the feast of the *aiōra* is modified by *eudeipnos* in Hsch., s.v.

19.   Many times there are springs inside sanctuaries (Paus., VII.27.9, VIII,29.1, VIII.42.12, etc., Rules for the Mysteries of Andania). The cult of Artemis is in this case associated with springs (Picard, op. cit., p. 454; W. Immerwahr, *Die Kulte und Mythen Arkadiens*, p. 155), as well as with high places elsewhere. We do not have to review all the evidence that shows the importance of objects in nature to Greek religion. It would be a large task! Before all else, one might note that objects in nature play a large role in Aegean religion. This is a general confirmation, but not an object of investigation for us. Our goal here is to examine documents that are, unfortunately, much later, in order to try to catch a glimpse of the psychology involved in the most ancient feasts.

20.   Pseudo-Dicaearchus (*Geogr. Min.*, 1, p. 197); Farnell, *Cults*, V, p. 79.

21.   See Cornford, in Harrison, *Themis*, p. 244. Perhaps the name of the Hyperboreans could be interpreted this way (O. Schröder, *ArchRW*, VIII [1905], pp. 69 f.). Alcman's description of a feast in the countryside has *en koruphais oreōn* (fr. 56, Page).

22.   Even when applied to the gods, these expressions at times merely designate the "arrival" of these gods into their town or their departure (Ath., IX.394 f.). It is especially true for Dionysus (see Prott and Ziehen, *Leges Sacrae*, II, p. 145). This symbolism conflicts with that of the *katabasis* to the underworld; it has some detectable antecedents. Thus we have the *anodos* or *anabasis* of the cult of Zeus Panamaros at Stratonikeia (see the comprehensive interpretation of A. B. Cook, *Zeus*, I, pp. 18 f.). Note especially the expression *ta anenenkhthenta tōi theōi d[ei]pna* (*BCH*, XXVIII (1904), p. 22, ll. 7f.).

23.   Only a few traits are ancient: the epiphany of Dionysus at Prasiai in Laconia (Paus., III.24.3; cf. Farnell, *Cults*, V, pp. 189 ff.); Dionysus in the basket and on the boat (H. Usener, *Die Sinthflutsagen*, pp. 115 f.); Thoas in Lemnos (G. Dumézil, *Le Crime des Lemniennes*, pp. 42 f.). For our purposes, the scope of these mythical changes allows for minimal definition. The fact that the Ephesian feast of Daitis took place at the seashore could be explained as having something to do with the history of colonization (see Picard, op. cit., p. 322); but it is only through the unique (and ambiguous) rite of the *lavatio* of the cult statue that the feast might be brought into some connection with the sea.

24.   A Theran inscription from the beginning of the fourth century B.C. (*IG*, XII.3, no. 452) reads: *Agorēiois de [de]ipnon [k]ai hia[r]a pro to samēio.* See Aesch., *Supp.*, 205 f.; Prott and Ziehen, *Leges Sacrae*, II, p. 316.

25.   This is the characteristic name that they have in a fragment of Euripides, one that deals with the famous landmarks of the Acropolis (*Erechth.*, fr. 362.46). For the *Lokalmarken*, and the secondary process whereby they are connected to heroic legends, see F. Pfister, *Der Reliquienkult im Altertum*, pp. 357 f.

26.   Harmod., *FGrH*, 319.1 (Jacoby): sacrifices are made to "heroes" (probably to all the heroes at once). The presence of slaves, a fact in some of the most ancient feasts, should be emphasized.

27.   Parth., IX.5. Dumézil (*Festin*, p. 257) goes too far when he traces these feasts back to the Indo-European banquet of immortality.

28.   Ath., XIV.622C.

29.   Sir R. C. Jebb, *Bacchylides*, fr. 17 and commentary.

30.   The will of an Epikteta (Michel, no. 1001). It should be noted that, following a custom that goes quite far back (as we shall see), the will deals with a "reception" for the entire brotherhood. The translation in R. Dareste, B. Haussoullier, and T. Reinach, *Inscr. jurid. gr.*, and Ziehen's interpretation are both unsatisfactory.

31.   Pind., *Ol.*, VII.

32.   See Prott and Ziehen, *Leges Sacrae*, II, p. 208.

33.   See, for example, Nestor's sacrifice in *Od.*, III. This type of sacrifice was practiced especially by the Achaean element (for its Indo-European characteristics, see B. Laum, *Heiliges Geld*, pp. 50 f.).

34.   See R. Hirzel, *Themis, Dike und Verwandtes*, pp. 216 ff. (note the strange inversion).

35.   This is what J. E. Harrison discerned (*Prologomena to the Study of Greek Religion*, pp. 78 ff.), in spite of the artificiality of certain constructs.

36.   I. Lévy (*Recherches sur les sources de la légende de Pythagore*, p. 44) has linked these traits to a certain type of Pythagorean legend: the pseudohistorical novel of the third century. This is not to deny that there were older survivals in this concept.

37.   Polemon, *ap.* Ath., III.138F.

38.   Paus., II.23.1. There are suckling pigs at the Laconian Tithenidia (the feast of the "wet nurses," with a banquet served by women): Polemon, loc. cit. The fish (see below) also should be mentioned.

39.   They were no longer eaten at the Anthesteria of the classical period (Theopomp., *ap.* schol. Ar., *Ran.*, 218).

40.   For example, *phusikullos* bread at the Hyakinthia (Polemon, loc. cit.); *ipnitai artoi* at the Tithenidia (ibid.); Delphic *dorata* in the regulations of the Labyadai; *obeliai artoi* (Poll., VI.75); *akhaine* bread (Ath., II.109E–F). I am sure that the food eaten together at country feasts gave rise to some lively images that have left their mark on the heterogeneous structure of classical ritual. In this connection, note the definition of *ambrosia* in Anticleides (*ap.* Ath., XI.473C), as well as the role of the *pankarpeia* (see Soph., *ap.* Porph., *Abst.*, II.9).

41.   *Georgics*, I.302. Concerning this expression, see J. P. Jacobsen, *Les Mânes*, II, p. 196.

42.   Alcman, fr. 17, Page. A social practice is indicated here, and not simply a constraint of nature, since there are no earth-born fruits during winter, the season Alcman has in mind.

43.   The *Thusiai* are currently thought of as sacrificial banquets.

44.   *Sunodois*: on this word, see Hirzel, *Themis*, p. 330. It persisted for some time in religious vocabularies (Michel, no. 710); it refers to *conventus*, which are the occasions for feasts and which point to an era older than that of the polis. These *conventus* pave the way for the polis: see *sunerkhesthai*, a concrete expression for the synoecisms (Artist., *Pol.*, I.2.1252b.20; Strab., VIII.3, p. 336); we propose translating it as *assemblées*, an expression of rural France.

45.   The subordinate role of the "naturalistic" element shows that the rhythm is,

properly speaking, social. It does not seem at all likely that the arrival of winter is marked by symbols of mourning. Indeed, the contrary seems true. Moreover, if the dead "rise again" at winter's end, it is not because they symbolize the spirits of vegetation returning to the light; they are sent back immediately; they are present only up to that time and can then be gotten rid of.

46.   See Nilsson, op. cit., p. 272.

47.   W. R. Paton and E. L. Hicks, *Inscriptions of Cos*, no. 34; *Inscr. jurid. gr.*, II, no. XXIV.B, side B, 1.30; Michel, no. 428.5 ff.

48.   Polemon, *ap.* Ath., IV.138F.

49.   Xen., *Anab.*, V.3.9.

50.   Bato Sinop. (Ath., XIV.640A): *thuontas Dii Pelōriōi...houtōs philanthrō- pon tēn panēgurin suntelein hōste kai tous xenous hapantas epi tēn thoinēn paralambanein.*

51.   Macrob., *Sat.*, I.7.25.

52.   *Daktuloi* according to Paus., V.7.7. See R. Vallois, *REA*, XXVIII (1926), p. 311.

53.   E. Maass, *Orpheus*, pp. 18 f. See Ziehen's discussion in Prott and Ziehen, *Leges Sacrae*, II, pp. 138 ff.

54.   *Stibas* means a bed of ivy, a sacrificial banquet, a banquet locale, and even the *dies festivus.*

55.   Note, moreover, that the statues of the gods are not always present, or so our sources tell us (L. Weniger, *ArchRW*, XXII [1923–24], p. 31).

56.   We know that this custom is later than Homer. It would be wrong to conclude (as some have done) that the notion of gods reclining at the banquet is also later. If one finds alongside this notion that of the *thronos* (E. Rohde, *Psyche* [French trans.], I, pp. 130 f.), this is an indication of two different religious bases.

57.   For example, in the testamentary endowment of Diomedon of Cos (*Inscr. jurid. gr.*, II, no. 24B, ll. 23 f.), the *xenismos* of Herakles is parallel to the *dexiōsis* of humans. Homer and Pindar are invited to Theoxenia.

58.   Hsch., s.v. *Theoxenia: koinē heortē pasi tois theois* (see *Hymn. Orph.*, XXV.27). This is a most valuable reference. Cf. the Thalysia in *Il.*, IX.534; Dumézil, *Festin*, p. 258.

59.   An old tradition maintained that at one time the gods were dinner guests of men (Hes., fr. 1 [MW]). On Apollo as the *Gastgeber*, see Weniger, loc. cit. Likewise, in the banquet of the dead, the latter are both the hosts and the guests (L. Malten, *Mitteil. d. arch. Inst.*, *R.A.*, XXXVIII [1923], p. 301). At the *xenia* of heroes, the latter are received by the gods (schol. Pind., *Nem.*, VII.68).

60.   Pind., *Paeanes*, 6.63 f. (see Puech's edition, IV, p. 113).

61.   See Dumézil, *Festin*, pp. 11, 134, 166. At Rome, the feast of the Cerealia also had the same origin (Warde Fowler, *The Roman Festivals*, p. 75).

62.   Polemon, *ap.* Ath., IX.372A.

63.   See O. Gruppe, *Griech. Mythol. u. Religionsgesch.*, p. 730, 1; p. 737, 4. The presence of Apollo at the Delphic Theoxenia is not even certain (Nilsson, op. cit., p. 160).

64.   Hdt., I.51; see also *BCH*, XX (1896), p. 625, no. 4, 1. 9. The Theodaisia have the kind of religious character that interests us; note especially the winter celebration at Andros, with its miracle of river water changing into wine.

65.   The themes of the Delphic hymns, the poems of Pindar, and those of Alcaeus (i.e., themes that touch on one or another of these feasts) are themselves related.

66.   For the connections between the myth of the Hyperboreans and the prehistoric conveyance of offerings, see Farnell, *Cults*, IV, pp. 100 ff. (even if his etymological conclusions are suspect).

67.   Himer., XIV.10.

68.   Naturally, it has an individual aspect, in that each person feels obliged to add

to the collection (*eispherein*). It is this notion that we will see dominate when we attempt to discern historical extensions.

69.   Strab., VIII.3, p. 337; XIV.25, p. 660. It is known that several of these systems are attested in Attica, where they survive into the historical period and serve religious ends (see especially Prott and Ziehen, *Leges Sacrae*, no. 26). For the festivals whose raison d'être are the relationships between the demes, one might consult a decree of the deme of Plotheia (Michel, no. 140). The deme is a peasant unit (see *kōmē*), one that the Homeric expression *dēmos te polis te* seems to denote (admittedly, the meaning could have evolved after Homer: see V. Ehrenberg, *Die Rechtsidee im frühen Griechentum*, p. 128). This unit is the village. For the characteristics of the primitive village, see Pöhlmann, *Gesch. des ant. Kommun.*, I, pp. 7 f. For the kinds of dwellings and the oldest morphology, see E. Kornemann, "Polis und Urbs," *Klio*, V (1905), pp. 75 ff.

70.   For the literary sources relating to the feast, see A. Mommsen, *Feste der Stadt Athen im Altertum*, s.v. Its *aition* is in Plut., *De exil.*, 6. The feast is unimportant in the classical period; still, the very existence of the month Metageitnion is an indication of its primitive importance (in our calendar, Metageitnion corresponds to August; but the rounds of the demes could not have taken place in August).

71.   The etymology has a very definite import: the *amphiktiones* are those who "live about," or those who have their *vicus* nearby.

72.   Michel, no. 986. For an interpretation, see Prott and Ziehen, *Leges Sacrae*, II, no. 45.

73.   Demetrius of Skepsis, *ap*. Ath., IV.141E.

74.   The Heraia, which are conducted by sixteen women, represent a very old element in the cult of Olympia (L. Weniger, "Das Hochfest des Zeus in Olympia," *Klio*, V [1905], pp. 28 ff.). The Sixteen organize the races for the young girls; they also set up two choruses, each named after a heroine (Paus., V.16.6).

75.   Prott and Ziehen, *Leges Sacrae*, II, no. 6, ll. 3 f.

76.   Dosiadas and Pyrgion, *ap*. Ath., IV.143B–E. Cf. *CIG*, no. 2554, ll. 60 ff.; *BCH*, XXXIV (1910), p. 331, l. 17.

77.   Ath., 173E.

78.   Tabulae Iguvinae, V.B., ll. 8 f. (C. D. Buck, *Elementarbuch der oskisch-umbrischen Dialekte* [German trans.], p. 155). See also the work of Bréal.

79.   We shall see the Spartans in Lemnos again. The story of the reception of the Argonauts in Lemnos was the subject of Aeschylus' *Hypsipyle* and *Kabeiroi*: Ath., X.428F, IX.373D; schol. Ap. Rhod., I.773 (where the idea of "wintering" is conveyed by *kheimazomenois*).

80.   Dumézil has shown the compelling nature of this interpretation (*Crime*, especially pp. 30, 42 ff.).

81.   Nilsson, op. cit., p. 271 (there is no reason, however, to restrict the reunion to the dead). The month Agrionios (*Agerrhanios* = Aeolic) is often attested in calendars.

82.   *IG*, XII.3, no. 452 (from Thera). The idea of a feast seems most probable. One sees an opposition between the Agoreia (an autumnal feast) and the Artamilia (a springtime feast). See Prott and Ziehen, *Leges Sacrae*, II, p. 316; and Hiller von Gaertringen, *Hermes*, XXXVI (1901), pp. 134 f. The Agoreia are a country celebration "in a place far from the town" (Hiller von Gaertringen, loc. cit.); their essential feature is a *deipnon*, a banquet offered to the gods. The ambiguity of the term is not surprising; the same use of Agoreia occurs in an inscription from Stratonikeia (n. 22 above).

83.   See Harrison, *Themis*, pp. 439 ff. ("Apollo as Megistos Kouros").

84.   Hsch., s.v. *Agrania*, *Agriania*.

85.   Ibid., s.v. *hōraia*.

86.   For the connection between the autumnal *pankarpeia* and the *panspermia* of the springtime celebrations of the dead, see Harrison, *Themis*, p. 292.

87.   See Rohde, *Psyche* (French trans.), II, pp. 13, 45. At Apollonia in the Chalcidice, the feast of the dead was first celebrated in Elaphebolion, and much later in Anthesterion (Hegesand., *ap.* Ath., VIII.334F).

88.   Concerning the Anthesteria, characterized as a feast of the dead, see Harrison, *Prolegomena*, chap. II. Her presentation in this work was rather one-sided, as she herself seems to admit in *Themis*, pp. 275 ff. The Anthesteria are a feast of the dead and also something entirely different.

89.   There is no need for us to examine this process. We simply observe, apropos of the word *hōraia*, the change in meaning it has undergone in the cult of the individual dead, where it refers to anniversary offerings (see Rohde, *Psyche* (French trans.), I, p. 251, n. 2).

90.   A regulation of the phratry of the Labyadai (*Inscr. jurid. gr.*, II, no. XXVIII, A, 31 ff.).

91.   A regulation of the phratry of the Demotionids (ibid., no. XXIX), A, 26 f.; Poll., VIII.107. The age was never specified (as was the civic age of majority). Pollux says: *eis hēlikian proelthontōn*. In the classical period, the age was perhaps somewhat indefinite (a pure conjecture is in *Inscr. jurid. gr.*, p. 212). For a more ancient milieu, the statement of Pollux would have a very clear application, without the need for specific figures.

92.   Quite evidently, the phratry is of Indo-European origin. Whether it corresponds to an Indo-European form of organization is another question. There are some parallels (in Sanskrit and, above all, in Slavic), but these are insufficient to justify mentioning, other than to say that the word *frère* seems to have had a narrow sense in the mother language. In any case, the phratry (which exhibits a "democratic" quality, as opposed to the *genos*) may well have been—but under a different name—the avatar of some very ancient groups.

93.   Steph. Byz., s.v. *patra* (N.B.: *hierōn koinōnikē sunodos*).

94.   Concerning the collective nature of the Athenian Apatouria, see Mommsen, op. cit., s.v. *Apatouria*, with regard to the *dorpeia*.

95.   It is strange that the subject is not even mentioned in E. Boisacq's *Dict. étymol.* Obviously, the root *(s)qer* is as phonetically correct as the root *ker* ("to increase").

96.   *Locus classicus* is in Plut., *Thes.*, 5.

97.   Hippolytus, the Hyperborean virgins, Iphinoe of Megara, the children of Medea, etc.

98.   *Il.*, XXIII.141 f.; Aesch., *Cho.*, 5 f.; Paus., I.37.3, VIII.20.3, VIII.41.3; Philostr., *Her.*, 13.4.

99.   Such is the case in the offerings of Hippolytus (Eur., *Hipp.*, 1425 f.; Paus., II.32.1) to the Hyperborean virgins (Hdt., IV.34) and perhaps also in the offerings to Eukleia (Plut., *Arist.*, 20: there is mention of a *prothusia* in her honor on the eve of a marriage). For the links between the rite of the cutting of hair and marriage (or the age for marriage), see Cook, *Zeus*, I, p. 23.

100.   Arist., *Pol.*, VII.1335A.35 f. In a nearby passage, it appears that marriages took place at a very young age during antiquity (ibid., 18).

101.   A. Brückner, *Mitteil. d. arch. Inst. R.A.*, XXXII (1907), pp. 114 ff. (his attempts to make precise certain constants in ritual seem illusory).

102.   Strab., X.20, p. 482 (following Ephorus): *gamein men hama pantes anankazontai par' autois hoi kata ton auton khronon ek tēs tōn paidōn agelēs ekkrithentes. . . .*

103.   Pl., *Leg.*, VI.771E. To be sure, Xenophon of Ephesus (see 1.2–3, where the *epikhōrios heortē* of Artemis is taken up) is a reliable source in matters regarding Ephesus. Note especially the following: there are separate processions, first of young girls, and then of young men, including Habrokomes, who is sixteen and who is "reckoned among the ephebes" (2.2); the order of the procession is broken up, the ephebes and *parthenoi* come together, and the two heroes quickly fall in love (2.9, 3.1).

104.   R. M. Dawkins, *JHS*, XXVI (1906), p. 204.

105.   None of the proposed explanations is satisfactory (see L. Beauchet's account in *Hist. du droit privé de la républ. athén.*, I, pp. 146 ff.). Still, despite the confusion in the testimonia of the lexicographers, here is the picture that emerges. The *gamēlia* are related to the *panēguris* and can even be called thus (*Lex. Seg.*, *ap. Anecd. Bekk.*, p. 128); the offering is similar to that of the *koureia* (ibid.) and is the prerequisite for "the entry of women into the phratry" (Harp., *ap.* Did., s.v.). On the other hand, as the name indicates, the *gamēlia* take place on the occasion of marriage (see schol. Patm. Dem., 57, 43); and since the regulations of the Demotionids consider them part of the *meia* (see *Inscr. jurid. gr.*, pp. 212, 226), they occur on the third day of the Apatouria, just like the *koureia*, with the latter being for young men and the former for maidens.

106.   See E. Fehrle, *Die kult. Keuschh. im Alt.*, p. 148. Demeter was united with Iasion at sowing time (*Od.*, V.125 f.).

107.   *Il.*, XIV.295 f. For the relationship between the myth of hierogamy and the *Kiltgang*, see Nilsson, op. cit., p. 53; idem, "Die Grundl. d. spartan. Leb.," *Klio*, XII (1912), p. 333.

108.   Schol., *Il.*, XIV.296: *phasi ton Dia en Samōi lathrāi tōn goneōn apopartheneusai tēn Hēran· hothen Samioi mnēsteuontes tas koras lathrāi sunkoimizousin, eita parrhēsiāi poiousi tous gamous.* The custom at Naxos (Callim., *Aet.*, I, fr. 75 [Pfeiffer]), which K. Kuiper (*REG*, XXV [1912], pp. 317 f.) failed to make clear, may have some connections with the Samian one (the scholion [loc cit.] does compare the two).

109.   See Farnell, *Cults*, II, pp. 461 ff.

110.   At Arcadian Orkhomenos (Paus. VIII.5.11; cf. VIII. 13. 1, 5), at first a virgin was assigned to the sanctuary; the rule was changed, however, after the priestess had been violated. N.B. these customs and the *aition.*

111.   Fehrle, op. cit., pp. 164 ff.

112.   Frazer's translation, "their husbands," is unacceptable, since the text does not read *tois heautōn andrasi.*

113.   *Badu* (or *Fadu*) = *hēdu* (Frazer, ad. loc.). There is a popular flavor to this designation.

114.   It is interesting to note that Crete is the classic land for hierogamies: see Harrison, *Prologomena*, p. 564; A. W. Persson, "Der Urspr. der eleus. Myster.," *ArchRW*, XXI (1922), p. 301.

115.   Diod. Sic., V.72.4: *legousi de kai tous gamous tou te Dios kai tēs Hēras en tēi Knōsiōn khōrāi genesthai kata tina topon plēsion tou Tērēnos potamou, kath' hon nun hieron estin, en hōi thusias kat' eniauton hagious hupo tōn enkhōriōn sunteleisthai, kai tous gamous apomimeisthai, kathaper ex arkhēs paredothēsan.*

116.   See G. Glotz, *L'Ordalie dans la Grèce primitive*, p. 72.

117.   Paus., II.38.2; schol. Pind., *Ol.*, VI.149.

118.   Perhaps in this connection a certain Lycian myth ought to be mentioned (Plut., *De mul. vir.*, 9). In any case, the Arcadian and Elean legend of Daphne (Paus., VIII.21.2–3) has some relationship with prehistoric customs: Leukippos, Daphne's lover, is told to dress like a woman; disguised in women's clothing, he wins the friendship of Daphne; one day Daphne and her companions, wishing to bathe in the Ladon, discover the identity of Leukippos and put him to death. One recognizes in this story the well-known rite of the sexes' exchanging clothes: see the *Hubristika* (Harrison, *Themis*, pp. 505 ff.), an obscure rite, but one that has bearing on the primitive marriage (the Spartan custom comes to mind) and also on ancient feasts. One is surprised to find that in games of an archaic character, the prize consists of clothing: cf. the Argonauts at Lemnos *before* their marriages with the Lemnian women (Pind., *Pyth.*, IV.252 ff.); the Theoxenia at Achaean Pellana (Paus., VIII.27.4); the garment woven by the "Olympian Sixteen," who organize the races that were instituted in honor of the marriage of Hippodameia (Paus., V.16.2 ff.). Weaving is the exclusive task of

women (see Gortynian Code, II. 51, III.26); this fact helps to clarify Plut., *Quaest. Graec.*, 58.

119.   Ov., *Fast.*, III.523 ff.; Mart., IV.64.16 ff. See H. Usener, *Ital. Mythen* (*Kl. Schr.*, IV), pp. 119 f.; Harrison, *Themis*, pp. 197 f.; Dumézil, *Festin*, p. 128. M. Granet (*Fêtes et chansons anc. de la Chine* [French trans.]), who generally eschews comparative statements, makes this one on pp. 212 f. We are guided by the same principle and defer to his otherwise full study.

120.   Ath., XIII.555C. The expressions are noteworthy: "Cecrops was first to establish monogamy, *anedēn to proteron ousōn tōn sunodōn kai koinogamiōn ontōn.*"

121.   In the will of Diomedon of Cos (*Inscr. jurid. gr.*, II, no. XXIV.B, C, ll. 23 ff.), an evidently human marriage is intended, one in which Herakles (who just received his *xenismos*) is involved. It seems likely that the couch, which had been prepared for the *xenismos*, had to be left in place for the marriage in which the hero acts as the host (Paton and Hicks, *Inscriptions of Cos*, no. 36).

122.   For the qualities of fertility (and later of an aphrodisiac) that were contained in willow leaves (which in turn were used by women for the Thesmophoria), see Fehrle, op. cit., p. 139.

123.   Hdt., II.64, claims it was the Egyptians who initiated this prohibition (the wording is too vague to allow for a comparision with the strictly Eastern custom of sacred prostitution).

124.   Prott and Ziehen, *Leges Sacrae*, II, no. 61 (an archaic law of Olympia): *hai de beneoi en tiaroi.* See A. Brand, *Hermes*, XXI (1886), p. 312.

125.   This, then, accounts for legends like that of the Garden of the Hesperides. See the excellent suggestion of Gruppe (op. cit., p. 457), who in studying the origins of the Herakles myth, reconstructs a feast on Mt. Aetna, together with a hierogamy in which sacred apples (symbols of conjugal unity) play a role. Contests with fruit seem attested (see Plut., *Quaest. Graec.*, 51).

126.   Pind., *Pyth.*, IX.111 f.

127.   See Farnell, *Cults*, II, p. 448, n. b; his intuition seems warranted.

128.   Dances continued to be a part of the cult of Artemis (Nilsson, op. cit., pp. 184 ff., 196 ff.). It is worth noting that Artemis had followers, who corresponded to the satyrs (*Hymn. Hom. Ap.*, 262 f.). Primitive poetry left behind even fewer traces. Still, see Semos of Delos (*FGrII*, 396.24 [Jacoby]), *ap.* Ath., XIV.622A. In describing certain popular practices, he speaks of the *autokabdaloi*, as though they belonged to the same category as the *ithuphalloi*; moreover, the former were called *iamboi* (along with their songs). These were probably improvised songs.

129.   See L. Preller and C. Robert, *Griechische Mythologie*[4], I, p. 718. The cypress trees that shade the tomb of Alcmaeon at Psophis were actually called *parthenoi* by the locals (Paus., VIII.24.7).

130.   Plut., *Thes.*, 13.2-3.

131.   Hdt., IV.145.

132.   As did Dumézil (*Crime*, p. 57) after translating the passage somewhat arbitrarily (ibid., p. 52).

133.   A schema might help us get oriented. In the ensemble, two processes are discerned: one (which we have been seeing throughout) is that of the concentration and appropriation by chiefs and noble *genē*; the second, exemplified in Sparta and partially in Crete, presents us with an identification between *phiditia* and *koina hiera* (D.H., II.23). This in itself is enough to show that a continuity exists. Even so, the primitive institutions are placed in a framework we know all too well, namely, that of a male society that is organized militarily (H. Jeanmaire, *REG*, XXVI [1913], pp. 121 ff.). The result is that the essential notions of a primitive substratum have undergone discernible changes.

134.   An explanation is due. The notions we have in mind had been elaborated well before the arrival of the Greek language in Greece. Still, vocabulary may be of help if the words applied to certain concrete practices convey certain sustained representations, and thus help extend a kind of psychology which is much older than the change in language. Subsequent facts in history prove this hypothesis. However, it goes without saying that when we find different meanings for the word *sumballein*, what we may regard as its underlying notion is not necessarily more ancient than the others in our sources.

135.   See Parth., IX.5 (on the Thargelia of Miletus). What we hope to rediscover in *pherō* (in connection with certain attested practices) is the concrete notion that appears in its most basic fashion in peasant feasts. Let us add that under diverse forms, the practice of the Spartan *sussitia* presents a lively image of this notion. See also the term *apophora*.

136.   See Prott and Ziehen, *Leges Sacrae*, II, p. 160 (the Latin *fertum* is compared).

137.   Soph., *El.*, 326.

138.   Dittenberger, SIG^3, no. 998.6, 24 (regulations of the Asclepium of Epidaurus from the end of the fifth century B.C.): *phernan to thioi krithan medimmnon*.

139.   See *REG*, XXX (1917), pp. 290 f.

140.   In the regulations of the phratry of the Labyadai, D, 29 f. (see Prott and Ziehen, *Leges Sacrae*, II, pp. 223 ff.), a whole series of religious outlays are attributed to the initiative of a legendary ancestor who in his daughter's dowry offered the objects enumerated as sacrifices.

141.   The *diaphora* in the regulations of the Mysteries of Andania are dues that come from the initiated: one part goes to the sacred treasury; another is kept by Mnasistratos, the last representative of the *genos* that had been in possession of the Mysteries. The sense of "interest" is attested in regard to a religious foundation (Prott and Ziehen, *Leges Sacrae*, p. 525).

142.   Several of them are still practiced in kind.

143.   In this usage, *eranos* is not special to groups of *eranistai*, properly speaking.

144.   Not necessarily. Even in documents from a late period, there seems to be an allusion to a recent reform that in one instance replaced the contribution in kind with an assessment in silver (Michel, no. 984; see P. Foucart *Assoc. relig.*, p. 43).

145.   It betrays an aristocratic contempt for customs foreign to Homeric society. The word *ageirō* was perhaps similarly discredited.

146.   Especially *Pyth.*, V.77 (naturally it underwent a change, but it continued to designate a feast celebrated by the city in common).

147.   Boisacq, *Dict. étymol.*, s.v. *heortē*.

148.   The expression *kharin pherein* could elicit some comparisons. In keeping with the bilateral notion of *timē*, Loxias is said to come to his worshippers *athanatan kharin Thēbais epimeixōn* (Pind., *Parth.*, II.23). On the other hand, in Eur., *Ion*, 1180, *kharin pherein* refers to a very specific type of homage: the presentation of a cup of honor *tōi neōi despotēi*.

149.   *Ol.*, I.39 f.: an *eranos* given by Tantalus at the summit of Sipylus.

150.   Callim., *Cer.*, 72, is once more precise in his archaisms. When he speaks of Erysikhthon's act of sacrilege (we recognize it as a ritual act), one for which he was plagued with insatiable hunger, he adds that no one dared to send Erysikhthon *oute...eis eranōs oute xundeipnia*.

151.   Pind., *Pyth.*, XII.14 (N.B. the scholion as well); [Apollod.], *Bibl.*, II.36. The latter seems to have an independent source; both contain the word.

152.   That is, the "hospitable" one (there is no reason to interpret him as Hades: Preller and Robert, *Griechische Mythologie*[4], I, p. 232).

153.   There is an interesting variant in Apollodorus: the requested *eranos* is not for him, but for the wedding of Hippodameia, which was, apparently, the occasion for a feudal service.

154.   *Thiasoi* or groups of *orgeōnes*. There is an ancient relationship between these and the demes (Michel, no. 1044; see P. Stengel, *Die griech. Kultusalter.*[2], p. 167). Even from a late period, religious confraternities are sometimes referred to as phratries. This certainly represents a very liberal use of the word (see F. Poland, *Gesch. des griech. Vereinsw.*, pp. 53 f.), and it is of some interest to us, since phratry, after passing through vulgar Latin, evolves into the French *frairie*.

155.   Concerning the *Festmahl* in the confraternities and its religious significance (often obliterated in late sources), see Poland, op cit., pp. 258 f. The *mutitationes* of some organizations are of present interest to us (H. Graillot, *Le Culte de Cybèle*, p. 90).

156.   The notion of *phora* is so central to these associations that it has given rise to the expression *sunodon pherein* (see Prott and Ziehen, *Leges Sacrae*, II, p. 132; Poland, op. cit., p. 159). On this subject, one should recall the semantic principle that Maurice Cahen demonstrated so brilliantly in his work on the Scandinavian libation.

157.   Boisacq, *Dict. étymol.*, s.v. (The meaning of "band" or "company" should be dismissed for linguistic reasons.) The fact that *telos* is traced back to the root *qwel* ("to turn"), and that originally it evoked certain spatial images (ibid., p. 952), should not concern us. To try to be precise would for the moment be in vain.

158.   Therein result some ambiguities that are a source of embarrassment to scholars: see R. Reitzenstein, *ArchRW*, XIX (1916–19), p. 191 (on the expression *tous kata tēn khōran telountas tōi Dionusōi*). The unity of the notion within the religious vocabulary can be illustrated by examples like Prott and Ziehen's *Leges Sacrae*, II, no. 88.25 (*suntelein tous khōrous eis ta krita*), and no. 46.67 f.

159.   Sometimes its relic surfaces, as in the endowment of Alkesippos of Delphi (*Inscr. jurid. gr.*, no. XXIII.D), *hōste thusian kai damothoinian suntelein tan polin*. See Bato Sinop. (Ath., XIV.640A) concerning the banquets of the Thessalians: *tēn panēgurin suntelein*.

160.   Concerning this notion, which was to become quasi-juridical, see, for example, Xen., *Anab.*, V.3 (a regulation inscribed on a stele to commemorate the founding of Skillous): *ton ekhonta kai karpoumenon tēn men dekatēn katathuein...*

161.   Dittenberger, *SIG*[3], no. 993.6, 12 (*to khōrion ekdōsounti dōtinas...praxantes tas dōtinas ek tou khōriou*); see also Dittenberger's commentary.

162.   *Il.*, IX.155 f.: *hoi ke he dōtinēisi theon hōs timēsousi kai hupo skēptrōi liparas teleousi themistas* (see Ehrenberg, op. cit., pp. 7 f.). On the subject of *themis* and its primary, concrete significations, it might be well to mention certain expressions within the religious vocabulary like *tithenai spondēn* (in the regulations of the Iobakkhoi: 111, 117, 127, 159 ff.).

163.   From her point of view, J. E. Harrison has already done this by showing the link between the most ancient notion on initiation and the notion that functions within the Mysteries (*Themis*, pp. 508 ff.).

164.   *Hēra teleia* = *numpheuomenē* (Paus., IX. 2.5, IX.9.3). On the subject of *teleumenais*, see Paton's discussion of a religious regulation from Cos (*Dialekt-Inschr.*, no. 3721; Prott and Ziehen, *Leges Sacrae*, no. 132), where it is correctly argued that women who marry for the first time are distinguished from those *epinumpheuomenais*. Cf. Dittenberger, *SIG*[3], no. 1006.

165.   See especially A. Dieterich, *Eine Mithrasliturgie*, pp. 121 ff.

166.   In the cult of Zeus Panamaros in Caria (Cook, *Zeus*, I, pp. 23 ff.).

167.   This is the current *communis opinio* (T. Reinach, L. Beauchet, and F. Poland); Thalheim (in K. F. Hermann's *Griech. Rechtsalt.*[2], p. 113, n. 1) has a better perspective.

168.   Thus we have words like *sunagein*, *eranon*, *plērōtēs*, and *phora*. They are used to describe both the assessments to the society and the contributions for a loan. *Phora* describes the restitution of the loan with staggered payments of the same sort as those of the members' *phora*.

169.   It is especially the idea of reciprocity that appears foremost both in the practice

of the loan and in the conception that is usually attached to the word (Eur., *Suppl.*, 361 ff.; Isoc., X.20; Dem., X.40, XVIII.312, XXI.101).

170.   Michel, no. 979. 17 ff.; *Supplementum*, no. 1562.6. Above all, note the use of *asumbolos* (no. 998.44).

171.   Of concern is the juridical protection of foreigners (an idea of great antiquity: Hes., *Op.*, 210). It recurs as a theme of praise in Pindar. In earlier times this protection was assured by the system of the *proxenia* (see H. Francotte, *Mél. de droit public grec*, pp. 169 f.).

172.   Immediately following, the author speaks of the feast of the dead in Chalcidicean Apollonia, a feast whose legendary basis he had recounted.

173.   See the testament of Diomedon of Cos *(Inscr. jurid. gr.*, II, no. XXIV.A, B.4); cf. Prott and Ziehen, *Leges Sacrae*, II, p. 355. In this cult the *apopuris* is a sacrifice to a hero, that is, an *enagismos* (Ath., IV.344C), and is therefore something consumed. Undoubtedly, from its very meaning, the *apopuris* was originally intended for consumption. And above all it is for the use (*tēn khreian*) of the inhabitants that the lake yields fish in such abundance. The remainder of Hegesander's text indicates just this.

174.   Our interpretation does not require us to assume that Bolbe was the name of a *kōmē*.

175.   On the Theodaisia of Andros (during the Nones of January), see Pliny, *HN*, II.231. For similar traditions, see Gruppe, op. cit., p. 736, n. 2.

176.   J. E. Harrison, "Delphika," *JHS*, XIX (1899), p. 208. The clearest formula is in Hippoc., *Somn.*, II, p. 14L.

177.   What evolved into rites of rain, for example, have close links with the feasts of spring: see the Arab *achourâ* in E. Doutté, *Magie et rel.*, pp. 426 f., and also the practice of tomb visitations (ibid., pp. 431 f.). The notion of the dead being thirsty (Gruppe, op. cit., p. 831), which belongs to this festival, is also connected with the Hydrophoria of the Anthesteria, with the myth of the flood, and with certain practices such as those that deal with the *manalis lapis* at Rome (see E. Samter, "Altröm. Regenzauber," *ArchRW*, XXI [1922], pp. 329 ff., for the meaning of *manalis*).

178.   On this belief, see A. Dieterich, *Mutter Erde*, pp. 48 f. The link between the concepts of river, flower, marriage, and death is particularly suggestive (Glotz, *L'Ordalie*, p. 72).

179.   See Dieterich, *Mutter Erde*, p. 56 f.

180.   From very early on, the representations of the celestial world were associated with this fundamental notion (for the relationship between the conjunction of the sun and the moon and marriage, see Gruppe, op. cit., pp. 163, 457, etc.). Characteristically, they are integrated in an essentially social representation. The term *sunodos* testifies to the derivation: "assemblies," "marriage," "solar conjunction."

181.   We come full circle with *telos*. See the suggestive observations in Harrison, *Prolegomena*, p. 356, concerning the words *epiteleios* and *epiteleiōsis*.

182.   See, in particular, H. Hepding, *Attis*, pp. 137 f. On the use of the *stips* (an evocative word) at Rome, see Graillot, *Culte de Cybèle*, p. 85. Our sources (Lucretius, Juvenal) show that the donors were generous.

183.   An amphictionic decree concerning the celebration of the Ptoia (Michel, no. 700.31) deals with the collection of funds for a national cult. Cf. the usage in a Messenian calendar, which goes back perhaps to a more ancient form of *agermos* (Prott and Ziehen; *Leges Sacrae*, I, no. 15.14 f.).

184.   P. Foucart, *Assoc. relig.*, p. 191, no. 4.8.

185.   *Dialekt.-Inschr.*, no. 3721.12 (a regulation in regard to the priesthood of Demeter at Cos).

186.   Michel, no. 713.11 ff.

187.   On the history of the word *pelanos*, see P. Stengel, *Opferbräuche der Griechen*, pp. 66 ff.

188.   See Ziehen's probing discussion in Prott and Ziehen, *Leges Sacrae*, II, pp. 279 ff. Note that the product of the *pelanos* is used at a *hestiasis* (Michel, no. 713.11 ff.).

189.   A. Dieterich, *Kl. Schr.*, chap. XXI (on *agermos*, pp. 337 ff.).

190.   For the connections between the stick laden with fruit and the *eiresiōnē*, the *xulon* of the Delphic *daphnēphoria*, and the Oskhophoria, see ibid., pp. 338, 340.

191.   Dawkins, *JHS*, XXVI (1906), p. 201.

192.   On this notion, see Dieterich, *Kl. Schr.*, p. 336. As usual, the views of Mauss ("Essai sur le don," *Année sociol.*, n.s., I [1923–24], pp. 53 ff.) are worth retaining. As for the special expression *tokos*, it brings to mind another series of rituals that are equally evocative of primitive feasts. On the remote antecedents of the marriage between Dionysus and the queen at the Boukoleion and its original significance, see E. Maass, *Hermes*, LXII (1927), pp. 1 ff.

193.   A. Piganiol, *Recherches sur les jeux romains*, pp. 92 ff.; see also H. Usener, *Kl. Schr.*, IV, pp. 117 ff.

194.   Zos., II.5.2 f.; note the citation of a Sibylline oracle, in which we find the expression *ta de panta tethēsaurismena keisthō, ophra . . . porsunēis*. (The *thēsauros* has a very old history; see Maass, loc. cit.)

195.   Usener (loc. cit.) makes a suggestive observation: the ceremony belongs to a group of preparatory rites that have to do with the *abtun* of the period just ended. Moreover, are not the primitive rites at the "closing of the year" simply those merrymakings where the products of that year are consumed in excess?

196.   Plut., *Quaest. Graec.*, 12.

197.   Schol. Lucian, *Dial. Meret.* (Rohde), *RhM*, XXV, p. 549: *hōn nomizousi ton lambanonta kai tōi sporōi sunkataballonta euphorian hexein*. This can be clarified through its similarity with the rustic Palilia at Rome, during which the remains of the October Horse and the ashes of the calves from the Fordicidia are distributed in order to fertilize the land (G. Wissowa, *Religion und Kultus der Römer*[2], pp. 165 ff.).

198.   Ath., III.109E.

199.   See Perdrizet, *REG*, XXVII (1914), pp. 266–70. Some links exist with the origins of coinage. The *obelias artos* of Poll., VI.75 (see a decree of Canopus in Dittenberger, *Or. Gr. Inscr. Sel.*, no. 56.73 ff.) orients us in the direction of the very interesting suggestions of Laum, *Heiliges Geld* (see especially pp. 109 ff.).

200.   Cf. Prott and Ziehen, *Leges Sacrae*, I, p. 51, with II, p. 123.

201.   As a rule, heroes' names have a transparent etymology and, accordingly, an Indo-European origin. The same is not exactly true for the names of gods.

202.   From another point of view, Gruppe (op. cit., p. 755) shows how certain prehistoric religious elements have been incorporated into the *Heldenlied*; in his well-known works, Usener adopts a similar stance.

203.   See Pind., *Pyth.*, X. The mode of mythical transposition can be recognized in this ode composed in praise of the Thessalians (cf. n. 66 above). It goes without saying that myths about the Golden Age belong to the same source. Like those of the Flood, these myths represent an *anthrōpogonia* that differs from those in aristocratic legends; it is heterogeneous compared to the latter (see Gruppe, op. cit., pp. 441, 444).

CHAPTER 3

Dionysus and the Dionysiac Religion: Inherited Elements and Original Features

Jeanmaire's book about Dionysus, although addressed to a wide audience, is a solid piece of scholarship.[1] It is rich in thought, and reexamines for purposes other than mere erudition an important chapter in the history of religion.

The author's method is not phenomenological. He does not try to establish the timeless essence of Dionysism; rather, he analyzes his theme within a carefully worked out historical context. However, the subject of his study does not easily lend itself to those more satisfying analyses that describe definite stages of "evolution." Laterally, Jeanmaire's book attempts to tell us the origin of Dionysus' cult; this is the purpose of the first chapter, which he bases on our most ancient testimony. In the later chapters, he tries to illustrate how myth and mystical thought developed even in a rather late period, and how Dionysus fared in a Hellenistic and Greco-Roman milieu. But over half the book—in fact its major section— is devoted to those elements that characterized Dionysiac religion as it existed in the archaic period.

With a cult such as this, questions of origin or dates of diffusion cannot be a starting point. Since these are only objects of hypotheses, they are mentioned later in the study, for example, when the author discusses a theory of Thracian origin (pp. 99 ff.) and the well-known affinities with Near-Eastern sources, which argue for an Asian origin (where the names themselves, god-son [= *nusos*] and Earth [= *Semele*], suggest a substratum of two divinities associated with earth and fertility). As far as chronology is concerned, any precision is impossible. According to Herodotus, the

This review originally appeared in *REG*, LXVI (1953), pp. 377–95.

Greeks conceived of the god's history as relatively recent. Jeanmaire does not, then, deal formally with problems of chronology; and at the very most he will note (p. 86) that the period of the Dorian invasion, which Rohde tried to link with Dionysism, is "especially remote in terms of testimony." For Jeanmaire, it seems that the religion he is studying should have been diffused sometime after the second millennium.

The author's investigation of traditional sources associated with the god's name produces more definite results. He examines first the beliefs and popular customs that have been placed specifically under Dionysus' patronage, and second the heortology or system of Athenian religious festivals, the only one about which we have considerable information. It is for this reason that he begins his book with a chapter entitled "Approaches to Dionysus." The purpose of this chapter, in its general and specific points, is to suggest areas of human activity where the conception of the god, the images evoked by it, and the accompanying emotional states manifest themselves with some immediacy. In the most archaic representations of his cult, Dionysus is associated with vegetation, and in this aspect he emerges from a religion which, though primeval, has at its roots a belief that will remain lively in him. The name *Bacchus* designates at the same time the god, the initiate, and the branch that is carried by the devotee and consecrates him to the god. Dionysus is more specifically associated with the cultivation of trees, especially the vine. This fact offers Jeanmaire an opportunity to show that in the history of Greek agriculture the cultivation of grains and that of fruit-bearing trees were in some way opposed to each other. Hesiod, a famous advocate of the former, describes "the peasant's life" as "tied down to the earth" (p. 31); there are no feasts and there is little room for the Graces. In contrast, the cultivation of fruit-bearing trees, because of the succession of seasons or the alternating rhythm of peasant life itself, creates a communal form of cheerful behavior, a sense of accord with the god of joy, *polugēthēs*.

With regard to Dionysus' prehistory, the author makes a penetrating observation: if Dionysus became the god of the vine, there must have been some "vacancy for him to fill," for in continental Greece, viticulture appears to have developed and expanded without a well-defined religious patron. But the author could have said more. Although the mythology of the vine is meager (p. 24), both in legend and in certain ritual patterns there exists a clear thread of evidence concerning the inventor of the vine and wine; this myth did not at first or always involve Dionysus. The tale of the vine's "invention" contains a recollection of royal or kingly magic power, and everything develops as if, between the ancient period and the "archaic" period (the period of the new god), there existed, as in the case of already constituted divine personalities, no stage involving the service of a religious group such as the Eumolpidai or even the Phytalidai.

The system of Athenian festivals—and it is possible to refer to a system, since the festivals can be described as Dionysiac feasts occurring in winter—gives preliminary support to some very important conclusions. First, Dionysus is found to be the patron of rituals much older than himself: the *phallophoria* of the Rural Dionysia, the more or less disorderly procession (*kōmos*), and the use of masks. Although a "new god," he is strongly represented in these practices. As Jeanmaire says, "The feeling of divine presence is essential in the conception one has of his interventions" (p. 38). But the religious activities associated with Dionysus prove that one is dealing with a complex personality. The season of his feasts is one of intense popular activity and gives rise to the joy and consolation of festive celebrations. But traditionally this same season also provides a period of contact with the world beyond, a world not only which the dead inhabit but which is also the source of the blessings they offer, or according to a Hippocratic text, "whence comes nourishment." The Anthesteria, especially, reveal this rich complexity of emotions. Another factor related to this is directly relevant to the religion of Dionysus. Earlier, Jeanmaire had pointed out that there was a prehistoric tradition of orgiastic rites in Greece, such as those associated with the cult of Artemis. But for us as well as for the Greeks, *orgiasmos*, "the celebration of orgies," suggests Dionysus most of all; according to the testimony from the festivals, it is associated with Dionysus himself. The Lenaean festival, more or less "in decline" by the classical period, could have gotten its name only from the *lēnai*, another name for the bacchants. (Jeanmaire cannot avoid mentioning the etymology *lēnos* = "wine-press," even though he thinks that the linguistic arguments against it are irrefutable.)

As far as one can ascertain, then, these appear to be the most general characteristics of a divinity at once single and multiple—surely unique in the Greek pantheon.

The "most ancient testimony about Dionysus" is from Homer. His reserve seems almost prejudicial; he barely mentions the god of wine and his *orgia*. But the Lycurgus episode (*Il.* VI.130–40), if only because of its allusive character, is evidence that a myth of definite shape had already come into being. It is a tale of the infant deity, the god "of rapture," escorted and protected by his "nurses," who bear the *thustla*, a kind of *thursos*. They are chased by the wolf-man to the edge of the sea, into which the small Dionysus in terror plunges for safety. It would be interesting to determine with some precision the date of this traditional tale. Jeanmaire tries to do so, and his effort has some merits. The passage in question can hardly be taken out of a context wherein one sees a stratum of "Homeric civilization" that is rather modern. There is, for example, mention of the *naos*, a type of sanctuary which can hardly be earlier than the seventh century's end. On the other hand, there is a scholion indicating that the episode was altered and adapted by many authors, "beginning with Eumelos in the *Europia*." Some reason exists to suggest that this poem, a natural place to insert the legend of Dionysus as part of the history of Cadmus' progeny, managed to establish "certain features that would eventually become canonical" in the life of the god. The Homeric parable, obviously an abridgment, is likely derived from it (p. 73).

In any case, from about 700 B.C., evidence exists of a mildly comic but edifying style of poetic tradition about Dionysus. Its origins might well be examined. Ritual themes of pursuit and escape appear in some cults, and they figure prominently in such legends as that of the daughters of Proitos. These involve a pre-Dionysiac scenario that shows up in certain religious practices: a "divine child" and the nurses who surround him are threatened by some menacing character. Jeanmaire would like to find the origin of this motif in the recollection or transformation of "rites of adolescence," the subject of his work *Couroi et Courètes* (pp. 76 ff.); but his arguments in this respect are unconvincing. The infant god of nativity stories is very different from the "subject" exposed to trials upon his emergence from childhood. The author is forced to assume that many scenarios combined to make a composite legend; but in other respects, he himself little appreciates the synthetic process as a principle of explanation. One must at least retain as basic the apparently Aegean ritual themes of women representing the god's nurses, and the pursuit to which they can be subjected. Equally important and a substantial piece of Homeric testimony about Dionysus is his epithet *mainomenos*. It almost seems to designate his nature in Homer, who was, moreover, not unaware of maenads and their ecstasies.

One characteristic of Jeanmaire's study is already apparent. One after the other, he selects certain testimonia, usually lengthy but restricted, and analyzes each within a historical context in order to discover some psychological facts. We should not, in my view, understand his method as literary-critical; it is more an inductive approach, one that is very personal; and it contrasts strikingly with the usually fastidious methods normally associated with philologists. Several times, one doubts that it is Euripides who supplies him with his material.

On the subject of orgiastic rites, Euripides' *Bacchae* offers a poetic tableau with a specifically didactic purpose, and within the context of other testimonia, one can place it geographically. The adventure of Skylas (Herod., IV.78–80) provides an example from a frontier region of Greece of delirium and possession in a male *thiasos*. A century later, Demosthenes attests that, among members of a *thiasos* dedicated to a foreign god, Sabazios (but one with analogies to the Greek god), there existed a form of behavior similar to that observed in the cult of Dionysus (XVIII.259). And in the vast area of the eastern Mediterranean, cult practices existed that characterized the bacchants of Greece as "an ancient Aegean substratum"—Asia Minor and its cult of the Magna Mater, Syria and its goddess, Canaan and its *nebi'im*. Perhaps these forms of orgiastic rites have to be distinguished. Even so, it is possible to show that in this region of the ancient world there was a similar kind of unity involving a yearning for ecstasy and trance. And if such a unity leads us to a period of prehistory, the classical problems are to a certain extent modified. When Rohde wanted to make Thrace the center for the diffusion of orgiastic practices, it was precisely because he needed to explain what he regarded as a disturbing element in an "Apollonian" Hellenism. It should be pointed out that for Jeanmaire the "origin" of Dionysus might be sought in Asia (surely he too easily minimizes the evidence from Greco-Lydian inscriptions concerning the name *Bacchus* [p. 58]); but for a historical understanding of orgiastic practices themselves, it is to his advantage to define an area or field of extension in which the Greek phenomenon, insofar as what is traditional rather than borrowed, should be situated.

This phenomenon can now be examined by itself; it can be defined as an act of possession. The Greeks speak of *mania* "madness" and they consider it divine. The *Bacchae* brilliantly illustrates such an interpretation and allows us to see the seriousness and profundity with which the Greeks invested *mania*. Although the significance of the *Bacchae* is a natural topic for Jeanmaire, he has managed to keep it more or less outside the scope of his main inquiry. Even so, he has some definite but nuanced things to say about it. What is Euripides' "real" attitude? Save for some of the philosophers, we know very few of the great figures of Greece "from the inside"; the tragic poets, for obvious reasons, are even less accessible. But in this case, we are not completely at a loss. The author cannot accept the thesis that Euripides represents a spirit of free thought sympathetic to Pentheus. Although Jeanmaire does not talk about a religious "conversion"—this would be too strong a word—the poetry of the drama, its tone and general movement, give the impression that Euripides is truly captivated, and is as sensitive as any poet could be to the ardor and rapture of Dionysiac religion, to the incomparable power of "divine madness." This view raises a question: just how far is the special kind of "sincerity" which characterizes literary works exceeded? Jeanmaire notes some reservations one must have about several parts of the play: the denouement of the play itself, the comic quality of Cadmus and Teiresias, representing as they do a certain form of piety, and the subtle irony of a forceful but absurd apologetic that attempts to justify the new scandal of Dionysiac religion by appealing to a tradition much older and more venerable. Perhaps, too, there is reason for some caution when the author speaks of a conflict between "religious fact" and the "rationalism that the poet and his generation espoused for so many years." Such a position, or at least the way it is stated, could very well contain some anachronisms.

One could really ponder the subject of the *Bacchae's* significance; but Jeanmaire deals with it in an *excursus* at the end of the chapter (chap. IV, pp. 138–56). There the author proposes to define and identify the psychological phenomenon of *mania*. The Greeks accepted the fact of *mania* with revealing complacency, and they spontaneously acknowledged the state of *furor* in many encounters as something "demonic." Euripides' account of Herakles' madness is an important example not only because of its religious or mythical interpretation of *mania* but because the dramatist describes the phenomenon in terms that are almost clinical. Symptomatic "fits" and stages of "hysteria" have their parallels in the "observations" of clinical psychiatry (pp. 112 ff.). Symptoms such as these are also associated with gods other than Dionysus. Here, however, they are expressed in the language of Dionysiac religion: the term *bakkheuein*, "to be a bacchant," is applied regularly. *Mania* is a category of religious thought and Bacchus is not only its symbol but in a way is its ordinary representative.

But the Bacchic delirium is defined not only in terms of mental pathology. Comparisons with experience from a different level can shed light on the Greek phenomenon; history and ethnography supply analogues to the Dionysiac religion. Jeanmaire analyzes some of the most convincing parallels. (It is interesting to note that his study of this material has already appeared in the *Journal de Psychologie*). The author singles out for special comment the cultivation and treatment of possession, which have been observed in recent or even contemporary periods within a broad region covering part of North Africa, Ethiopia, and a section of the Sudan. Despite their differences, the practices, known according to their regions as *zar* and *bori*, have this in common: each uses possession itself for the treatment of possession. This corresponds to a kind of homeopathic care. Detailed testimony regarding the Corybantes shows that possession played a similar role in Greece.

Once Jeanmaire has created an introductory frame of reference by drawing on history, clinical psychiatry, and ethnography, he can direct his attention to the major institutions of the Dionysiac religion. He does this in a series of chapters that form the book's central part.

The subject of the first of these chapters (chap. V) is maenadism. It seems a historical oddity that in a period of enlightenment the figure of the liberated or unchained maenad appears so frequently and with such force. From a psychological viewpoint, it is difficult to understand that a society that confined women to lives of domesticity could give them license to indulge in temporary but public frenzy. Some modern skeptics have responded to these difficulties by suggesting that the bacchants are inventions of myth or poetry. But maenadism is a fact for which there is no lack of attestations. The iconography of the maenad herself provides us with what can only be described as a realistic portrayal. Well-known practices in North Africa should remind us that phenomena that do not fit our preexisting notions of a given civilization should not thereby be dismissed as impossible. It is necessary to realize that certain female practices existed in Greece—just how extensively we cannot say, but they were certainly not isolated instances—which, though intermittent, were nevertheless institutionalized. They were institutionalized in the sense that they occurred at definite times and places and allowed a certain minimum of hierarchical organization to appear—that is, there were "degrees in the initiations"(p. 173). Their singular and yet paradoxical quality was the existence of a "culture of feminine *mania*." All the terms designating a maenad (p. 158) connote hypnotic practices, wild ecstatic behavior, and most especially the mad forays into the wilds of nature which the *thuades* of Delphi, among others, best exemplify.

At the same time, the phenomenon of maenadism should be located within the realm of religion. Two questions on quite different levels must be asked. The first deals with origins. A cultic practice is usually grounded in myth; in this case the myths point to a background older than history. They attribute the *aition* of maenadism to Dionysus; he himself is a first bacchant, seized by the madness he imparts as punishment or cure. They also confirm the fact that this strange divinity is a god of inspiration and a paragon of *enthousiasmos*. So, it is truly remarkable that myths exist which attribute to divinities other than Dionysus the power to cause madness. In some tales, the roles of Hera and Dionysus are interchangeable. The truth is that in terms of maenadism, Dionysus' cult belongs to a much older religious tradition, one involving orgiastic female dances that are associated with cults of vegetation. The question of "origin," then, raises yet another: what is the significance and primitive function of this earlier ritual behavior? Jeanmaire looks for the answer in the complex of initiatory rites he studied in an earlier work. Using an induction that he formulated there, he tries to give an account of the trieteric rhythm of many Dionysiac cults by alluding to the biennial pattern, which sparsely populated societies find more suitable for the rites of initiation of youth (pp. 218 ff.). But does this explain their obligatory quality, one essential to a religious rhythm such as this? There is some doubt that it does. However, there is something very attractive in a theory that suggests that maenadism could originate from certain forms of initiatory practice. For there is proof that these rites are normally conducive to religious feelings and on occasion are open to genuine ecstasies. Since the scope of this review is limited, let it suffice to note that maenadism is far more an affair of *gunaikes* than of *parthenoi*. And if it is possible to believe that, in the beginning, maenadism functioned for the purpose of winning new female recruits, then, given the present state of our knowledge, one can do so only by extrapolation.

The second question is about the connection between Dionysus and Delphi or, put another way, between the practice of divination, as it is generally depicted in the "ministry" of the Pythia, and the state of possession, which is the index *par excellence* of Bacchic *enthousiasmos*. This is still a much discussed problem (see his p. 492 for a brief discussion of P. Amandry's recent thesis), and Jeanmaire's treatment of it is cautious but decisive. Prophetic inspiration at Delphi is a phenomenon that is perhaps earlier than either Apollo or Dionysus. Whatever accommodations it was forced to make with the utilitarian and political goals of the "all too human" milieu of the fifth and fourth centuries B.C., it was still considered by the Greeks to be an essential part of the Apollonian institution. That the two gods were associated is a verifiable fact, but this does not imply that Dionysus conquered the oracle's sacred precinct, after which Apollo would have borrowed his ecstatic divination. For Dionysus is not properly an oracular god. What should be seen here is a sharing of tasks, a kind of "entente" between two gods of very different character who have in common their "expansionism," which is openly that of "usurpers" (pp. 192 ff.).

The language of Dionysiac religion is rich in words that are instructive. The term "dithyramb," for example, leads to an examination of another set of facts. Maenadism is a female phenomenon, but the *dithyramb* is a masculine one. Perhaps, as Jeanmaire suggests, behind this "opposition" there lies another that is geographical. It can at least be seen within a cycle of myth and ritual belonging to the Aegean islands (especially Naxos), which are more or less independent of continental Greece. It is, of course, a question not of dualism but of complementarity, and in fact the materials in the chapter on the dithyramb complement those in the preceding chapter on maenadism. The word *dithurambos* is an ancient one from the Aegean basin. In the classical period, it refers to a literary and musical genre that we know has a prehistory. Behind its standardized form, which has been shaped and assimilated by a Greek esthetic norm, one can detect several elements: memories that the word itself evokes, echoes of the pathetic, and, above all, the depiction of a very primitive Dionysus. These elements evoke a religious practice that, despite its original features, appears to resemble those making up the complex of *maenadism* and those that have been compared with them. Direct testimony— about the cult of Dionysus—or indirect (cult vocabulary) permits us to make a reconstruction. Its central act was the sacrifice of an ox; the dance to which it gave place was frenzied and "inspired." The ritual culminated in the victim's dismemberment and the eating of its raw flesh. In this case, too, clarification of these phenomena can be found in ethnographic parallels: for example, the *zikir*, as observed in the last century among Cairo confraternities, reveals the same kind of communal ecstasy; the *frissa* of the Aissaoua, still practiced on occasion in North Africa, reaches its climax in a *diasparagmos* and omophagy.

In examining this typical pattern, Jeanmaire has observed something that triggers the study of an important phase of the Dionysiac religion, for it deals with its literary possibilities. He says that in a milieu that is above all civic, the religious drama easily takes on the character of an exhibition; and precisely because of the audience, the cyclical choruses tend to become *spectacles*. However, before the question of Dionysus' connection with the theater is raised, it is appropriate to explore in some depth a specific conception of Dionysus involving the actions he performs for souls and the means he uses. As has been seen, Dionysus has certain selected affinities with the world beyond and the world of the dead. The chthonian Dionysus appears as a leader of a "chimerical hunt," and this conception of him is inseparable from that of his coterie, the demonic band, which is the mythical expression of the human *thiasos*. Even in our most common depictions, those containing the fantastic and burlesque figures of the satyrs, there still persist some connections with an equine demon whose very shape could be a symbol of the underworld forces (a theory Jeanmaire has developed following Malten's lead). At its most profound, this symbolism underlines the idea, or rather feeling, that the intoxicating ecstasy of Dionysus gives one access to a world that is supernatural. This is confirmed by the testimonies about the popularity, effects, and even specific character of a type of dance which is essentially bacchic—a dance that, for purposes of "purification" and "initiation," contains elements of *mimēsis* (Pl., Leg., 815C). Is this what the Attic theater owes to the cult of Dionysus?

Of the four theatrical genres that we know were performed during the great March festivals in the precinct of Dionysus, it is the satyr drama to which Jeanmaire devotes the most time. He postulates a "preliterary form" in which the "imitation" takes the form of orchestrated leaps and gambols. This would be the chorus of the possessed, which is the manifestation of the divine mania and at the same time the means of its cure. Although the author believes that satyrs of the type we find depicted in art are essentially characters of myth, he does not dismiss the belief that the mask played a role in this primitive stage, a role that G. Dumézil has illustrated in his discussion of the Centaurs. In any case, there may have been an "organic relationship" (p. 312) between the cult of Dionysus and the origin of the dithyramb. As for comedy, it could naturally have been placed under the patronage of Dionysus, whose traditional festivities were accompanied by a frivolous form of behavior that issues in comedy. Only tragedy remains for discussion, and here Jeanmaire is reserved. In his rapid survey of various theories (see his additional note on pp. 321 ff.), the author seems at least provisionally to lean toward skepticism. The theories in question were originally inspired by a literature that was ethnographic. But drama is a quasi-universal phenomenon; it is a specifically Hellenic type of drama that must be explained; and evidence from contemporary Thracian folklore is of little help. However, despite the Greek precedents that are said to be of value in studies by Ridgeway, Dieterich, and Nilsson, one always runs into the same question, or better, the same mystery: the transition from the vague and often undynamic elements of folklore and religion to the tragedy of Aeschylus or even Thespis remains inexplicable.

Finally, in an attempt to present some idea of the "birth of tragedy," Jeanmaire resorts to an analogy from biology: biological species exhibit forms of mutation that explain the sudden appearance of a new life form. It may be, then—and I hope I am not misinterpreting the author—that the historical problem, that of the origin of tragedy, might be a pseudoquestion. One can discern a milieu and catch a glimpse of some antecedents; but the creation of tragedy is an original event of the same order as the other discoveries so characteristic of Greek humanism. It is probably for this reason that tragedy's origin cannot be found in a specific moment of history. It should be quickly said, however, that such a semiagnostic view does not prevent Jeanmaire from taking some definite positions. He recognizes that commemoration of legendary events at anniversaries of heroes must have had an important role to play in the prehistory of tragedy. And he is strongly opposed to the thesis that states that there is a "primary and fundamental relationship" between Dionysus and the literary genre which circumstances ended up placing under his patronage. Notably it is impossible to admit that the initial themes of the tragic poems "dealt with the suffering" of the god.

Up to this point, little has been said about the mythology of Dionysus. Actually, this mythology in part eludes us, and in some respects is irrelevant for our understanding of the god's personality. For his mythology reveals no features that are original. In the portrayal of most Greek divinities, the strictly mythical element (which is rather limited) consists of themes or remnants of themes of obscure origin that, except for an occasional reference to a few moments in a cultic act, have lost their original significance and survive only in a poetic tradition in which they are freely embellished. Dionysus' case is admittedly rather peculiar. The themes of his myths happen to be very ancient; they are adapted for the use of a god who arrives late on the scene (p. 78), and they are organized into narratives in which archaism itself is a sign of artifice. But because the work of the imagination has been redirected, the intentions that now dominate them give these tales an emotional force that is certainly more vital than that in the tales of Zeus or even of Apollo. Dionysus has been provided with a biography that puts him in close contact with the human world, and with a "history" that is no longer a timeless myth. In the version that has turned out to be almost canonical—it is not the only one, nor is it likely the most ancient—mythical motifs of the thunderbolt and the second pregnancy are echoes of states of society and religious thought which are "primitive," but which essentially emphasize the eminent dignity of a god, who is the preferred son of the supreme deity, although he is like so many heroes born of a mortal, and has close ties with men. Semele and Ariadne are avatars of goddesses (they can return to their goddess forms); but depicted in their sufferings, they represent the element of the feminine which plays so large a role in the cult. On the other hand, the myth develops in two directions. From its beginning, the tale of such a god, because of his unique magical power, remained open-ended: a certain gospellike quality asserted itself in developments that formed the data for a divine biography. This was at first spontaneous, but later on, contemporary history exerted its influence. Alexander's expedition to India inspired a new chapter in Dionysus' biography, and it enlarged his sphere of activity to fit the geographical and fantasy-filled world of conquest—and all this, of course, favored every form of syncretism. Dionysus, it must be observed, was already by his vocation a conquering god, a god of lightning journeys; and the theme of his peregrination in the East, even the Far East, is already present in the *Bacchae*'s prologue. In the version found in Apollodorus' *Bibliotheca*, one that can be described as pre-Alexandrian (p. 308), it is an integral theme.

But the mythopoeic process has also operated on another level, and there is another sort of Dionysus which must be considered: the mystical Dionysus. It is curious that for both the mystical and ancient Dionysus the tales told are of the same kind. The basic myth is one of dismemberment of the god. This has been specifically interpreted as a myth belonging to a "religion of salvation," itself derived from "agrarian rites" (Cumont and Frazer complement each other here). Jeanmaire offers a very judicious critique (pp. 373 ff.) of a theory that makes much of vague analogies and employs a form of schematization which is hardly applicable to the concrete themes in the legend of Dionysus. At the very least, it can be said that the myth is connected with the practice of *diasparagmos*, and that, based on the facts of the cult, there has been speculation of a gnostic type which finds in the destiny of the suffering but resurrected deity a model and promise for his followers.

But the legend is not at one with the rite: undoubtedly the connection had been established in antiquity, but only secondarily (p. 387). In fact, the mythical theme of boiling in a cauldron or passage through fire appears frequently in heroic myths; and though it has several meanings, its basic one is rebirth or immortalization. In its most typical form, it is a myth explicative of a ritual of initiation of the young. Such a view appears well founded; and though Jeanmaire does not cite it, the tale of Pelops provides the closest analogue. Is it not then correct to say that one form of Dionysism has established its own mythology with some ease?

But the myth has been put to use: that is to say, it has been incorporated into a "mystical" doctrine. Such a word as "mystical" can cause doubt or discomfiture, but avoiding it is difficult, although each time it is used it must be defined. The question of mysticism had already been discussed by Jeanmaire in its Platonic context (pp. 295 ff.). There it was the vital movement, characterized by pathos and intelligence, toward the world of ideas; Plato describes it in the myth in the *Phaedrus*. The author has been able to demonstrate that this form of "Platonism" owes its general inspiration and its idea of *mania* to Dionysus. But something else is involved here which the still-crude term "mysterious" might better describe (if one understands it in its ancient context and within the restraints of a critique as informed as Jeanmaire's). The most important question is simply that of Orphism, long a controversial subject. There is little reason to speak of an Orphic religion, if one means by that an organized religion: there is no evidence for the existence of "Orphic communities." However, there does appear to have been a specific unity of tradition; there must have been a transmission of teachings and consequently a society that, though diffuse, still had its books. This is the society of the so-called disciples of Orpheus, and there are other movements from the same period which are analogous but which ought not to claim the same name. This society propagates a doctrine that contains a cosmogony (Aristophanes alludes to it) and a soteriology wherein the myth of Dionysus has acquired dogmatic consistency. For one belief appears to have been well established since the sixth century B.C.: the belief that salvation could be gained through initiatory and ascetical practices by the descendants of the Titans, the murderers of Dionysus. Whatever else the fantastic theology that had long been under Orpheus' literary patronage could supply—or add—to the general concept of rebirth, this concept was the ancient one, and in the framework of Hellenism the important one.

The book's last chapter is the natural place to consider, in the context of the religious movements of the Greco-Roman period, the belief in immortality, which is so intimately linked with what one calls the Dionysiac "mysteries." How does the belief in immortality relate to those "mysteries"? Jeanmaire does not answer this question (p. 423), but notes only that within the circle of these mysteries a "teaching that dealt with the future life" is not attested before Plutarch. In sum, such aspirations and tendencies—already affirmed in ancient "Orphism"—would be satisfied in a new milieu, one more vast, more open to the syncretism of "religions of salvation," and in more or less new forms.

The capacity for renewal, and the diversity and richness that it presupposes, are quite properly the themes of this final chapter. Dionysus is a god who has benefited from the crises or turning points in the ancient world, for example, the period following Alexander's conquest, or the establishment of the Roman Empire. The polymorphous religion that remains attached to his name has a universal quality; but it also appeals to the individual. Within the Hellenistic monarchies, the cult assumes the shape of state religion but still flourishes in confraternities of devotees. The life of the cult continues in Greece and develops in Italy as well. Historical sources abound for the period from the end of the fourth century B.C. to the triumph of Christianity; but it is impossible to reconstruct a history. All that Jeanmaire can do is to retain in his fashion a few significant phenomena in succession.

The development of associations of *tekhnitai* shows that a special artistic and dramatic vocation still continued under the god's patronage. The paean of Philodamus celebrates a universal Dionysus who is linked with the institutions of Delphi and Eleusis. The religion of Dionysus also benefits from the favors, even initiatives, of the kings of Pergamum and Egypt. (Why, in contrast, is there no evidence of this in Syria?) Parallel with the official and often spectacular appearances of Dionysism, it is possible to catch a glimpse of private associations. The amended regulations of the Athenian Iobakkhoi belong to a genre of documents which captures the author's fancy. It is along similar lines that Jeanmaire describes the different blossomings of Dionysism in a milieu that is Roman or soon world-wide; and new proofs of its adaptability appear which always reveal a definite line of development.

After the initial shock of the "Bacchanal affair," there was a period of subtle penetration in which Dionysiac motifs became quite the vogue in household art. But the crisis that immediately preceded our own era revealed the most traditional and yet troubling powers of Dionysus, if it is true (see his p. 415) that the quasi-messianic expectations of this period, along with a concept of perpetual renewal, owed part of their vitality to the god of rejuvenation. In a peaceful Empire, however, the Dionysism of the first century A.D. has "become wise." In the centuries that followed, Dionysus had to find a career in a cosmopolitan religion of *thiasoi*, characterized by a theology of the occult and a poetry of artificial sincerity, such as Nonnus' *Dionysiaca*. The author is keen on demonstrating that the life of Dionysism continues; but one ought perhaps to say that it is no longer renewed; and it is remarkable that Neo-Platonism borrows nothing original from it. However, Dionysism had to be destroyed nonetheless; Jeanmaire attributes its defeat to an intransigent and iconoclastic adversary that used force, the kind of force employed by successful revolutionary movements.

Jeanmaire's book is a new approach; but there is nothing outlandish about it. He does not overthrow any "methods" or offer careless "hypotheses." If one means by a hypothesis a supposition of facts that are only indirectly attested, there are very few; and even these could be omitted from the book without affecting the study as a whole. In the way it is organized, and in the subtle treatment the material calls for, the book presents itself as a history. Jeanmaire has kept the word "history" in the title, and he obviously observes the rules of the historical genre, which are rules of sound judgment. One might add that this gives him the opportunity, without being polemical, to remind his readers that hasty analogies are often misleading, and chronology must be respected. Each of his chapters is indeed that of a historian as far as contents go.

Put more simply, Jeanmaire's work is new because he takes analysis in a direction not taken since Rohde, and he utilizes sources that were unavailable to the latter, and perhaps even with different purposes in mind. After all, the author feels strongly that *Psyche*, although it is somewhat outmoded in its historical views, is still a great book and that he is writing the sequel. To get a fix on Jeanmaire's views, it might be good to compare his approach with that of another historian, one who is known for his vast knowledge, rigorous critical sense, and the sound scholarship of all his works: Martin P. Nilsson, whom Jeanmaire himself praises. In comparing the two, one is struck by the fact that Nilsson is not concerned with the same category of problems as Jeanmaire is, and his purpose does not require that he produce the kinds of interpretations the other does. (On this point it might be good to mention a kind of explanation Nilsson easily turns to, one whose origin would make an interesting subject for study: an accidental synthesis between elements that are more or less heterogeneous, for example, the Dionysus of spring and the Dionysus of winter, joyous drinking bouts and a feast of the dead, funeral laments and *mimēsis* as origins of drama, etc.).

There is a psychological theme that has a very important place in Jeanmaire's book and that seems to have furnished the point of departure for his whole study: What is the significance of this phenomenon of *mania*? For Plato felt obliged to defer to its magic power, and though he recognized that it operated on various levels, he found its most authentic form dominated by the name Dionysus. Surely this is a question about a human reality, as strange as it may be to us at first inspection. How are human realities grasped in history? Jeanmaire is one of those who poses such questions, and he has already touched on them in *Couroi*. The reflection that precedes his analysis is worth quoting: "To comprehend in history is always to interpret texts (and sometimes monuments) by way of experimental forms of knowledge, with the understanding that our direct experience of man and social realities...must be supplemented and illuminated by disciplines that are basically descriptive in their methods of inquiry. Here one is dealing, in the case of a religious form of behavior which has to do with what the ancients understood by the term 'orgy,' with some psychological realities that depend in part on clinical observation, and with the connection of these with social realities, the analysis of which comes from ethnography or sociology" (pp. 105 ff.). In other words, human events have many dimensions. So, in his own study, Jeanmaire devotes one part of the effort to the psychological element that research in mental pathology allows him to identify, and another part to the religious manifestations of a *mania* that has analogues in other societies. Although he recognizes the plasticity of the psychological states in question, or better, their diversity of contents, he still insists on the phenomenon's unity—a unity grounded in the fact that pathology has a certain primacy, for which a "hysterical temperament" provides a fundamental explanation.

But here, perhaps, there is cause for caution. For the most part, Jeanmaire is justified in referring to the concepts and terms of psychiatry; Rohde himself utilized the earlier work of Pierre Janet. However, could there not be a suspicion that there is some equivocation in the exposition, if not in the basis, of his thesis? He emphasizes the "possession," whose subjects are the sick, and the "cure," which the "culture of *mania*" effects. Since he emphasizes these, it could appear that his point of departure should be discovered in certain individual cases, provided more or less frequently by the areas under consideration, depending on the relative density of numbers of mental disorders (a datum, by the way, which is social). In a convincing fashion, Jeanmaire has asserted that nothing more closely resembles individual delirium proper than the manifestations of Dionysism; and what is more, they are really the same phenomena, but in different contexts. Greece provides us with a means of distinguishing. The bogus cures of the Corybantes are directed, at least in principle, to depraved subjects who are, by hypothesis, individual. But the Corybantism that is elsewhere linked to Dionysus is different; the particular mark of maenadism is the collective or communal quality of the trance; the messenger's speech in the *Bacchae*, a "rather fine document" in its own way, allows us to speak about an organized delirium without exaggerating. For there is unanimity in the frenzied movement: it is the concerted action of a single group, but also an involuntary one resembling gesticulations by possessed persons. Were all these women mentally disturbed to begin with?

It is true to say, as Jeanmaire opportunely reminds his reader, that madness is not only a medical phenomenon but an important human event that has been the subject of endless reflection. It has a genuine function in certain human conditions and it operates on many levels, depending on whether the madness is ordered by the society and whether it is recommended or tolerated, at least in its traditional form, where it manifests itself, and whether it is accepted with a kind of amazement.[2] In regard to the *furor*, which is a necessity in the training of the warrior, some have spoken of a "principle of human activities."[3] Concerning maenadism, which is part of a vast complex, it is necessary to say that it is defined not only by its psychological character (probably psychophysiological) but also by its institutional nature, already recognized in the phenomenon of collective autosuggestion (p. 107). It is a reality that is strikingly singular, and Jeanmaire exposes its different aspects.

There are some negative points to make. It is surely necessary to preserve in Dionysism a heritage of phallic cults such as are found in the Rural Dionysia; it is a heritage obviously very ancient (though the symbol is not found in the Aegean basin) and one associated, in a "primitive" system of religous thought and conduct, with the female and with agrarian fertility. It remains, however, on the fringe of the normal Dionysiac phenomenon; for in maenadism, especially, there is nothing sexual: the *libido* is absent.[4] Pentheus' incorrect insinuations in the *Bacchae* bring this out.

Nor does intoxication, at least in its current sense, appear to be a factor. One always thinks of Dionysus as the god of wine, then as the god of drunkenness; and it is true that drinking bouts are important in the traditions of his feasts: the *kōmos* could perhaps be a staggering drunken band. But the *mania* should not be seen as owing its force and magic powers to the consumption of wine (or of any other substances, since the evidence we have about these is really feeble). The maenads are not women intoxicated with wine; on this point, Pentheus' other insinuation is presented by Euripides with the same implication as the previous one. The bacchants, and less so the celebrants of the ancient dithyramb (see his p. 236), are not beings in the throes of drunkenness. In other words, it is delirium in a pure state, one of those instances of "collective ecstasy," the kind of phenomenon de Felice writes about in one of his well-known books. Admittedly, however, this is a delirium brought on by the traditional and equally communal means of suggestion: the intoxication of the dance and hypnotic music.

What place ought we to assign to *mania* within the complex of Dionysiac religion? In answering this question, we encounter a curious contradiction. At first, *mania* seems to be an essential ingredient of Dionysiac religion; and even when limited to one group, the Bacchic delirium can still be viewed by the rest of society not only with a more or less benevolent curiosity but with a genuine and participatory sympathy. It is sometimes explicit, but at least implied, that the *thuades* involve a kind of delegation; and Jeanmaire has underlined the important and dynamic force of the "spectacle," which, even before the theater, is one means of access to the Dionysiac experience. The well-known *katharsis*, after all, exists for those other than the actors: its fundamental efficacy is its ability to cure *mania* by means of *mania* (pp. 316 ff.). Delirium, then, has a religious function that could be described as generic.

There are many other elements in Dionysiac religion besides that of maenadism; but the more remarkable thing is that maenadism is associated, or better, coordinated, with some very different elements that have an affective tone and content almost contrary to it. Tranquil liturgies coexist with the violence of ecstasies and sometimes even replace them. Evidence of this can be found not only in the history of such an organization as the Iobakkhoi, who performed a toned-down version of the ancient *bakkheion*'s "tumultuous practice" (p. 436), but also in the Athenian religious calendar, where all traces of the "mad women" who gave their names to the Lenaia were erased. And just what does the world of the *Bacchae* have in common with periodic festivals characterized by a form of joviality, boisterous and even coarse at times, but basically peaceful?

It would not really suffice simply to point out these contradictions, for Dionysism's special character consists in the extreme variety of psychological attitudes it either authorizes or demands. In order to give an account of its richness and the possibilities it offered the Greeks, it should be enough to say that the cult of Dionysus "fills up the 'in-between,' " for while it moves in a highly individual religious direction, it also finds its fulfillment in the social order when that order has been stirred up by the Bacchanal (*thiaseuetai psukhan* [Eur., *Bacch.*, 75]).

Yet another aspect of Dionysism is episodic in appearance, but possibly revealing. Jeanmaire mentions the role laughter plays in the complex experience of *katharsis* (p. 321); and by doing so, he reminds his reader of the importance of the question of laughter itself, a phenomenon hardly studied since the old and rather superficial study by Salomon Reinach. But here the question, an even more general one, concerns the function of "play," or the *paidia*, in Dionysism. If Dionysus has become a symbol *par excellence* of the theater, it is because he is a god who plays and who makes others play. Even in a festival as popular as the Anthesteria, one might almost say that Dionysus "plays" or frolics with a kind of equivocation between the "real" and the other world.

Jeanmaire conveys to his readers a sense of the unstable and shifting quality of Dionysism; but he communicates a sense of its unity as well. Even so, little light is shed on the significance of *mania* because for *mania* to be so emphasized at certain moments, it cannot be totally absent from others. One can sense some kind of perplexity within this religion, which is not to say that it is oriented toward a form of hysterical pantheism or inspired by a desperate need for communion with a world of mystery. There is little risk of this happening among the Greeks; and Jeanmaire notes several times that joy, not pessimism, is the dominant theme. There is perplexity because the god himself is an entirely restless and disquieting one (p. 118), and his major occupation is madness. His revivals and advances are those of orgiastic rites. The full classical period witnessed a new outbreak of maenadism (pp. 163 ff.): Alexander's history or legend—they are the same—depicts an army completely swept up by force of Dionysus' *furor*. With Dionysus, so long as one believes in him, one is always on the edge of madness.

Nevertheless, this madness is a good thing: the moral of the *Bacchae* is the exaltation of divine *mania*. But the very term "bacchants" is significant, and the singularity it evokes helps us understand the profound nature of Dionysism, for the most striking quality of this religion is the importance of woman. It is most often women who are the subjects of the aberrant and frenzied behavior described by the term "orgy," and in figurative art they alone appear at the awesome moments of the cult. How should these data be interpreted? It is well known that women provide "favorable terrain" for this kind of behavior; but such a predisposition is no explanation. Perhaps our information is by chance tendentious; depictions of *mania* are in some way designed for artistic ends.

Perhaps also there is a difference, which Jeanmaire would be willing to admit, between the cult of Dionysus on the Greek mainland, more properly a cult of maenadism, and the island-centered cult, where men played a larger role. But there can be no doubt that, whatever its setting, the Bacchic delirium was not an exclusively feminine phenomenon. Still, the most striking manifestation of the cult, to judge by its name, was a feminine monopoly—a monopoly that was only indirectly consecrated by an official and somewhat toned-down form of Dionysism. If there existed associations of bacchants and, even from early on, some mixed groups, the only *collegia* were maenads.

What lies at the base of all this is the opposition of the sexes. It functions in all forms of religious life, where it occasionally translates itself into symbolic antagonism. It can also be found in mythical transformations of ritual dramas, where hostility is carried as far as possible: for example, in festive practices involving the exchange of insults, or in myths such as those about the crimes of the Lemnian women and the Danaids. This is a very general concept that Dionysism utilizes; but it gives it an importance that ought to have its own special significance. There is something antimasculine as well as revolutionary in the *Bacchae*. The opposition of the sexes is less explicit in Dionysism, but perhaps more profound. Nothing characterizes its legends more than the liberation of women, whether promised or imposed: they are delivered from domestic life, its joys, and its life of servitude. What they realize, by the grace of Dionysus, is an "escape"; and the word appears many times in Jeanmaire. Its recurrence serves to point out one of the most obvious goals of Dionysism itself. And it is possible to understand woman's preeminent place in the cult because she is best suited to embody it: women are less involved, less integrated in society, and are called upon to represent a principle that is opposed to society itself, but that society needs. Such a need, one has to believe, was keenly felt by the Greeks on a religious level.

Upon examining Dionysus' personality, these suggestions seem confirmed. Within the Greek pantheon, his personality is magnetic, and yet, remarkably, it is made up of elements that for the most part lack any originality. A Greek god's profile is usually discovered in the types of religious activities he presides over and in the myths in which he partakes. It has already been shown that Dionysus' mythology is, from the beginning, prefabricated. His only peculiar quality, and that which has any bearing on the understanding of this god, is the complex of "heroic" motifs that have attached themselves to him (and as is often the case, evoke memories of prehistoric social conditions with motifs of child exposure, foster parents, maternal aunts, etc.). But none of this helps to individualize Dionysus; quite the contrary.

As far as his cult is concerned, save for the parts set aside for *mania* (where he appears in the role of an heir), Dionysus borrows some ancient traditions for his own use. As was seen earlier, he emerged as a new deity from prehistoric cults of vegetation; but it has to be said that he gave some old things a new accent. An element of *pathos* that is Dionysiac appears in certain rites of sacrifice, that is, those involving the ox and the goat (in the case of goat sacrifice, there is a curious contrast: the goat belongs to Dionysus, but the important ritual cycle of the ram is almost completely foreign to him). Ritual practices such as "the hurling in" or the capturing of victims have been carefully examined by the author. Other practices could be grouped under this heading; but upon examination they would only show more clearly that it is not Dionysus' cult that really makes him unique. In any event, the god's personality is something more or less "outside": as Jeanmaire says so well, there is no semblance of any quest for a "communion-sacrifice" in Dionysism. But if in spite of the commonplace quality of his myth and ritual Dionysus dominates souls with such force, it is because this aspect of personality is affirmed in his case more than in that of any other. There must be profound reasons for this, and Jeanmaire brings some of them to light.

Dionysus is a god with many sanctuaries but very few temples (p. 20): he did not easily enter a form of civic religion that magnified and depersonalized divinity. This observation leads to another point that occurs as a leitmotif: except by accident or contrivance, Dionysus is foreign to the world of the affairs of state; not hostile, but peacefully foreign. He alone among all the gods is associated with no function of the state; nor does he even figure in any moment of the past life of the city. The other side of this is his direct link with the world of nature, especially its wild and un-civilized side. His followers yearn for abandoned and uncultivated places, and the most ancient depictions of his triumph or his marriage procession put him in the company of animals of the forest, or even wild beasts. Here it is enough simply to note that a fundamental tendency continues to be satisfied even in the private and urban forms of the cult by use of snakes or by feebler but still suggestive symbols, the *stibades*. Among the most im-portant deities (where Artemis no longer has her place), this trait is exclu-sively Dionysiac.

Another definite characteristic of Dionysus is his rapport with the world of the dead. This is not to say that no other god has connections with it, but that Dionysus' is different. There are the goddesses of Eleusis or of related institutions; but they are goddesses of that particular city and represent a specialized element of religion. And Demeter herself, through her enormous number of universal cults, is involved with man's earthly existence. Certain of Zeus' aspects, the divinity of Hades, the permanence of Hermes *Khthonios* or *Psukhopompos* (no more than a minor god)—none of these contradict the important belief, almost poetic and mani-festly profound, that the society of great gods, the Olympians, is opposed to death and repelled by the dead. Dionysus, who plays a large, even grand, role in this society, and—more importantly—who has made a grand entry into it, is the only exception. It is all the more remarkable, then, that he does not appear as an addition to the Olympian society or as a god with some particular "mystique," for he is neither a god of death nor a god of immortality: "He is not at home in the kingdom" of Hades, and "it would be inaccurate to say that his disciples were on a journey to a paradise of the elect" (p. 273). His dealings with the world of the dead are those of a "ubiquitous" god, and his presence alone creates a sense of the *hereafter*.

There are other side issues that are significant. Jeanmaire under-lines (p. 311) the originality of a god "of many powerful illusions" in a system "where gods almost never act like magicians." Would it be exces-sive to find in the *Bacchae* a god of *maya*? After all, it is there. Here there appears a definite perspective in which Dionysus, in the intellectual con-text, appears to be opposed to the world of ideas. The author often men-tions the problem of Plato's attraction and yet wariness with regard to the god. Dionysus brings to mind the *Other*. He would at least be its symbol, since he is, in terms of his function and nature, a god who is beyond our reach.

There are always subtle connections between a mode of thought and a community's character or *ēthos*. For a long time, scholars misunderstood the character of the Greeks when they perceived, along with the famous serenity, only the feeling for and the necessity of the Forms. Such a view has been corrected: there is an opposite view, which Dionysus everywhere intimates, whether at the level of religious activity, art, or the very view of the world. But it complements the other view: what one can observe about the meaning of the god retrieves what one could say of *mania*; and there corresponds to the theme of "escape" the theme of a divine "presence," one that is truly alien.

If Dionysus belongs to a system precisely because he represents in it a principle of opposition, the significance of this paradox cannot fail to be perceived. In the organization where he finds his place, he had to be there consciously and deliberately. The function of Delphi has been known for some time; and Jeanmaire's suggestions about the division of labor that made it possible for Apollo and Dionysus to associate in some harmony are known. There are some minor pieces of evidence about this peaceful usurpation (p. 197) which are nonetheless very informative precisely because they tell us about the process in some detail. Above all, there existed a continuous effort in which we can see the history of the cult as a whole: an effort to integrate the most typical elements of Dionysism because they needed to be integrated. But it should be noted that this was beyond a doubt an effort to tone down, even to neutralize, them. However, marginal existence was given to the anarchy of an independent maenadism, which was able to assume authority in the shadow of a maenadism of the *collegia*.

It is, then, only a question of accommodations? The truth is that the new god determines this system's economy and stability. Teiresias' apologetic in the *Bacchae* (272 ff.) is relevant. The old priest's tirade is a remarkable example of religious philosophy: it contains a design for a divine-world map, or at least a section of it, in which the entire "Orient" is Dionysus'. The god's vocation is also to assimilate a number of functions that need no longer be differentiated. In addition, the speech gives the distinct impression that the god's new roles were not assumed gratuitously and that some impulse had to be at work. This is the point of that magnificent antithesis at the end of Teiresias' speech, the antithesis between the *dunamis* of the god and the *kratos* of traditional powers.

What remains is the historical question. After uncovering the elements that seem integrated in Dionysism and that characterize it from its beginning, and after determining the cult's place and raison d'être within a system that is more or less directly known, a question still remains unanswered: how does one explain the success of a religion that Herodotus found "incompatible with the Greek temperament" and whose recent introduction he could only explain as a borrowing? Jeanmaire does not pose this question; and it is admittedly an obscure one. But it cannot be avoided. The cult of Dionysus must have had its origin in a genuine religious *movement* with a fully deliberate desire for renewal; otherwise, how can the extraordinary popularity of a new god and his message be explained? In the history of his cult, Dionysus is a god of *revivals*, and such a trait must have been his from the beginning. His legend itself is instructive. Jeanmaire's claim—that the tales of resistances to the god, their violence and eventual defeat, are mythical themes—is probably true; but there must have been a more or less rapid diffusion of the cult, which involved the concept of a militant religion of conquest. In any case, it is not a religious movement that comes essentially from the outside. And the indirect testimony we have about it suggests that it is indeed a spontaneous movement.

Within this context, it is possible only to allude to a very general but troubling question about human history: on one level, it is the question of revolutions, or at least one of mutations and sudden internal renewals. In his analysis of short-lived phenomena analogous to Dionysism, Jeanmaire touches on this problem. Speaking of the "extension" of practices like *zar* and *bori*, he notes that the word can take on a dynamic meaning: "it [extension] refers to a movement that gains ground." Phenomena comparable with religious renewal or innovation observed by ethnographers seem to be the results of nearly explosive forces. Such is the quality of an innovative Dionysism, which is simply not subject to coercion.

The reader who is unwilling to accept these facts without question will be tempted to examine their bases in a specific stage of Greek society when the cult was first diffused. The vastness of the phenomenon permits us to establish some correlations. However, we are dealing with a period of "protohistory," a term that is itself a litotes. Even so, it is important to keep in mind two kinds of facts about Dionysism and the phenomena surrounding it.

The semantics of words like *orgeōn* and *thiasos* suggest that in connection with the religious renewal, social groups have been dislocated and recombined. On the one hand, these terms are discovered in religious forms independent of every civic organization or, in the absence of a political structure, in the nobility. On the other hand, they are also used to describe certain groups that had to be admitted into the phratries; and these, it must be said, were opposed to the associations of warriors from which the phratries originated, just as they were opposed to the religious clans of the nobility such as the *genē*. The second term, *thiasos*, is a characteristic of Dionysism. This is not a new observation, but perhaps this theme could be studied anew with some profit.

What can shed some light, even if feebly, on this critical *moment* of social and religious history is the observation that Dionysism is not the only

cause of it. Jeanmaire singles out one phenomenon associated with Dionysus (p. 398) which is usually referred to as "Greek shamanism" (but we
know of it only in terms of derivatives and legends). It refers to magicians
such as Abaris and Epimenides (cf. Pythagoras), who practiced purificatory rites or magical forms of medicine that involve the idea of a religious
reformation. Their pattern of activities resembles that of Dionysus and
may even have had some influence on his cult.

There is at one point in the *Bacchae* (ll. 466 ff.) an example of true
shamanism; but a distinction must be made with regard to the methods of
recruitment, the divine patronage, and, curiously enough, the form of
psychological therapy. In all this one can detect an unsettling form of agi-
tation or ferment within different forms of religious propaganda. These
indicate the different kinds of change that accompanied the emergence of
Greece as a culture, and within the religious scheme, Dionysism would be
one of them.

Even though it does not deal with some of these questions, the book
still has its own value. One of its obvious merits, stated earlier, is the
author's sense of history and his genuine ability to interpret historical
events. In light of this, I admit some puzzlement at the skepticism of the
book's last lines, where Jeanmaire speaks of *"histoire inactuelle."* There is
no such thing. There is an undefined series of human experiences in which
Hellenism has an important place.

NOTES

1.   H. Jeanmaire, *Dionysos: Histoire du culte de Bacchos* (1951).
2.   See M. Mauss, *Sociologie et anthropologie*, p. 327.
3.   G. Dumézil, *Horace et les Curiaces*, pp. 23 ff.
4.   See M. P. Nilsson, *Geschichte der griechischen Religion*, I, p. 261.

PART II

FORMS OF MYTHICAL THOUGHT

CHAPTER 4
The Mythical Idea of Value in Greece

There are some human activities, such as law and economics, whose intellectual nature it is possible to forget. In our society, law and economics operate so mechanically that man himself seems absent from them. To discover that certain phenomena are nonetheless products of the human spirit, we must not look first at their modern manifestations. They possess a rich past that an unconscious philosophy of *Aufklärung* can make us disregard. But it is this past that is actually the cause of their development. And one of the best reasons for the existence of history as a discipline is the reconstruction, where possible and as much as possible, of the ancient circumstances wherein we can better understand creations of the human mind; and such an enterprise is primarily a psychological one.

Among those creations, the concept of value merits an investigation. In the state in which we know it, the process of quantification, universal and necessary, makes of it an abstract concept *par excellence*. But in situations that we identify, for better or worse, as primitive or archaic, the opposite is true. There, the evaluation of objects in terms of possession or consumption is dominated by a number of different ideas and sentiments; and behind them lie all sorts of ramifications and reverberations. The range of material in this area could at first bewilder us; all the more reason to examine it. The concept of value is one that is global in scope; it has to do with an object of respect, even reverential fear; it has to do with the source of interests, attachment, or pride, provoking that wonder that Descartes would call the first "primitive passion." The idea of value also presupposes or signifies a psychological tone more elevated, more diffused, than in our own human nature. We are dealing with actual complexes,

This article originally appeared in *Journal de psychol.*, XLI (October–December 1948), pp. 415–62.

that is to say, with forms in which the classical "faculties" have an interest and are entangled. Physical and mental attitudes here are connected with the same idea of value, one where there sometimes exist, in a state of equilibrium, a tendency to be apprehensive and a recoiling in the face of danger. Rules of conduct, similar to those that govern reciprocal gift-giving, give it a specific quality and enhance it; and its deep emotional qualities are accompanied by images whose function and very nature deserve our attention. We will discover, as a mediating factor of value (no doubt disguised but nevertheless having the effectiveness of guiding principles), those general representations that belong to a society, contribute to its definition, and constitute for it the necessary framework of all its thought. In addition, these are situations that are particularly favorable for the study of the function of symbols.

No doubt, the experience has only more interest if it has some bearing on the period that borders—chronologically—on the "positive" age of value, where psychological forms survive nonetheless, revealing a very ancient tradition. This experience is offered to us—and is the basis for the following observations—by an ancient civilization, concerning which these types of questions pose themselves everywhere.

I

The problem of money's origin is a special one in the case of ancient Greece;[1] for it is there that we find for the first time in human history the widespread use of inscribed money, *sensu stricto*. One aspect of the problem is this: if we accept the distinction between the symbol and the sign[2] (the symbol retains immediate and emotional significance, whereas the sign is spent or appears to be spent in its very use), it becomes clear that what we are talking about when we refer to the origin of money is actually the transition from symbol to sign. In effect, we are not ignoring the fact that many societies, where money in the real sense of the term is not used, do reveal some typical elements of the phenomenon of value, all of which function more or less analogously, but are by comparison with the use of money essentially concrete.[3]

It is possible to point to a parallel development in law, where ritual precedes and sets the stage for procedure. If the parallel is valid, it is precisely because it tells us something about the situation in Greece in terms of an institution whose social importance is manifest: the public games. In the legendary competitions *(athla)*, where epic found its favorite themes, the behavior and attitude to which the awarding of individual prizes gave rise are preludes to the regular kinds of acts and gestures that characterize archaic law.[4] As a specific example, it is possible to show an antecedent of *mancipatio*.[5] This gesture of "seizure" is connected with the thing over which it is expressed. In a kind of limited example, where an ox is the prize, the *mancipatio* consists in seizing the animal by the horns; and it is the direct continuation of an act that is specifically religious. The object—as a rule the material for sacrifice—has religious value. The other objects awarded as prizes are no less qualified, even though they signify something evidently more profane. The notion of the ownership one acquires of these objects is inseparable from that of the value one attaches to them. The representation of these objects, the concept of law applied to them, and the forms of conduct governed by the acquisition or defense of this right all involve a reciprocal relationship. Now the objects in question, namely, customary forms of recompense, already suggest money. We could say that in the funeral games of the *Iliad*, for example, we are the same distance from money as from legal procedure. It is always interesting to call attention to this kind of connection.

※

In effect, the things that are given as prizes—especially goblets, tripods, bowls, armor, etc.—belong to the category of "premonetary signs," to which the work of Laum has called our attention.[6] These objects are frequently numbered: the ransoms, the gifts of hospitality, bear amounts that attest to some traditions and norms. In a custom such as the Homeric games, where all competitors were rewarded, there exists hypothetically a hierarchy of values among the prizes. Moreover, several of these objects are related directly to the first appearances of money. Even in Crete in the fifth century B.C. fines are calculated in tripods and cauldrons. If these were to be interpreted (and the subject is still being debated) as tokens used as substitutes for money, the tokens themselves and their designation would be equally informative. The iron sickles given as prizes in the Spartan games have at times been identified by modern scholars as Spartan money. On the other hand, contests are often the themes imprinted on those ancient coins that are sometimes issued on the occasion of the games.

Objects given as prizes belong to a rather large category, but it is one that is also rather well defined. We find them, or things comparable to them, in several parallel groupings: customary gifts, gifts of hospitality, ransoms, offerings to the gods, funeral offerings, and objects placed in the tombs of leading men. Taken together, all these things constitute the substance of a noble commerce. By implication, this system of classification contrasts these items with another category of goods which is inferior and functionally different. If we could borrow the terminology of Roman law (but Roman law, in a basically rural civilization, accordingly formulates this distinction in another way), we might say that these inferior items are the *res mancipi par excellence*. And there is a correlation in the ownership system where these same items create a special sphere, namely, that of individual ownership understood in its strict sense. For one particular class, such as the warrior class of Epic, this sphere is defined in terms of its own mores and practices, and in opposition to other legal or quasi-legal areas (ownership of land, ownership of herds). The right of disposition that applies to it is absolute, as is eminently clear in the practice of burial: the items in question follow the leader to his tomb. Finally, this specific concept is translated into the vocabulary where *ktēmata*, by preference, applies to this category of goods. *Ktēmata* accentuates the idea of "acquisition," that is, of things acquired as a result of war, the games, or gift-giving. The term never gives primary emphasis to the idea of commercial gain.[7]

This combination of preferences, exclusions, and norms defines one particular area of value. Within a historical perspective, where this sphere of value is attached to objects that are *par excellence* premonetary signs, we will examine those objects that have twofold characteristics: first, they have a "circulation" value (in contrast to the "money" in livestock, which had above all to function as money on deposit);[8] second, they are products of human industry—especially the metal industry, and on occasion, the textile. To limit "value" in this way is intentional. The ideas pertaining to livestock, its special religious value, and its use in rituals—these have furnished the theme for Laum's essay on "sacral money" and form the basis of a theory of the religious origins of secular money. We do not intend to discuss this theory. Nevertheless, it does appear that outside the cultural and even, in principle, the sacrificial areas where his theory is legitimate, Laum has not been able, without some contrived arguments, to integrate the precise group of objects whose nature and function we have been discussing. Such a group has its place in research concerning the origin of money; and in a study about judgments of value, these objects should be considered apart.

We are dealing, then, with economic value, or at least with its antecedents. But we ought to be prepared to say that our topic is quite simply "value." The expression "economic value" tends to eliminate the very idea of value by substituting the idea of "measure," elsewhere an essential ingredient of the concept of the measured thing. But we are not concerned with value as something "banal" or abstract. We are dealing with a preferential value embodied in certain objects, a value that not only predates economic value but is its very precondition.

There is no longer any need to justify treating the different spheres of value as a homogeneous entity. It is possible to recognize their common "purpose," and they all equally presuppose a process of idealization. Social psychology attests to this on various levels.

But first let us begin with the language of value. There is a word that in its most ancient usage implies the idea of value; it is *agalma*. It can refer to all kinds of objects, even at times to human beings to the degree they can be considered "precious." Most often it refers to wealth, especially aristocratic wealth (horses are *agalmata*). It is inseparable from another idea suggested by a still-discernible etymology. The verb *agallein*, from which it derives, means both "to adorn" and "to honor." Applied especially to the category we have been examining, it refers to personal objects and furnishings. We should add that in the classical period the verb regularly refers to the offerings to gods, especially such objects as statues of the divinity.[9]

On the level of technology and economics, we must underline the fact that if the objects we are examining are products of industry, the industry would best be termed a "luxury" one. An indirect witness of these objects' extraordinary and singular value is their mass-produced imitations, substitutes made of cheap material. Under the title of a votive offering, they are like a symbol of a symbol. Archaeology provides many examples of them. As a counterpart, archaeology has also noted the significant revival of commerce and production in the goldsmiths' trade in the protohistorical period. In addition, K. Bücher's views concerning the character of Greek industry argue for their establishment in the archaic period.[10]

In the area of religion we have already remarked that the *agalmata* are designed especially to be offerings. In Homer, where the word does not yet mean an offering in the proper sense of the term, it refers— and this is very instructive—to "precious objects" that are spontaneously used as offerings. Here we are witnessing a form of religious commerce that is of special interest. As soon as the idea of value is set apart and elevated— and becomes specialized[11]—we find it associated with a concept of sumptuous generosity, indeed an aristocratic generosity of the kind Aristotle attributes to a class for whom "*noblesse oblige.*"[12] On the other hand, we will not forget that this kind of wealth, insofar as it is the property of the gods, remains a well-defined category in the classical period. In criminal law, sacrilege (*hierosulia*) is something other than the theft or diversion of funds belonging to the divinity; it is a special and unforgivable offense. It is the crime of laying one's hand[13] on a more revered kind of "sacred goods," among which we can readily recognize the same series of *agalmata*—tripods, vases, jewels, etc..

II

There is yet another area in which we can observe the workings of the mind, workings that lead to the formulation—that is to say, to the objectification—of value. It is the category of mythical representation.[14]

We know for sure that precious objects play a role—in a way a central one—in some legends. In legend these objects are always endowed with special power. This is not just a Greek phenomenon. But it is remarkable that this kind of imagination is especially found in the same stage in which we find the notion of value; that is, the premonetary period, which immediately precedes that of abstract thought. There is perhaps something to be learned from all this; in any case we have some material to analyze.

There is no special method of analysis. We must simply read the myths. They do, however, presuppose or suggest certain attitudes, and it is important to keep this in mind if we want to read them as they should be read. One tale leads to another; similarities exist which we should not dismiss because of some a priori fear that connections are arbitrary. What we are basically asking for is permission to say that mythology is a kind of language. The way "signifiers" function in language is well known.[15] Fortified then—at least a bit—with the teachings of the linguist, we might say that we have first to give an account of the connections that exist between the specific elements of the same legend (and we can at times presume that the more profound the connections, the more difficult it is to find their raison d'être, which sometimes seems even to elude the storytellers). Second, we must account for the association by virtue of which one episode, motif, or image evokes another similar group. Connections and associations help us to understand—to some extent at least; but we must not be in a hurry.

The Tripod of the Seven Sages

It will be easy to start with a story that purports to be a bit of history; actually it introduces onto the stage some historical figures who are by hypothesis no earlier than the sixth century B.C. In addition, it has a reasonable and edifying allure that captures the spirit of the period. It would be difficult to regard the story as legend, since it seems to have been invented simply as an illustration of a type of wisdom. Still, it remains a legend because of the recognizable persistence of certain traditional ideas or images, and because of the mythological basis it retains (more or less faithfully, depending on the authors). Without such a foundation, the narrative would lose the minimum emotional and poetic interest it has. The legend at least invites us to stress from the beginning certain features, certain elements that we may discover some time later. This much by way of introduction.

The legend is known to us chiefly from Diogenes Laertius, who did not hesitate to give us a good many versions.[16] It seems that within a very ancient tradition the variants of the tale proliferated until a late date. Most of the authors cited by Diogenes date from the fourth century B.C., but the materials they make use of appear to be ancient. And had they been invented only for the purpose in hand, they would still be in the category of mythopoeic imagination; and this is enough for us. Roughly, the legend is concerned with a reward to be given to "the wisest man," which each of the Seven Sages receives in succession. (The "catalog" of the Seven is handed down in more or less variable form through the whole of antiquity.) The reward sometimes takes the form of a tripod, sometimes a cup or golden goblet. Most often the initial recipient is Thales, who then yields it to someone whom he knows to be wiser. The second gives the prize to a third, and so on, until the object is in the hands of the seventh Sage; it then goes back to Thales, who consecrates it to Apollo.

As far as the story's setting is concerned—one might even say its lighting—we should first emphasize the fact (more or less explicit and without being dictated by the general theme) that the tripod or the vase is regarded as a prize awarded on the basis of a *competition* of "wisdom," indeed, a contest of "happiness."[17] Here the basic idea of rivalry appears in a new form. The pattern of the games is adapted spontaneously; the games constitute the precious object's favorite social context. There is another pattern that also has social implications, since it forms, as best it can, a unit with the pattern of the games. This is the pattern of successive acts of presentation where the object passes from one hand to another. Concerning the participants and the ethic of the gift, Plutarch's text is particularly rich in information. The expressions "yielding" (a term that implies deference), "noble generosity," and "circulation" are all worth examining. The concrete expression—and it is pleonastic in Plutarch—"circular passing around" is noteworthy. The Seven form a group (the number itself is significant); elsewhere the tradition brings them together at a "banquet," and the banquet, according to practices inherent in legend, is the choice place for acts of generosity, agreements, and challenges. The banquet, then, is the ultimate background for a kind of circulation, like the passing around of the cup with accompanying calls of *"prosit."*[18] In the legend concerning the tripod of the Seven Sages, we find a very traditional representation in a latent form.

The object itself has a special value, and it is associated with religious value. In the end (and as if the religious value were increased simply by passing it from hand to hand) the tripod is consecrated to a god. Earlier, in a most remarkable version of the legend,[19] the tripod figures as a religious object of a well-known type: an oracle has ordered it taken "to the house" of a sage,[20] an event that reminds us of the cult practice of having the *sacra* kept successively in the hands of various specially designated persons.

This background and these comparisons give us a mythical representation. In several versions, the object has a history, an almost civic status, as is often the case with prize objects in Homer. The object is divine in origin, and has been fashioned by Hephaestus—a commonplace invention that almost all myths share. But there are also some more-pertinent elements. When the object is a tripod, the standard theme is that it was discovered in the sea and brought back in a fisherman's net. Here we should make a point we have already alluded to; it is a compelling one. Not only is it the sea that carries or casts up the god, the dead man raised to the status of hero, the child hero, and especially the chest in which the child hero is placed;[21] but there is also the fisherman's net in which the divine beings or the magical objects are either discovered or miraculously rescued. This is what happens in the case of the young Perseus and his mother, Danae, when they are exposed at sea in a chest.[22] Telephos and his mother, Auge, provide a parallel example.[23] The shoulder bone of Pelops, an important part of the bone collection of heroes, is recovered in the same way, as a condition for the conquest of Troy.[24] And the same situation holds true for the statue that comes to life, is at times accursed, and at other times compels devotion from the people.[25]

There is something else we would emphasize. In our tales, this mythic image has a connection with another one, which is its counterpart, at least according to a version that is richer than the present tradition.[26] The tripod was originally a divine bridal gift presented in this form to the family of Pelops and finally kept by Helen. It was thrown by her into the sea "in conformity with an ancient oracle" and at the end of a predetermined period was miraculously recovered.

The mythical aspects of the precious object immediately—almost spontaneously—stand out in the moralizing tale of the Seven Sages. Such an object is conceived of as something that is actually *valuable* and *useful* to society. Both these aspects characterize the premonetary phase of society. Among the most typical examples are the tripod and the cup; in legend they are interchangeable and equal in value. The only difference is that the tripod has a stronger association with myth; the golden cup seems to have other associations. The cup (unlike the tripod) is not merely a rare object or the privileged sign of wealth in a mainland milieu where poverty is the rule.[27] In the version of Eudoxus of Cnidus,[28] the Lydian king's initiative in organizing the competition indicates that this kind of object— especially the cup[29]—was used in the early phase of commerce.

The legend of the Seven Sages' "tripod" should lead us to see that there are somehow two different poles in the legendary depiction of the *agalma*.

＊

Our review would not be complete, in terms of the legend's mythical significance, if we failed to note one element that on the surface seems accidental. Before being given to one of the sages, the tripod is generally the object of a dispute that turns into a war between cities. This is not really an essential part of the story; it could have been passed over. Nevertheless, it is part of the legend, as a revealing detail indicates.[30] Helen, in throwing the tripod into the sea, predicted that it would be the stake in conflicts. Thus the tripod seems endowed with a mysterious power; more precisely, it exercises an ominous influence. If this aspect, which is not essential to the legend, was nevertheless retained as a part of it, we can only presume that it was because such a theme belongs to the very notion of the "precious object."

There is something else worth noting. We are dealing here only with versions of the story involving the tripod; those involving a cup lack this additional element. There may have been a special affinity between the tripod's symbolism and a basic feature of the mythical idea of value. In fact, the theme of the "dispute over the tripod" is illustrated in the well-known legend that pits Herakles against Apollo. In that instance, the tripod is the one at Delphi and possession of an *agalma* can therefore be related to the establishment or claim of religious authority. At the same time, it is just as easy for the possession of the *agalma* to have a "political" significance. A tripod sent by the Argonauts to the Libyans or the Hylleis guarantees these people the peaceful ownership of their territory.[31]

The symbolic meanings we have derived from one and the same image have really led us in different directions; but in myth they are closely connected.

The Necklace of Eriphyle

There are other points of contact where similar connections regarding the object of value appear in legend.

According to the most ancient tradition of the games, substantial and very real prizes are offered. Among them we sometimes find arms. These are not intended for "practical use," but belong to the category, long recognized in anthropology, of "arms for display." The "shield of Argos," which lent its name to one of the competitions at the great festival of Hera, furnishes us with the most striking example. Pindar uses the "bronze of Argos" as its synonym and thus indicates its value as a metal object, which is primary in its depiction. But all this has its own back-ground. The shield in question is related to the one King Danaos conse-crated in the sanctuary of Hera after he had carried it as a youth.[32] The annually decreed recompenses appear as a kind of mintage of the shield.[33] From what we find in the legend, the object has the nature of a talisman, and plays a role in both the installation and transfer of royal power. Upon Danaos' death, his son-in-law removes the shield and hands it to his own son (the latter being the qualified representative of his maternal grandfa-ther). On the other hand, the same object provides protection for the city to whose sanctuary it belongs. This protective power is miraculous in times of war; the sight of Danaos' shield is enough to put the enemy to flight.[34] We are back to the theme of magical weapons; this motif appears again and in precisely the same form in the story of Aristomenes' shield. It too was consecrated, and being placed on a memorial erected in full view of the enemy, gave the Thebans victory at Leuctra.[35]

※

But the ambivalence of the precious object is particularly attested in certain modes of social behavior.

In Aeschylus' *Agamemnon*, when the play has almost reached its climax, there is a scene that, from the way it affects us, still has all of its strange power. Agamemnon, only recently returned to Argos as the con-queror of Troy, will soon be assassinated by his wife. But Clytemnestra is devious; she welcomes her husband with extraordinary hypocrisy. Let us outline the scene: Agamemnon is immediately invited to walk on the richly purple cloth on his way into the palace. He hesitates and is afraid, but finally he gives in. As the door of the palace closes behind him, we know that he is as good as dead.[36]

In the exchange between Agamemnon and Clytemnestra, we find several themes that are very old and yet stunningly alive. They manifest themselves in allusions to the past that are filled with innuendo and in a rapid cadence where the apparent discontinuity of dialogue is actually the indication that the ideas are all inextricably linked. What Clytemnestra asks the king to do is to manifest his divine power.[37] A king's foot must never touch the ground directly; this is a well-known taboo. But the splendid cloth, which he will besmirch by walking on it, is the material part of an actual rite; by stepping on the hide of a victim, on a tomb, or on hereditary ground, one actually designates something as religious, seizes power, assumes ownership. In this case, the item Agamemnon befouls has its own deadly properties. What troubles him at first and makes him hesitate to follow his wife's wishes is the thought of hostile forces that can be aroused by so extraordinary a display—reproach from the gods for whom these kinds of processions are reserved, and who are angered when men usurp their honors. Agamemnon thinks of the "envy" that manifests itself in the "blame from mortals"; but it is really seen as the impersonal "numen," an occasionally all-powerful force that emanates sometimes from gods, sometimes from men. At one moment it takes concrete form in the magical concept of the "evil eye." But what directs and underpins all these confused thoughts is the idea of wealth. The qualities of power and danger are attached to something that is a valuable and precious possession. To know whether or not it will be wasted—or more precisely trampled on—is crucial. For while wealth as such is an object of religious awe (*aidōs*), it can also be sacrificed deliberately. And Clytemnestra forces Agamemnon to recognize that in the critical situations where one must run the risk of extraordinary sacrifices, he himself could have made a vow to offer just such a sacrifice. The wife's treachery triumphs. Agamemnon accomplishes his own destruction by likening himself to the gods and by accepting the sinister consecration that contact with the purple cloth brings with it.[38] And if, before admitting defeat, Agamemnon's last word can be taken as an expression of shame over the waste of such a thing of luxury, we can find in this scene, if we so desire, witness to a bourgeois form of avarice. But there are also quite different elements involved.

In a story about a necklace in Theban legend we find the most representative example of the precious objects' destructive force.[39]

In order to return to Oedipus' son Polyneices the rightful patrimony that Eteocles had usurped, seven Argive chieftains undertake the famous war against Thebes. One of the seven, Amphiaraos, participates only reluctantly. To obtain his cooperation, his wife Eriphyle has to be used as a go-between; she receives a *peplos* and a gold necklace for her effort. A series of catastrophes ensue: Amphiaraos dies during the expedition; his son, Alcmaeon, avenges his father's death by killing Eriphyle. Polluted with his mother's blood, Alcmaeon too has a tragic end. The objects around him (which are gifts to two successive wives) bring about men's deaths, and the curse continues until the middle of the historical era. When the Phocians pillage the temple at Delphi, a general's wife wants to adorn herself with these jewels that had been offered to the temple. She perishes in flames.

It is good to point out that at the core of this story there is a certain connection with social reality. The necklace and the *peplos* have a long history. They had been given to Harmonia, the grandmother of the Theban kings, when she married Cadmus. They had been handed down in the royal family all the way to Polyneices; according to an isolated but nevertheless remarkable piece of evidence, he obtained them as a share of his patrimony by yielding the kingship to Eteocles first.[40] These objects, then, are basically in the category of wedding gifts, a category that itself belongs to the cadre of customary gifts and is, as such, subject to a form of protocol. We know that in other instances these gifts came in pairs. In the *Medea*, the Corinthian king's daughter receives a crown and a *peplos* from her rival. (The same combination of a gold crown and a purple *peplos* is still suggested in the first century A.D. for an imperial offering at Delphi.)[41] Remember too that Theseus receives from Amphitrite a crown and a robe, which are more or less gifts for his wife-to-be, Ariadne. Then there is Alcmene, who received from Zeus (who had taken her husband's shape) a necklace and a goblet.[42]

We notice that certain gifts of custom, especially those presented on the occasion of marriage, are handed down by inheritance. In addition, we can say that everything—at least in our story—happens as if the deviation caused by the act of Polyneices sets the *agalmata* on a course of disasters. But it is necessary to examine just how, at the decisive moment, the power of the *agalmata* is set in motion. Why did Amphiaraos have to join the expedition of the Seven? On this point the legend's tradition is unclear and complicated. One after the other, terms like "persuasion" and "obligation" appear in alternation. But the persistent theme is that Amphiaraos, when he leaves, is told what has taken place and that he must go nonetheless. As far as the obligation imposed on him is concerned, an attempt has been made to explain it in terms of the "right of arbitration" that has been recognized beforehand for his wife. But philologists note that this would render the theme of corruption through bribery useless.[43] The obligation remains unexplained; persuasion is ineffective. The two are in contradiction. It seems that at the moment the legend becomes part of the epic poetry referred to in our sources, a laborious and ingenious attempt is made to justify this central element, which, though no longer understood, is in effect the true ingredient of an explanation. And sometimes, though only fleetingly, it gives all the indications of being sufficient in itself. When in works of art we see the portrayal of Amphiaraos' departure, with Eriphyle standing in front of her furious husband, quite obviously adorned with the fatal necklace;[44] when we are told that Amphiaraos, precisely in order not to leave, prohibited his wife from accepting the gifts of Polyneices;[45] when we read in Homer that the hero's death was caused by "feminine gifts"—an expression that is at first obscure but in another context refers to a theme of legend[46]—we recognize the basic idea of the "compelling force of the gift."

The notion of the formidable force inherent in a gift is fundamentally inseparable from the one we have just been referring to.[47] But it is remarkable that it is missing from a typical legend about an *agalma*. The origin and *raison d'être* of the mythical theme are already more or less obscured, but the theme itself survives, and the depiction of the "object of value" cannot be omitted.

There exist other aspects; and other forms of imagination receive definition in certain series of legends.

III
THE RING OF POLYCRATES

Can such wealth, an object of religious awe, be destroyed? On occasion it has to be. Such is the case in the scene of the *Agamemnon* where we see that the very vow to destroy such an object is the acceptance of a perilous ordeal.

Polycrates is a tyrant from the second half of the sixth century B.C. Nonetheless, the legend associated with his name contains some very illuminating motifs. Herodotus, in his version, adjusted it to fit the moralizing kind of piety he so freely exemplifies.[48] According to the tale, Polycrates' unmitigated happiness provokes the gods, and he is advised to deprive himself of part of his wealth. More precisely, he was to give up "the object that he valued the most." Accordingly, Polycrates, in the course of an actual ceremony,[49] throws the famous ring—the object he treasured the most—into the sea. But despite all efforts to the contrary, the ring is recovered. The renunciation that Polycrates had agreed to was impossible to fulfill; he thus becomes a condemned man. Only complete ruin can atone for such continuous prosperity.

To understand this legend's makeup, we should note that when all is said and done, the metaphysical concept of *nemesis* does not distort too badly the traditional elements that even the intrusion of "folk tale motifs" cannot prevent us from perceiving. Some attempt has been made to define these elements in terms of comparisons that, though not without some relevance, are too indeterminate to be really informative: as when we call to mind the ceremony of the marriage between the *doge* and the Adriatic, symbol of the imperial claim over the sea. It is more useful to deal with the myth as myth, analyze its components, and emphasize its connections with other Greek legends.

First, it is worth noting that in the Theseus legend too a ring is thrown into the sea. True, the context is quite different, but it could all the better represent the ritual character of a gesture. During the voyage of the ship bringing the victims destined for the Minotaur, Minos and Theseus have an argument. The reason behind the argument is of little immediate interest (especially since the pretext is immediately forgotten), but the argument itself appears as a conflict between two kings over prestige. Minos obtains a favorable sign from his father, Zeus; it affirms his divine parentage. Theseus must obtain the equivalent from his father, Poseidon; in effect he does so after diving into the waves. But this trial or ordeal involving a leap into the sea—it is familiar from other legends and sufficient on its own—is motivated in our story by a unique request from Minos. His request is not an essential (it is of so little importance that it is omitted in the principal source), but it is nevertheless striking: Minos throws his ring into the sea and dares his rival to recover it.[50]

The first thing we observe is the role of the ring in an episode concerning a *contest* over regal status. In the tale of Polycrates, the trial is one-sided; with Theseus it is two-sided. But in both tales there is a trial: the tyrant's power is at stake in one, the king's legitimacy in the other; the gesture is the same; and the same object is the substance of a ritual.

But another legend about the magical ring allows us to pinpoint the significance of the symbols in the tyrant's biography: the legend of Gyges' ring in the form in which Plato first tells it.[51]

Gyges, a shepherd in the service of a Lydian king, enters a cave through an opening that has suddenly appeared in the earth. Inside the cave he finds a bronze horse, and within it a naked corpse with only a ring on its finger. He takes the ring and departs. He discovers that by turning the ring's stone toward himself, he becomes invisible. He uses this to his advantage and kills the king, thus usurping the throne.

In a legend that, according to Plato, preserves the most traditional elements (murder of one's predecessor and marriage to the queen), the ring is the means of gaining royal power. But in this kingdom of Lydia, which is sometimes credited with having minted the first coins[52] (the event itself is thought to have occurred during the quasi-historical period, namely, the seventh century B.C.), what we must observe is what makes the tale unique. We note that the essential part of Gyges' ring is the flat part that bears the seal.[53] In addition, the ring of Polycrates—and on occasion that of Minos—is called a "seal." Beginning with the Mycenaean period, the ring fitted with an engraved stone was an important possession in Greece; it was the kind a ruler took with him to his tomb.[54] The relative antiquity of the use of seals (well known from the earliest days in Eastern civilizations) can thus be presumed true for Greece as well. In any case, what is certain is that the seal is directly linked to the most ancient kind of money, since it preceded the striking of coins.[55] The seal is an attestation—more precisely, a *mark* of ownership—and on this basis it is endowed with a primitive magical power.[56]

It is in a cave the Greeks describe as a "treasure house" that Gyges found his ring, a powerful tool for the acquisition of wealth and power.

In a form that the rational context eventually makes appear quite naïve, the ring of Polycrates appears as the epitome of wealth in the possession and service of the tyrant. What qualifies as a precious object in the Samian legend is the thing that can be risked as part of an enormous gamble where all power and possessions are at stake. Polycrates throws his ring into the sea—"in such a way that it can never return to mankind," Herodotus has his adviser say to him. The question is, Will this offering be agreeable? It is not, and Polycrates does not obtain the favor or approval he seeks. One has no difficulty in interpreting this rejection as a manifestation of *nemesis*; in principle, it is the conclusion of a trial by ordeal, one that is related to divination.[57] According to it (where the use of the ring is preserved), when an object that is submerged does not go to the bottom but "reappears," it is a fatal sign.[58]

Of course the trial is also related to the sacrifice. We need only remind ourselves that in a religious event, which is something like its equivalent, the custom of the *ex voto*, in the form of coins thrown into a fountain, survived in the cult of warrior-heroes. But what is significant now is the seemingly royal custom of throwing into the sea, as part of a sacrifice, one of the symbolic objects like the golden cups and other precious vessels. This practice is attested in the legend of Alexander.[59] Upon his arrival at the mouth of the Indus, Alexander goes into the open sea[60] and—following the immolation of victims—throws the golden cup used for libation and a golden crater into the waves. Herodotus has Xerxes perform the same rite during the crossing of the Hellespont.[61] After a libation, a cup and a bowl, both made of gold, are tossed into the sea along with a scimitar.[62] The very close analogy should be noted, but it is highly unlikely that Alexander *imitated* Xerxes.

One will observe that, in such a case, one theory of sacrifice—where it is understood as an intellectualized justification for a religious act—would be misleading. The divinity that is the object of sacrifice can be unspecified. Admittedly, Xerxes, hoping for a successful European campaign, is understood to be addressing the Sun. But Herodotus wonders if there actually was a "consecration" to the Sun, and not rather an offering to the Hellespont. Xerxes had ordered the Hellespont flogged and might have wished to offer it a propitiatory "gift." Alexander himself sacrifices bulls to Poseidon; but the presentation of the cup and the bowls to the Ocean—after the libation that follows and has no connection with the animal sacrifice—is an act that appears to be self-sufficient. The goal for which the offering is designated remains poorly defined, not only in Xerxes' case, but in Alexander's too, which involves at one and the same time "acts of thanksgiving" for an expedition's happy outcome and "prayers" for the success of yet another. To the degree to which the action is deliberate, we will say only that the deliberation justifies a posteriori—and with some incertitude—a practice to which the legend of Polycrates has given the sense of a royal trial: the practice is the complete consecration of a precious object by immersion.

While the rites reported by Herodotus and Arrian are considered "sacrificial," they are not sacrifices in the ordinary sense of contractual acts. As their depiction lacks the definite outlines one finds in descriptions of regular sacrifices, so too they reveal a different purpose and outlook. It is the idea behind this outlook which can give rise on the cultic level to a whole series of practices that sometimes—almost spontaneously—attract agalmata. Indeed, in some sacrifices the offering is completely consumed. It is consumed, one might say exclusively, by fire or water. The essential characteristic of these sacrifices, in terms of what is perceived in them, is not the fulfillment of a handing over or the idea of getting rid of something; rather, it is an intense need for destruction. And destruction in this instance has as its object not only animal victims but at times, and intentionally, precious items and symbols of wealth. This is what happens in rituals that form part of the "bond fires."[63] In an early Phocian festival, animals from the flock, clothes, gold or silver, and statues of the gods are thrown into the flames.[64] The ritual of throwing things into the sea can be seen in the same light: harnessed animal pairs are the material for a "sacrifice,"[65] for they are par excellence a sign of privileged wealth. There is the chariot whose mythical significance need only be mentioned; there are the horses (sometimes outfitted with their harnesses). These play a role only in sacrifices of a very special sort known in the classical period, and they are glorified in legends, where they are set apart for the most spectacular immolations.[66]

Whether we are dealing with sacrifices involving conspicuous consumption in extreme forms or with offerings to the sea of the ring, the cup, or the tripod; whether the sacrifice is meant to be total or whether it is focused on an object that is singular and symbolic, sacrifice within an entire vein of rituals and legends involves a destruction of wealth. But one has the impression that in myth the expression of destruction can have only provisory value. What destruction signifies, among other things, is that the act is not necessarily addressed to anyone. We might even suggest that "destruction" does not evoke the image of a divine recipient. In the legend, at least, the notion of a divine recipient is almost excluded by hypothesis. There can be no doubt that this is so in the extreme case of the Polycrates legend,[67] as well as in the tale of Helen's tripod. Still, even if the act has no destination, it does have a direction. And it is in this connection that mythical thought as such will be most easily comprehended.

The ring of Polycrates should no longer return to the world of men; but there is another world that stands opposed to the world of men. It is even possible to say that the world of men presupposes another one.

It is a recurrent theme in religious thinking that an act of destruction need not be an annihilation. Of course, we have to consider this in the concrete. For our present purpose, a curious legend in Herodotus might offer at least some suggestions. Let us observe that once again it concerns a tyrant: in fact, the tyrant is Periander of Corinth.[68] It seems that Periander consulted a necromantic oracle (it is perhaps significant that the consultation concerns a thing left in his charge but which he cannot find). Melissa, his late wife, appears to him, but refuses to reveal the hiding place because she is cold and naked; her clothes, which were buried with her, serve no purpose, since they were not burned. Periander then summons the women of Corinth, who, dressed in their most beautiful garments, proceed to a sanctuary "as though to a festival." There Periander orders his guards to strip the women. Their clothes are burned and the ghost of Melissa gives Periander the requested information.

It is the narrative itself which gives us the imagination's starting point. We know that the institutions regarding the dead were not displaced by the practice of cremation. Indeed, in order that the dead man be provided with the things he can carry with him—because they are his "belongings"—they *must* be burned with him.[69] When they are destroyed by fire, they are assured for the dead man. But in Herodotus this idea is somewhat altered and takes on a new significance, one more indefinite in orientation but more particular in terms of the material used in the sacrifice. No doubt Melissa is the beneficiary of the act; but the sacrifice—one that is prodigious, thus befitting a tyrant, and also disproportionate to its immediate purpose—is directed toward the world of the dead, the world of which Melissa's ghost is a part and which from the very beginning was the reason for the sacrifice. The essential element in the legend is the sacrifice itself, an immense holocaust that has as its special material the symbols that characterize wealth and for which the finery of an entire city's women is not too much. By definition, tyrants are the grand "collectors" of property: they excel in appropriating the goods of their subjects. But these goods, especially these prize objects, can be efficaciously consumed if their elaborate destruction is intended for the "other world." Periander knows what he is doing: a tyrant of legend can exist only within a line of mythical thought.

This thought reveals itself little by little in the plot of legends; but we have other means of approaching the subject. On a completely different level, we can recognize the theme of things swallowed, but not destroyed, in its original import in the legendary prehistory of Cyrene. It does not involve an *agalma*, a sign of value; it concerns an object whose magical properties exhaust its significance. But this object has a quasi-functional relation to a characteristic *agalma*.

The Argonauts, in the course of their voyage, land in North Africa. There Triton, the sea god, receives them and they offer him a tripod[70] or, in another version, a golden bowl. But it is also said that Triton himself gives one of the Argonauts, Euphamos, a clod of earth (*bōlos*).[71] At first glance, these two features seem independent of each other; but both are equally rooted in an ancient tradition. If we find that these presentations are connected and actually dovetail,[72] it must be for a reason: gift and return gift exhibit the idea of reciprocity. The tripod, whose psychological connections are suggested by its equivalent, the golden bowl, is for the donor a pledge of safety in the country where he sets it up.[73] The *bōlos* guarantees to its recipient (perhaps in a parallel way with a view to the legend) the right of ownership of the land from which it was taken. In Greece, the *bōlos* has this well-known significance in several legends where there is a relic of the rite of *traditio per glebam*.[74] In the legend of Euphamos, the *bōlos* conceals "*mana*" for the use of its owner. For the owner to take advantage of this power, the *bōlos* must be thrown into the sea.[75] Pindar gives us the details:[76] the date of possession had been delayed through the inadvertence of Euphamos' companions; they allowed the glob of earth to fall into the sea in a bad location. They should have thrown it into the sea near Cape Tainaros, *into an opening leading to the underworld*.[77]

When someone throws a magical object into the sea, he knows what he is doing. The motif is a long-lasting one. To survive, in the legend of *agalmata*, it does not have to retain reminders of the fanciful inventions that first surrounded it. It is enough that an imaginative format continues to exist. Its mythical power will appear again in a kind of counterstory.

Obviously a motif of folk tale, the ring of Polycrates returns in the special form in which legend presents it. Meanwhile, we may assume something else that a chance discovery tells us about the idea of the trial. We find this other element in an altogether different area, and the connection guarantees that in legend its meaning is not unique. We know that the tripod Helen threw into the waves had to come back; she herself intended this. And in effect it is returned, "discovered," in the way mythical objects usually are.

The *agalmata* can come directly from the "other world." One legend tells us that one *agalma* was thrown up by the sea itself.[78] Lesbos was colonized by seven kings who were commanded by an oracle to offer sacrifice at a specific place on the coast. This was a "foundation sacrifice," which involved a human victim: one of the kings' daughters was thrown into the sea. Enalos, a young man who loved her, dived into the sea with her and reappeared only after a long time. He told of how the girl was living with the Nereids and that he himself drove the horses of Poseidon to pasture. Then he let himself be carried off by a wave, but soon emerged with a golden cup "so admirable that the gold fashioned by men was only copper in comparison."

The tale may well have been given its form by some Alexandrian. But the "erotic" motif does not prevent us from recognizing certain fundamental elements in it. First, some connections should be pointed out. In Plutarch's version (it is the most complete), there is not only human sacrifice, but a bull is also thrown into the sea. Moreover, as we have seen, the form of whole offering, especially when it is in itself complete (that is, not preceded by immolation), characterizes certain isolated but persistent rituals that are parallel to that involving the "hurling in" of horses.[79] And it is not an arbitrary use of the imagination if we use the horse story to shed some light on the purpose of the Lesbos legend;[80] the context makes one think of some already established patterns. We should also note that the young girl is thrown into the sea wearing her splendid clothes and gold jewelry.

On the other hand, Enalos, the principal character, has a name that obviously designates him as a sea hero. He belongs to the same category of figures we frequently find elsewhere, like Glaukos, whose name is roughly synonymous, and is associated with the rite of leaping into the sea (and particularly, it seems, with the memory of "prophets" who specialize in the ritual plunge). Glaukos gained immortality through magic. In fact, the depiction of a "marine paradise" (one not as well attested among the Greeks as among Celtic peoples) is at least implied in the legends of Enalos and Theseus. The idea of immortality is suggested by the presence of the Nereids[81] in both legends; and this is especially true of the role they play in the Enalos legend. Now Theseus, having gone to the bottom of the sea (as we have already seen), receives two striking *agalmata* from Amphitrite, the Nereid who is the wife of Poseidon: one is a valuable garment, the other a crown. The crown has a different destiny or significance in the Theseus legend, but in particular it is visualized as an expensive bit of jewelry.

In this series of tales, in which we see the representation of the "other world" taking shape, this latter notion figures especially as the place of the *agalma*'s origin. The legend of Enalos and the gold cup returned by the waves illustrates the idea of a gratuitous gift from the world beyond. And this is not an isolated suggestion in legend; it appears in two other instances, but in a somewhat different format. Still, the parallel is all the more striking since the objects are different.

Although generally regarded as an episode of history, the second Messenian War is no less fitting as material for myth. Aristomenes, the national hero, is known through a tradition of popular songs; as we have seen, his shield was supposed to exercise destructive power over his enemies even several centuries after his death. There is a legend about the shield. Aristomenes had lost it in battle in a mysterious fashion (through the work of the Dioscuri). The Delphic Oracle advised him to recover it by descending into the underground sanctuary of Trophonios. There he recovered his shield and with it he accomplished even more valorous deeds than before.[82] Trophonios is an oracular hero; how do we explain his involvement in the tale?

In one episode of the Bellerophon legend—one concerning an *agalma*—we might ask the same question. Pindar tells us that the hero, after his efforts to tame the horse Pegasus were frustrated, received a gold bit from Pallas. There immediately follows mention of a dream, one that is in some way real, wherein the goddess gave him the bit.[83] In fact, at the spot where Pallas gave Bellerophon the bit, there exists a sanctuary of Athena Khalinitis (*khalinos* = bit); this episode serves as a foundation legend for the sanctuary.[84] On the other hand, the Bellerophon tale is regarded as being about a "prophetic dream." But the goddess does not simply supply a piece of information or revelation; she supplies the object itself. What could appear equivocal in the legend of Aristomenes is quite clear in the tale of Bellerophon: Aristomenes "recovered his shield at the place of Trophonios"; the god's gift comes directly. The object comes from the world beyond, a world that is alternately the realm of dream and the underworld region of an oracular hero.

In Bellerophon's case, we have an object whose powers are suited to its wonderful function. But the harness of the horse—in particular, the bit and headstall—is one of the most significant objects of wealth for a warrior. A thousand-year-old tradition demands that it be buried with its owner. There are specimens of these from Olympia; Cimon of Athens, "a skilled horseman," makes a solemn and symbolic offering of his harness on the Acropolis on the eve of Salamis.[85] Just as other mythical objects, but especially prize objects, which by custom are symbols of wealth, have a necessary relationship with the other world postulated by religious thought, so one by one these objects descend into this "other world" and arise from it.

IV
THE GOLDEN FLEECE

We have deliberately limited ourselves to more or less recent legends or to bits of a legend which show us the mythical imagination at work in the very period preceding the arrival of what one calls "positive" thought. But one feels one ought to be able to go back to more-ancient forms, to rich sources wherein the scattered concepts that have been highlighted along the way are found to be in harmony with the general idea (a profoundly mythical one) of wealth. Here the image of the golden fleece might serve as a typical example. It appears in what is tantamount to the same form.[86] Some of the settings, though, are fairly different; and it is found in two traditions that have no connection, that is, the legend of the Argonauts and that of the Pelopidai.

The legend of the Pelopidai involves a drama in the true sense. On its own, it is perhaps more understandable. We find the legend in Euripides (one of the few ancient poets interested in legend), and particularly in a lyrical setting in the *Electra*.[87] Let us say in passing that we are fortunate when we find a topic of mythology dealt with by lyric. Greek lyric proceeds by a process of recollection, that is, through suggestions or "snapshots" of scenes, or fragments of scenes, which can thus retain their proper significance. When necessary, the poet (especially Pindar) can make these scenes follow without any regard for chronology. But in the case of continuous narrative, the *look* is different. A case in point is Pherecydes, one of the most ancient mythographers. By way of Apollodorus, he gives us a classic example of this kind of narrative. The two approaches (lyric and narrative) each have their own appeal. Naturally, narrative will always involve a degree of reconstruction; still, its basic lines are not entirely dependent on the discretion of the narrator or his literary sources. Even in the connections that are invented, it is possible to find a tradition in the narrative. But because we are afforded the convenience of a dramatic vision, we return to the *Electra*.

A miraculous golden lamb is born on the estate of Atreus, who is a contender for the throne of Mycenae. The god of the herds leads the lamb down from the mountains of Argos to the sound of his pipe. The herald, standing on a rock in the agora, calls an assembly of the people in order to contemplate the "apparition," this sign of a joyous reign. Throughout the city there is the gleam of gold and the glare of fires on the altars. One hears flutes and hymns of celebration. Suddenly it appears that the golden lamb has been stolen by Thyestes, who, before the assembly, boasts of possessing the lamb. It is then that Zeus changes the shining course of the sun and stars.

True, a poet has the right to express himself through allusions. Still, it is worth noting that Euripides, so elliptical that we must fill in certain details, so little concerned with things psychological or the story's motivation, is nevertheless quite intent on retaining certain spectacular and essentially ceremonial images. Consciously or unconsciously, he is restoring a scenario. And the role of the golden lamb in it is quite clear: we are dealing with a talisman that gives its owner a claim to royalty, since it is a pledge of prosperity for the people. As such, the talisman is brought out during the celebration of a festival.[88] The very incoherence of what one can barely call a story only helps to underline the importance of this element. It is the first act; the second, and even more the third, are mentioned only summarily. One could ask whether they too are not relics of a scenario. In any case, we may well ask what the connection is between the two successive miracles.

The coherent narrative that we have in Apollodorus[89] is explicit about material that the chorus of the *Electra* presents in synthetic form. Atreus vowed to sacrifice the most beautiful animal that was born in his flocks; subsequently the golden lamb "appeared." This motif has its analogue in the legend of Minos, where his brothers contest with him the royal succession, and Minos asks specifically for the miraculous apparition of an animal (which he promises to sacrifice) as a decisive sign in his favor.[90] Both kings violate their oaths (without affecting the right of succession). The golden lamb is strangled by Atreus and locked in a chest (*larnax*). But Thyestes steals the animal[91] and presents himself to the assembly. He has the assembly agree that royal authority should be given to the one who has the miraculous lamb in his possession. Thyestes then produces the animal. At the urging of Atreus, Thyestes agrees to a revision of the rules; the kingship will revert to Atreus if the sun changes its course. And that is what happens.

However artificial the connection between the two episodes—and precisely because there is one—it is quite clear that the second is both the analogue and the counterpart of the first. Perhaps it would not be too far-fetched to see in these episodes two acts of an investiture ceremony. In any case, they represent two successive manifestations of royal power. Power over the elements is an essential attribute of a "king's magic," and it is well attested especially in Greek mythology. In our tale, this power exists in a form and with associations we need not analyze: it is exercised over the course of the sun and stars. What is the origin of the kind of synthesis (attested in the legend) between this power and the power that is signified and founded by possession of the talisman? Euripides suggests the answer when he evokes from one word, apropos of the golden lamb, the traditional theme of a beneficent royalty, prodigal with its wealth. In fact the two manifestations are of the same type.

But the significance of the talisman is enriched—or developed—in the myth that forms the basis for the legend of the Argonauts.

The Argonaut legend is actually more complex than that of the Pelopidai. Or rather it has many phases, and correlatively many aspects. The golden fleece comes from the ram that saves Phrixus, who is threatened with sacrifice as a result of his stepmother's intrigues. She has provoked a famine that can be warded off only by the sacrifice of a king or a king's son. The king's son, Phrixus, is designated as the victim, but the golden ram appears miraculously and sweeps him up into the air. The motivation in the legend is too bizarre and complicated not to reveal a necessary connection between the miraculous animal and the cult realities that are themselves transparent. To bring about sterility,[92] the stepmother persuades the local women to roast the seed corn. According to one suggested variant, she herself gives them the roasted seeds. Here, indeed, we have the relic of very ancient agrarian rites, as well as a reminder of ceremonies that custom has kept alive in certain festivals where the king (or as in this case, the queen) figures in the distribution of grain. The complement to royal beneficence is the responsibility of the king, who can be sacrificed or is obliged to sacrifice his son if the general welfare is threatened. It is into this milieu (institutional or mythical) that the legend itself introduces the golden ram. Finally, the ram (which according to the legend is sacrificed immediately) plays the role of the substitute victim.[93] In this case, the victim is magnified in the form of the miraculous animal and is connected with the divinity who causes its appearance and with the king or queen for whom it is a substitute.

As for the golden fleece, it appears in another mythical function; and this correlates with the symbolism of the miraculous animal. In a way, the legend of the Argonauts assumes that the fleece can be viewed as a royal talisman, since Jason, who lays claim to his throne, must go on a quest for the fleece as a precondition. But this element also appears in a different but concrete form. After his arrival in the far-eastern region of Colchis, the country of the Sun, Phrixus gives King Aietes the skin of the sacrificed animal that saved him. It is from Aietes, then, that Jason demands the fleece. Of the dramatic images arising from Jason's claim, the clearest is supplied by Pindar.[94] The golden fleece is the prize in an ordeal Jason is subjected to: he must yoke two wild bulls to a chariot and plow a piece of land with them. Aietes is the first to do this; Jason also succeeds and qualifies, according to the terms of the contest, for possession of the prize object. This is all. But for this brief dramatic composition to be complete, Pindar must harmonize it with the traditional imagination by bringing together two elements of the story: the heroic trial of ploughing and the miraculous fleece. Tradition among the Athenians has perpetuated the practice of sacred tillage, which was the monopoly of religious *genē*; these were the ploughings of seeds (as was the case with Jason); and the pelt of a sacrificed ram, called the "hide of Zeus," figures in the ceremonies accompanying the seeds. The transformation in the myth shows that the important qualification of farm labor and the possession of a talisman (originally the hide of a victim) are associated.

﹡

When these two legends are studied—and put side by side—they attest to a link between the symbol of wealth and the themes of royal power or royal investiture. They also allow us to see how this symbol functions in the mythical imagination. In the legend of the Pelopidai, it is associated with the magical quality of a kingship that is legitimated through its power over the Sun. In the tale of Jason, it is associated with the prosperity of the land which is guaranteed by the exercise of a religious monopoly. It is also associated through these tales with a rich mythical and ritual background where we find the idea of an effective concentration of agrarian and pastoral wealth in the hands of the king. The long-lived rites of the Boukoleion at Athens, the cattle shed at which the marriage of Dionysus and the Queen is annually celebrated; the powers attributed to the sacred herds; the preeminent value (with all its implications) one finds in the image of the sacred or royal field (like the field where Aietes' ploughing occurred)—all these bear witness to a kind of thought that we merely point out, since the question it raises is this: If the representation of the golden lamb or the golden fleece belongs strictly to a theme of agrarian wealth (which is also a theme of royal responsibility), is there in this representation only the spontaneous and free embellishment of a ritual object?

The composite character of the image is itself sufficiently significant. What lies behind the fleece, or better, the animal of *gold*? Here we need not emphasize the uncertainties and contradictions in the legend. Instead, we should keep in mind the synthesis of the two significant components of wealth, that is, livestock and precious metals. These are the very components that make up the mythological theme formerly studied by Usener, who called attention to their relationship and fusion in the legends of Atreus and Phrixus.[95] The image is so open to suggestions from a guiding philosophy that it is free from the limits and coherence its own autonomy would necessitate. It is an image that penetrates a system of representations and motivations from which it is inseparable. Depending on the inclination of the mythical thought process, this image will go in one direction or another. Atreus locks the golden lamb inside a box as he would an object made of precious metal. In the depiction of the golden fleece, it is its precious metal that seems to be most important. Inversely, it is the animal's nature that is emphasized when the talisman of kingship is specifically considered as part of the king's flock. In fact, these two elements are inseparable. It is curious to observe, in an avatar of the ancient myth, a modern tale from Epirus,[96] how—in a more or less unconscious way—the suggestion of gold and its real worth slips into a category where it seems oddly out of place. A king's daughter is enclosed in a subterranean palace; in order to be married, she must first be discovered. A young man clothed in sheepskin and sold to the king as if he were a sheep succeeds in reaching the girl. The skin in which he is clothed is a "golden fleece." Now the echo or reminiscence in this tale might seem superficial. Still, the king's daughter is locked up in the way that Danae was; and Zeus entered her prison in the form of a golden shower. The reference in the tale of a "fleece" must have been to a "golden fleece." A "golden fleece" naturally belongs to the underground, since treasure has its proper place below the earth. Even in a mythical fantasy that aims only to please, traditional associations continue to play a role.

In reality, the expression "composite image" is merely a label. These are not different images that come together, but multiple meanings of a single representation, which is, in the proper sense, "plastic." We are not interested here in analyzing all of these meanings; but we must at least identify them briefly. In this way we can discover what the idea of *agalma* is associated with, an idea that is the most remote aspect of the conception of the golden fleece.

🌿

Our point of departure is very remote: one of the cults most characterized by archaism is the cult of Zeus at Pelion, quite near the land of Phrixus.[97] The officials of this cult annually climb to the top of the mountains wrapped in hides of recently sacrificed rams. This rite occurs at the rising of Sirius, a critical time that is not, in this case, only the occasion for meteorological magic. On the cultic level, skins of sacrificed animals have all kinds of powers.[98] But the miraculous fleece has a special connection with a category of mythical objects whose purpose is easily recognized. In the case of the famous aegis, the defensive weapon that the skin of the animal represents, it is a magical one. In Zeus' hands, the aegis causes panic, as if releasing a supernatural force. But Zeus also moves it in the fashion of a *rainmaker* from Arcadia,[99] and it has effects on the sky and atmosphere. Even when held by Athena, it has some qualities of fertility. The aegis is the hide of a goat. The goat Amalthea, which nursed Zeus, is most often regarded as a benign creature; its horn became the horn of plenty, and in myth it supplies a designation for other symbols of agrarian wealth. But sometimes the animal is terrifying, and Zeus must "hide" it. The goat's hide served as a weapon for Zeus when he undertook the celebrated war against the Titans; at the war's end Zeus instituted a new monarchical order.[100] However, the Chimaera, the monstrous creature destroyed by Bellerophon, is also a goat, as its very name suggests. In its country of Lycia, the Chimaera appears as a coat of arms;[101] the lamb of the Pelopidai might also have been one.[102] A ram sculpted in rock over a tomb in the Argolid was known as the "tomb of Thyestes."[103]

These few comments can at least put these themes back into a specific zone of mythical representations. The concept of "royal" efficacy has already been seen to have associations with the mythical image of the fleece; such a concept seems complex, and almost unlimited in its ramifications. Still, it has—on a basis that is prehistoric—a kind of unity that can be seen in the very plasticity of the symbol. In the legend of Aietes, king of the mythical Orient, the connection between gold and the sun —which elsewhere consecrates royal power in a unique way—is especially close. In the legend of Atreus, this association appears in another way; it is less direct and yet more suggestive. But to be sure, the fleece is not always "golden"; it is sometimes purple. Within the Etruscan tradition of divination, the apparition in a flock of an animal of this color is the sign of a new reign that will be an age of fertility.[104] In a comparison with its variant, this theme, which hearkens back to a heritage of "Aegean" beliefs, agrees to the letter with what we find from the very beginning in the legendary chronicle of Mycenae.

✿

Here is a remarkable case of inflexibility. One of our sources, who to a high degree preserves mythological meaning, is Pindar. He recalls "the fleece, glowing red and with fringes of gold."[105] These "gold fringes" are the detail that Homer retains in his description of the aegis of Athena.[106] Homer knows their number and their value. His is a decription of a ritual garment; worn by the goddess herself, this object contains all sorts of qualities, *including* beauty and value. The mythical representation evolves into an image of an *agalma*, all the time preserving—if one can use the term—its substance.

This shift of the imagination, conditioned by the symbol's permanence, is a rather widespread phenomenon. Its analogue can be encountered in the case of real objects or, on occasion, actual practices. The kings of legend or epic carry a scepter[107] that is not only the sign but the instrument of their authority. In Homer's language, the scepter contains some of Zeus' power, which is the source of royal power. In fact, there is a necessary connection between the carrying of the scepter and the power of issuing the *themistes*, the ordinances and judgments that are in the nature of oracles. The real antecedent to the scepter is the prophet's staff; it is cut and shaped from a special tree through which the divinatory faculty is infused. But the royal scepter becomes the work of a craftsman. The one Zeus hands down to the Pelopidai was fashioned by Hephaestus, god of the forge. Understandably, it eventually becomes a scepter of gold. Still, there exists in the metal object (and the object of value) a quality related to that contained in the orginal material.

The practice of the offering, on the other hand, sometimes reveals a functional continuity in which one can observe the same kind of transition. The offering to be consumed is replaced by a copy of the offering done in precious metal. Typical examples are the sheaves of gold that were consecrated at Delphi by several cities.[108] (One of these cities, Metapontum, was to keep the symbol on its coins.) Indeed, the representation that is mentioned is of an animal of sacrifice, especially one of gold; it is characteristic that the legend preserves a parallel kind of substitution apropos of the golden lamb of the Pelopidai.[109]

All of this testifies to what, for want of a better term (since in fact there is continuity), can be called "transfer." The same representations, on occasion the same dispositions, and the same attitudes are required or suggested by an object that is considered identical but that nonetheless brings with it certain basically new elements. Thus, we are seeing the transition to the distinctive notion of value. Legend is a source for one of the objects that functions in religious commerce and plays a role in human commerce under the heading of *agalma*; it is associated with the kind of features found in the golden fleece theme; and this is certainly not something we expected. In the inventories of temples, one sometimes finds mention of a "golden vine."[110] This is the same kind of transformation as that which occurs, for example, in the case of the ear of grain made of precious metal. The vine stock, as such, appears in a series of rites and myths and is itself part of a rich complex at whose core exists the theme of a fruit-bearing tree that a god or hero has planted or made to grow. This whole complex is connected with myths of kingship—indeed, with survivals of certain scenarios that are vigorously preserved in rituals. These representations live on in the corresponding object of gold. A golden vine stock allows for the recognition of two heroes: the son of Jason the Argonaut, and the grandson of Thoas, the latter having received the object from Dionysus, god of the vine. The object here involves a "showing"; it must be made to appear at a critical moment, and it functions as a hereditary talisman.[111] But we also find that this object is a typical *agalma*. One of the most obvious illustrations of the constraining force of the gift is furnished to us by an episode taken from the conclusion of the Trojan War. In order to obtain military assistance from his nephew (the son of his sister), Priam sends him a vine with golden leaves and silver grapes; it is the product of Hephaestus' labor and had earlier served as ransom for the kidnapped Ganymede.[112] It is a typical example of the "feminine gift" theme;[113] and the legend is presented in the same way as the tale of Eriphyle's necklace.

The finely wrought object that *represents* the thing full of magical properties and fulfills the function of a talisman is in this instance the same object wherein one finds "economic" value.

There exists, as it were, a projection of the ideal notion of the other world onto the human plane. Treasure is a social reality, one might even say an institution, but it is also a mythical reality.

The legend of the golden fleece has been linked—and correctly so by Usener—with the theme of treasure. And in fact, since the double significance of talisman and value reinforce each other, the object is guarded by Aietes in his palace or sealed in a box by Atreus. The symbol of wealth is by definition something more or less hidden; its power is inseparable from its almost secret nature. No doubt, it must be "produced" at certain times, unlike the ultrasecret *Palladia*. Still, protective objects with functions like that of the *Palladia*, and objects whose legends suggest, inversely, the image of priceless furniture as treasure, are nevertheless similar. The bronze urn that contained a lock of Medusa's hair, a pledge of security for a royal city,[114] suggests a whole complex of associations in which the idea of wealth or riches alternates or converges with that of magical power.

Precious objects are often beneath the earth. A Delphic treasure, which was miraculously discovered, had been buried. But buried in the earth we find things that conceal a force that is both "political" and religious: for example, the knife that was used at the sacrifice over a treaty;[115] the arrow of Apollo, hidden among the Hyperboreans and made of gold, but also a sign of recognition for Abaris the prophet;[116] the tripod of the Argonauts; the she-goat Amalthea; the thunderbolt that is presented to Zeus upon his accession to the throne as a symbol and guarantee of his power.[117]

The very lines of development of the word *thēsauros* are indicative. The most ancient *thēsauros*, or "treasure," is the silo: it remained a depository where jewels and precious garments were stored along with provisions. The word takes on a special meaning in the religious domain, but this occurs—and remarkably so—through a kind of "self-secularizing" process whereby the notion of a secret repository eventually disappears. However, there is one type of sanctuary/*thēsauros* worth emphasizing: this is the kind of vault for offerings which was dug into rock and covered with a lid. The same structure is used for other purposes as well: for the protection of cult implements (objects of great sanctity in an archaic religion),[118] and, in legend, for the concealment of objects used for investiture.[119]

The room where the ancient wealth of rulers was stored is called a *thalamos* (and it is worth noting that the word applies equally to the living quarters of the wife or daughter). It is spontaneously represented as an underground chamber, and the legend of Danaos has preserved its mythical connotations. The same implications are true for the *thalamos* of Aietes,[120] the keeper of the golden fleece. For Mimnermus[121] there is a golden *thalamos* "in which the rays of the sun repose." Euripides speaks of a *thalamos* where the king, the alleged father of Phaethon, keeps his gold locked up, and where the body of Phaethon himself (in reality, the son of the Sun) is placed at the tragedy's conclusion.[122] The Queen, according to Euripides, has the keys to it. In a parallel fashion, Athena, Zeus' daughter, has the keys to the treasury where Zeus' thunderbolt is kept.[123]

The idea of a royal treasury, a storehouse for riches and *agalmata*, is based on a belief in protective *sacra*, which, kept in a safe corner, are guarded by a mythical king or king-god.

V

We will be forgiven for making a detour that in the realm of legends always risks the appearance of getting off the subject. But it serves a purpose if we can discover some parallels, even some common denominators, which are more or less telling ones. This deviation was inevitable, since representations of value and precious objects develop in the context of social behavior. That this is the situation goes without saying; but nothing is more worthwhile than offering proof in the case of a given culture, especially one that is, as here, the prehistoric background of civilization. The practice of gift-giving at specific moments in the social life of a people; the outlay and, if need be, the destruction of wealth for purposes of gaining prestige; the practice of investiture or expiation; the functioning of an authority whose essential quality involves the "magical" promotion of the general welfare—without the principles that regulate such activities, and without the forms themselves, one could not understand the exaltation in myth of objects that are simultaneously the material and the instrument of human and religious commerce, all within a milieu that must be reconstructed. But if legend helps us reconstruct this milieu, we must realize that the testimony it offers is already multivariate and even capricious. We must look to concrete variations and regard the implications of each story. This is the case even when we pay less attention to a story's content than to its psychological workings.

If an ancient concept of value finds itself illustrated in legendary tradition, there is one good reason: the very concept of value is mythical in its mode of thought. What from the beginning signifies different functions—or, more precisely, what appear in the end to be differentiated functions—is more or less confused; the mythical notion of value tends to be total, and it touches the whole ensemble of economics, religion, politics, law, aesthetics. But one may still try to discover within this mythical notion a specific type of thought,[124] inasmuch as we have already found, at least to some extent, specific tendencies in it. What, then, can we say with any precision about the notion of the *agalma*? To what other ideas is it related? And what are these relationships?

A Greek word may be suggestive here, since it sometimes refers to the objects we have seen, and the notion it leads to forms part of the basic pattern of imagination that interests us. The word is *teras*.[125] At first sight, the approximate meaning of the term corresponds to the idea of something exceptional, mysterious, even frightening. In Homer, the doublet *pelōr* designates a monster such as the Gorgon; and after Homer (who uses *teras* more in the indefinite sense of "marvelous"), it is with this specialized meaning that *teras* is frequently used. On the other hand, the term is associated—one might say almost as a rule in the most ancient usages—with the idea of a "sign" or token. We should add that this "sign" sometimes makes us think of "signs" appearing on weapons, shields, or armor. In such instances, we often hear of depictions of monstrous beasts; and there is a special connection between the monster or the omen and the images on coats of arms. Finally, the etymology of the word itself is an important source of information; it permitted Osthoff to discover, behind the idea of the marvelous, the notion of *zauberisch*: the root (q^wer) expresses in Indo-European the idea of "doing," especially "doing" in a magical sense. In summary, there exists in this complex a mode of thought, implicit or explicit, but always central: it involves the supernatural power that belongs to a sign, and is the idea of a religious force that can be concentrated in the thing denoted by the term *teras*. Not surprisingly, the golden ram also can be called a *teras*,[126] as can the bit given to Bellerophon by Athena[127] and called by her a *philtron*.

In summary, the idea of religious force can be recognized as fundamental in the mythical transformation of the *agalma*, and normally the *agalma* is found associated with the realm of the sacred. It is even represented according to lines of thought that are religious. With the image of the treasury being somewhat equivocal, the idea of the thing hidden, in the case of precious objects, is modeled on that suggested by cult practices. The idea of transfers between the divine and human worlds such as are found in the legends of precious objects is a concept that the life of religion constantly puts forward. There are, at times, some helpful parallels. Thus we find a Boeotian cult in which the victims were thrown into ditches, and are believed to have reappeared at Dodona.[128] This is a down-to-earth and naïvely physical interpretation of a standard practice in "chthonian" religion. On the other hand, the image of the *agalma* often comes into contact with things that are distinctively religious; it can be associated with cult instruments, and from this association it derives some of its prestige. The cup, which appears so often in legend, is usually termed a *phiale*: it is the cup of libation. The woven garments, which count as *agalmata*, have a very ancient function in cult. It is possible that the games, at which garments were sometimes presented as prizes in the historical period, could be descendants of ancient tribal contests; in any case, the exchange of garments between the sexes, which remained standard in some feasts, constitutes an instructive archaism. The offering of the *peplos* to certain goddesses, a practice that seems to be of ancient organization, is also one in which the specialized cultic aspect of the object is most striking.[129]

There is, therefore, a kind of religious quality attached to precious objects in general. But the imaginative thought about *agalmata* moves in a specific direction. There is a principle of selectivity in it, and—if we want—a principle of freedom. It has its own particular sphere inasmuch as the objects touched on in the representations of myth all have something in common: they are all objects that are handled and more or less passed around. This underlines a singular notion of value, one in which the "aesthetic element" predominates. In a story such as that of Enalos, this is primary: "transfers" are acts of enhancement in this tale. Myth, on occasion, allows these same recognitions: social customs sometimes permit us to determine their mechanics and true nature. When there is a gift of food, especially on the occasion of communion between equals or between the chief and his "companions," the giving of *agalmata* is an added feature—a gold cup is the magnificent complement to a toast—and it can even be a substitute.[130] But the relationship with religious objects is reversible. It is not only because an object has a religious use that it has value; it is because it is precious that it can be consecrated.[131] This is the origin, in myth, of certain images that are, from the beginning, symbols of wealth and nothing else. The *larnax* in which Atreus locked up the golden fleece is the piece of "furniture" in which vestments and precious objects are stored; it is the typical instrument for the "exposure" of infant heroes or even gods.[132] It seems that the tripod, at least in the beginning and in and of itself, did not have any cultic significance. It was essentially an *agalma* in the most ancient meaning of the term. Only later did it become a gift object, and therefore an offering. Thus, its association with the prophetic power of Apollo was only secondary,[133] as was its use as the normal symbol of the god in his mythical iconography.[134]

Along the same line of thought, there is a small but suggestive point:

it is the use of the adjective *timēeis*, which is, for example, the Homeric epithet applied to Eriphyle's necklace. In the case of an object that is characteristic of legend, the complex notion of *timē* (honor, social prerogative, religious quality) is concentrated on the specialized and somewhat banal notion of the "precious." This represents a turning point: as late as the pseudohistorical period, the same objects that remain charged with mythical potential also represent what we might term the external signs of wealth. This view is much less positive than one might have been willing to believe. But from its origins and constant associations, it reveals a mode of thought in which the objects mentioned above not only signify wealth; there is a mysterious power embodied in them as well. And it is not unimportant that the methods used to maintain treasures in the classical period still reveal traditional attitudes.[135]

VI

Attempts are made to survey a mythical notion. But the essential feature of mythical thought is not only that it is accompanied by images but that the images constitute a necessary instrument of the thought itself. What we are saying specifically is that it is possible to recognize a distinctive function for the imagination.

Legends about precious objects supply us with the primary material. These derive, more or less directly, from themes of magical kingship. The inherent efficacy and force of the *agalma* is first and foremost a social one, and the oldest representations of authority seem to feed the imagination. But is this survival a dry fact of tradition, and must we view it as something jejune? It should have its own raison d'être, since we are able to establish that it survived in the subconscious well beyond the mythical age.

Being especially associated with objects made from precious metals, the idea of value is linked with the oldest notion of "wealth" and, like it, moves toward an ideal center. In mythical representations of kingship, and in the scenarios that revive and sustain it, the king, who is responsible for the life of the group and plays an important role in the prosperity of field and flocks, is also the one privileged to hold the kind of wealth signified by the golden fleece. The possession of treasure is the testimony and the condition for the possession and exercise of beneficent power, as are the possessions of the sacred field, the sacred tree, and the sacred herd (with all of which it remains in contact). This formulation of a center, where the talismanlike object (in a certain sense already transformed into a precious metal) appears as both an expression and a guarantee of value, persists in a way even into the historical period. A treasury of a god, which is also a treasury of a city and holder of its reserve (like Athena's treasury at Athens), contains not merely coined money, which is specifically labeled for the city-state's use in time of need, but also the heart of the city's defense, goods that are otherwise sacred: the *kosmos* or ornamentation of the goddess, and all the precious materials that the financial acumen of a Pericles, and a Lycurgus one hundred years later, could put to use in time of supreme crisis.[136] The mythical expression of this mentality survives even in a later period. Callimachus' *Hymn to Demeter* ends with a litany in which the poet formulates the symbolic significance he attributes to the liturgical procession that is his theme. The four horses carrying the goddess's basket promise blessings on the year and its four seasons; the garb of the officiant signifies the desire for health and prosperity; and finally, "as the *kanēphoroi* carry the baskets filled with gold, so may gold abound for us beyond measure." In this period of a Ptolemaic monarchy when a political-religious and somewhat artificial mentality is still rooted in prehistory, a dilettantish court poet rediscovers the sense of kingly sumptuousness linked with a spectacular cult. The display of gold objects is the sign of power; it benefits the community and is exercised in the same way as is the power of mythical kingships.

The social memory that functions in legends of *agalmata* does not function gratuitously. In a notion of value which is in the process of becoming independent, a traditional imagination assures some continuity with the magical and religious idea of *mana*.

In social history, in as ancient a period as we can examine directly, the symbolism already ceases to be multiple. No doubt it is interesting to note that when Homer describes or calls to mind certain jewels—which he seems to enjoy doing often—value is attached to those objects whose religious or legendary implications are emphasized by the poet himself or can easily be supplied by the audience.[137] We would also point out that the kind of bridle and bit mentioned in the tale of Bellerophon (in fact, it owes its suggestive poetic power to an earlier legend) is in Homer essentially a sample of an industrial product, one that is exhibited as such for its market value.[138]

The evolution of this kind of thought presupposes social conditions about which we know little; but we can at least see that such conditions favored a certain diffusion of the "external signs of wealth." Because these signs are no longer the privileged possession of a class in which the heritage of mythical kingship and the power of these symbols survive, economic value begins to impose itself, and for its own sake. Even in the premonetary stage, the saying "silver makes the man" had force; the saying crept into the legend of the tripod of the Seven Sages.[139] Thus the way is made clear for the revolution created in the life and thought of society by the advent of money. Still, at the end of our study, it is worthwhile to recall evidence of continuity in the midst of abrupt change, a continuity which those involved in that revolution at first failed to recognize.

There is little doubt that the invention of money was possible only because of an abstract notion of value. There corresponds to this new state of affairs the use of an instrument whose substance, understood in the philosophical sense, could seem unimportant. It fell to Plato and Aristotle, men who were in general ill-disposed toward a mercantile economy, to construct a theory of money as sign and convention. It is a logical theory, since the philosophers retain only the functions of exchange and circulation (they forget or fail to recognize that metallic money found one of its most ancient uses in religious commerce, where it granted individuals dispensation from acts of thanksgiving, customary offerings, or expiatory acts). And it is certain that the instrument, once created, lent itself well to the task of circulation, which so soon became widespread in Greece itself. But in the historic milieu, when the sign first appeared it was a "certificate of origin," certifying that the religious, aristocratic, and agonistic symbols retained their original patterns. Up to the very point where its creation had become possible there survived a form of mythical thought. This is what allows us to understand how in value, and later in the very signs representing it, there is a core that cannot be reduced to what is commonly called rational thought.

NOTES

1.   See B. Laum, *Heiliges Geld*.

2.   On the impossibility of a universally useful definition, see I. Myerson, *Les Fonctions psychologiques et les oeuvres*, pp. 75 ff.

3.   On these primitive forms of money, see M. Mauss, "Essai sur le don," *Année sociol.*, n.s., I (1925), pp. 62 ff., 119 ff.; F. Simiand, "La Monnaie, réalité sociale," *Annales sociol.*, ser. D, I (1934), and his talk to the Institut français de Sociologie, ibid., pp. 59 ff.

4.   F. de Visscher, *Etudes de droit romain*, pp. 353 ff.

5.   L. Gernet, *Revue histor. du droit*, XXVI (1948), pp. 177 ff. [= L. Gernet, *Droit et société dans la Grèce ancienne*, pp. 12 ff.].

6.   Laum, op. cit., pp. 104 ff.

7.   On the realm of ownership that is strictly individual and the themes operating therein, see E. F. Bruck, *Totenteil und Seelgerät im griechischen Recht*, pp. 39–74.

8.   Laum, op. cit., pp. 10 f. For the Romanist viewpoint, see H. Lévy-Bruhl, *Nouv. Rech. sur le très ancien droit romain*, p. 99.

9.   This follows a concept that is rather aesthetic and "positivist"; it is opposed to one of Aegean origin which sees in the cult statue a receptacle of "mystical" qualities. The word *agalma*, according to the latter concept, also contains the notion of a thing mysteriously alive. In this regard, one notes a curious development that lies at the base of a metaphor in Plato's *Laws* (XI.930E).

10.   K. Bücher (*Die Entsteh. der Volkswirtsch.*, pp. 50 f.) shows how ancient pro-

ductivity, unlike that of more modern milieus, was directed to an aristocratic and restricted clientele. He also explains how the Games, especially, had a large role in the fame of certain material objects.

11.   The practice of the "anathema" appears at a relatively recent phase of religious life (Laum, op. cit., pp. 86 f.). Laum connects it with the notion of gods having permanent personalities, as opposed to the concept of *Augenblicksgötter*, for whom consumable offerings are appropriate. One might ask whether the reverse is not true: in fact, there is a tendency to objectify on two fronts, that of the cult practice and that of the representation of divine beings.

12.   Arist., *Eth. Nic.*, IV.1123a.5. In contrast, Plato limits wealth to an extreme degree in the city of the *Laws*, and restrains equally the extravagance of private and public offerings.

13.   In this regard, the notion of the "objective crime" more or less survives into fourth-century Athens (see pseudo-Demosthenes, *Contra Aristogeitona*).

14.   There is no need to quibble over this word. Even if one wishes to qualify myth more specifically in terms of a different kind of narrative, one is still faced with the same type of representation, together with themes that are at times common to the different stages of invention, stages that are designated by time-honored words like "myth," "story," and "legend." From the psychological point of view at least, this is all that matters.

15.   See F. de Saussure, *Cours de linguistique générale*, pp. 170 ff. ("rapports syntagmatiques et rapports associatifs").

16.   Diog. Laert., I.27–33; Plut., *Sol.*, 4.

17.   See K. Kuiper, "Le Récit de la coupe de Bathyclès," *REG*, XXIX (1916), pp. 404 ff.

18.   M. Mauss has studied this series of usages and representations for a neighboring civilization, but apropos of a very suggestive Greek text (ibid, XXXIV [1921], pp. 388 ff.).

19.   Diog. Laert., I.33.

20.   The "sage" is curiously termed as one of an ancient sort, or as an inspired soothsayer.

21.   Paus., III.24.3, has a typical example (the chest of Dionysus and Semele). For the general theme, see H. Usener, *Die Sintfluthsagen*, pp. 138 f.; F. Pfister, *Der Reliquienkult im Altertum*, I, p. 215.

22.   They are saved by Dictys the fisherman, whose name has been traced to the word for "net" (see the goddess Dictynna, who was herself rescued in a net); C. Robert, *Die griech. Heldensage*, p. 232.

23.   G. Glotz, *L'Ordalie dans la Grèce primitive*, p. 51.

24.   Paus., V.13.5–6.

25.   Ibid., VI.11.8.

26.   This is what was preserved by Plutarch (*Sol.*, 4). His account is parallel to that of Diogenes Laertius (I.32). These are two variants of the same story, a fact that indicates it was highly regarded.

27.   See Kuiper, op. cit., p. 424.

28.   Diog. Laert., I.29 (following an Eastern tradition, the intermediary is one of the king's "friends").

29.   Even as late as the beginning of the fourth century B.C., a golden cup, a "*sumbolon* received from the king," serves as a "letter of credit" (Lys., XIX.24).

30.   Diog. Laert., I.32.

31.   Hdt., IV.179; Ap. Rhod., *Argon.*, IV.532 ff.; Diod. Sic., IV.56.

32.   Robert, *Die griech. Heldensage*, p. 273.

33.   See A. J. Reinach, *RHR*, LXI (1910), p. 221.

34.   Serv., *ad Aen.*, III.286.

35.   Paus., IV.32.5–6.

36.   Aesch., *Ag.*, 905–49.

37.   The image evoked is that of the goddess who is an escort to the king. It is an image recognized elsewhere as a triumphal scene.

38.   The same type of self-consecration is found in the ritual of the "great oath" at Syracuse: see G. Glotz, *Dict. des Antiq.*, s.v. *Jusjurandum*, p. 752.

39.   Robert, *Die griech. Heldensage*, III, pp. 915 f.; cf. idem, *Die Oidipussage*, pp. 20 ff.

40.   Hellanic., *FGrH*, 4.98 (Jacoby).

41.   Paus., II.18.6.

42.   Concerning this cup of special form and designation, see Ath., XI.474F, 498A–B; Macrob., *Sat.*, V.21.4. The gifts under discussion have the special quality of a *pretium concubitus*, as do the crown (Hdt., VI.69) and the ring (whose mythical properties we have already noted); the latter serves as a talisman in the service of the male child both in historical legends and in ordinary ones (Just., XV.1.3).

43.   See Robert, *Die Oidipussage*, p. 208.

44.   This is the depiction of a Corinthian bowl from the sixth century B.C.; it reproduces the same scene as the chest of Cypselus (Paus. V.17.7–8).

45.   Apollod., *Bibl.*, III.61.

46.   *Od.*, XV.247, XI.521.

47.   Mauss, "Essai sur le don," pp. 45 ff., 153 ff.

48.   Hdt., III.40–43.

49.   It is similar to the one that occurs (in a cult situation that is different) at the end of Euripides' *Helen*. One could also compare it to a nautical rite, one involving the same conditions, whereby a cup is thrown into the sea (Ath., XI.462B–C).

50.   The most detailed text is that of Bacchylides (XVIII [Snell]). It is worth recalling that the legend of Theseus, as we know it, must have developed in the sixth century B.C..

51.   Pl., *Resp.*, 359D f. The episode has been dealt with from a special point of view by P.–M. Schuhl, *La Fabulation platonicienne*, pp. 79 ff.

52.   On the premonetary functions of gold rings, see P. N. Ure, *The Origin of Tyranny*, pp. 145 ff. (a work that follows the lead of Babelon and Ridgeway).

53.   See E. Cassin's interesting article, "Le Sceau: un fait de civilisation dans la Mésopotamie ancienne," *Annales*, XV (July–August 1960), pp. 742–51.

54.   Bruck, op. cit., p. 8.

55.   G. MacDonald, *Coin Types: Their Origin and Development*, pp. 46–52.

56.   Ure, op. cit., pp. 149 f. For the legend of Gyges' ring, see ibid., p. 151; cf. Laum, op. cit., pp. 140 ff.

57.   See P. Saintyves, *RHR*, LXVI (1912), p. 70, for an interpretation of the Polycrates legend. A very suggestive comparison can be made from an entirely different civilization; see E. Mestre, "Monnaies métalliques et valeurs d'échange en Chine," *Annales sociol.*, ser. D. II (1937), pp. 46 ff.

58.   See Paus., III.23.10, concerning the oracular methods used in the Laconian sanctuary.

59.   Arr., *Anab.*, VI.19.5.

60.   This is the same ceremonial form that has been noted in regard to the story of Polycrates (see pp. 85 ff., above).

61.   Hdt., VII.54.

62.   It is regarded here as a precious object. When Xerxes makes an offering of it, we are to understand that it is an exceptional gift (ibid., VIII.120).

63.   Concerning this group, see M. P. Nilsson, "Der Flammentod des Herakles," *ArchRW*, XXI (1922), pp. 310 ff.

64.   Paus., X.1.6; see M. P. Nilsson, *Griech. Feste*, p. 222.

65.   Festus, s.v. *October Equus*; Paus., VIII.7.2; Serv., *ad G.*, I.12.

66.   E.g., Paus., III.20.9; *Il.*, XXIII.171. The striking consecrations of the chariot and its horses are complements to their mythologies.

67.   See P. Stengel, *Die griech. Kultusalter.*[3], p. 113.

68.   Hdt., V.92.

69.   For the Homeric application, see Bruck, op. cit., pp. 28 ff. Cf. E. Weiss, *Griech. Privatrecht*, I, pp. 146 f.; C. W. Westrup, *Introduction to Early Roman Law*, II, pp. 167 ff.

70.   Hdt., IV.179.

71.   Pind., *Pyth.*, IV.28 ff.

72.   Ap. Rhod., *Argon.*, IV.1547 ff.

73.   See p. 81 above.

74.   M. P. Nilsson, *ArchRW*, XX (1920), pp. 232 ff.

75.   Ap. Rhod., *Argon.*, IV.1756.

76.   Pindar, *Pyth.*, IV.45.

77.   In this regard, one notes that bulls are thrown into a spring near Syracuse at the spot where Hades plunged into the underworld following the abduction of Persephone (Diod. Sic., IV.23.4). Horses are thrown into the sea in the Argolid near a certain Genethlion (Paus., VIII.7.2), that is, a "place of births" (where souls come for reincarnation?). In Pindar, the *bōlos* is the "immortal seed of vast Lybia."

78.   Anticl. (third century B.C.), *ap.* Ath., XI.466C; Plut., *Conv. sept. sap.*, 163B.

79.   See p. 88 above.

80.   Here, as elsewhere, horses are linked to Poseidon, especially in his role as a sea god. But they are also connected to Hades, god of the underworld. See P. Stengel, *ArchRW*, VIII (1905), pp. 203 ff.

81.   In regard to this significance of the Nereids, see C. Picard, *RHR*, CIII (1931), pp. 5–28.

82.   Paus., IV.16.7.

83.   Pind., *Ol.*, XIII.63 ff.

84.   Paus., II.4.1.

85.   Paus., V.20.8; Plut., *Cim.*, 5.2.

86.   In the context of the Pelopidai, the animal (the "golden lamb") and its fleece are, as it were, independent entities. In stories of the "golden fleece," the animal itself is ignored.

87.   Eur., *El.*, 699 ff.; equally lyrical passages are found in *Or.*, 812 ff., 996 ff.

88.   The memory of a celebration of royal investiture, along with choruses and sacrifices, had not vanished in fifth-century Sparta (see Thuc., V.13.6).

89.   Apollod., *Epit.*, II.10 ff.

90.   Apollod., *Bibl.*, III.8. The legend allows us to see here the drama of royal investiture, together with the "struggle" between brothers.

91.   For this he seduced the wife of Atreus (in Euripides' version). We will merely mention here the importance of the role of the woman in the transfer of the talisman or the precious object.

92.   On the mythical concept of barrenness (antithetical and homogeneous to that of abundance), see the important work of M. Delcourt, *Stérilités mystérieuses et naissances maléfiques* (1938).

93.   A dramatic symbol of substitution appears in a kind of corresponding situation; see Hdt., VIII.197, on the subject of certain practices (ostensibly, human sacrifice) that occurred in Thessaly at a place where the legend has sometimes been localized.

94.   Pind., *Pyth.*, IV.224 ff.

95. Usener, *Die Sintfluthsagen*, pp. 183 ff.
96. A. B. Cook, *Zeus*, I, pp. 412 ff.
97. The connection was made long ago; see Nilsson, *Griech. Feste*, p. 12.
98. J. Pley, *De lanae in antiquorum ritibus usu* (1911).
99. See *Aen.*, VIII.351 ff.
100. Eratosth., [*Cat.*], 13 (Robert).
101. L. Radermacher, *Mythos u. Sage bei den Griechen*, p. 97; L. Malten, "Bellerophon," *JdI*, XL (1926), pp. 125 ff.
102. J. G. Frazer, *Pausanias' Description of Greece*, III, p. 187.
103. Paus. II.18.1.
104. Macrob., *Sat.*, III.7.2.
105. Pind., *Pyth.*, IV.231 (cf. Ap. Rhod., *Argon.*, IV.1143).
106. *Il.*, II.447 ff.
107. See L. Deubner, "Die Bedeut. des Kranzes im kl. Alt.," *ArchRW*, XXX (1933), p. 85.
108. Plut., *De Pyth. or.*, 16; see W. H. D. Rouse, *Greek Votive Offerings*, pp. 66 ff.
109. Anticl., fr. 10 (C. Müller, *SRAM*, p. 149).
110. *BCH*, VI (1882), p. 146 (Delos).
111. *Anth. Pal.*, III.10; *POxy.*, VI.852 (Euripides); see C. Robert, *Hermes*, XLIV (1909), pp. 376 ff.
112. Robert, *Die griech. Heldensage*, pp. 1222 ff.
113. *Od.*, XI.5; see p. 84 above.
114. Apollod., *Bibl.*, II.144.
115. Eur., *Supp.*, 1205 f.
116. Eratosth., [*Cat.*], 29 (Robert); see Delcourt, op. cit., p. 89.
117. Hes., *Theog.*, 504 ff.
118. Paus., VIII.15.3.
119. The Rock of Theseus: Plut., *Thes.*, 3.4–5.
120. See Pind., *Pyth.*, IV.160.
121. Mimn., fr. 11.5 f. (Diehls).
122. Eur., fr. 781 (Nauck).
123. Aesch., *Eum.*, 826; see Radermacher, op. cit., pp. 277 ff.
124. Concerning this function of myth, see H. Usener, *ArchRW*, VII (1904), pp. 6 ff.
125. See H. Osthoff, *ArchRW*, VIII (1905), pp. 52 ff.
126. Eur., *Or.*, 1000; cf. *El.*, 716.
127. Pind., *Ol.*, XIII.73.
128. Paus., IX.8.1.
129. We refer here briefly to a whole "primitive" background of religion, one which deals with weaving, the women's craft.
130. In this regard, we have pertinent evidence concerning religious brotherhoods from a curious fragment of the memoirs of Ptolemy VII (Ath., XII.549E; cf. ibid., IV.128A–B, XI.466B–C).
131. Concerning offerings from the classical period; concerning "symbolic offerings"; concerning the fact that most consecrated vases are indistinguishable from those intended for ordinary use, except for the dedication and the locale—see T. Homolle, *Dict. des Antiq.*, s.v. *Donarium*, pp. 368 f., 372 ff.
132. Glotz, *L'Ordalie*, p. 45. It is worth noting that the brand, which is the "measure of life" for Meleager, is kept in the *larnax* (Bacchyl., V.140).
133. See Reisch, in *RE*, V. 1687; K. Schwendemann, *Arch. Jahrb.*, XXXVI (1921), pp. 169 f.; P. Guillon, *Les Trépieds du Ptoion* (1943), pp. 90 ff.
134. For the tripod as a winged conveyor for the god, see A. B. Cook, *Zeus*, I. pp. 334 ff.; II. p. 205.

135.   See Ath., XI.465C.

136.   Thuc., II.13.4–5; [Plut.], *X orat.*, 852B–C.

137.   For example, *Il.*, XVI.225 f., XI.632 ff.

138.   *Il.*, IV.141 f. (The change in meaning for *thalamos*, whereby it comes to denote a "storehouse," is noteworthy. Moreover, in Homer the *agalma* is reserved for a "king.")

139.   Diog. Laert., I.31.

CHAPTER 5

The City of the Future
and the Land of the Dead

In the Hellenistic age, the social utopia seems to have flourished. In ancient Stoicism, a concept of the ideal city was expressed on occasion by certain Stoics who personally favored the socialistic or communistic experiment. Moreover, there existed so-called ethnographic literature in which the description of faraway and imaginary countries was the pretext for a description of a happy and egalitarian society. There is a link between these two intellectual phenomena, and J. Bidez has recently indicated that what makes them similar is the concept of a celestial city, one that the Stoics—of Eastern origin—introduced into the Greek world.[1]

However, it is interesting to point out that even at that time, social utopia was part of a long tradition. If Bidez is correct in suggesting[2] that there must be more than a similarity of words between the Heliopolitans of Iambulus' *novel* and the state of the same name, which Aristonicus claims to have founded with the slaves of the kingdom of Pergamum,[3] then one should also bear in mind that the novel in question comes at the end of a whole series of romantic writings, to which Rohde dedicated a chapter of his classic work.[4] Let us go one step further: one needs only to establish a link between this series of examples and the tales of Elysium and the Golden Age[5] to grasp the deep and seemingly essential continuity between myth and utopia.[6]

The novel of Iambulus should have a privileged place among the utopias of the Hellenistic age. It is the work about which we know the most; it is also apparently the most recent; and it is noteworthy that even though it is addressed to a Greek audience, its author came from the Orient,[7] or was a Greek who claimed to be an Oriental.

We know this from a rather confused account of Diodorus (II.55–60). We will spare the reader an analysis of these chapters. It is enough to

This article originally appeared in *REG*, XLVI (1933), pp. 293–310.

know that the heart of the story was the description of the happy isles, situated somewhere in the South, below the equator—the vague land of Taprobane, otherwise known as Ceylon. There were, of necessity, facts about natural history, and a number of precise and more or less localized details. With regard to ethnography, there were some details that could not have been invented.[8] In brief, it is a work that in principle is connected with the literature of exploration, which was naturally in favor after Alexander.[9] But this is only an alibi: in fact, the Heliopolitans lived in a dream world that was itself a product of fantasy. This imaginative genre always follows certain rules. In the present case what are they?

Some believe that the author was influenced by Stoic thought. It is possible. It is especially possible that even the name "the City of the Sun," which is applied to this imaginary people, and even more their religion, which in essence involves the adoration of celestial powers, had some connection with the Stoics and their conception of the *kosmos*. Perhaps the most characteristic sign of this is the term *periekhon*, which though minor, in the summary of Diodorus seems appropriately to indicate the divine sky. The word also belongs to the vocabulary of the Stoa.[10] But an influence does not mean the essential inspiration. For one thing, the comparisons made are rather vague;[11] for another, they are not topical. It has already been noticed[12] that the sharing of the women and children in the novel of Iambulus is not necessarily derived from the writings of the Stoics, but can be explained from the teachings of Cynics and Platonism.[13] In any case, in taking contemporary speculations into account we must recognize here an ancient tradition that is in no way dogmatic.

For this reason, we must not separate the country from its inhabitants: in the account of Diodorus, the description of the first is at least as important as that of the second. The land of the Heliopolitans is first of all described as an exotic land, and as one existing at the ends of the earth: in a word, beyond this world.[14] It is practically inaccessible. Iambulus could reach it only after several unique and quasi-miraculous adventures. Since he was judged as undesirable, he could not stay there. This land certainly belongs to the same category as the land of the Hyperboreans, which Hecataeus of Abdera managed to bring back to popularity again at the beginning of the Hellenistic era;[15] or if we go back a little further,[16] it is in the same category as Theopompus' fantastic island, which was beyond Oceanus in the unknown regions of the Hyperboreans.[17]

Let us examine this last point more closely. We see some remarkable similarities between Iambulus and Theopompus; but this is not to say that—in this case—the first is a product of the second. In the land of Theopompus, men are twice as large as normal and they live twice as long. In Iambulus' land, the inhabitants are of an extraordinary height and they live 150 years—twice as long as a healthy person's life.[18] It goes without saying that neither of these races is familiar with sickness.[19] But they both have a rather unique way of dying. In Meropis, which is part of Theopompus' imaginary continent,[20] there is a place called Anostos, which is fed by two rivers: the River of Sorrow and the River of Happiness. Trees grow in the neighborhood of these two rivers. Whoever eats the fruit of the one is consumed by sorrow; the fruits of the other have the opposite effect. What is even more remarkable is that a meal of these fruits is all that is needed to make one forget any object of attachment and to relive the course of one's life in reverse, becoming young man, child, and newborn, after which the only course left is to vanish.[21] We shall return to this; let us merely remember for the moment a specific image of death. What do we see in Iambulus? It seems that in the Land of the Sun there grows a special and miraculous plant;[22] whoever has completed the normal course of life lies down on this plant and falls quietly asleep in death.

There are similarities here which one cannot ignore. A certain general affinity can hardly be disputed: to understand the tale of Iambulus, one can study the fantasy of Theopompus.

There is no doubt that the tale of Iambulus was composed from mythical remembrances. The author himself warns us of this in the episodic passage about the city of warriors, the Makhimoi.[23] Despite some unique traits,[24] the "warriors" are the counterparts of the "fourth race" of Hesiod's poetry. One of their significant traits corresponds to the invulnerability of the heroes of legend. More precisely, these men cannot be harmed by iron; only rocks and wood can destroy them—a fact, that is very reminiscent of legends such as that of Caeneus.[25] Besides, the men of the other city—the city of the Eusebeis, which strikingly resembles Iambulus' utopia—die happy and in laughter. This is a trait that is attributed to the Hyperboreans by Pomponius Mela who permits us to interpret it as the confused recollection of prehistoric customs. Among the Hyperboreans, it was a matter of ritual suicide, and we are familiar with the custom to which the proverbial phrase "sardonic laughter"[26] applies. Theopompus makes no mention of this suicide; but it is indeed curious that Iambulus, in a contradiction that does not seem to bother him,[27] prescribed ritual suicide for those Heliopolitans who were stricken by any illness—yet further evidence of the underlying layers of development by which the story of Iambulus is related to old traditions.

But the continuity of tradition, the persistence of mythological descriptions—these must be seen before all else in the imaginary geography that is involved in this kind of story. In Iambulus' tale, the very vague localization of the land of the Heliopolitans does not mislead us. We would be surprised to learn that this country, situated under the equator, enjoyed even there a temperate climate,[28] if the name of the equator itself, *isēmerinos*, were not a reminder of a traditional fact, namely, that of the equality of night and day in the "Land of the Blessed."[29] And surely there is nothing more obviously mythical than the alleged topographies of countries situated at the ends of the earth, at one or another of the four cardinal points,[30] and accessible only by miracles (for they are properly inaccessible).[31] In reality, these contain the notion of the other world.[32] There is no room here—a reference to Usener will suffice[33]—to illustrate the close parentage, or rather the deep identity that exists between the depiction of the land of the gods, the Land of the Dead, the land of miraculous fruit, and also, naturally, the Golden Age.[34] It is this type of imaginative concept which one finds in a fantasy such as that of Theopompus, and beyond that, in a description of the kind we find in Iambulus.[35] In these exotic lands, where men are no more acquainted with sickness than with want,[36] not only does the earth blossom spontaneously[37] several times a year[38] and produce marvelous fruits, as in the Garden of the Hesperides, but also, in the description of Meropis,[39] and in a passage already mentioned from the story of Iambulus, we recognize a similarity with certain topical details of the Land of the Dead. If the fruits that grow near the River of Joy[40] make those who taste them forgetful—and if it is significant to find such an idea and the very word in Iambulus (*lelēthotōs...eis hupnon katenekhtheis*)—it is not only the tale of the lotus-eaters that one should think of, a tale which itself could be another version of the same mythical idea.[41] In addition, we know that in the underworld there is a place called *Lēthē* (Forgetfulness), and in particular a fountain of *Lēthē*. We also know that before entering the Orphic paradise, one comes near a spring (shaded by a white cypress) that in all likelihood is the Spring of Forgetfulness,[42] and that would, if need be, corroborate the testimony of Plato.[43] This image, much older that it would seem,[44] is associated with rites found in the mystery cults, such as that of Trophonios.[45]

Let us return, momentarily, to the final feature in Theopompus: when one has tasted the fruit of the River of Joy, one begins life over again in reverse. This concept of regression appears in a Platonic myth about the age of Kronos, a myth that appears in the *Politicus* (270D f.) The connection seems obvious; and it can justly be admitted that Theopompus borrows from Plato.[46] But there is another question besides the philological one: if Theopompus has taken this bizarre invention for his own benefit, it is because it suits a whole ensemble of mythical ideas, and also because Plato did not invent it.[47] In a general way, the cosmological or eschatological myth in Plato[48] has its sources in the more or less popular and reworked myths. These involve two principal elements. On the one hand, there is the notion of successive and antithetical periods of the world, a notion that no longer appears in Theopompus but is the raison d'être of the Platonic myth. For in Plato, regression is experienced by all men at a time determined by the celestial revolution. In the classical age, this idea of cosmic periods is somewhat repressed except in philosophy, where it is sometimes used for speculative ends. But it reappears later.[49] Revivified by theories that are Eastern in origin, it will offer to man, in the form of millenniarianism, hope for a joyful renewal of humanity.[50] On the other hand, the myth of the *Politicus* cannot be separated from a whole series of Platonic myths whose mythical substrata are known. Because they treat of death, these myths also treat of rebirth: in the world beyond time, symmetrical to that which is beyond our space, unattached souls are ready for reincarnation, *scilicet immemores supera ut convexa revisant*.[51] (So it happens that in Virgil's underworld we meet not only the past but—what is surprising— also the future.) Thus, if the men of Meropis became newborns, one can say that there is, in the image of human larvae, the obscure memory of souls who will have a new existence. Perhaps without meaning to, Theopompus has clarified the infernal nature of the surroundings; the Anostos,[52] the place haunted by dreamlike beings, resembles an abyss (*khasma*) over which hangs a mist, the mist that also rules in the land of the Cimmerians.[53]

We can see the kind of imaginative thought Iambulus must have inherited in an authenticated continuum from the myth of the other world to the fantasy of the historian, and from the historian's fantasy to the utopia of a romantic novelist. The continuity is even more certain because the land of Taprobane, about which Iambulus conjectured more or less precisely, must have been equated expressly with the Isles of the Blessed.[54] What might have seemed the most novel thing in Iambulus' story, and what led him to look for a philosophical and religious inspiration in the speculations of the Hellenistic age, is the very idea of a City of the Sun. Without wanting to deny such an inspiration, we believe it is useful to look for other traditional themes that complement it.

We have pointed out the symmetry—one could say the relationship —between the imaginary lands situated at the four cardinal points. The northern land, where Apollo exercises supreme rule, belongs to the Hyperboreans. Apollo was more or less a sun god, and was particularly so in the geographical myth, especially in his relation to the North.[55] On the other hand, he is connected with the South and the Southeast[56] correlatively. The Sun, the supreme divinity of the faraway region described by Iambulus—the Sun to whom the inhabitants of this region are devoted[57]—was not about to leave Greeks in the dark about the Heliopolitans. Can it be by chance that the Apollonian number 7 appears twice in the tale? And Iambulus stayed with the Heliopolitans for seven years—and it was for the sake of a communal expiation that he was sent to their land.[58] No less important is the fact that the Blessed Isles themselves number seven.[59] But what really matters is a general reflection: with or without Apollo, *the other world* is always a Land of the Sun; and—at the same time—it is the Land of the Dead itself, or in its vicinity. Not far from Circe's[60] island is the land of the Cimmerians.[61] The last three labors of Herakles have one common theme: they are voyages to a land beyond. On the one hand, the theme of a descent to Hades is superimposed on the adventure of the Hesperides, an incident that could logically end the career of the hero.[62] On the other hand, there are unquestioned similarities of motifs between the expedition to Hades and the quest for Geryon.[63] But the land of the Hesperides is a Land of the Sun;[64] even the name of the island of Geryon, Erytheia, suggests this idea.[65] It is curious that by means of a rather awkward but revealing compromise, Theopompus harmonizes the two tales, which in a fairly scrambled tradition like that of the Greeks, could have seemed to run afoul of each other. The mist covering the *khasma* where life vanishes into forgetfulness—or so he says—is something intermediate between light and darkness. It is linked with redness, *eruthēma*, a name that suggests the term designating the land of Geryon. But when the land of the Makares (who are the dead and the happy)[66] is viewed through the most ancient myth, we know that it is illuminated by pure light.[67]

Land of the Sun. In Herodotus, there is a very significant legend, in that it tells us of the distant origins of this whole group of myths and stories. It is of little importance that it figures in the story of an Oriental king; the exotic legends—especially in Herodotus,[68] where they are not simply Greek—are of a kind familiar to the Greeks, and one can see in them a traditional schema.[69] Herodotus, then, tells us that Cambyses sent an expedition to Ethiopia (the Ethiopia that is one of the favorite places in mythical geography)[70] to find out, among other things, about the famous Table of the Sun. He does not judge it appropriate—and we do not hold him responsible—to tell us the result of this inquiry. "Here is what is said about the Table of the Sun: there is a flatland on the outskirts of the land where one can find an abundance of boiled meat of all kinds of animals. Those in charge of the city have the job of bringing meat there every evening. In the daytime, anyone who wishes may feast upon it. The inhabitants say that the earth itself continuously produces these gifts."

Almost every word of this text calls for a commentary. First is the use of the term "table." There is actually no table, at least expressly; the feast is on the plain. But the word *trapeza*,[71] which in the classical period designated a ritual object,[72] could at first be applied to any flat surface—for example, the flat rocks on which the Greeks continued their prodigal feasting, notably in the cult of the dead.[73] In any case, the term suggests the idea of a collective feast.[74] According to ancient custom, flatlands were natural for these feasts. So it is not by chance that they are the same for the Heliopolitans of Iambulus;[75] the image was regularly retained in portraits of the other world.[76] It is worth noting that Herodotus' flatland was on the outskirts. We find a similar statement in one of Pindar's fragments describing the life of the Blessed.[77] The food itself is interesting. The Greeks generally do not consume boiled meats; and religious practice does not normally allow it. Signalized as they are by Iambulus,[78] they are found in a ritual that must be very old.[79] There is every reason to believe that the legend is a relic of a prehistoric practice.[80]

Moreover, in a characteristic way, the abundance of food disposed beforehand,[81] participation of the whole society and the freedom of all to eat, the implicit idea of a miracle by which the meals are renewed[82]—in all this, the portrait painted by Herodotus represents, in a certain way, one of those *euōkhiai* that belong to the most remote past of Greece and that turn up of necessity in the life of the Makares.[83] The Heliopolitans do not deprive themselves of these,[84] despite the sobriety Iambulus attributes to them. In connection with the theme of the multiplication of the loaves, the horn of plenty, and so on, Saintyves has illustrated the importance of this passage.[85] In truth, his interpretation is a bit cursive, as is the following formulation: "It involves a festive ritual: they offered meats, cakes, and fruits to the Sun and Earth, just as in ancient Europe." The insight, at least, seems justified; in Herodotus' slightly confused rendition—the confusion is instructive—we find included in the concept of the lordly gift of nourishment the memory of seasonal rites wherein the consumption of the goods of the earth, issuing from collective offerings, was attributed to the generosity of the Earth. These customs and prehistoric beliefs, and their connection with the concept of an ideal world (which is the other world), have been emphasized before. What is particular to our legend, and what permits us to recognize from its point of departure the utopia of the Land of the Sun, is the fact that the Sun is precisely the principal mythical character.

So we once again confirm the antiquity and the persistence of a myth of the beyond—home of the gods, home of the dead, and a marvelous land. At the same time, we confirm the equally old and continuous presence in this myth of a "solar" element that links the social dreams of the Hellenistic era with the most ancient images of Greece. Which Greece is another question: it would no doubt be better to speak of a Greco-Oriental origin. Such an expression, although not specific, gives some authority to the hypothesis of a foreign and pre-Hellenic tradition. This is not the first time such a hypothesis has been offered to explain this complex of myths.[86]

We have wanted to emphasize an observation that is not perhaps very new but that would be interesting to apply in a specific case. This observation could apply to a condition that is favorable to social development.

An almost essential theme, which resurfaces throughout the centuries as a leitmotif in the Greek concept of faraway and ideal lands, is that their inhabitants are the just. This is true of the people of the North in Homer, just as it is true of the Hyperboreans in Hecataeus. Naturally, this was implied in the mythical notion of the other world, whose inhabitants, living in the heart of abundance and idleness, do not know the hardships of real society. Hence, the transition from myth to utopia. One has to believe that the groundwork had been prepared by the time of the Hellenistic age, and that in the human perceptions of that time there were desires to find somewhere the place of goodness and justice. We know that some slave revolts incorporated this idea, and it would appear from the example of Sertorius in his search for the Isles of the Blessed that such a concept could affect the entire Greco-Roman world. About the time of the Christian era, something else would be needed—a promise in time, and no longer a perspective of place. But the same vein continues to be mined to new ends; images of the Golden Age will live again in the *Fourth Eclogue*.[8] What we find in all of this are sentiments, more or less suited—depending on the period involved—to one particular form of thought. Undoubtedly, this kind of thought was not remote even in Hellenistic times, and it scarcely left the realm of dreams. The only thing is that in certain cases there will be occasion to look for the mythological substrata of social revolutions. There is an example not far from our own times: it is very interesting to note the activity of a "mysticism" in prewar Russia, a mysticism in which one can discover some concepts and images that differ from those we have seen, but that strangely enough are analogous and undoubtedly no less ancient.

NOTES

1.   J. Bidez, "La Cité du Monde et la Cité du Soleil chez les Stoïciens" (abstract from *Bulletins de l'Acad. roy. de Belg., Cl. des Lettres...*, 5th ser., XVIII [1932], pp. 244–91).

2.   Ibid., p. 49. Cf. W. Kroll, in *RE*, s.v. Iambulus, col. 684.

3.   Diod. Sic., fragment from bk. XXXIV. One cannot say whether Iambulus' novel is earlier or later than this attempt; see Kroll, loc. cit.

4.   E. Rohde, *Der griech. Roman*, pt. II, chap. 3.

5.   See P. Capelle, *ArchRW*, XXV (1927), pp. 245 ff.

6.   This continuity is clearly demonstrated in E. Rohde, *Psyche* (French trans.), p. 259, n. 3.

7.   Concerning the author's ethnic background, see Kroll, loc. cit.

8.   On the funeral practices, see Diod. Sic., II.59.8; on the vertical mode of writing, ibid., II.57.4.

9.   See F. Susemihl, *Gesch. der griech. Litter. in der Alexandrinerzeit*, I, pp. 649 f. Euhemerus' *Panchaia* (which Rohde takes up in the same chapter) fits well into this ensemble. On the other hand, there are reasons for Eratosthenes to connect it with Theopompus' Meropis and Hecataeus' Hyperboreans (see U. von Wilamowitz-Moellendorff, *Der Glaube der Hellenen*, II, p. 270).

10.   J. von Arnim, *SVF*, I, p. 33, no. 115.

11.   Rohde (*Der griech. Roman*, pp. 240 f.) and others who follow his lead show that in the Land of the Sun there are no families, no organized justice, no temples, no public games—in brief, none of the things that constituted the Hellenic State, properly speaking, and that had been criticized by Zeno. This amounts to negative testimony, and one can say as much of descriptions such as those of a Theopompus. Concerning the suicide of the infirm, see below. In regard to the *politeia* of Zeno (which we now know comes from the early phase of his career), one can only say that except for a more conscious—or more real—cosmopolitanism, it does not comprise elements other than those of traditional Cynicism. Still, we can glean from it (Plut., *De Alex. fort.*, I.329B) the comparison between society and a flock of sheep, one that is an old symbol in what might be termed the political mythology of philosophers (see A. Espinas, *Les Orig. de la technol.*, pp. 239, 284 f.). Concerning Chrysippus, see E. Bréhier, *Chrys.*, p. 53.

12.   Rohde, *Der griech. Roman*, pp. 240 f.; Kroll, loc. cit.

13.   What Iambulus speaks of here is doubtless what Zeno and Chrysippus have in mind (Arnim, *SVF*, I, p. 62, no. 269; III, p. 183, no. 728). Even more so, this is perhaps what Plato intends in *Resp.*, V.462A f. (see Diog. Laert., VIII.131; Rohde, *Der griech. Roman*, p. 231, n. 2).

14   Diod. Sic., II.55.3, 6.

15.   *FGrH*, 264.2 (Jacoby). See Rohde, *Der griech. Roman*, pp. 208 ff.; Capelle, loc. cit.

16.   A favorable condition was the tendency (one that goes far back in the history of Greek thought) to invent ideal *politeiai*. For the fifth and fourth centuries B.C., see L. Robin, *La pensée gr.*, pp. 239 f.; G. Mathieu, *Idées polit. d'Isocr.*, p. 129.

17.   Ael., *VH*, III.18. This description is part of the *Thaumasia*, a collection of *mirabilia* which appears in book VIII of Theopompus' *Philippics*. There is no reason to think (see the Commentary of Jacoby, p. 365) that the *Thaumasia* is a specific work that was put together from the extracts of Theopompus in the Alexandrian period (this seems to be Susemihl's opinion, op. cit., pp. 478 f.). But what we know of the contents of this considerable digression (it deals with the doctrine of the Magi, the legend of Epimenides, the legend of Pythagoras, etc.) is quite revealing of a certain spirit and of certain curiosities that prevailed in the fourth century B.C., a century already quite modern.

18.   See Ael., *VH*, III.18.2. If we interpret *huperagein tous tettaras pēkheis* as "surpassing by four cubits [men of our time]," Diodorus Siculus supplies exactly the same data; cf. Ael., *VH*, III.18.2, and Diod. Sic., II.57.4.

19.   Ael., *VH*, III.18.4 (*hugieis kai anosoi*); Diod. Sic., II.57.4 (*anosous*). On the contradiction that is presented here by Iambulus, see below.

20.   It belongs there, although it is difficult to see in Aelian what its connections are with the other parts of the continent. Moreover, the section in Theopompus that deals with Meropis is the most heavily mythologized. Concerning the name Meropis, see n. 39 below.

21.   Ael., *VH*, III.18.7–8.

22.   Diod. Sic., II.57.5. The traditional reading is *diphuē botanēn*. The adjective is odd, even though Rohde tried to account for it (*Der griech. Roman*, p. 230, n. 1). The emendation *idiophuē*, mentioned by Rohde himself, had been accepted before him. In the

Hellenistic period, collections of *mirabilia*—in particular, one attributed to Orpheus—were entitled *Idiophuē*; see Susemihl, op. cit., I, p. 465.

23.   Ael., *VH*, III.18.5.

24.   Such as the overabundance of gold and silver that one observes among them, a condition that links them to other legendary races.

25.   Concerning the legend of Caeneus, whom the Centaurs buried under trunks of pines and rocks, see C. Robert, *Die griech. Heldensage*, p. 10; O. Berthold, *Die Unverwundbark. in Sage u. Abergl. der Gr.* (*Religionsgeschichtl. Vers. u. Vorarb.*, XI.1), pp. 17 ff.

26.   Pompon., III.5. On the traditions concerning the sentencing to death of the old and the sick, see Rohde, *Der griech. Roman*, p. 330; A. Piganiol, *Essai sur les origins de Rome*, pp. 149 ff.

27.   The inhabitants of the Land of the Sun avoid illness. In order to introduce the theme of suicide by the ill, the author is obliged to add (rather awkwardly) that there are exceptions to the rule. This passage was thought to exhibit another relic of Stoic moral philosophy. However, the subject at hand is an imposed suicide, of exactly the same sort as Pomponius mentions (see Rohde, *Der griech. Roman*, p. 230, n. 1, for the legendary tradition).

28.   Diod. Sic., II.56.7. On the word *eukratotaton*, see Hecataeus, *ap.* Diod. Sic., II.47.1 (on the Hyperboreans).

29.   See Pind., *Ol.*, II.67 f. (and fr. 7 [Snell]).

30.   Changes in the same representations are not uncommon, not only because of progress in geographical knowledge (for what happened to the Hesperides, see U. von Wilamowitz-Moellendorff, *Herakl.*[2], II, p. 97), but also because these regions are sometimes spatially interchangeable. Such is the case with the Isles of the Blessed, which were situated almost everywhere. The land of the Hyperboreans, seemingly situated in the North, was at times moved to the West, and was even identified with the Garden of the Hesperides (see O. Crusius, in W. H. Roscher, *Lex.*, I, pp. 2815 ff.).

31.   This datum, which is present in both Theopompus and Iambulus (and which moves their alleged geography *exo toutou tou kosmou*, as Theopompus states), is to be understood as a souvenir of a mythical source, such as the one in Eur., *Hipp.*, 744 (apropos of the Hesperides).

32.   The very name that Theopompus gives to a certain part of Meropis, Anostos ("from where there is no return"), already designates it as a Land of the Dead. The same notion is found in modern Greek folklore (see B. Schmidt, *Das Volksleben der Neugr.*, I, pp. 235 f.).

33.   H. Usener, *Die Sintfluthsagen*, pp. 197 ff., 214 ff.; *RhM*, LVII (1902), pp. 181 ff. The Garden of the Gods is sometimes situated in the North (see A. Dieterich, *Nekyia*[2], p. 20) or in the West (Eur., *Hipp.*, 742 ff.).

34.   Rohde, *Psyche* (French trans.), p. 88, n. 1; p. 259, n. 3.

35.   The country where Iambulus and his companion must land is described in characteristic terms (Diod. Sic., II.55.4): *hēxein gar autous eis nēson eudaimona kai epieikeis anthrōpous, par' hois makariōs zēsesthai.*

36.   See pp. 113–14 above.

37.   Ael., *VH*, III.18.4; Diod. Sic., II.57.1 (*trophas automatous pleious tōn hikanōn*). On this notion and its expression, see Hes., *Op.*, 117 f. N.B. in Theopompus the following description: *geōrgein de kai speirein ouden autois ergon einai.* This lends itself to comparison with Pindar's description of the land of the blessed (*Ol.*, II.69) and with an anonymous, fourth-century author's description of a fabulous land situated to the East (Latin translation in C. Müller, *Geogr. gr. min.*, II, p. 514).

38.   Diod. Sic., II.56.7, II.47.2 (on the Hyperboreans); cf. Hes., *Op.*, 173.

39.   The very name of the Meropes, the inhabitants of this land, is significant. We do not know whether it was Theopompus or tradition that conferred this name on them. It is pre-Hellenic and is often used in Homer (where it is no longer understood) in reference to

mortal men. Because of this, it was destined to be used in designating mythical beings like the Makares. Corresponding to the Meropes and the Makares are two legendary heroes, Merops and Makar (or Makareus), who are not without analogues. More on this later.

40.   Here we encounter themes that are both mythical and ritualistic. Pliny tells us that near Kelainai there was a spring called *Klaiōn* and another called *Gelōn* (*HN*, XXXI.13); through their very names, these correspond to the two rivers of Theopompus. The two types of trees facing each other lead one to think that in Greece there was a myth similar to the one that J. G. Frazer discovered in his reading of Genesis (*Le Folklore dans l'Anc. Test.* [French trans.], p. 16). In Iambulus, it is no longer a question of trees but of herbs: the theme of the magical herb is mentioned in Apollod., I.35 (cf. Hes., *Theog.*, 640; see J. G. Frazer, *Apollod. Libr.*, I, p. 42).

41.   Lamer (*RE*, s.v. *Lotophagen*, XIII, 1514) realizes that this episode is essentially a kind of fairy tale. Excessive philological zeal keeps him from admitting that the episode, together with other elements in the Odysseus story, are relics of the voyage to the other world. Even if the text of Homer is not explicit on the notion of "forgetfulness," the latter appears in several proverbial expressions dealing with the "fruits of the Lotus-Eaters" (see Jessen, in Roscher, *Lex.*, s.v.). On the subject of the lotus, mention should be made of certain of the observations in A. B. Cook, *Zeus*, II, pp. 772 ff.

42.   Orph. *Fr.* (Kern), no. 32a–b. The mythopoeic mind, which seeks a coherent system, has, of course, labored over these notions. According to the "Orphic" tablets, this spring must be avoided and the dead must drink from the Spring of Memory.

43.   *Resp.*, X.621C; the link between the story of Er and myths of the Orphic variety is quite evident.

44.   L. Preller and C. Robert, *Griechische Mythologie*[4], I, p. 827; Rohde, *Psyche* (French trans.), p. 260, n. 2 (where the author recognizes, at least, that Aristophanes, the first to mention the "plain of Lethe," can only "allude to an ancient invention").

45.   Paus., IX.39.8. See J. E. Harrison, *Prolegomena to the Study of Greek Religion*, pp. 574 f.; idem, *Themis*, pp. 511 ff.

46.   E. Rohde, *Kl. Schr.*, II, pp. 22 ff.

47.   Concerning the ancient elements within the myths of the *Politicus*, see P. Frutiger, *Les Mythes de Platon*, pp. 241 f. The datum that interests us most is the one furnished by Hesiod, *Op.*, 181 (men will be born with white hair).

48.   The two are interchangeable in Plato.

49.   It resurfaces in the second century B.C.: see the mythical portion of the history of his country by Zeno of Rhodes (Bidez, op. cit., p. 289, n. 4).

50.   It is an essential element in Virgil's *Fourth Eclogue* (see J. Carcopino, *Virgile et le myst. de la IVe Egl.* [1930]).

51.   Concerning the substance of the religious ideas that Virgil was first—among Roman writers—to incorporate into literature, see E. Norden, *P. Vergilius Maro Aeneis Buch VI*, p. 295.

52.   See note 32 above.

53.   The comparison is made by Giringer in *RE*, XV, 1058. We shall see what compromise Theopompus made in order to safeguard altogether the "Homeric" representation of Hades and the image of the blessed dead. Once again, it is evident that we are dealing with a conflict in traditions: the antiquity of the second cannot be questioned, and its persistence is all the more remarkable.

54.   See note 35 above. Rohde (*Der griech. Roman*, p. 239, n. 2) points out that in a passage from Palladius (*ap.* pseudo-Callisth., III.7.8), where Taprobane is described with characteristics that are remarkably similar to those in Iambulus' novel, Ambrose's Latin translation of *hoi legomenoi Makrobioi* reads *illi quibus Beatorum nomen est*, a translation that suggests a reading of *hoi legomenoi Makarioi*.

55.   See G. H. Macurdy, "The Hyperboreans," *CR*, 1916, pp. 180 f.

56.   Eur., *Phaëth.*, fr. 781.14 (Nauck); cf. Verg., *Aen.*, IV.143 f., and Serv. ad loc.

57.   Diod. Sic., II.59.7. Similarly, the Hyperboreans in Hecataeus are consecrated to Apollo: idem, II.47.2.

58.   Diod. Sic., II.60.1; cf. idem, II.55.3. It is especially in the rites of collective purification, the ones dedicated to Apollo, that the number 7 plays a role: see W. H. Roscher, "Die Seben- u. Neunzahl im Kult. u. Myth. d. Gr." (*Abhandl. d. philol.-histor. Kl. d. kön. sächs. Gesellsch. d. Wiss.*, XXIV, pt. 1), pp. 10 f. However, Iambulus and his companion (they are two, like the *pharmakoi* of the Thargelia) play the role of scapegoats for the Ethiopians.

59.   Diod. Sic., II.58.7. The fundamental characters of the script are also seven in number (II.57.4). In Zeno of Rhodes there are seven Heliades.

60.   Concerning the septentrional parts, where this island is situated, and their link with a myth of the Sun, see M. I. Rostovtzeff, *Iranians and Greeks in South Russia*, p. 62. On the other hand, the land of Aietes, Circe's father, is in the West (Mimn., fr. 11 [West]), where "the rays of the sun repose."

61.   See U. von Wilamowitz-Moellendorff, *Homer. Untersuch.*, p. 165. It goes without saying that, in the Homeric representation, the Land of the Dead is a shadowy world apart. The spatial connection with the Land of the Sun is, therefore, all the more significant. Here, as often, there are heterogeneous traditions at work in Homer.

62.   In fact, it usually comes last (the order is inverted in Apollod., *Bibl.*, II.122). On the nature of these two episodes (that are regarded as "doublets"), see M. P. Nilsson, *The Mycenaean Origin of Greek Mythology*, pp. 203 f., 214 f.

63.   See Robert, *Die griech. Heldensage*, pp. 465 ff.

64.   Mimn., fr. 12 (West). Of course, the fruits from the garden of the Hesperides are to be compared with those of the "tree of life" (see note 40 above).

65.   Robert, *Die griech. Heldensage*, p. 467. Erytheia is also the name of one of the Hesperides (Hes., *ap.* Serv., *Aen.*, IV.484). We know, moreover, that Herakles borrowed the disk of the Sun in order to go to the land of Geryon.

66.   For the use of words in this family in regard to the dead, see Rohde, *Psyche* (French trans.), p. 254, n. 4 (for their derivatives in modern Greece, see B. Schmidt, *ArchRW*, XXV [1927], p. 58). It is appropriate to observe that Makar(eus) is the son of Helios and Rhodos (see Schirmer, in Roscher, *Lex.*, II, 2288 f.). Moreover, if the Meropes of Theopompus are parallel to the Makares (see note 39 above), then it should be pointed out that Meropis, a land in the vicinity of Rhodes, has also been observed to have associations with the Sun (W. R. Paton and E. L. Hicks, *The Inscriptions of Cos*, pp. 360 f.). On the other hand, in Euripides (*Phaëth.*, fr. 771 [Nauck]), Merops is a king of Ethiopia and the putative father of Phaethon, whose divine father is Helios.

67.   Pind., *Thr.*, fr. 7 [Snell], 1 f.; Ar., *Ran.*, 454. Concerning the representation in general, see Dieterich, *Nekyia*[2], pp. 20 ff.

68.   For example, those that deal with the origin of Scythian power (IV.5 f.) or the infancy of Cyrus (I.108 ff.).

69.   See W. W. How and J. Wells, *Commentary on Herodotus*, I, p. 261.

70.   Basically, it is the Land of the Sun: Mimn., fr. 12.9 (West); Eur., *Phaëth.*, fr. 771 (Nauck). Iambulus leaves from Ethiopia on his voyage to the Islands of the Sun.

71.   It is doubtful that *trapeza* originally meant "a piece of furniture." The current etymology (*tetrapeza* = "on four feet"; see E. Boisacq, *Dict. étymol.*, s.v.) should be treated with caution; cf. M. Murko, "Das Grab als Tisch," *Wörter u. Sachen*, II (1910), pp. 115 ff.

72.   The *trapeza* is precisely distinct from the altar. One places on it those offerings that have not been burned and that are on occasion eaten by the priest (since they are consecrated to the gods); see J. de Prott and L. Ziehen, *Leges Sacrae*, nos. 24, 98, 118, and com-

mentaries. Moreover, the word is applied to tables at which the worshippers feast (schol. Lucian, *Dial. Meret.* [Rabe], p. 280).

73.   For the derivatives of this custom, one that is perpetuated not only in Greco-Roman antiquity but also among Balkan Slavs (where the word *trapeza* continues to designate a funeral banquet and also the very large group of "relatives" who participate in it), see Murko, op. cit., pp. 79 f.

74.   There are examples in a practice at Ephesus and in the legend that is related to it (*Etym. Magn.*, s.v. *Daitis*).

75.   Diod. Sic., II.57.1: *toutous d' en tois leimōsi diazēn, polla tēs khōras ekhousēs pros diatrophēn.*

76.   *Od.*, IV.563. Cf. Rohde, *Psyche* (French trans.), p. 86 (Bidez, for his part, has drawn the comparison [op. cit., p. 282, n. 3]; Orph. *Fr.* (Kern), no. 222.3; 32 f. 6.

77.   *Thr.*, fr. 1.2: *phoinikorodois d' eni leimōnessi proastion autōn.*

78.   Diod. Sic., II.59.1. At issue here are boiled and roasted meats. Is it the same meat in both cases? Perhaps. One might recall that a mystery rite, which we know only through its interdiction, has provisions for both cooking procedures at the same time (S. Reinach, *Cultes, mythes et religions*, V, p. 61).

79.   Philoch., *ap.* Ath., XIV.656A. On the antiquity accorded to this sacrificial practice, see A. Tresp, *Die Fragmente der griech. Kultschriftst.*, p. 71.

80.   Evidently a usage of the type that characterizes a civilization. In this instance and others, primitive Greece must have experienced this practice differently according to regional and ethnic considerations.

81.   For the social and religious import of the word *tithenai*, see Chapter 2, n. 162, above.

82.   Cf. the themes of certain miracles that occur at annual feasts (Hegesand., *ap.* Ath., IV.334E; Plut., *De Pyth. or.*, 409A; Pliny, *HN*, II.231; Paus., VI.26.1–2).

83.   *Makarōn euōkhia* (Ar., *Ran.*, 86 and schol.).

84.   Diod. Sic., II.59.6 (the same word, *euōkhia*).

85.   P. Saintyves, *Etudes de folklore biblique*, p. 265.

86.   L. Malten, "Elysion u. Rhadamanthys," *JdI*, XXVIII (1912), pp. 35 f.; cf. M. P. Nilsson, *Min.-Myc. Rel.*, pp. 542 f.

87.   Similar speculations are kept up for some time in literature. The theme of the *Saturnia regna* (see Pohlenz, in *RE*, XI, 1999, 2007) is popular among the Augustan poets.

CHAPTER 6
Dolon the Wolf

The *Rhesus* has become very popular. Recently it has had its citizenship restored; and its date of birth and authorship have been determined with some probability.[1] The brilliant scholarly endeavors of Goossens and Grégoire have focused attention on its historical interest; but I would like to show that the *Rhesus* has mythological interest as well. It is not Rhesus himself who will occupy us; it is Dolon.

We know that the plot of the drama is borrowed from the "Doloneia"; and in general, Euripides adheres closely to his Homeric model. Not that he follows Homer slavishly. When he departs from his model or adds to it, he may very well draw from other sources.[2] There is even some possibility that the Rhesus episode had been treated in the Epic Cycle.[3] In any case, we need not consider the details that are, in our tradition, peculiar to Euripides as the poet's free additions.[4] For they can provide us with precisely the primitive meaning of a legend whose mythical and ritual substrata, as it happens, were more or less unrecognized by Homer.

The passage describing Dolon's outfitting in the *Rhesus* (ll. 208 ff.) is one of these cases. The author of Book X of the *Iliad* mentions almost in passing, but quite clearly, that Dolon dressed himself for his night expedition in the skin of a gray wolf (X.334). Usener, because he was preoccupied with the "religious origins" of epic, underlined this detail and correctly saw that it could be significant.[5] Unfortunately, he created one of those somewhat ethereal/mythological constructs of which he was so fond, the sort of interpretation which seldom contributes anything, because it is so subjective. It contributes what one chooses it to.[6] So one has to look elsewhere, all the while staying close to the concrete data, which in this case is ritual. It is here that Euripides' text is so valuable to us.

What could have passed for a bizarre outfit becomes in the *Rhesus* a

This article originally appeared in *Annuaire de l'Institut de Philologie et d'Histoire orientales et slaves*, IV (1936) (*Mél. Franz Cumont*), pp. 189–208.

genuine disguise. The text is clear on this point: the chorus carries on an iambic exchange with Dolon, and obviously enjoys making him speak. Dolon tells them all the details: "I will put the skin of a wolf on my back, its gaping jaws over my head.[7] I will attach its front paws on my arms, the rear paws on my legs. Unrecognized by the enemy, I will imitate the four-footed tread of the wolf as I approach the trenches and ramparts that protect their ships. When I arrive at some isolated stretch, I will go upright. That is the ruse I have planned!"

Patin finds the tone of this interlude comical, and for good reason. But he also, and not incorrectly, judges it a somewhat strange one. The *Rhesus*, it is true, like the *Alcestis*, has been thought by some to have taken the place of a satyr play.[8] But such a hypothesis hardly recommends itself.[9] The citation of one brief and isolated passage can scarcely support it. Let us then regard the *Rhesus* as an ordinary tragedy. Euripides is being amusing, that is certain; but this is incidental. What exactly is he being amusing about? Does he intend some parody of Homer? Homer offers nothing to parody; he only mentions a wolfskin that Dolon uses for a cloak.[10] On the other hand, the way in which Euripides would have developed such a simple bit of information could not be categorized as innovative, *epi to pithanōteron*.[11] Therefore, the poet must have had in mind a tradition more explicit than the one in Homer. Such a view is no longer hypothetical, since archaeology provides substantiating evidence. On a fragment from a vase of Euphronius (earlier than Euripides), Dolon is depicted dressed completely in a wolfskin.[12] Euripides himself provides a supplementary bit of evidence, one based on similarities between the *Rhesus* and its contemporary, the *Hecuba*.[13] One of the most curious things in his *Hecuba* is the allusion to the animal disguise of Polymestor, which is very much like the disguise of Dolon.[14] This description was haunting Euripides' mind in this period because it had been suggested to him by the subject of the *Rhesus*.

What is the origin of this tale about a man disguised as a wolf? It would be a waste of time and, for our purposes, impossible to collect every myth in which the wolf plays a role. There is no lack of them.[15] For the moment I mention simply the principal legend, that which is attached to the Arcadian cult of Zeus Lykaios.[16] Whether or not the god's name should be explained by the wolf's[17] should not concern us here. What is certain is that after sacrificing a child, the legendary Lykaon became a wolf; and there is from the historical period well-attested evidence of the belief that whoever performed the human sacrifice required by the cult also became a wolf. Without having to consider all the cult's mythical data—and they are very complex—it is still possible[18] to recognize, among other things, a relic of a fraternal rite.[19] After a sacred act,[20] the newly promoted member abandons human society to live as a "wolf." He hangs his clothes on a tree, crosses a lake, and undergoes a prescribed period of segregation from society, one that is necessary for an initiate.[21] In order to make our hypothesis more precise, let us add that several pieces of evidence allow us, in effect, to catch a glimpse of actual "wolf" confraternities. One well-delineated example is the Latin Luperci,[22] who, as has been demonstrated in a prehistoric period, had "some connection with the power of the state."[23] Lykaon, undoubtedly an ancestor of the confraternity Anthidai and a type of mythical king, founded a town named after the wolf, Lykosoura.[24] On the slopes of Mount Parnassus there is a town called Lykoreia, a name from the same root. The legend of its foundation parallels remarkably that of Lykosoura's, and is naturally connected with a story about wolves.[25] (It happens elsewhere that mythical guilds are involved in the founding of cities.) The same motif applies to Athamas, who, before founding a city bearing his name, accepted "hospitality" from some wolves.[26]

As far as Greece is concerned, there have to be good reasons for these wolves being called wolves. The metamorphosis of the Arcadian sacrificer belongs to a well-known group of tales. On the subject of werewolves, doubtless not all the Greeks of the fifth century B.C. would have been as skeptical as Herodotus;[27] and it is this theme of folklore which bears striking resemblance to the Arcadian legend.[28] Dumézil's persuasive study lets us recognize, behind the whole series of animal demons from Greece and other cultures, an Indo-European tradition involving the use of animal disguises at certain times of the year.[29] Among the demons (*Kallikantzaroi*) of modern Greek folklore who perpetuate the memory of a prehistoric custom, the demon-wolves, sometimes called *lykokantzaroi*, or at times simply *lykoi*,[30] play an important role. Another fact that could bolster our hypothesis comes from south German folklore: the werewolves prowl about in the period of "Twelve Days" between Christmas and Epiphany, precisely the period of the *Kallikantzaroi*, which also corresponds to the time of year in which Dumézil locates the "Indo-European" practice of wearing animal disguises.[31]

But even with all this, there is no direct evidence of wolf disguises from Greece. At most, the story of the Arcadian sanctuary would allow us to infer or allege for this sanctuary a ritual practice: whoever has performed the sacrifice then *removes his clothing*—all of which brings to mind Petronius' famous story about the werewolf.[32] The circumstantial evidence from Euripides will be more useful if we assume premises that are difficult to challenge.[33] Some mythical and ritual themes have been transformed in the epic. In this particular instance, an episode that is only clumsily interpolated into the story of the Trojan War[34] could build upon an old description—one retained for its picturesque quality—by using confused but more or less coherent relics of a "primitive" practice. This is not the first time that the nucleus of a Homeric tale has been discovered in post-Homeric sources.

In the Doloneia, are there traits that ought to be explained by such reminiscences? There are, in my opinion, a certain number of these that Euripides, in this case, will help us discover. Nevertheless, within an episode that has been incorporated into a legendary narrative, it is impossible to recognize, at least on the surface, a complete and ordered series of ritual themes, for the descriptions we have are composite and complex; they are images preserved by a collective and fairly capricious memory.

The theme that serves as the starting point in the epic narrative is the nocturnal expedition. Dolon prepares himself for an exploit that should not be, as Homer sees it, simply a successful act of espionage. Euripides is very instructive here: Dolon hopes to bring back the head of either Odysseus or Diomedes (ll. 219 ff.). There are a goodly number of lopped-off heads in this tale; in Homer's version one of them will eventually be Dolon's. In the meantime, however, the chorus in the tragedy, enthusiastic about Dolon's departure, wants to know on whom the blows of the "earth-treading slayer" (*pedostibēs sphageus*) will fall. They already imagine the Trojan placing Agamemnon's head in the hands of Helen (ll. 254 ff.).[35] Head-hunting is a well-known practice, and the memory of it in Greece has not been entirely lost.[36] It is a practice well attested among certain Indo-European peoples such as the Celts[37] and Scythians;[38] and it is an obligatory rite for one being initiated into the "secret societies," which are normally brotherhoods using animal masks. We know that the same societies were, on occasion, organized for war,[39] and that their disguises were considered helpful precisely for that end.[40] The very name Dolon (the "Trickster"), which can hardly be a legitimate one, and which Euripides plays on with good reason,[41] is connected with this practice and belief.

In Dolon's case, there could also be a relic from some part of a festival. Unfortunately, we are limited to one piece of evidence, as annoying as it is suggestive: how good it would be to know what the Delphic *Dolonia* was about! The name actually designates[42] the route along which the torch-bearing procession passes in silence as it escorts the young boy-officiant (*koros amphithalēs*), before the "hut of Python" is put to the torch and the "table" is overturned.[43] Usener has also noted the strange similarity of vocabulary in the Stepterion ritual of Apollo, which he thought could be placed in the month of Ilaios—that is, the month of

Ilium—and which he has linked with the story of the fall of Troy. His thesis rests on somewhat shaky ground; but for our purposes we may merely choose to retain from it the word *Dolonia* itself, which connotes a procession, perhaps a nocturnal one, in a festival consecrated to the same divinity invoked by the chorus of the *Rhesus*,[44] where a young man is protagonist and the central theme is victory. Despite the associations between the Delphic Apollo and the wolf, nothing allows us to say that the *koros* who represents Apollo is disguised as a wolf. Still, might not the figure of Dolon, dressed in such a way, preserve the memory of an officiating figure from a more ancient rite, or from some analogous ones?

However, Dolon also turns out to be playing another role, which we will understand quite well if we continue to admit that the data from the epic are related to the practice and concept of animal disguises. But it is also necessary to adopt the very specific logic—one that is well attested[45]— that controls this practice and the ideas behind it.

Dolon comes to a bad end; he ends up a wretched wolf; in short, a wolf who has failed. From the narrative's context and structure, I am convinced that the brilliant success of Diomedes and Odysseus was the necessary counterpart to the miserable defeat of Dolon; and this antithesis underpins and conditions the simultaneity of the episodes and their "unity of action" as they existed in the primitive material inherited by Euripides and Homer. At the hands of Diomedes and Odysseus, Dolon suffers the very fate he wished to inflict on them. The Greek heroes crown their exploit with the capture of Rhesus' wonderful team of horses. Ironically, it is the brilliant team of horses of Achilles which has been promised by Hector to Dolon as a reward. In Homer, Diomedes and Odysseus are especially armed for the expeditions;[46] and this agreeable description[47] is not without its oddities.[48] From another point of view, the *Rhesus* of Euripides, despite its historical allusions (and there are many), has a pronounced mythological color. Rhesus is hailed by the chorus as one whose birth is divine; and standing in his chariot drawn by white chargers,[49] he is compared to Zeus the light-bearer. The dreamlike image with which his catastrophe is announced is one of wolves who throw themselves with gaping jaws on the hindquarters of horses.[50] The image is precisely a mythical one: the ravenous wolves have their regular victims.[51] It seems that they have something to do with the cult of Zeus Lykaios, where the human victims are *elaphoi*, who might well be represented as wearing animal masks.[52] Finally, before killing Rhesus, Diomedes executes a *dozen* of his companions; the number is a ritual one and is worth noting at least for its ritual value.[53]

But let us return to Dolon. He has not succeeded; so he must die, and his head is cut off. There are other ways for a wolf to meet its end, but it seems they are all ritualistic. A point should be made right away: the wolf represents an *outlaw* in the twofold sense that the data from the Arcadian cult permit us to define. The newly initiated wolf withdraws immediately and cuts himself off from human society. But the sanctuary of Zeus Lykaios is a place of asylum, and we can conjecture that here, as elsewhere, the wolf had some connection with the exile, the *vargr*.[54] Among the Scandinavians, this last word is the equivalent of *friedlos*, which in eastern and western Germanic is a taboo word that designates the wolf.[55] Here there is a strange, paradoxical mix. In any case, the roles seem interchangeable: the animal is the hunter and in turn the hunted. What does this mean?

The evidence from German folk tradition provides us with a point of comparison, or at least a very useful suggestion. It shows that there is a close connection between capital punishment and human sacrifice,[56] and (what especially interests us) between the rites accompanying them and the ceremony of initiation into "secret societies."[57] The masked brotherhoods (among the Germans they are fraternities of warriors) are, above all, distinguished by their connection with the world of the dead. The title *exercitus feralis* in Tacitus (*Germ.*, 43) designates one of their most characteristic features.

This point deserves more consideration. It is a universal phenomenon that a special connection exists between masks and the world of the dead. Dumézil noted this in his study of the Centaurs. On the subject of the wolf, and especially the wolf of the Mediterranean world, the character of Dolon provides us with a literary and more or less comical avatar, one who is related to depictions of the world beyond.[58] Through Euripides' good graces, one can identify an element of prehistory which sheds light on mythology. The *Aidos kunē*, the "cap of Hades," makes its wearer invisible.[59] Where does this notion come from? From the popular etymology that makes Hades mean the "invisible one"?[60] Perhaps popular etymology did in fact play a role. But such an answer seems inadequate, since Hades is made invisible by means of some object; such an object is a sign of power and resembles a mark of investiture. The Cyclopes, a mythical brotherhood, gave the cap to Hades at the beginning of his reign. At the same time, they gave Zeus the thunderbolt, and Poseidon the trident.[61] S. Reinach has successfully demonstrated that this animal headgear is a substitute, an abbreviated symbol, representing a wolf-god or a wolf-demon.[62] Such a symbol sometimes appears in Greece itself, where it stands for the god of the underworld.[63] Examples of the same type can be found elsewhere: for example, in the Etruscan *genius* of the dead, and in the *Dispater* of the Gauls.[64] The representatives of the world of the dead, demon-men dressed as animals, have good reason for belonging to the domain of the invisible. To the degree they are in costume, or "demonized," to that same degree they are unrecognizable; and they cannot be recognized because they have lost their old personalities. It is not accidental that it is precisely in the sanctuary of Zeus Lykaios that one loses one's shadow, that is, becomes magically invisible.[65]

All this indicates once more that the wolf can represent a demon who is pursued and driven out. We come back to the widespread theme dramatized in the rites of masked societies, where one sometimes sees the new dignitary "hunted" and submitting himself to a mock death (witness the Green Wolf of Jumièges).[66] All this also makes it possible for us to understand that a similar theme operated in rites connected with capital punishment. The Germanic *vargr*—about which it is said, "Per silvas vadit, caput lupinum gerit"[67] (from which comes the derivation of the Anglo-Saxon *wulfesheved*)—denotes a *friedlos*, that is, one who is to be put to death. Elsewhere we are told that criminals who are to be executed wear a coating of tar or a black cloth on their heads, which makes them demons. For with these emblems of their punishment they represent demons in this "savage hunt," which is the function of the *exercitus feralis*.[68]

There are no attestations of comparable practices in Greece. Still, the dramatized action of punishment has an analogue in Greek religion: the ritual chase of the condemned and their ritual execution resemble practices of the *pharmakoi*, the "scapegoats" of many cities. In Homer and Euripides, Dolon comes from a good family, but Homer stresses his ugliness and Euripides insinuates that he is a sorry fellow.[69] He almost reminds one of Thersites, who himself has all the earmarks of the *pharmakoi*.[70] Deprived as he is of a fine physique, Dolon has only one advantage: he runs fast. And it is important that he does. Earlier we had seen a vague relic of a *pompē*, but it is the theme of pursuit[71] that stands out. Might the *pharmakoi* have worn masks? At Athens, it does not seem so, and in other cities there is no report of it. We do not know everything; far from it. A word in the *Suda* apropos of a *pharmakos*—*estolismenos*—as suggestive as it might be, does not help bridge the gap. Given the nature of the animal demons, let us at least agree that such a hypothesis cannot be discarded. In the case of Rome, it seems quite justified: Mamurius Veturius, who was led through the streets and beaten with sticks, was dressed in animal skins. The comments of Usener and Frazer on this rite—most likely a rite of Expulsion of the Former Year—are known; but it is attested only by Johannes Lydus, and very scrupulous philologists hesitate to regard it as ancient.[72] All the same, the rite cannot have just been invented. From the silence of Varro and Ovid, we can presume that in their period it was not celebrated at Rome on March 14. But we are obviously dealing with a rite of "popular religion," which did not appear all of a sudden in the fifth century A.D. And in the case of Greece, the theme of the chase, together

with the relic of human sacrifices,[73] is found in a series of religious practices[74] in which, as it turns out, an episode from the Trojan War could actually have served as an *aition*,[75] but in which it also happens that the
individuals who are pursued represent demons in a rite in which we know
indirectly that disguises were used.[76]

There is also a fine story in Pausanias.[77] Even though it is quite edifying, philologists hardly credit it with any truth.[78] The town of Temesa in
southern Italy had been haunted by a certain hero (usually referred to,
quite simply, as the Hero: a common instance of anonymity). During his
life, he had been a companion of Odysseus. One day he landed in the region and raped a local girl; he was then stoned by the population. But his
daimōn[79] made life difficult for his murderers by "attacking people of all
ages" (it should be noted that according to what comes before and what
follows, the *daimōn* preferred the young girls of the town). The people of
Temesa consulted the Delphic oracle, which told them they had to come
to terms with the Hero; he would be content with the annual tribute of a
young girl, and of course the most beautiful one. So it was done. But one
day a superb athlete, Euthymos,[80] was passing through Temesa, and he
saw the young girl who had been promised to the Hero. Pausanias tells us
rather facetiously that what began in pity ended in love. Euthymos lay in
wait for the coming of the demon; it goes without saying that he defeated
it. "As he was chased from the land, the Hero plunged into the sea and
disappeared." The story culminates in a marvelous wedding feast. Pausanias had seen a depiction of the Hero in an archaizing painting: his flesh
was horribly dark, his appearance as terrifying as could be, and he was
dressed in the skin of a wolf; at the bottom of the painting, as clear as day,
was inscribed his name, *Lykas*—that is, the Wolf.[81]

A good book of images, with some legends thrown in for a bargain,
should not need a commentary. But for someone really interested in pur-
suing this subject, provided he is familiar with the common structures and
themes, underlining a few things here and there should suffice. The story's
pattern has been supplied by the fairy tale about the splendid hero who
wins the princess by saving her from the monster. Such are the stories of
Herakles and Hesione, Perseus and Andromeda. In Pausanias' narrative,
however, the fairy tale becomes particularized—as we shall show—by an
important element: namely, the appropriately "demonic" character of
the adversary. But first let us examine some other remnants of myth which
have been integrated into the tale.

There is one that is immediately apparent: Euthymos lies in wait
for the demon, much like Herakles, who ambushes *Thanatos* in order to
steal Alcestis, likewise a woman condemned to death. Euripides' *Thanatos*,
a character who belongs to folk religion, has parallels with the Etruscan
genius of death, a *genius* who wears the head of a wolf (whatever his

name may be).[82] The Greek *Thanatos* has certain connections with the wolf.[83] And the demon of Temesa has all the earmarks of playing a similar role. Its wretched behavior during its life, and even after its death, is adequate proof that in its character there is a relic of the carnival-type demons. In addition, its undue sexual liberties connect it with the Centaurs and the *Kallikantzaroi*. These demons also share natural bonds in mythology with the underworld. And this is not all. The theme of the "Centaur," who claims a new bride rather brutally and must therefore be defeated in order that the young girl be saved, is one of the most typical in the whole collection of mythical themes.[84] In the Greek material, it is illustrated not only in the episode of the marriage of Deidameia but also in the legend of Herakles,[85] who for Deianeira's sake must deal successively with Eurytion and Nessus. But there is still more, and it is here that we will conclude. The Hero was stoned; and stoning is a rite of execution used for the *pharmakoi*.[86] It appears again in the cult of Zeus Lykaios,[87] and in the legend of the Centaurs.[88] And the Hero has a second death: he plunges into the sea. The victim of the "Leap from Leukas" is also thrown into the sea, and can be considered a *pharmakos*.[89] It is also striking that in certain European vestiges of the carnival some "Centaurs" or monsters of the "Twelve Days" end up the same way.[90]

The observations we have made on the Doloneia episode should in some way clarify the deep-seated ambiguity of animal demons.[91] The episode itself may have its remote origins, quite forgotten by Homer, in prehistoric rites and beliefs that have been completely transformed by the epic. I do not believe I must justify once more this principle of interpretation. But I would willingly repeat what Pierre Roussel said in an analogous situation:[92] I do not think that it is out of date.

NOTES

1.   R. Goossens, "La Date du *Rhèsos*," *Ant. Class.*, I (1932), pp. 93 f.; H. Grégoire, "L'Authenticité du *Rhésus* d'Euripide," ibid., II (1933), pp. 91 f. In the same historical circumstances mentioned by Goossens, I believe that, without referring to his thesis, I have found a chronological clue to the subject of Sophocles' *Tereus* (*Mél. Navarre*, II [1935], 207 f.).

2.   Concerning the family background of Rhesus, we know that Euripides follows a different tradition than Homer (C. Robert, *Die griech. Heldensage*, p. 1171). Homer's version is not necessarily "the most ancient."

3.   See A. Severyns, *Le Cycle épique dans l'école d'Aristarque*, p. 417.

4.   See U. von Wilamowitz-Moellendorff, *Homer. Untersuch.*, p. 413.

5.   H. Usener, "Die heilige Handlung," *ArchRW*, IV (1901)[= H. Usener, *Kl. Schr.*, IV. pp. 447 ff.].

6.   As we shall see later, one intuition of Usener's should constantly be kept in mind: the mythical being represented by the wolf is in turn the victor and the vanquished.

7.   *khasma thēros:* note that the expression makes one think at once of the head-dress of the Etruscan genius of death (see A. B. Cook, *Zeus*, I, p. 98, figs. 72 and 73).

8.   By G. Murray, for instance; see Grégoire, op. cit., p. 118.

9.   See Grégoire, op. cit., pp. 123 ff.

10.   In Homer, Dolon's cap is made from the skin of another animal (*Il.* X.335: *ktideēn kuneēn*).

11.   This is how one can explain divergences between the *Iliad* and the *Rhesus*; see Goossens, op. cit., p. 103.

12.   See W. H. Roscher, *Lex.*, s.v. Dolon, I. 1195. Moreover, in this portrait, Dolon wears a metallic helmet. As for Euripides, he insists on a hat made of animal skin.

13.   These have been examined by Grégoire, op. cit., pp. 125 ff.

14.   Cf. *Rhes.*, 255, with *Hec.*, 1058; the comparison is made by Goossens, op. cit., p. 132.

15.   See R. de Block, *Rev. de l'Instr. publ. en Belg.*, XX (1877), pp. 227 ff., and especially the work of W. H. Roscher, *Kynanthropie*. For divine mythology, see the evidence collected by M. W. de Visser, *Die nicht menschengestaltigen Götter d. Griechen*.

16.   The passages that deal with it are collected in W. Immerwahr, *Die Kulte u. Mythen Arkadiens*, I, pp. 1–12. Cf. Cook, op. cit., I, pp. 63 f.; and F. Schwenn, *Die Menschenopfer bei den Griechen u. Römern* (*RGVV*, XV.3), pp. 20 ff.

17.   The opinion that the god's name is explained by the wolf's is probably correct, even after Cook's exegesis, which gives extensive treatment to the theory of a heavenly god, or rather a god of light. The linguistic argument, which has been used often, is not very impressive. A certain contradiction must be faced: on the one hand, the wolf plays the essential role in the cultic myths of the Lykaion, and on the other hand, at least supposedly, the god represents an entirely different concept. In the ancient cults, the personality of the god is generally not the starting point; it is rather the cult itself which gives the god existence. In other words, what should be explained here is not only the name *Lúkaios* or *Lukaîos* but also, and especially, the name *Lukaōn*, that of the hero who becomes a wolf. Thus, *Lukaōn* is neither more nor less difficult than *Lukaîos* (it is also known that proper names ending in -*aōn* constitute a separate group: P. Chantraine, *La Formation des noms en grec ancien*, pp. 162 f.); but it is possible to connect it to *Lukas*, the name of a demon we shall soon encounter, one that is certainly a wolf. As for what to do with *Lukaîos*, it is true that according to a "correct" derivation it should be linked to *luka* (*lukē*), and that this feminine noun for the she-wolf (which is not an Indo-European type, but could be ancient just the same: see A. Meillet, *Linguist. histor. et linguist. génér.*, p. 212) is not attested in isolation but appears in the compound *Mormolukē*, which designates a mask. Still, the word *lukē*, "light" (see Cook, op. cit., p. 64), is hardly better attested. There is no really "correct" derivation, but there is nothing to prevent us from saying that *Lukaîos* is connected to *lukos*, given the composite character of the group characterized by the suffix -*aios*: see Chantraine, op. cit., pp. 46 f., where we find that similar cases are in no way unusual (except for *lēnaios*, which is not derived from *lēnos*). Even accepting this etymology, we can still admit that there are "naturalistic" elements in the portrayal of Zeus *Lukaîos*.

18.   I imagine that this interpretation has already occurred to others; I discovered it too late in G. Murray, *Anthropology and the Classics*, pp. 72 f.; cf. the *Agrioi theoi* in Cook, op. cit., II, p. 971.

19.   In tradition, human sacrifice, as it continues to be offered in cults, is performed by the new member of a specific *gens* (Pliny, *HN*, VIII.34), and on this occasion it is

possible to speak of a priestly clan (Cook, op. cit., I, pp. 73 f.). On the other hand, there is the matter of the *congénères* with whom the new wolf goes to live.

20.   It is possible to suspect that here, in an essentially legendary version, there is confusion between the one sacrificing and the victim of sacrifice. We can even be skeptical about the reality of human sacrifice in the classical period (without denying that the memory of a ritual cannibalism was joined to the legend). The new wolf must of necessity undergo trials that are believed to kill him; this is a normal thing, especially in other "wolf societies" (see J. G. Frazer, *Baldur le Magnifique* [French trans.], II, pp. 237 f.). And we have in Greece another tale of cannibalism, that of Tantalus and Pelops, which it seems must be interpreted in light of a similar ritual (F. M. Cornford, in J. E. Harrison, *Themis*, pp. 243 ff.).

21.   This is to say that the man changed into a wolf cannot regain his earlier form until nine years later (Paus., VIII.2.6, VI.8.2; Varro, *ap.* August., *De civ. D.*, XVIII.17; Pliny, *HN*, VIII.34). In the stories having the same foundation there is also a definite time (seven years) during which one must remain a werewolf (see Frazer, *Baldur le Magnifique* [French trans.], I, p. 353, n. 761).

22.   The name, in any case, is connected with *lupus*; for the etymology, J. Carcopino's hypothesis in *Bull. de l'Assoc. G. Budé*, no. 6 (1925), p. 16 (*lupus + hircus*) seems very appealing (although one would expect that the *i* from the second part of the word would be kept within a closed syllable; the *h*-sound would pose no problems, since it disappeared very early in some dialects). There is nothing to prevent us from thinking that the second part also means *wolf*: the duality of the words could be compared with the duality of the *collegia*. In any case, the Romans saw in the Faunus of the Lupercalia a *Pan Lukaios* (see G. Wissowa, *Religion und Kultus der Römer*[2], p. 209, no. 1). Although the analogy has been contested (ibid., p. 559, n. 1), one would naturally have to link the Lupercalia with the *Hirpi Sorani*, which Mannhardt and Frazer discussed from another point of view, and whose etiological legend is quite telling (Serv., *ad Aen.*, XI.785).

23.   G. Dumézil, *Le Problème des Centaures*, pp. 219 ff.

24.   Paus., VIII.2.1: a descendant of Lykaon lives in a town named Lykosoura (Paus., VIII.4.5).

25.   Paus., X.6.2. For the connection between Zeus *Lukaios* and Zeus *Lukoreios*, see Immerwahr, op. cit., p. 22. The parallelism is affirmed by the fact that the foundation of the Lykoreia is linked to the story of the deluge, and that the latter is part of the story of Lykaon: Paus., VIII.38.1, concerns the very foundation of the Lykosoura.

26.   Apollod., *Bibl.*, I.84.

27.   With regard to the Neuri, a Scythian (or Thracian) people who celebrated a "lycanthropy" once a year for several days, see Hdt., IV.105.

28.   See p. 126 above and n. 32 below.

29.   Dumézil, op. cit., pp. 174 f.

30.   J. C. Lawson, *Modern Greek Folklore and Ancient Greek Religion*, pp. 203 ff.: the word *lukanthrōpos*, which is the most direct expression of a man changing into a wolf, seems to have been replaced by *lykokantzaros* (ibid., pp. 241, 384). It is worth noting that it has as its synonym the common noun *lukaōn* (Paul. Aeg., III.16).

31.   See Frazer, *Baldur le Magnifique* (French trans.), II, p. 354.

32.   Petron., *Sat.*, 62.5. On this matter, Frazer observes the inherent interest in the word *versipellis*, "werewolf" in Latin.

33.   See M. P. Nilsson, *The Mycenaean Origin of Greek Mythology*, pp. 75, 170, 203.

34.   See P. Cauer, *Grundzüge der Homerkritik*[3], pp. 526 f., 658 f. Already in antiquity, Book X was thought to be a more or less late addition. Modern separatists base some of their arguments on the Doloneia. We do not wish to take sides except to note that it is doubtful our Doloneia existed separately before the *Iliad*, and doubtful that it was not put together in order to fit the *Iliad* (see Wagner, in *RE*, V, 1288).

35.   This is so she can sing the *thrēnos* of a kinsman. Perhaps there exists here a trace of the ritual practice whereby the head of the enemy (or in other instances the spoils of the enemy) is brought to the woman.

36.   There are some examples in L. Gernet and A.Boulanger, *Le Génie grec dans la religion*, p. 84.

37.   A. J. Reinach, *Revue Celtique*, XXVI (1919), pp. 274 f.; H. Hubert, *Les Celtes depuis l'ép. de la Tène et la civil. celt.*, pp. 231 ff.

38.   Hdt., IV, 64 ff.

39.   In the organization of its young, Sparta represents a relatively evolved form of "male societies," with their characteristic segregation and licentiousness (H. Jeanmaire, "La Cryptie lacédémonienne," *REG*, XXVI [1913], pp. 121 ff.).

40.   See Tac., *Germ.*, 43: Harii...insitae feritati arte ac tempore lenocinantur: nigra scuta, tincta corpora...formidine atque umbra feralis exercitus terrorem inferunt, nullo hostium sustinente novum et velut infernum aspectum.

41.   For derivatives in *-ōn*, *-ōnos* (an ancient form that includes surnames and qualificatives), see Chantraine, op. cit., p. 161. For *dolos*, *Dolōn*, see Eur., *Rhes.*, 158 ff., 215.

42.   Plut., *De def. or.*, 418A. See Usener, loc. cit.; M. P. Nilsson, *Griech. Feste*, p. 152.

43.   *tēn trapezan anatrepsantes*: it is striking that a completely similar episode is found in one of the major sources for the Lykaon legend (Apollod., III.99: *Zeus...tēn men trapezan anetrepsen*), one that Immerwahr (op. cit., p. 14) calls Hesiodic.

44.   Ll. 224 f. The expression *pompas hagemōn*, instead of just *hagemōn* or *pompaios*, is rather noteworthy.

45.   The dualism within the mythical conception is one of Dumézil's themes; on the Centaurs in particular, see op. cit., p. 174.

46.   As if by chance, they do not have their own weapons; this is a fate that would be especially appropriate for Odysseus, who returns from his mission. Indeed, the description seems to have forced itself on the poet.

47.   *Il.*, X.254–65.

48.   Naturally, what exists in Homer is the notion of a special kind of armament that is suited for a night mission. Diomedes' helmet is called *kataitux*, a *hapax*; it is a piece of headgear that protects the heads of *thalerōn aizēōn*. The word *aizēos* sometimes signifies a "young man" (that is, someone from a young-age group). The special helmet of Odysseus is plainly Mycenaean (see *Dict. des Antiq.*, s.v. *galea*, p. 1142; on the tusks of the wild boar, see Kluge, cited in M. P. Nilsson, *Homer and Mycenae*, pp. 77 and 138, fig. 7.

49.   Ll. 355 f.: *su moi Zeus ho phanaios hēkeis diphreuōn baliaisi pōlois*. Cf. ll. 301 f.: *Rhēson hōste daimona...; pōlōn...khionos exaugesterōn*.

50.   Ll. 781 f. As noted by Goossens, there is an analogous motif in the dream of Hecuba (*Hec.*, 90 f.), where the wolf's victim is a deer (*elaphos*).

51.   Besides the wolves of Athamas (see p. 127 above), one thinks of the wolves that attack the herds of the Sun (Hdt., IX.93; see Cook, op. cit., I, pp. 409 f.) and the story of Danaos (Paus., II.19.4).

52.   This is Cook's conjecture (op. cit., I, p. 67, n. 3). W. R. Halliday's skepticism (*The Greek Questions of Plutarch*, p. 172) seems excessive.

53.   *Il.*, X.488. It would be ridiculous to link this number with that of the "Monsters of the Twelve Days." As in the case of Achilles' vengeance, what is at least indicated here is some religious schema.

54.   O. Gruppe, *Griech. Mythol. u. Religionsgesch.*, p. 918, no. 7. This interpretation has already been postulated: see Immerwahr, op. cit., p. 22; see also G. Glotz, *La Solidarité de la famille dans le droit criminel en Grèce*, p. 23.

55.   Wilda, *Strafrecht der Germ.*, p. 396. Finally, see Klein, *ArchRW*, XXVIII (1931), p. 171.

56.   K. von Amira, "Die german. Todesstrafe," *Abhandl. d. bayer. Akad. d. Wiss.*, XXXI, no. 3 (1922).

57.   L. Weiser-Aall, "Zur Geschichte der altgerm. Todesstrafe," *ArchRW*, XXX (1933), pp. 209–27.

58.   See W. H. Roscher, *Abhandl. d. phil. -histor. Kl. d. kön. sächs. Gesellsch. d. Wiss.*, XVII (1897), pp. 44 f., 60 f. On the connection between the Lupercalia and the spirits of the underworld, see A. Piganiol, *Recherches sur les jeux romains*, p. 103. Cf. F. Altheim, *Terra Mater*, pp. 48 f. ("Maske u. Totenkult"); and Weiser-Aall, op. cit., p. 212. Socrates' Apollo is an infernal god (Wissowa, op. cit., p. 238).

59.   [Hes.]., *Aspis*, 227:...*Aidos kuneē nuktos zophon ainon ekhousa*. This is the helmet that Athena and Hermes wear to become invisible (*Il.*, V.455; Robert, op. cit., p. 225). It is also the helmet of Perseus ([Hes.], *Aspis*, 227; Apollod., II.38), the veritable *Tarnkappe*, which, curiously enough, has given rise to some bizarre representations in art (see G. Glotz, *Dict. des Antiq.*, s.v. Perseus, p. 405).

60.   See P. Mazon, *Hésiode* (Coll. des Univ. de Fr.), p. 141, n. 1.

61.   Apollod, II.7. The thunderbolt and trident are *kratē*, symbols and instruments of power.

62.   Glotz, *Dict. des Antiq.*, s.v. galea, p. 1430.

63.   For the headgear of Hades, see ibid.; for that of Thanatos, see n. 83 below.

64.   For the former, see the tomb portraits at Orvieto and Corneto (Roscher, *Lex.*, I, col. 1805); for the latter, see the Bonn statuette (S. Reinach, *Bronzes Figurés*, pp. 135 ff.).

65.   See Halliday, op. cit., p. 173.

66.   Frazer, *Baldur le Magnifique* (French trans.), I, p. 165; II, p. 24.

67.   See Weiser-Aall, op. cit., p. 222.

68.   Ibid., pp. 217–18. Cf. p. 227: "Die Verurteilten mussten die Kennzeichnen des Bundes tragen und wurden dadurch ursprünglich mit den Toten identifiziert."

69.   Interestingly, he becomes a character in comedy in the fourth century B.C.

70.   H. Usener was of the same opinion ("Der Stoff des griech. Epos," *Sitz. Wien, phil-hist. Kl.*, CXXXVII [1898], p. 3).

71.   Pursuit and procession are associated in the rite of the *pharmakoi*, one that is essentially a *pompē* (from which comes the term *apodiopompeisthai*: Lys., VI.53).

72.   See the reservations of W. Warde Fowler (*The Roman Festivals*, p. 49), who had originally followed Frazer's and Usener's theory. These reservations, however, concern only the literal exactitude of the information transmitted by Lydus. Wissowa (op. cit., p. 148) adopts the same critical attitude. But the "late nature of the testimonium" should not concern us, since the existence of the rite seems to be confirmed by the rustic religious calendar.

73.   It seems very probable that the feasts that called for masks also involved human sacrifice from time to time. Within popular rites (and even from a later period), we have indirect testimony of such sacrifices, especially in the case of the martyrdom of Timothy of Ephesus (Lawson, op. cit., pp. 222 f.). The events regarding Timothy are similar to those of Dasius, a saint well known from the works of Cumont and Frazer. For the link between the *Kallikantzaros* and human sacrifice, see Lawson, op. cit., pp. 267 ff.

74.   Schwenn (op. cit., pp. 43 f.) studies them in connection with the *pharmakoi*, since "pursuit" also has the sense of "elimination."

75.   As in the case of the maidens of Locri (ibid., pp. 47 ff.).

76.   As in the case of the *Oloai* at the Agrionia of Orkhomenos (for the type of expelled demons, see ibid., p. 57). Legend has them being chased by the Psoloeis; the latter (cf. *psolos* and the adjective *psoloeis*) most likely derive their name from the black smoke in which they are enveloped (see L. R. Farnell, *Cults of the Greek States*, V, pp. 234 ff.). We

have here the relic or the equivalent of an animal disguise, which explains the name of one of the Centaurs, Asbolos (a name misunderstood by Lawson, op. cit., p. 250, n. 2). One of the rites that Schwenn has grouped within this ensemble is the sacrifice of the Athamantid at Halos (Hdt., VII.197); the link between Athamas and wolves has been noted. See also the story of a wolf chase, which accounts for the institution of the *hirpi Sorani*.

77.   Paus., VI.6.7–11 (= the *Suda*, s.v. *Euthumos*); the story is retold more briefly and in a different way by Strabo, VI, p. 255, and Aelian, *VH*, VIII.18 (the two are in close agreement).

78.   Frazer's commentary is brief. On the Hero as Wolf, see Roscher, *Abhandl. d. phil.-histor. Kl. d. kön. sächs. Gesellsch. d. Wiss.*, XVII (1897), and E. Rohde, *Psyche* (French trans.), p. 159, for some pertinent and correct remarks. What is interesting, in recent times, is the historical substratum of the legend, which has been reconstructed (perhaps in a somewhat "rationalized" way), principally with the help of Strabo and Aelian. There is no room here to refute this kind of interpretation, in spite of the diversity of results to which it has led (see E. Maass, *JdI*, XXII [1907], pp. 39 f., an essay that W. Kroll [in *RE*, s.v. Lykas] labels "*phantastisch*"; E. Pais, *Ricerche di storia*, II, pp. 79 f.; E. Ciaceri, *Storia della magna Grecia*, I, pp. 258 f.; G. De Sanctis, *Atti d. R. Accad. di Scienze di Torino*, XXII, pp. 154 f.). What interests us is the mythical theme itself, as transmitted by Pausanias.

79.   Paus., VI.7.8: *tou kataleusthentos de anthrōpou ton daimona*. For this last term, see J. G. Frazer, *Pausanias' Description of Greece*, IV, p. 24. Here the idea of demon and that of the evil hero are practically the same.

80.   He is a historical character whose victories at Olympia are dated, and who was known because of the statue Pythagoras of Rhegium had made of him. Consequently, the mythical schema was still productive after the middle of the fifth century B.C.

81.   The reader should be warned that this name is challenged, and not without good reason. The point is of secondary importance, since the nature of the demon is not in doubt. When Maass (op. cit., p. 40) writes "ein Wolfsfell hat er um die Schultern, darum ist er noch kein Wolf," one cannot help being dismayed. Nevertheless, we must say a word about the reading *etitheto de kai onoma Lukan ta epi tēi graphēi grammata* (Paus., par. 11). The MSS have *Lubanta*; the reading *Lukan* is Bekker's emendation, one that is very simple from the palaeographic point of view; long accepted, it is now in dispute. What is weighty is that the *Suda*, which draws on Pausanias, has *Alubanta*. This reading finds favor because the name Alybas is known in southern Italy. Still, it is so poorly attested as a personal name (Alybas, father of Metabos, founder of Metapontum: *Etym. Magn.*, s.v. Metabos) or as an ethnikon (*Anecd. Bekk.*, III, p. 1317) that in order to account for its existence, scholars have identified it with *alibas* = death (De Sanctis, op. cit., p. 166; Tumpel, in *RE*, I, p. 1708; cf. ibid., p. 1477); this assimilation has not met with general acceptance. We see that the reading *Alubanta* is far from satisfactory, necessitating as well an emendation in the text of Pausanias. Overall, Bekker's emendation is preferable, since it has the advantage of being in accord with the story itself, a story that supplies us with a name corresponding to that of the Athenian hero Lykos and that could be corroborated by the mention of a *Luka pēgē* within the same context. (I wonder if *Luka* is a nominative, as is currently thought. In the numerous passages from Pausanias where springs are discussed, there is no example of a parallel construction. Usually, the proper noun in apposition *follows* the word *pēgē*, while a proper noun in the genitive *precedes* it: IX.31.7, VII.22.4; cf. the *Hippou krēnē* of Boeotia and Troezen. *Luka* could thus be a Doric genitive—Pausanias sometimes has such local forms—and *Luka pēgē* could thus mean "the spring of Lykas.")

82.   See F. de Ruyt, "Le Thanatos d'Euripide et le Charun étrusque," *Ant. Class.*, I (1932), pp. 61 ff.

83.   See A. Furtwängler, *Meisterwerke* (English ed.), I, p. 80, n. 1. Especially interesting is a statuette from the end of the fifth century B.C. (*AthMitt*, 1882, pl. XII) which depicts a demon wearing a wolf head and carrying off a young girl.

84.   See Dumézil, op. cit., pp. 228 ff.

85.   One may recall here that Euripides (*Alc.*, 50) has *Lykaon*, the brother of Kyknos, as one of Herakles' defeated adversaries.

86.   Schwenn, op. cit., p. 39; stoning is employed also against evil demons (Roscher, *Kynanthropie*, pp. 33 ff.).

87.   Plut., *Quaest. Graec.*, XXXIX.300A.

88.   This is the story of Caeneus: Robert, *Die griech. Heldensage*, I, p. 10.

89.   Strabo, X, p. 542; see Schwenn, op. cit., p. 41. Moreover, this is a mode of execution for real *pharmakoi* at Marseilles (Serv., *ad Aen.*, III.57). We note that at Leukas the victim of the Leap has feathers fastened to his body; this may serve the purpose of an ordeal, or it may function as an animal disguise.

90.   Dumézil, op. cit., p. 171.

91.   We see at least a parallelism within the same area of mythical imagination. There is a comparable dualism in the representation of the Giants as a mythical projection of a warrior class (F. Vian, *La Guerre des Géants*, 1952, pp. 280–82).

92.   *REG*, XXXII (1919), p. 487.

PART III

LAW AND PRELAW

CHAPTER 7
Law and Prelaw
in Ancient Greece

The history of institutions has for some time familiarized us with the idea that the most ancient laws, ones very different from our own, have this in common: they have been strongly marked by "religion." This is an idea that has been in need of definition, and for some years now, it has received definition—surprisingly, at the hands of the Romanists.[1] Accordingly, it has received its definition within a specialized area (the field of Roman law) where we can generalize from some "obvious facts." This generalization is most clearly stated by Pierre Noailles: at Rome "consecrated law" preceded the appearance of "civil law," and the latter is distinguished from the former at the same time that it emanates from it. Remarkably, this thesis has recently met the opposition of another Romanist, but not as a result of prejudice. Henri Lévy-Bruhl[2] accepts the formula that "in the archaic period, it is ritual that creates law." But he adds that ritual is imposed by society; that juridical forms, whether they be religious or not, are equally products of due process (in the larger sense of the word); and that these forms have the same principle and the same functions. There are not two phases to be distinguished; or at the least there is no qualitative difference to be discovered.

There will doubtless always be some reluctant or resistant Romanist, as might be expected from the object of their studies. The indices for "very ancient Roman law" (clues that are not very plentiful and that, while being suggestive, remain at times irritatingly enigmatic) almost never take us directly or all the way back to a very ancient stage. An excision was made in the social memory, which—from set purpose—does not go beyond a late event, namely, the "founding of the City." Moreover, it is

This article originally appeared in *Année sociol.*, 3d ser. (1948–49), pp. 21–119. It was dedicated "to the memory of Marcel Granet."

part of Rome's originality that a properly juridical mode of thought was elaborated early; and it turns out that the very notions the legal historian would be tempted to work with are tainted with the possibility of a kind of anachronism. Thus the expressions *reus* and *damnatus*, technical legal terms, are also applied to two phases of a religious situation in which the devotee is successively pledged (tentatively) and then constrained to the fulfillment of his vow.[3] It is possible that this terminology perpetuates the very ancient notion of an obligation that is not yet a legal one.[4] But it is also possible that in a society already penetrated and, as it were, invaded by law, the formula for intercourse with the gods had been marked by the later categories of *ius*. The practical solution for us must be to enlarge our inquiry. For the problem remains, and facts alone can answer it.

What are the delimitations of the problem? One will always be able to fill an archaeological dossier; one will always be able to collect—both in ethnology and in history—evidence for practices and beliefs through which we might see law functioning in its "primitive" forms. If this were our only concern, then we would be able to renew the *ethnologische Juris-prudenz* of not long ago. But the whole of these archaic data will remain a closed system, one without an intelligible connection with the state of law that in the course of evolution is thought to have "succeeded" it. The question posed by the Romanists goes further: can one see a situation in which the relationships that we designate as "juridical" might have been conceived according to a mode of thought other than the one inherent in law as such? Also, what relationship does this legal situation seem to have with the state of law itself in cases where we observe a succession? We see at once what interest this problem might have here. Juridical function, as an independent one, is easily recognized in a large number of societies in which it naturally presents many variations but an undeniable unity as well. We mean here not only a social function (in the quasi-external sense of the word) but also a psychological one, that is, a system of *Weltanschauungen*, habits of thought, and of beliefs that are grouped around the specific notion of law. Will one say that this juridical function exists, by definition, in every society, notwithstanding certain appearances that it can assume and certain justifications that men give for it? Or must we conclude that the juridical function appears at certain points of historical experience as something new with respect to what we shall have to call "prelaw"?

※

Certain questions of this sort have already been examined in a methodical inquiry. This study was centered on a single category. (We need not remind the reader of the work of Davy on the prehistory of the contract.)[5] The inquiry included a very large area of juridical data: Huvelin studied the connections between the practices and notions of magic and the most ancient forms of "individual law."[6]

Huvelin's work, written in 1907, calls certain correct observations to mind. As to the central ideas in the book, Huvelin and Mauss were involved in something approaching a polemic on the subject of the respective roles of the "magical" and the "religious." It would seem that the term "magic" was misused at first. Above all, one should bear in mind that in matters such as these there is no need to be a slave to definitions formulated in advance: the notion of "magical force" (or magic religious force), if it characterizes a certain kind of thinking that is different from that of law, can still be put to use properly. Moreover, an excessively exclusive attention to the picturesque side of magic can lead to the inversion of the sequence of facts: Huvelin, for instance, considered magical acts as procedures that predate legal terms, whereas the former are really the result of the latter, as in the case of *defixiones* and other magical spells. On the other hand, the notion of "religious," a notion under which is included—in archaic law—all that does not pertain to individual (magical) rights, is an ill-defined notion, one that can be deceiving. It is ill defined because for Huvelin it is only a kind of counterpart to collective sovereignty in the ancient periods, and because one does not see the connection that it can have with the "magic" that might dominate in another realm.[7] The notion is also potentially deceptive, for in the end, what is it that one should call "religious" within law? Certain practices and beliefs that are positively religious can be closely linked with laws that certainly have nothing primitive about them. What is of interest to us is not "the religious" in general, but the type of *mentalité*. Let us note in this regard that the very notion of "consecrated law," valid perhaps for ancient Rome, might be too narrow a notion for other archaic cultures.

As for the material he chose to study, Huvelin defined it in a way that was typical of his era. He deserves the honor of recognition for having noted a large number of facts, unnoticed up to that point, from which he drew the most suggestive conclusions. He discovered these facts almost everywhere, in the most diverse cultures. In this way he was able to draw attention to an entire series of human realities; doubtless, this was a good procedure to adopt at the start. Today we see these facts differently: we see them differently at least in terms of the question we posed at the start and to which we shall return. Finding the roots or bases of the juridical function should be the aim of a scientific research program; but this can be attempted only under certain specific conditions. In such a case we should not set out to find the general history of mankind, determined and justified by the law of the evolution of human societies.[8] Our type of study involves an analysis of specific civilizations. Obviously we cannot forget that the phenomena we shall encounter are susceptible to generalization: analogies or parallelisms are always capable of suggesting or reaffirming. But the general phenomena are observed and are understood only within a limited segment of humanity.

❋

The domain we shall examine here is the one in which the legal systems of the ancient Mediterranean world developed,[9] and most especially—without neglecting the "concordances" that ancient Roman law might present—the legal system of Hellenic societies. Obviously there are some personal and imperative reasons for this limitation; nevertheless, it is legitimate to say what we propose to study is of interest in and of itself, for we shall examine societies where on the one hand the evidence for prelaw is not wanting, and where on the other hand, from early on and across the society, practices and formulations acquired the aspect we shall call "juridical." One can also assert that the developments in these societies are central to their historical evolution, and that the human significance of this experience is, in the end, of general importance and fundamental.

Again, the experience itself is limited. The present contribution is even more so: it applies only to two essential series of experiences; and even on the subject of these experiences, our contribution does not aim to be exhaustive. Other facts or other noteworthy aspects might be emphasized and discovered. One cannot hope for anything better than to have one's work continued and surpassed.

I
DEBITUM ET OBLIGATIO

At first we shall examine an aggregate of formulations and modes of behavior in which we may legitimately look for the antecedents to a juridical mode of thought, one that may be called fundamental, since it is this mode of thought that has to do with obligation. By way of an introduction, it would be a good idea to recall two concepts that have seemed to be at work both in history (even in the most ancient history) and in dogma.[10] The analysis of juridical obligation in general has distinguished two elements: the *debitum* (*Sollen*) and the *obligation* (*Haftung*). Objectively, *debitum* means "owed satisfaction;" but subjectively it is the "duty" of the debtor. The *obligatio* (in a strict sense *Haftung*) is the control that is guaranteed to the creditor and that in primitive times is applied to individuals; it is the "engagement" (in the fullest sense of the word) of the one who owes. This theory is not at issue here; but we would like to indicate the interpretation the theory took on in regard to "origins." In terms of "origins," one of the two elements tended to be absorbed: the element of constraint is emphasized, and it is a constraint that is occasionally exercised on someone other than the debtor, namely, on the countersigner or person who offers surety. The *debt*, therefore, takes on the aspect of a moral duty. "Moral" can be pejorative: in this context one might use it to mean "ineffective." We might add—still on the subject of origins—that the material (and not the moral) force is the only one that counts.

In the Greek language, one would look in vain for the dualism that the terminology of Germanic law and even, to a certain extent, that of Roman law allowed. We find that the word *khreos*, a word that signifies debt (and that has no equivalent), is applied to a global notion in which there appear, one by one and from ancient times, four related ideas: the idea of a constraint that weighs on the debtor; the idea of an obligation that is punishable in case of default; the idea of the very thing that, once received, "obligates"; the ideas, in addition, of propriety, duty, and even religious observation. But let us analyze some of our data.

The Myth of Protagoras

Deeds present themselves as societies wish. In a context that is remarkable in itself, a word that has no apparent connection with our topic will nevertheless allow us to follow a lead.

In the Platonic dialogue named after him, Protagoras is asked to justify his assertion that statecraft (or the correct way to live in the city) can be taught. The Sophist, who has more than one trick in his bag, offers to reply, and answers at first with a myth and then with a theory.[11] The myth is as follows: Prometheus has conferred on men the gift of fire, and from this an entire series of technical achievements. But men remain no less ill suited to social life, injustice reigns among them, and it is necessary that the favor of Zeus, which is "of another type" than the benefaction of Prometheus, intervene; Zeus grants to men two virtues that will be distributed to all (and will no longer be distributed according to the principle of the division of labor): *aidōs* and *dikē*. The latter is quite clear: *dikē* is justice, such as is manifested above all in judgment; hence it is sentence and implementation. Moreover, *dikē* is also—through an implicit or explicit reference to another term—something like the *ius strictum*. The word *aidōs*, on the other hand, is not translatable (as is often the case for key words that supply the fullest evidence). But through the multiplicity of the uses of *aidōs*[12] one can say that it designates a feeling of respect or of restraint, which comes close to religious awe and which, in point of fact, can have a divinity as its object. *Aidōs* is a feeling arising from the realm of human relationships, where it demands certain abstentions or attitudes with respect to a parent, a being of great dignity, a suppliant, and so on. It is a sentiment that is both social and moral, since it is both mindful of public opinion (of which it often seems to be a corollary) and preoccupied, in a willfully aristocratic sense, with what the subject owes himself or herself. It is certain that in the myth of Protagoras this varied notion, already known in its mythical guise in Hesiod, is determined, more or less, by the notion behind *dikē*. Through the gift of fire, moreover, man had already reached an altogether human condition in which religion itself is constituted. Now, there is in the *Protagoras* a question of the organization of relationships between men and, accordingly, of justice (in the larger sense), where—outside of the observance of rules for their own sake—room must be made for a more intimate feeling, one that is more personal, but one in which the law does not cease to play a role.

This is a very general concept, one that emanates from philosophical reflection. Nevertheless, it is worthwhile to observe the direction the word *aidōs* takes here, along with the traditional meanings that are latent in it. At a more ancient stage and in a more popular mode of thought, we find a particular and very specific use of *aidōs*, one that is certainly connected with the question of the "origins of juridical obligation."

The verb *proaideisthai*, a curious compound, occurs twice in Herodotus (and nowhere else); surely Herodotus did not invent the word. Soon after the accession of Darius, a Greek, declaring himself to be Darius' benefactor (*euergetēs*), asks for an audience. Darius is surprised: he knows no Greek to whom he has obligations (*tōi egō proaideumai*) or to whom he owes a debt (*khreos*). The foreigner is brought in and he explains his situation: one day at Memphis, Darius, who was then a mere member of the palace guard, wanted to buy the splendid cloak the Greek was wearing; the latter refused to sell "at any price," but gave it to Darius "for nothing." Darius showed boundless gratitude by offering the Greek all the gold and silver that he wanted. The Greek refused, but asked instead that he be installed as tyrant of Samos.[13] There is also the story of Peisistratus. Banished from Athens, he withdrew with his sons to Euboea, from which they prepared their return. They were amassing money; specifically, they were gathering the gifts (*dōtinas*) from cities that were obligated to them (*haitines sphi proaideato*). Herodotus adds that of the large number who brought their contributions, the Thebans were distinguished or outdid themselves (*huperbalonto*) by their generosity.[14]

Thus, in apparently normal conduct, *aidōs* is a feeling of obligation that is repaid to an associate or acquaintance, a feeling that constitutes an "advance" for a gift freely given. The counterpayment, at an indetermined date, is not equivalent in the mercantile sense: it emanates from a generosity that does not calculate. The very composition of the word indicates the mechanisms that are at play; a revealing opposition shows that obligation in this case is precisely correlative to the duty of exacting vengeance.[15]

※

There are other affirmations of this type of morality in this same period. We remember the story in Herodotus of the Spartan king who forced his friend to give his wife to him—indeed, he obligated him—through the gift of his possessions, which he offered the husband. This very peculiar commerce is started by a proposition backed by an oath, and it automatically sets in motion the associated gift. The receiver does not even know what will be asked of him, but he is nevertheless obligated.[16] In the international sphere, it happened that the acceptance of a gift involved an alliance that could not be refused. Croesus sent to Sparta certain envoys bearing presents. He then asked the Lacedaemonians, or more precisely he required or "called" them to friendship in a verbal ceremony that had an effect. The Spartans would not have known how to get out of this demand, since earlier they had waited to *buy* some gold in Lydia, and Croesus had given it to them for free (*edōke dōtinēn*); as a result of this (and Herodotus chose his words carefully),[17] the Spartans were "constrained" by the favor they had received (*eikhon euergesiai*).

It would be interesting to learn more about the sixth century B.C.: many things must have survived in terms of *mentalités* and morality, at the dawn of the period we call classical because it seems modern to us. The fact is that after the sixth century, except for archaisms such as those noted in writings as late as Aristotle's *Ethics*,[18] the rule of law became the universal norm. Unfortunately, the archaic period is one about which we know the least, and what we do know comes only from later texts. Other than sporadic mentions, we have only the *Histories* of Herodotus. Their authenticity is immaterial; one must regard them as psychological documents. They show that in various places an "ethic of gift-giving" survived in the memory (preserved in the historian's period) of only slightly earlier generations. Moreover, the *Histories* presuppose certain circumstances or conditions. An Ionian like Syloson takes advantage of a code of ethics, like the one mentioned above, more than he practices it. Knowledge of a custom that Eastern civilizations kept alive better than his own suggested to him a veritable speculation on finance capital.[19] Elsewhere, in dealings among groups from different nations, ancient codes of conduct remained in force. This is not quite yet the age of international politics. On the other hand, the code of "condottieri" might be based on an ideal that remained very much alive, outside the framework of the cities, within a kind of chivalrous class. This is an interesting datum, insofar as the arena for this relic could be the military class, which has behind it, sociologically speaking, a glorious past.

During the same time, in other areas, and even in places where the rule of law was established, we see that law sometimes found support from a code of ethics that preceded it. There are certain operations that partly elude its purview, since they take place outside the city and thus evade the normal possibilities of enforcement. We see this phenomenon in the regulations concerning the reconstruction of the temple of Apollo at Delphi. The accomplishment of this task could take place only through the initiative of an exiled Athenian family, the Alcmaeonids. According to Herodotus, they had the resources. These aristocrats were both knights and capitalists. Like several contemporaries, they entered into an entrepreneurish contract with the administration of the sanctuary. They received half the price in advance (this became a more widespread custom as time went on). They used this advance to buy weapons (and perhaps to bribe the Pythia); they planned to finish the temple at a later time.[20] The Alcmaeonids all but pass for scoundrels in the eyes of modern historians, but such moralism is out of place. The Alcmaeonids were linked to Delphi with a personal bond. For sure, they were under some obligation, but this obligation was more free, as we would say, than one protected by a legal system. They did not discharge their obligations like merchants, for this is how the story turned out: "They built the temple more beautiful than the blueprints called for." They were obligated to use limestone, but ended up using marble.[21]

There are, then, relics of the period, survivals that bring us to the very threshold of the rule of law. As for those survivals that remain marginal, it is toward the past that they direct us. We have seen their power to confirm or suggest. The mode of thought that is found in these survivals should be put in context, if possible. Our investigation should go further back in time.

❦

The Greek experience is in fact unique. The reader will doubtless have already inferred that there is little direct evidence; the testimony of the primary texts is naturally worth remembering when it deals with institutions, but such testimony is not all that ancient and is, by nature, poetic (and therefore artificial within the limits of Greek poetic practice); moreover, such testimony must be interpreted on the basis of notions that are not always explicit. In contrast, even though they are literary hand-me-downs, the data of legend are precious. They lose nothing by being mythical; rather, this is what makes them interesting. Not only have very odd ways of thought come down through the ages in legend; not only is a good deal of the collective subconscious stored there; but in matters of psychological or archaic complexes, nothing can give so clear an image as mythical transformation. Legend functions freely, and it transmits what has been of real interest to the practitioners of myth. Therein lies a double advantage. Obviously the freedom of myth makes us feel that benevolent complicity which makes us participate in the narrative. But there is a serious aspect to the game.[22] Thus, it is mythology that we wish to retain as our prime material. We use "mythology" in a larger sense: it pertains not only to the stories but also to the symbolism in folklore and, indeed, to the very plot lines of tragedy.

The Feast of Tantalus

In the juridical forms that have to do with *commercium*, the fact of circulation is implicit. *Commercium* involves a certain dynamism that is necessary for its functioning. We know that there are cultures (those that were examined in *Essai sur le don*) in which the accent falls on the initiatives that trigger this trade. Mauss has indicated that the real question is not just the response (to trade), but is above all the appeal (to trade). A Greek word is suggestive in that regard, namely, *proïenai*. In the fourth century B.C. it was assimilated into the most modern business language, and meant the "advance" of valuables[23] in a system of law where it was ensured and had a kind of built-in mechanism. Hence, *proïenai* designated a specific yet abstract notion. But when the bourgeois phraseology of Isocrates evokes the "good old days" with its customer who paid for business at a good profit, the same word, applied to the advances of the wealthy, suggests something quite different. The vocabulary of Aristotle also indicates something different yet again when *proesis* is used to designate the "prodigality" that is opposed to "liberality," inasmuch as the former is an exaggeration of the latter.[24] Let us add that by its very composition the verb *proïenai*, which means "to throw" or "to let fly," can be applied, at least in theory, to a special type of gesture, one that is more or less ritualistic, as for example, in the symbolism of the gift. In any case, the idea that is basic in *proesis* is that of abandonment or the surrender that constitutes gratuitous generosity. Implicit in this is the understanding that the counterpart must be of the same sort (i.e., gratuitous generosity in return for gratuitous generosity).

Legendary acts of generosity occur readily at feasts and in forms that are more or less close to real life. We note in Homer and elsewhere that it is the business of the chieftain to "nourish" his "companions," and that the business of the king is to put on a show for his subjects. There is the feudal practice of banquets for vassals, and the aristocratic practice of religious banquets. In all this we catch a glimpse of very precise practices or at least the extensions in time of these realities. Mythological stories are spin-offs from these institutional bases.

The most colorful is the story of Tantalus, and it is quite complex. But legendary syntheses are seldom so artificial as learned mythologists are tempted to postulate. As heterogeneous as the elements of a myth may appear, still there is often an organic bond to be discovered between them. In this case there is already a link between the two chronological phases of the story: the first being the one in which Tantalus is received among the gods; the second being the one in which he receives the gods at that famous banquet in which his son Pelops, properly prepared, was the meal.

Everyone knows that Tantalus underwent an exemplary punishment in Hades.[25] But no one has ever seriously maintained that Tantalus was damned for having had the curious notion of giving the gods his son to eat. According to a very clear source, one that supplies us with "the most ancient text,"[26] the crime of Tantalus—his *hubris*, in Greek terms, or his being above the law—consisted in the wish he had expressed in front of the divine assembly, a wish that was justified in principle but that was extreme in fact. Zeus had asked his guest to make whatever request he wanted: Tantalus' request was to participate in the life of the gods. Zeus was obligated to fulfill this request, but evil awaited the maker. We see the interplay of notions and modes of behavior in this first act, an interplay with which we should be familiar through our acquaintance with history and ethnography. In the exchange of gifts, countergifts, offers, and promises that characterizes the "archaic form," there is an a priori obligation to accede to the request of another party, whatever the request.[27] But it is up to the other party to play by the rules. The theme of meeting one's match, which for various and converging reasons appears often in heroic myths, finds its natural application in such a case. One does not compete with the gods. Tantalus will join other extremists in the underworld.

Meanwhile, Tantalus is going to try to set himself apart through the enormity of a gift that according to one of our sources will make the greatness of his hospitality apparent to all. Legend concocted a whole series of elaborations that seem singular at first hearing.[28] The limbs of Pelops were served to the gods; but the gods did not want their meal. Zeus had them put it back in a cauldron: therein Pelops is revived (only his shoulder is missing, and it is rebuilt with ivory); his good looks seduce Poseidon, who takes him away in his chariot and then presents him with a chariot. The story ends well, though indeed one might add—in fact one has[29]—that episodes of *teknophagia* recur as a rather obsessive theme in the "lineage of Tantalus." It is not for us to analyze here such a rich legend, one in which certain multiple "motifs" overlap, motifs such as the "monster banquet," institutionalized pederasty, royal succession, hereditary birthmark, resurrection, and the infant who is dismembered and boiled in the cauldron. Besides, the essentials of this story have already been told by Cornford, then by Jeanmaire.[30] What does interest us is the definition, through those motifs, of the mythical formulation of certain milieus or of certain conditions where this notion of the demand of Tantalus might have seemed appropriate. After all, the claim of Tantalus is our point of departure.

This mythical formulation is itself multiple and doubtless contains several levels. But the central feature is an initiation that is figured as death followed by rebirth. The feast given by Tantalus seems at once to be connected with initiation. Precisely for this reason we may even call it a kind of potlatch.[31] Moreover, initiation is a versatile notion, and it is natural for the mythical imagination not to reproduce the design of one or another social form but to magnetize them simultaneously from many directions. Analysis (of myth) lets us catch only a glimpse of remembrances of royalty, of religious societies, and of "adolescent rites." The evidence from legend concerning prelaw can be explained if one views it in the context of certain data that historical Greece can still supply here and there. By nature, the legend can deal only with residual elements: one finds these elements in the milieus that remain on the margins of *civic* organization and in which a prehistoric tradition lives on as a lifeless shadow.

From Diodorus Siculus we know about a cult of the hero Iolaos in the Sicilian town of Agurion, where Diodorus himself was born.[32] The ephebes of Agurion make an offering of their hair, which they grow from the time of their birth until such time as they can reconcile "the god" to themselves through "a magnificent sacrifice." The historian adds that the youths who do not perform this sacrifice become voiceless and resemble the dead. They return to a normal state only when a vow is made on their behalf to acquit them and a pledge of obligation is made. What we have in this case is a secret cult[33] based on an initiation that is a rebirth and that is necessarily accompanied by an opulent sacrifice offered by or on behalf of the initiates.[34] It is noteworthy that Diodorus, in the deliberately confused account that he left behind, spontaneously related in legal language a situation that is not at all juridical. A "pledge" is made, but that pledge, which is neither partial payment nor a sign of passage, must consist in the offering of hair (or a lock of hair),[35] an offering that has the power to create a "mystical" link by symbolizing the gift of the person. As for the final gift, its nature is traditionally defined, but its size is left, in theory, to the discretion of the one under obligation.

This last characteristic is equally typical of a somewhat different sort of society. Moreover, this society has been brought to mind in the case of the Tantalus legend because it pertains to an entire religious system, a system that corresponds to a geographic area that comprises a very ancient cult linked with the very locale of the legend.[36] We know of a collegium in Ephesus that is dedicated to a "mystical" cult: the society of the Kouretes.[37] In an organization that seems hierarchical in the way that mystical organizations normally are, the Kouretes represent the most exalted grade, even the ruling one (*arkheion*). Their role is to celebrate annual sacrifices during which "they hold banquets." But we are also told of the role of the "young men" who constitute traditional associations in Asia Minor, and who, in the present instance, "compete to give the richest feasts," with panegyreis supplying the opportunity.[38] Similar customs lead us to a prehistoric social formation in which authority is held collectively.[39]

Although this milieu is equally traditional, it is different from the milieu of the Attic phratries. The latter are "quasi-family" groups that maintain a very important function, but a marginal one in terms of the law: the enrollment and legitimation of new members of the family. In fact, this integration is the modern and trivialized form of adolescent rites, which prehistorically must have included a genuine initiation.[40] Moreover, one of the preserved rites is the hair-offering we have already seen. The Attic feast of Apatouria—at which new phratry members are presented—requires the ministry of the so-called *oinoptai*,[41] who, entrusted with various offerings, are primarily supposed to superintend the wine offerings that are made at the first day's banquet. In this reunion of the phratries, which is synonymous with feasting, the sacrificial food and wine provided by the fathers of newly admitted children make up the banquet meal.[42] This contribution of wine is called the *oinisteria*: the same word designates the libation the ephebes offer to Herakles when they have their hair cut, a libation that is accompanied by drinking paid for by the ephebes. We see in these customs, upon which the intervening public authority tends to impose the quasi-fiscal form of a tax, traces of those obligatory acts of generosity that are the antecedents of "liturgies" and that are carried out in this case in order to acknowledge the passage of the young to adulthood.

In an analogous situation within a more archaic context, one that in any case exemplifies the originality of so-called Dorian societies, a Cretan custom must be considered. In a well-known passage quoting Ephorus, Strabo relates rules for the male lover (rules that he alone relates).[43] After emphasizing the abduction of the young boy and the protocol involved in all this, Strabo makes special mention of the gifts the "abductor" has to give. Strabo specifies that the young man receives these from his abductor when he is brought to the countryside where he must live for two months in a hiding place, hunting and feasting with his abductor and the abductor's followers. The boy receives even more lavish gifts when he is freed. These "regulation gifts" include armor, an ox, a cup,[44] "as well as other very costly things." Initiation assumes a singular form here, a form that is by no means unexpected in this kind of society.[45] The custom of gift-giving is related to initiation: the relationship is as narrowly defined here as in the marriage custom. It is, in fact, for the benefit of the initiate that the practice exists. But the abductor himself acquires a "page" in a prelegal arrangement that is of exactly the same sort as "marriage through purchase," in which one finds the same mix of regulations and gratuitous generosity.

One other characteristic of the Tantalus legend might be mentioned. Poseidon, who is in love with the young Pelops, abducts him and makes him a gift of a marvelous chariot. The legend draws its material from a parallel theme.[46] But the very data that we gather and that—in the context of the historical period—seem like mere tangents or curiosities, are still connected with the psychology and social situations that we glimpse in the legend. We find in the legend an attenuated reflection of prehistoric milieus that do not come to us directly but on which legend has much to say. The violent humanity that we see in action in the legend of Tantalus/Pelops gives us the impression of an antiquity that has nothing to do with Hellenic reasoning. And yet we realize that this humanity has its own norms and its own ideas of "obligation." What is more, we are going to see that these ideas have a connection with a type of collective behavior in which there is a kind of anticipation of the concept of law.

🌿

The banquet of Tantalus is known, in the poetic and mythographic tradition, as an *eranos*, the "*eranos* of Mount Sipylos." The word *eranos* has diverse meanings, and this diversity may at first be puzzling. But for our purposes the diversity is a source of richness.

One of the first meanings is that of the great feast. The grand festival of Apollo at Cyrene is thus called an *eranos* by Pindar. The central element of a festival is the collective banquet, or the *dais*, to use the most ancient word, a word that is divinized by Sophocles and that evokes the following gloss in Hesychius: "a banquet that takes place through an *eranos*." What does this mean? In regard to the banquet of Tantalus, Pindar supplies a commentary when he uses, along with the term *eranos*, the expression "banquet given in return."[47] This is an important bit of evidence, one that makes precise what is at the base of the legend: the cyclic offerings of food (such as these, which survive in religious societies up to the Greco-Roman, and even the Roman, period).

Here is another testimonium, one from a legendary milieu that is probably not very different. The exploits of Perseus have as their starting point an *eranos*. The scene is the court of the king of Seriphos, Polydektes. Now Perseus is a grown boy who belongs to a group of royal banqueters. A banquet is given by Polydektes, but requires something in return: the other banqueters offer horses; as for Perseus, he commits himself to bringing back the head of the Gorgon. The word *eranos* is applied to the banquet itself, but it also designates the group of people Polydektes brings together as well as the personal contribution of the hero.[48] Instead of offering an analysis (for which there is not space here), we should at least note, through data that are at times confusing and even contradictory, the obvious articulations of the original story. The king's invitation gives an "advertising" quality to the feast/assembly where promises are to be made. Similarly, it is within this same framework of publicity, and following the invitation, that Perseus fulfills his promise by bringing back the head of Medusa, which turns the king and the others at the banquet into stone. (It is a "sinister *eranos*," according to Pindar.) The payments of the vassals, made in the customary and aristocratic form of horses, are explicitly connected with the king's generosity. These payments are made in a solemn way the day after the banquet. The presumptuous young Perseus wants to outdo the others: he declares that he will "accept" the exploit conditionally. The "promise" that he makes is the kind of thing that is done in the heat of a banquet, at a time when boasting and wagers are routine. But it is also a time when these boastings and wagers confer an advantage on the person who makes them to the chieftain, a chieftain who holds sway over his vassals through his hospitality and who accepts from them—to his future destruction—the competition for the most impressive gift. In the legend's formulation, the image of the banquet is at the center of a series of behavior types that today are called "classical." What gives unity to this series of behavior types is the force of a mutual obligation, one suggested by the word *eranos*.

It is solely through legend that a feudal milieu such as the one in the exploits of Perseus is evident. In historical Greece this feudal milieu is forgotten.[49] But in historical Greece the idea of the *eranos*, always more or less on the periphery of law, remains quite alive. It receives its definition— in diverse and related ways—at several social phases.

The Cretan custom does indeed involve the *eranos*. In the abovementioned section of Strabo, one feature needs to be made more precise: the splendid gifts that are added to the customary presents require an assessment on the part of the "abductor's" friends. The confirmation the abductor makes is designated by the expression *suneranizein tous philous* ("to gather an *eranos* among one's friends"). This idea of an assessment is what we find, in totally different spheres, to be characteristic of an operation that was certainly more widespread, even at Athens, than a theoretical exposé of law might lead one to suppose.[50] The *eranos* is a loan, but one that has at least two particularities: it carries no interest—it is what we call a loan based on friendship; and the multiplicity of the lenders is normal. The equality of the contributions is occasionally noted; and it seems that a person pays his debts in staggered payments. There is the expression *sunagein eranon*: the debtor is the one who can bring together the *eranos*, but so can a friend who heads the entire group and who determines the assessments for the participants if necessary. In the classical epoch, the *eranos* is sanctioned by law: we do not know at what point and under what conditions this came to pass. What the law can sanction is debt as such, a debt that is contracted following a "borrowing," whose mode of contracting matters little in law. But it is the mode of contracting that gives the "borrowing" a sense of vital reality. Doubtless the *eranos* was used in commercial practices at least from the end of the fifth century B.C., when it appeared as a kind of limited partnership; finally, it completely enters the realm of law, where its original character is lost. But in a persistent practice, one in which we see traditional elements (ransom, gathering of a dowry, etc.) and participants who are "friends," there is evidently an entirely different situation. In principle, the *eranos* in these cases is not an executory operation in a legal sense, nor does the element of obligation depend on the means for a legal recovery.

On the other hand, *eranos* is applied to one of the species, or rather types, of "religious associations" with which we are familiar above all in the Hellenistic epoch, but which, in fact, predate this period by a good deal.[51] These are freely constituted societies, often established among humble persons, and they involve gatherings that are more or less religious in character. The *eranos*, in these cases, is the contribution (originally in kind, it seems) to the meals that accompany the gatherings. From this comes the term that denotes a category of societies—namely, the societies of the *eranistai*. One should add that even if this type of association was not established—as used to be supposed—for the purpose of practicing the "free loan" (a loan that is designated by the very word *eranos*), still, this type of association seems to have offered an especially favorable milieu for this practice.[52]

There is yet another use of *eranos*. Already in Homer it designates a meal at community expense, a meal of a humble sort as opposed to the banquets of great pomp and those of wedding feasts.[53] This meaning survives in comedy. Aristotle, using the same contrast as Homer, alludes to a practice that is both different and yet analogous.[54] This is the custom of treating members of the same group as *eranistai*. It is like a pale, almost-carbon copy of the *amoibaia deipna* Pindar mentioned in regard to Tantalus.[55]

In this mixed picture, it is still possible to see clearly. It is striking that the same word and the same phraseology are used in the exploits of Perseus, in the practice of the friendship loan, in the custom of religious associations, and in private life. At different stages and under different conditions a common notion emerges, the notion of contribution. Not an abstract notion, it is defined, in terms of certain types of collective life, as a multiple exchange that is assured of repayment, but of which the principal psychological support is nonetheless free generosity. The literary uses of the word *eranos* are very instructive in this regard, for through these uses a veritable category of moral thought emerges for the classical period. Ancients like to express, through the metaphor to which *eranos* lends itself, the idea of give and take in social or political life; it is the compensatory mechanism that causes citizens to accept advantages gained and sacrifices made.[56] The most noble of these sacrifices is that of life itself, a sacrifice that Thucydides describes as complete liberality.[57]

Words have their destiny too. This one fell early, but in a singular way: bastard offspring, meals at common expense, suffered the contempt in Homeric poetry that peasant culture often suffers in the eyes of military aristocracy. Yet they are the progeny of very ancient practice, where the idea of the "offering" and the "collection," with all the resonance of their religious and moral meanings, is almost a prefiguration of *eranoi*.[58] However, we shall have to content ourselves for the present with an examination of survivals.[59] The first thing we see, in different uses and with widely varying value judgments, is the single signification of which the use of the word assures us: the feeling of obligation, the idea of an obligatory gift or offering, is joined in a necessary synthesis to the idea of commerce and more precisely to the image of a cycle that depends for its movement on gifts that are simultaneously gratuitous and necessary—all this at different levels in different uses. However different the situations in which we see this idea at work may be, there is here a unity of *form* that orders the way speakers can imagine human social relations. The form is not juridical; it is not isolated from a coherent social formation from which its autonomy cannot be separated, nor does it imply the kind of organization that puts a specialized bureaucracy at the service of the law. For both these reasons the idea of debt and the idea of obligation (*debitum* and *obligatio*) are submerged in this form.

It is not a juridical form, but it carries juridical possibilities. First, the very multiplicity of the *eranoi* is almost the symbol of a society in which the associations and the freedom with which the associations are formed testify to a particularly Greek ideal for Greece:[60] it is worth noting that the *contract* for associating in a "society," in which a juridical relationship was stated, was recognized in all its applications as early as the law of Solon.[61] We have also seen how very archaic survivals make themselves felt in historical periods in the form of a contract for a loan—a sort of *mutuum*, if we want to use the Latin word. I had my reasons, though, for taking as a starting point the evidence from legend which gave us the image of an *eranos* larger than life. The reader will doubtless have already noticed that in order for law to make its appearance, preclassical societies needed more than the popular practice of mutual help and communal meals, which beg comparison with egalitarian societies in which this level of contract-making would not have been surpassed without outside intervention.[62] To return again to Latin terminology, in association with *mutuum* there is *nexum*, with all the rigor it implies. In Greece, at least, alongside the plebeian practice of *eranos*, distant from the world and the morality of the nobles, we find a code in which the game of gifts and gifts-in-return was linked with the acquisition and exercise of power. Insofar as it is possible to see this evolution clearly, I am tempted to say that it is this code that is at the basis of the first calling into being of the law—the one that ended with the bondage of the debtor. But we have other questions to consider.

The Sword of Hector

In the transmission of property and in contractual relationships there is an act to which ancient laws attach a special importance and that they sometimes subject to real formalism. This is the act of handing over (*traditio*). Even laws that have been refined, that evade or dilute this act, nevertheless have something to do with it. Handing over has certain conditions for its recognition: it involves a ritual at the start, and it contains certain legal consequences; it is effective in its own way. Moreover, its value apparently predates that of law itself; law did not bring it into being.

First, a person receives; he therefore owes. In other words, a person is contracted by what he receives. A *pistis*—to use the Greek expression— or a *fides* is created by this act. We may wish to recall an expression that quite nearly describes this mentality, one penned by a Sophist in the fifth century B.C.[63] But it is an abstract expression. At a much more ancient stage, what kinds of mechanisms can be observed?

In Book VII of the *Iliad* there is a duel between Hector and Ajax, a duel that has no conclusion. After the two separate they exchange armor in order to create a truce.[64]

The exchange of armor occurs in another episode of the *Iliad*, one in which it seals a bond of hospitality between the two warriors who are about to meet face to face; it is a bond that neither knew existed.[65] Still other examples can be found in Homer.[66] But the exchange between Hector and Ajax has a special effect, one that is attested in a legendary detail that is important even though it is after Homer. This detail is made specific in Sophocles' *Ajax*. The subject of this play is the suicide of the hero, who, having become a public enemy by plotting the deaths of certain Achaean leaders, and having been dishonored by the crisis of madness into which he has just plunged, can only bring on himself his own proscription (*atimiē*, or *sacratio*) through a suicide/execution, an act that is also suicide by vengeance. Three times Sophocles insists on this dramatic detail: namely, that the instrument of death is the very sword Hector had presented to Ajax.[67] Sophocles adds that the belt the former had received from the latter is the one by which Hector is tied to the chariot that drags his cadaver around Troy.

The theme in all this is the pernicious potential of gifts. Whoever the donor is, this potential is immanent. Stories such as the one of the necklace of Eriphyle show the disasters that can result.[68] This pernicious potential is unfailingly evident when the gift is from an adversary. "Presents from adversaries are ill fated," according to Ajax, who cites an adage that attests to a popular tradition. An extreme case highlights a general notion and helps us recognize a certain mentality. It is because the gift transfers some part of the donor's being that the gift is efficacious and can be dangerous. One can even detect in Sophocles the notion that Hector's present has made Ajax a stranger to his own people: his mana is neutralized by a hostile force. The force in question is long lived. Emanating from Hector, the force is in truth Hector himself, who, although dead, causes the catastrophe.[69] At the climax, this force also partakes of the power of the "enemy land" in which the hero has planted his weapon.[70]

Without having to insist on this point, it would seem that this mode of thought is quite recognizable. It calls for exceptional stories, stories full of pathos. The extension of this mode of thought continues to the very threshold of law. In a relatively late practice, and in the "history" of the archaic period, one can still observe, at least at an implicit stage, the double notion of the symbolic importance of actual contact (which is actualized by the *delivery* in the most concrete sense) and the constraining efficacy of the thing that is received and kept.

The first notion is attested for us, *a contrario* one might say, in a curious rite that is validated in the Gortynian Code. It concerns the severing of the tie of adoption by the person who adopts. The adopted one then has a right to compensation in the amount of ten staters. No contact is any longer possible between the two; the disavowal has just been pronounced solemnly. The ten staters are deposited (*anthemen*: the word elsewhere signifies consecration, an act often conceived of as "abandonment") and are later paid by a magistrate to the adopted one.[71]

As for the other half of the double notion, a legendary tale in Herodotus interests us because it already describes in legalistic vocabulary a situation in which one of the parties is all the more involved because the object of his gift is religious. The Epidaurians obtained from the Athenians some wood from the sacred olive trees in order to build some idols that, once set up on their land, would ensure fertility. In return, the Epidaurians were required to send annual victims to certain Attic divinities (in a sort of religious vassaldom that is attested elsewhere). When war broke out between Epidaurus and the Aeginetans, the latter removed the statues and set them up in their own land so as to take advantage of the statues' beneficence. Accordingly, the Epidaurians stopped paying tribute. When the Athenians demanded it, the Epidaurians replied that they had regularly discharged their debt so long as they "had" the statues "in their land," but that having been robbed of the statues, they were now freed from their obligation. The Epidaurians added that the Athenians should go to the Aeginetans, who now had the statues (this is exactly what the Athenians did, but that is another story). Thus we see in a parallel case what the "source" of the "obligation" is.

Two series of remarks suggest themselves, one on the thing exchanged and the other on actual contact. Clearly there is an abstraction involved here; the two series of facts are related, but the abstraction is convenient.

※

In the first series, the category of clothing is stressed: in a unique way it illustrates a mythical theme. The famous robe of Nessus had been given by the Centaur to Deianeira, and then given by her to Herakles, causing his death. In *Medea*, Euripides utilizes the same motif of a murderous robe. It has been argued that this motif is autonomous in tradition and a determinant in tragedy.[72] Both Herakles and Medea had recourse to magical potions;[73] but the "sorcery" of the gift can do without them. In the story of Eriphyle the necklace is almost always associated with a robe. One should add that in rites, as in legends, the type of vestment has special significance. These robes exercise an ambivalent effect of consecration: they either sanctify the one who wears them or they make him accursed. The *pharmakos*, who plays the role of the scapegoat, is sometimes dressed in "sacred robes."[74] In Lemnian legend it is these sacred vestments, the ones of the god himself, that are put on by a royal personage, who doubles at once for the god and for the scapegoat.[75] Clothes can validate priests, as in the case of the Eleusinian hierophant. The purple cloth, consecrated to the gods, promises to them in the ritual oath the perjurer who is dressed in it.[76]

This mythical theme, to which a brief reference is sufficient, is interesting not merely in itself but should be studied as a sign. There is reason to suppose that in more or less regulated or stylized social practices clothing can be an object of special interest, one that has its own role. This is, in fact, what we observe in two series of customs.

Certain of the "fatal presents" that are mentioned in legends are wedding presents (in which the pairing of the gifts and the similarities from one case to another might indicate a kind of protocol): Eriphyle's peplos is a wedding present many times in the course of its long career, as is the peplos that Medea offers to her rival. Other analogous gifts figure in legends where they are not necessarily wedding gifts, like the robe that Theseus receives from Amphitrite. In fact, in a persistent practice, gifts of clothing have a natural role as wedding gifts. We should not forget that wedding gifts represent a kind of trade that is not at all unilateral. Husbands and wives and their families take part in this trade; the gifts even go from women to men, as in the case of the Lemnian women who sent clothes to the Argonauts at the moment they took them in marriage.[77] On the other hand, as witness to the value attached to this practice in the ruling class, it is worth remembering that the alleged law of Solon forbidding dowries is in reality a disposition that aims to limit the accumulation of "clothes and jewels," things that constituted the ancient *phernē*.[78] This disposition is similar to the so-called sumptuary law, which restrained expenses in which gifts of clothing played a major part. This reaction of the civic group at the moment when it achieves full self-awareness recalls, together with a contradiction in its world view, the ancient import of a theme that is at once social, familial, religious, and aristocratic.

Another occurrence of a gift of clothing is seen in a custom that might loosely be termed feudal, a custom that has some connection with the preceding one. According to Apollonius of Rhodes, Jason and Medea received from the Phaeacian women certain wedding gifts that were specifically called "feminine gifts"; the most important of these gifts were fine vestments.[79] Concerning the custom in general, we have indirect testimony, above all from foreign but neighboring peoples with whom prehistoric Greece had some contact. To be sure, the Greeks of the classical period no longer understood a mode of exchange in which the noble receives, but by definition gives as well, and in which they function according to a market they refuse to acknowledge.[80] At any rate, the classical Greeks observed this sort of exchange at Cyprus, for example, and at the other end of the world, Thrace.[81] And when they witnessed it, once again gifts of clothing were most important. We discover among the Macedonians, in a stage of kingship that has often been compared to that of prehistoric Greece, a counterpart where the worth of the present is accentuated. Incidentally, Plutarch tells us that the gift of rich robes was a customary method for kings to secure the adherence of their followers.[82]

In the picture that develops we see the emergence of an abstract idea of value, an idea that orders the contractual mode of exchange at the juridical stage. But we also see an ancient stage in which intermittent trade is governed by social forms that have nothing to do with economics, and by a notion of obligation and efficacious operation that is no closer to economics as we now understand it. Briefly we behold a "mystical" notion of the thing that is exchanged. We thus have an opportunity to grasp one of the bases of civilization, one in which we see this notion functioning in an incontestable and intelligible way.

The offering of vestments is generally considered to be a markedly archaic custom, one often seen in religious life. However modernized, the grand celebration of the Panathenaia still included as a central element the quadrennial offering of a peplos to Athena.[83] The weaving of the peplos, which lasted for a definite period, was assigned to certain officiants.[84] The same arrangement prevailed at Olympia, where a college of Sixteen Women was charged with the weaving of a robe offered to Hera, likewise every four years.[85] At Sparta there was a place called "Khiton,"[86] where "the women" (obviously select ones) wove the annual robe for Apollo at Amyclae. Other similar customs are in evidence.[87] What we see in these examples is a form of religious life derived from very ancient practice and more or less adapted to a civic organization. In all our examples the offering comes from women. What comes to mind at once is a social fact whose significance is far-reaching (and doubtless associated with the mythical theme of the accursed dress). In the division of labor among the sexes, weaving is the task of women.[88] Even in a rather late period this social fact continues to exist and to have juridical consequences.[89] But in prehistory it must have had a very different import, since it appears in connection with the structure of primitive feasts in which the rituals of clothing play an important role.

The Sixteen Women at Olympia were not only charged with the manufacture of Hera's robe; they also presided over the women's choruses and they organized in honor of Hera a race between young girls, a kind of race that is typical in local religion. Dances and foot races are among the most ancient elements in the Hellenic tradition of festivals, a tradition where at times within the same complex certain rites of adolescence, which are, in part, rites of collective marriage, and certain practices that have to do with clothing are brought together. At Achaean Pellene the festival of the Hermaia offered a prize of locally made mantles.[90] Although this is an isolated locus, it is still significant. One might discover the *aition* of an analogous celebration in a detail in the story of the Argonauts: after landing at Lemnos, the latter took part in games organized by the island's women, with clothing offered as prizes.[91] Moreover, there were no longer any men on the island, so naturally the Argonauts married the Lemnian women.

The marriage rites (explained poorly by the Greeks) consisted of disguises or the exchange of clothes.[92] This system has often been noted; a unilateral interpretation is not warranted, but we can easily recover the reflex of rites of passage. A festival in Cretan Phaistos was called the Ekdysia; the name indicates the act of shedding one's clothes. We know the story behind this festival: a certain Leukippos, transformed miraculously from a girl to a boy, shed his girlish clothes.[93] Suffice it to recall that the childhoods of heroes regularly involve the ritual theme associated with the mythical theme of a change in sex.[94] A trace of both themes is found even in the romanticized legend of Achilles and the daughters of Lykomedes.[95] To review, there are rites that accompany the passage to the state of manhood; there are also rites that are connected with group marriage, the memory of which persists in the tradition of the most ancient festivals;[96] there are rites in which girls also participate. In this system of rites, there are the symbolisms of clothing being shed, given, and exchanged. Once again, clothing is women's work; the old festivals are opportunities for collective expenditures. One might hazard to say that in the most ancient system of exchanges, the exchanges between sexes form a nucleus.

We arrive, therefore, at some basic forms. Faced with a series of noteworthy data, it has not seemed useless to go so far: in the ensemble of notions that are associated with clothing,[97] we have at least been able to see (and this was for certain) a mode of thought that is rooted very deeply, one that attributes a unique value to the transmission of certain objects.

In the practice of exchange of arms, we have noted the concept of "participation." The arms themselves are the means for this participation; but the primary instrument is the hand. The hand can act independently: the symbolism of the joining of hands (which survived, especially in a system parallel to the legal one) stems from an idea of intimate association brought about through (physical) contact, and even from an idea of contagion.[98] In Greek, the word *enguē* retains traces of a contractual or precontractual mode that might be thus explained; for even if the word hardly deals in our sources with anything other than differentiated types of contract (pledges, the marriage contract), we may still doubtless infer that the etymology has to do with the joining of hands. Inversely, there is a word that is not perpetuated in law, but that is still very much a vital word in Homer, where it is used to designate an agreement. This word has kept its specific meaning: it is *dexiai* ("right hands"). Our purpose here is not to consider the gesture itself;[99] to do so, we would have to distinguish certain variations that correspond to certain different symbols, for there are different ways of joining hands. What we do wish to emphasize is the idea of "delivery," insofar as it is like the notion of *enguē* and is associated with it.

Certain "expressive" modes of religious commerce already have the quality of a sign. The ritual from the classical period[100] still includes the custom of placing "in the hand" of the god—or of his statue—a part of the *splankhna* ("entrails" of the sacrificial victim). Or it happens that the priest, prophet, etc., who represents the god receives the entrails "in his hand."[101] As the ritual becomes more symbolic in character, a piece of coin takes the place of the *splankhna*.[102] It is possible that this custom stems from a precontractual practice whereby the divinity, through an intermediary, receives that which will become "earnest money" from someone making a promise (pledge).[103] In any case, it is evident that in the direct dealings between man and gods, the preliminary offering, which has the property of beginning a commerce at the same time that it can be fulfilled separately,[104] is itself accomplished by a transfer, no less direct and specific, of a piece of the victim.

At the human level, the characteristic modes for handing-over serve to establish, through the efficacy of the gesture, social relationships of various sorts; but all are equally old.

In Homer, the expression "to place in the hand" (*en kheiri tithenai*, or *engualizein*, a word that is related to *enguē*) is found frequently. It is interesting to note that quite often this is a figurative expression, since it has as its object abstract things such as power, victory, or privilege.[105] This suits the intellectualized language of Homer, but one senses that in a more ancient time these abstractions were made real in symbols, that is, in the very objects that contain the corresponding properties and that are actually "placed in the hand." Such is the case, in Homer at least, regarding the scepter.[106] These two series of examples help to explain one another: the scepter is not only the sign but the seat of a religious force.[107]

An entire series of examples is suggested in which the properties, linked and as it were synthesized between the right hand and the object, confer on the handing-over its true value. This series deals with situations in which the handing-over corresponds to a transfer of power and to a consolidation of authority or prestige. Besides the scepter, which in Homer is all but stylized, there are diverse attributes of power that get their meaning when one bears them (*phorein*, an "intensive" of *pherein*) and, correlatively, when one transmits them from hand to hand. This is what we see with the club of Ereuthalion, a club of iron that figures as a weapon in Nestor's boast, but that we see elsewhere as an "attribute" of the god of the underworld.[108] Such is also the case with the double ax that the Lydian kings—according to legend—carry as a "sacred object" and that one of their number once "gave to carry" to one of his faithful.[109]

Investitures of this sort can accomplish a hereditary transmission. A fine passage from Euripides shows us how Herakles had arranged the succession among his three sons.[110] The symbols of power that correspond to various parts of the kingdom are placed in two of the sons' hands: the club and, implicitly, the arrows. The case of the remaining son reveals the equivalent symbolism of contact and clothing: the hero dresses this son in the skin of the Nemean lion.[111]

The opposite of investiture is suggested by a ritual that among certain peoples evolved into a formal procedure, namely, the *traditio per glebam*. In Greece, we know of this ritual only through legend,[112] that is, under another aspect and with the most ancient significations. The giving of a clod of earth seems to mean not the giving up of ownership but the recognition of an overlord who will provide protection and assurance. We might say that it is the principle of *pars pro toto* that is at work here. But this would be an incorrect translation. On the one hand, there is in our examples the question not so much of territorial possession as of the "kingship" that is exercised over the territory; on the other hand, the territory is nevertheless represented both in the most concrete way and yet in a highly "mystical" way, that is, as a nourishing force. The clod of earth is sometimes a sham gift, one that is given in lieu of bread.[113] Moreover, the symbolism can take another turn; it is particularly full in the very well known legend reported by Pindar: one of the Argonauts receives from a sea god (near the shores of Libya) a piece of earth that is in some way the title to the future establishment of Greeks in Cyrene. The clod of earth is compared to a presage:[114] the prophecy to which it corresponds shall be fulfilled according to a mystical order of time. As the sign and actualization of an allliance, the clod of earth is endowed with an efficacy that connects it and even identifies it with the prophecy that has the force of bringing it about.[115] But the ritual that is mentioned in our sources is no less suggestive. It takes on two forms: the clod of earth is either received in a sack or contained in the lap of a robe;[116] or, in the Pindar version, the handing-over of an object is not merely associated with a gesture of the palm (of the hand), as in the Homeric tale,[117] but is mixed up with *enguē* itself.[118]

Here and there, lyric poetry or narrative can keep a very primitive notion alive. The notion under consideration is pretty well obsolete in Homer, who often shows us, in formulas loaded with ancient symbolism, a *traditio* that might be described as banal. Even so, this *traditio* is still very striking in its "solemnity," and it remains charged with meaning in its secular applications.[119] Additionally, the Greek is mischievous enough to regale himself early with reminiscences. The sixth-century *Homeric Hymn to Hermes* uses the word *engualizein*, with a sort of humor verging on parody, to describe the grants of attributes as though they were acts of investiture or homage.[120] The young Hermes was expert in these activities; but in a timely way the poet recalls the ultimate vocation of the god: he is the divinity who "sanctifies exchanges between men."[121]

The Sacrifice of the Kings of Atlantis

In the customary forms of gift commerce the obligation need not be explicit. We hear sometimes of "promise" or of "oaths."[122] This is revisionism on the part of moderns who do not understand how obligation is implicit in the rules of the game of gift exchange. But there are moments and occasions where a specific accord must be sealed with a special procedure, when the parties are more or less strangers to each other. The *form* [of this procedure] is precisely the one that will be perpetuated in "international law," but is also the form in which we see, concentrated in a single act that is the direct antecedent of contract, the forces that are responsible for the vitality of prelaw: it is the oath.[123]

The word "oath" needs definition, its familiar notion notwithstanding. This notion is intellectualized and it presupposes law itself (where, moreover, the oath is still used occasionally). One must be open-minded when dealing with a notion that is more ancient than the historical epoch.[124]

In one of the best-known myths, that of Atlantis, Plato reports how this huge island was governed more than nine thousand years before him. The ten kings who ruled it gathered periodically to discuss common matters. To ensure that justice would be rendered if any one of them had committed an infraction, they pledged themselves to one another.[125] For the purposes of this pledge, they sacrificed a bull, slaughtering it on top of a pillar (on which was inscribed the law that governed them) in such a way that the blood flowed over the inscription. While the victim was consecrated in the holocaust, the kings poured into a bowl containing a mixture of water and wine a drop of blood for each of them. Then they drew from the bowl with golden cups, poured a libation over the fire while swearing to conform to the laws, and drank the rest of the cup.

It would be contrary to the very intentions of Plato for this ceremony to have been totally contrived; and, indeed, the relic of genuine practices has been discovered in this legend. The grouping within the legend may be fictitious, but the elements are not. We see in the latter many themes of ritual, almost all of which deal with oaths. Deliberately archaic, the description is all the more helpful to us.

※

In the perspective that it affords (as an artist Plato chooses more or less at will) the mixing bowl is central. It is, by itself, the symbol and instrument of union/communion, such as with the Ionian cities that periodically renew their alliance.[126] Pouring into the same bowl wines brought by two contracting parties is one of the expressive modalities of Homeric oaths.[127]

These two cases are, in a way, the inverse of each other. The first is collective drinking, which has the effect of a communion service. The second case, which is the Homeric one, is an oath-sacrifice, in which the wine is poured in a libation but cannot be consumed—and this is the operative principle in the classical period. Still, this distinction is not absolute. The kings of Atlantis drink from the liquid that serves as a libation, and the drink they consume is exactly the same as the one drunk by the Greek mercenaries who, according to Herodotus, entered into a contract sealed by human sacrifice: a mixture of wine and water, together with the victim's blood, was consumed.[128]

The mode of thought manifested here can also be seen in other guises. There is no attestation of communion through blood in Greece; but we do know of practices in which the victim's blood, through contact or absorption, serves to create a reciprocal bond. The seven warriors in Aeschylus' play dip their hands into the blood of a sacrificed bull;[129] the Greek leaders and the barbarians plunge their arms into the victims' blood that had been collected—as in Aeschylus' play—in a shield.[130] Aristophanes, mocking the theme of the *Septem*, shows us the conspiring women who were supposed to have sacrificed a victim animal, for which was substituted a jug of wine that one of the seven wanted to taste individually, since she thought the word "swear" was the facetious equivalent of "drink." This same mentality is indicated in a text that is quite late, to be sure, but that still has a genuine link to the past. In the *Argonautica* of Orpheus the warriors make compact with one another by drinking a mixture of barley, bull's blood, and sea water.[131] The name of the beverage, *kukeōn*, also designates the drink that is consumed by the future initiate at Eleusis, and it could have denoted the drink given to the boy who won the prize in the race at the Athenian Oskhophoria.[132]

A victor in games is consecrated through his victory; an initiate, through the preliminary rites at his initiation. We can see what is behind a certain type of oath. The word "communion" would be inadequate; we are dealing here with a change of state. Obligation requires such a change, and the primitive oath brings it about by means of a substance.

This substance, in the cases that we have just considered, is alternately or simultaneously blood and wine. The one is the equivalent of the other;[133] both belong to the same group, which is clearly opposed to the group composed of milk-and-honey libations,[134] which do not involve the oath (a contrast that can perhaps be accounted for by differences in social or ethnic milieus). This presents us with an opportunity to confirm (and to fill out) the notion of the property inherent in blood and, in particular, the idea of its precontractual significations. To use the vocabulary that

Hubert and Mauss applied to the subject of sacrifice, the effects of blood are not only subjective—involving only the participants—but also objective; they have an effect apart from the participants. The ritual of soaking weapons in blood would already indicate this. In Plato's Atlantis there is a very suggestive detail: the column on top of which the victim is slaughtered bears the text of the laws and the oath itself; it is this inscription that is restored by periodic anointing. The conclusion to Euripides' *Suppliant Women* offers a striking analogy: with a view toward a perpetual alliance with Argos, Athena orders Theseus to slaughter some victims "in a tripod" —in other words, to make the blood flow there—and this tripod was from then on to bear the inscribed text of the oath.[135] There is a trace in all this, recalled as well perhaps in the Argonauts' story,[136] of a very particular form of contract *litteris*.

꿏

There are other forces and other modes of action. The act of libation ought to be considered in and of itself. It is of singular importance: in Greece and in Rome it gave a name to a method of contract;[137] and even where the oath is no longer used to create an obligation, the etymology of *sponsio* holds the memory of the central place that libation has in the sacramental ritual. Indeed, the libation by itself often appears as the equivalent to the oath, concentrating in itself the properties of an oath. It is *through* a libation that an oath becomes effective;[138] in everyday practices the oath can be reduced to the libation;[139] and by recalling sacrifice, a synthetic expression such as *spondas temnein*[140] evokes the important datum of libation as the basis for accords.

The ritual of libation uses the power of wine,[141] but especially of pure wine—wine which is charged with a particular mana and over which there sometimes hangs a general prohibition. This also applies to blood. Especially for oaths of a serious nature, the custom of pouring blood over the victims survives for a long time.[142]

Blood is poured over victims who are in the process of being consumed; it is poured over the fire, according to Plato. In Plato's account, the ritual of libation, in certain respects a communion that is directed to an Olympian, requires a mixed wine, which is also consumed by the officiants. Elsewhere—that is, in nearly all our sources—the demands of religious law are especially significant: the wine, which cannot be consumed, is poured out completely and all at once.[143] The fire consumes the entire offering: *di' empurōn*, in the words of the cult codes. Still, to whom is the offering directed in such a case? No divinity is involved in the transaction, not even collectively; there is only complete anonymity. It would appear that the destruction by fire suffices in itself, unless, as some modern critics have suggested,[144] the pouring of wine (and blood) is meant to arouse the infernal and avenging powers. But even this is saying too much. Vengeance will occur if there is need. From this point on, we have an obligation through consecration; and punishment for faithlessness to the obligation, if that ever happens, will be the automatic result. Might not the destruction by fire[145] have a positive and immediate effect?

In an extreme case, one in which the libation itself is sufficient, the liquid (not "burned" but "volatilized") has such an effect. It is contained in a myth, and it involves an affirmative oath by which the traitor, who had intended to violate it, was immediately condemned. This is the famous swearing by the Styx, a common practice among the gods. The Styx is water of the underworld. One swears while pouring the entire contents of a golden pitcher into which the Styx water has been drawn; and if the water is poured while "laden with a false oath," the faithless god will fall down paralyzed.[146] In the promissory oath that seals an agreement, how is it that a force of a similar nature is not immediately aroused? The force is not felt through contact—the water of the Styx might act as poison in a trial by ordeal—[147] but acts by a process of elimination in the religious sense. The infernal nature of the water is the symbol of what is at work in libation oaths: through the libation, the oath is linked to the other world. It is there, ideally, that the oath creates something through the special quality of a gesture, which is part of all forms of cult, but which assumes unique significance in this case. If libation has a central role in the prehistoric contract, it is because through it, and under variations that the ancient mentality can accommodate, the contract truly acquires objectivity.

※

Ritualistic destruction or "elimination" with a positive effect; communication established by it with the other world, conceived in particular as the underworld, where there is a reservoir of forces, some of which are, by nature, dangerous—this is the mythical code of behavior that we can also see at work on other levels.[148] In the ritual of the oath itself there are additional practices worth noting, ones that also help us recognize it.

A Cyrenean inscription contains the oath that guaranteed the reciprocal obligations between the home city Thera and colonists leaving for Africa. A curious ritual was performed. Figurines (kolossoi) were fashioned from wax, then thrown into the fire as the following formula was intoned: "May he who is unfaithful to this oath be liquified[149] and made to disappear, together with his people and his possessions." The kolossoi are images that have the property of representing (in the full sense of the word) the persons whom they figure,[150] as an equally telling inscription from Cyrene shows.[151] Obviously, the destruction of the statuettes symbolizes, or rather predetermines, the eventual fate of the perjurer, even as the knife that cuts the victim's throat is an efficacious image and is formally recognized as such.[152] But this anticipated carrying-out does not exhaust the meaning of the act: if the threat is not merely postponed, or if something is at once accomplished by the fire, it is because the contracting party himself is immediately brought under obligation through his "double."

Many rituals, undoubtedly no less suggestive, must have been lost. But of those that we do know there is another system to consider, and it is doubly instructive.

What happened to the victims' remains after their death? In theory, the oath-sacrifice belongs to the category of chthonian sacrifices that are total, ones in which the victim is entirely "abandoned." According to Plato there is a "holocaust," and the positive sense of the sacrifice is perceived anew through destruction by fire;[153] but other procedures are no less instructive. Following the oath between the Achaeans and Trojans,[154] Priam brings the cadavers of two sacrificed lambs on his chariot, evidently to bury them. Moreover, certain places in Greece preserve the memory of victims buried there following an oath-sacrifice.[155] We are face to face with a ritual of elimination; but the earth represents the powers of another world, a domain where the force inherent in an oath will remain deposited and alive, just as the sacrificial knife, buried in the ground, makes the pledged troth eternal.[156] As for the Achaeans, they are not natives of the Troad and thus have no earth that can serve as a recipient; so after Agamemnon has taken his oath, the remains of the victim are thrown into the sea.[157] But the sea is also "another world."[158]

Aside from producing this "objective" effect by destruction or elimination, the body of the victim can act in another way, directly and on the very existence of the contracting party. By body of the victim we mean parts of the victim's body (notably the testicles). Some very specific and instructive rituals are attested.[159] One holds in one's hand the *splankhna*,[160] or one places a foot on them.[161] There is not only action by contact, there is action through radiation. A practice familiar outside Greece, but found only rarely within it, seems to have been used in the sacramental obligation.[162] It involved making the oath-taker pass between the parts of the victim, from which certain lines of force radiate and converge. An army can thus be "purified" or "consecrated."[163] Through the act of consecration, though, one takes an oath: Plato plans for his city a comparable ritual, one with similar value.[164] Perhaps it is to this practice that we should relate the primitive sense of a nearly constant expression in the oath formula, namely, *ta tomia*, "the cut up parts." This is an expression to which a lively symbolism continues to be applied.[165]

❧

We can see how far removed we are from the classical concept of the oath. Even Homer is no longer at this stage.[166] It would be wrong, however, to reduce the opposition between the two epochs to that between "magic" and "religion." As far back as we go, it seems that the major divinities have assumed the role of presiding over oaths; but one can observe that even the ritual does not attribute to the gods an active function at the moment of giving. It is not the gods who create the obligation; nor is the sacrifice addressed to them. They have merely come to be called, in a characteristic expression, the "guarantors"; they can intervene only in case the return gift is past due. If, in the historical period, we see the gods in the foreground, it is because the oath tends to be concentrated in the affirmatory or promissory formula, which is substantially the same as that seen in a contract or in (legal) testimony, but which adds to itself the divine guarantee.

It is this formula that in a multitude of examples is called *horkos*, "oath." But the first sense of *horkos* is not "oath." We have seen the forces at work in the most ancient oaths, emanating from various beings or substances; and the list of these substances is open ended. For example, when one swears over a rock (a practice often mentioned by Pausanias), one actually swears by the rock.[167] Strictly speaking, the *horkos* is the thing with which one comes in contact when one swears an oath. Both the components[168] and the many uses[169] of the word show us this. Ultimately, the pronouncement of a formula can be superfluous; we know of oaths that dispense with it.[170] If the pronouncement seems usually to be indispensable, this is because the pronouncement is needed to make the oath clear and explicit—unless the quality of the utterance (understood in the same way as a *carmen*) constitutes a particular force but is nevertheless one of the many forces at play, converging with the other forces and being of the same order.[171] The oath is quite different from a mere declaration that is reinforced through an appeal to a divinity.

It seems that the most ancient forms of obligation make the oath effective. They provoke a change of estate among the parties, and they create something between them in the world beyond. In order to create, they bring forces into play. But these forces are not specific. They emanate from the victim; they are in the blood; they are released by the destruction of the victim, and so on. These are so-called religious forces, whether or not there is absorption of blood, burial of sacrificial remains, the ritual of the *kolossoi*, the ritual of the *tomia*, and all the characteristic practices we have seen which attest a variety that is greater in proportion to how far they are removed from the stereotyped forms of the historical era. And while we are not greatly endowed with testimonia, one may still point to a tight analogy with various religious practices. What is basic in the most ancient obligation is the *intent*[172] with which these forces are directed: as we have seen, intent determines certain particularities of ritual. But intent does not put other particularities into effect. And if one wants to define prelaw in this domain, it is here, in the examination of intent, that the definition will be made.

II
THE ORIGINS OF DUE PROCESS

If there is a domain where we have a chance of seeing the juridical mentality develop, it is the area of procedure, or due process. One cannot overemphasize the importance of procedure for the foundation of law or for our own knowledge of archaic laws. For a fairly clear sense of their importance, all we have to do is examine the Homeric poems, in which we can sometimes see the evocation of a past that is more ancient than the poems, one that is only sketched, but nevertheless very lively.[173] From the moment that a plaintiff is instructed to formulate a claim, and the defendant is instructed to deny it before a court—however rudimentary—what we call the "idea of law" develops. The conditions and, to coin an expression, the "social space" are quite different from those prevailing when this idea of law was satisfied in traditional legal fulfillments—that is, in activity that is totally private and, in a way, a priori legitimate. This is the basis for the parallels and even for the communality in nature between the forms of the defense in law and the forms of the creation of law. That is why in legal claims the "prosecutory formula" of Roman law is applied to *mancipatio* or *in iure cessio*, what we would call the transfer of property, or to *nexum*, which is the basis for an obligatory bond.[174]

Judiciary actions and juridical acts—in the beginning there were connections between the two.[175] These connections are particularly clear, for within the archaic forms of both, law is the object of an affirmation that is deliberately and "fictitiously" absolute. At the same time, judiciary actions create the reality of a law that does not have to refer to the past, a law that appears at precisely that moment by virtue of certain gestures and spoken words. This is what we observe in the Roman action involving the pursuit of a claim,[176] and in the analogous situations that Greek tradition reveals.[177] Such situations are produced similarly in Roman *mancipatio*[178] (and in the analogous modes of behavior that we see in archaic Greece)[179] through a formula of *meum esse*, one which is ipso facto authoritative.

We must recognize in all this the efficacy of the formula. The formula is not the product of "superstition" or blind obedience to *mos*; it is essential to the birth of the law. It not only restrains the parties to a dispute, but it also demands respect from third parties and gives the indispensable feeling of a guarantee. It is not an exaggeration to say that the formula is creative psychologically, in the fullest sense of the expression, and not merely in its function of making a decision known.[180] The virtue attached to it is that of establishing law or—and it comes down to the same thing—unquestionably calling forth the categorical statement.

Still, the formula is not creative *ex nihilo*.

The Judiciary Scene on the "Shield of Achilles"

An examination of the beginning of due process in Greece allows us to formulate the problem. According to a well-known and until now widely accepted theory, judgment comes as a result of arbitration.[181] Let us note at once that the theory is more or less consciously in keeping with a "naturalistic" concept according to which only the law of force reigned at the beginning. The first attempts at procedural law would thus have been attempts to bring about peaceful solutions to conflict by regularizing and neutralizing the manifestations of struggle and *Selbsthilfe*. Accordingly, although voluntary at first, arbitration would have gradually become obligatory.

This thesis does not seem acceptable. The confirmation that was thought to exist in Roman law disappears upon examination: the suit does not conjure up the image of a fistfight, as has been argued. The seizure of a thing or of a human cannot be interpreted as a manifestation of brute force. Instead, it is the fulfillment of a ritual. Apart from its presumptions, the above explanation at once runs into difficulty. This is not to deny the extent and the frequency of arbitration during the most ancient periods; and the question of the links between arbitration and judgment remains quite complex. The earliest judgment could not have been made without one of the parties acquiescing to the judgment in some fashion in advance. Roman procedure retained traces of this kind of collaboration, which at least in theory was freely entered into. On the other hand, when it led to a judgment, arbitration was able to pattern itself on a socially founded practice of judgment.[182] In any case, there is a specific difference between arbitration and judgment: the latter emanates, directly or indirectly, from a collective authority, and is effective in and of itself, instead of depending on the good will of the interested parties. There is discontinuity between the two institutions: the one could not have been derived from the other through some "spontaneous evolution," an evolution about which it is very difficult to be specific in any case.[183]

Concerning the conditions under which judgment appears, and at the same time concerning the first function of judgment, the most ancient version we have is the famous scene of the *Shield of Achilles*,[184] as described and commented upon by Homer (obviously with some abridgments and things left understood). Let us recall this story without getting involved in some discussions that are, by now, dated. In the agora, where the people have assembled, a dispute arises between two men over the subject of *Wergeld*, or "blood price," that is owed following a murder. One man, explaining his case to the people, claims that he has paid in full; the other man denies ever having received anything. Both have recourse to a judge for a verdict, which it is the duty of the Elders, who are seated on stone benches in a sacred circle, to pronounce. The heralds hold back the crowd. One by one the judges rise to make pronouncements: two talents of gold have been deposited (on the ground); the gold will belong to the man who makes the most righteous decision.

We do not have to ask ourselves here what the basis of the "right to a debt" was. The amount of the *Wergeld* might have been fixed through arbitration or defined in advance through custom; the latter is most probable. At any rate, a private arrangement has been made in order to place limits on the right to vengeance through a settlement-payment. We also do not have to search out what might have been the verdicts of the Elders among whom a competition arose; if we accept that the poet knew what he was talking about, then we can agree that our task is not to settle the question of the fact but to propose criteria for decisive proof. Here is the essential point: a judgment is solicited not from an individual person but from an agent of the collectivity (the recourse to justice was not absolutely required but was suggested and practically imposed by the atmosphere of the agora).[185] The judgment itself—or at least that which takes its place—is not to be discussed. How can this be so? In other words, under what circumstances is judgment imposed? In the circumstances presupposed by the Homeric episode, there is no question of trying the murderer. Murder calls forth private vengeance. An arrangement[186] was agreed to whereby the exercise of vengeance was conditionally suspended: if the ransom were not paid, the avenger would again be free to act and could kill his adversary. As Glotz points out, this is what gives dramatic interest to a scene that might seem to be reduced to a "simple question of payment." From this comes the kind of pressure that finally calls for the appeal to justice. Theoretically, however, the initiative comes not from the one we might call the "plaintiff," from the one who has the "right to vengeance": the initiative comes from the one who has submitted to vengeance and who "tells the people about his case."[187]

We have here the image, at once schematic and poetic, of a primitive procedure whose mark is preserved in later law. Even in the law of the classical period, the question posed to the judge is whether a party is or is not qualified for fulfillment; the judgment confirms the right to fulfillment.[188] Privileged rights are defined by the fact that they do not have to be enforced by the law (for example, the right to one's inheritance, to buy property from the state, etc.). Laws are involved only if the fulfillment they legitimate is impeded by the adversary, and only under the form of penal action that is directed against the adversary:[189] proof positive of the primacy of the power to execute a sentence. Similarly, a question like that of the status of the free man, at Athens, as at Rome, is provoked by the freeing gesture of an *assertor* who opposes the seizure of an alleged slave, a seizure that has an effective force by itself, but that is provisionally neutralized by an equally ritualized intercession. On the other hand, let us consider the forms of archaic law: they involve situations that are similar to those in the *Shield of Achilles*. If the city was able to impose a judiciary system for trials of homicide, it did so by controlling the rights of the avenger, at the initiative of the person who was liable to vengeance,[190] and in tribunals that were sanctuaries and that had presumably been places of asylum. Practices such as a house search for a stolen object involve immediate consequences, without recourse to justice. Recourse to justice occurs only upon the protest of the adversary if he can plead a rule violation. This is the case in the *Homeric Hymn to Hermes*, which is a historical document despite its buffoonery.[191]

Thus, judgment first appears in special circumstances. An entire series of routine acts theoretically takes place without judgment: for example, arrest, seizure, execution. What provokes judgment is not the exercise of "private justice" but the opposition of the other party, who contests its legitimacy. The function of justice is to allow or deny the application of law. A public authority cannot at first do more than control a customary means for personal action. To be able to do this, the judging authority must affirm its role as the public one. In this way the act of judging defines an understandable role for itself at its earliest stages and, at the same time, its eternal nature.

A question poses itself. Rules that are both respectable and compelling; rules that are imposed on litigants; those forms that constitute procedure and that are effective in themselves; that entire system whose development seems gratuitous in a hypothesis where the institution of judgment emanates from specific and arbitrary arrangements—all this fits together with a system of legitimate fulfillments. What is more, these fulfillments are represented in law. The essence of procedure derives from their essence: a *manus iniectio*, the validity of which is its reason for existing, affirms, before being adjudicated, an unconditional value.[192] In other words, all the activity that was subject to a regulation was also endowed with an immanent power. Whoever made a house search always had to observe certain conditions, but if he observed them, then, by virtue of a correct act, he started with total power over the adversary. This example is worth pondering, since beneath procedure we catch a glimpse of ritual, a glimpse of a kind of "magic."[193] In short, if the efficacy of symbolisms predates procedure, then it makes sense to study the forms in which what will become the affirmation and the rule of law presents itself very early. We will examine at least some of these forms, as far as allusions and reminiscences will permit.

Orestes at His Father's Tomb

In Athenian law from the classical period, the heir is designated by the fact that he "comes into possession" (*embateuei*). The same verb is applied to the creditor who upon default takes possession of mortgaged property. A related verb, *embainein*, at times indicates (even at a late period) a "taking possession" by the purchaser.[194] There does not seem to have been in this any special, solemn ceremony, one demanded on pain of voiding the contract. But there is here the relic of an act that belongs to a group of actions that are efficacious in themselves, in whose functions we must find the most ancient uses of judiciary action. The right to inherit one's property is especially protected. This is so, first of all, because of a curious procedure, *diamarturia*, which consists of inviting witnesses whose "testimony" is enough to stop a petition of inheritance that runs counter to a *suus*.[195] Second, the right to inherit one's property is protected through that *dikē exoulēs* which is called forth in opposition to a regular "taking possession." A passage in Isaeus shows the direct and specific link that could exist even in the fourth century B.C. between taking possession, the role of the witnesses, and the "expulsion" by an adversary.[196] But what are the antecedents to *embateusis*? The question may well be asked, for etymologically the word signifies the act of "entering" or "placing the foot on."

In Aeschylus' *Khoephoroi*, Orestes, having returned in secret to Argos to avenge Agamemnon's death, at first pays homage at his father's grave. Orestes' sister, Electra, who was agonizingly awaiting his return, did not know that he had indeed returned. She then recognized the lock of hair Orestes had placed on the tomb, as well as the footprints he had left behind. She became convinced that the hair was the same as hers, and likewise the footprints.[197] In a scene from the *Electra*, Euripides took the time to criticize this rather ancient element in the Orestes story.[198] This parody is but a joke.[199] In fact, there is in the situation a kind of presupposition that is common to the three tragedians, namely, that only Orestes has been able to come in this way to his father's tomb. Only he was qualified to climb to the top of the mound and perform the hair-offering, a ritual that especially establishes a religious link between the male heir and his ancestor.[200] Orestes' *embateusis* has its sacrilegious counterpart in the act of the usurper Aegisthus, who dances on the tomb of Agamemnon, a ritual act in its own way, but, of course, one with an opposite sense.[201]

One must not forget that these are (as has been pointed out)[202] "dynastic" problems that are sometimes posed in legend and even in tragedy. Succession, properly speaking, has always been the concern of the sons of "kings," chieftains, priests, or prophets. The act that confirmed succession had a definite value: when we consider how the Homeric poems use so often the patronymics that are like a trademark for these poems, we are better equipped to understand an expression such as the one in Herodotus, *embateuein tou onomatos*, which means, for such conspicuous persons, the act of claiming for oneself at once filiation and a name. Through its etymological sense, the verb highlights the idea of the ritual that in primitive times had established the rule of law.[203]

There are other symbolisms in the act of taking possession; but they are sometimes very closely related. Thus we have those that are denoted by certain compounds of *bainein* ("march"). Even some figurative uses make us recognize something like the rites of succession or investiture: for example, the use of *epibainein* in Homer and Hesiod.[204] In the expression concerning royal or divine property, the word *amphibainein* brings to mind the custom of walking around, one that is familiar in religions where it has a purificatory or consecratory effect.[205] But there is a symbolism at work here that we must recall for two reasons: first, because it furnished a legendary motif for which the signified ceased to be clear; and second, because it can take on, in its own form, a dynastic signification. When Jason, who comes to claim his paternal heritage, presents himself incognito before the usurper Pelias, the latter is dumbstruck, since the new arrival is "the man shod on only one foot," about whom an oracle had warned Pelias.[206] In trying to get at the essentials of this myth, scholars have formulated hypotheses that are not always necessary.[207] The legend communicates its meaning directly enough. For Pelias, threatened by dispossession, the latter is signaled by the accouterment of a rival who is going to install himself as the legitimate successor by a ritual of *embateusis*. It is a special ritual here, and one for which we shall see analogies. Besides, footwear as such has the same symbolic functions: in the legend of Theseus the hero's father has left hidden away, for his son's sake, shoes and a sword. These are the "signs" by which the son, when he is of age, will make himself known—and this is a double sense, since in the legend itself Theseus is declared by his father the presumptive heir.[208]

We have enough information from Greece concerning mythical enthronement—of which Ireland or India also offer us glimpses—to recognize the affinities of these practices. The symbolism of the foot and footwear in religious life is very widespread. In the mass of facts that have been collected,[209] there are some pertinent indications. First, it is of interest to establish that the word *embateuein* has its own use in certain ritual forms.[210] It corresponds to the gesture of putting the foot on an object that has a religious signification and import. He who takes an oath has the foot on the *tomia*. The purification of the suppliant, the qualification for marriage, and the consecration in the Mysteries are all accomplished by the same gesture on the hide of a victim.[211] The same specifics, which can be seen in legendary rites of enthronement or those involving the taking-over of an inheritance, are evident in a practice that pertains to a kind of common religious basis, but that also finds singular applications in the stories of heroes. Many cult regulations prescribe that feet be bare or that certain footwear be worn; but there are instances in which one of the two feet, unclad, designates the officiant, or the faithful. Sometimes the foot puts one in communication with the source of some religious energy, such as the hide of a victim in the case of an initiate.[212] The practice is the same as the one in the legend of Jason. It reappears elsewhere with other significations: at the moment when he is about to qualify himself by his initiatory exploit, Perseus receives some notable attributes from several divinities. Deserving of special mention are the sandals of Hermes. But we have a revealing variant, according to which the hero receives only *one* of the two sandals.[213] One cannot help but think also of that custom in military societies, where the same practice really seems to have a sense of consecration—in one instance perhaps in the context of what has been termed *devotio*.[214] Another form and another application of the same symbolism can be seen in an example of the legend of magicians, one of the products of archaic Greece: one found at the rim of Mt. Aetna's crater the sandals that Empedocles left behind before hurling himself into an apotheosis.[215]

Thus we have diverse projections of this thought at diverse levels of society and belief. But the thought is the same. In order to penetrate (*epibainein*) into a domain that is religiously qualified,[216] the spatial dimension (space of the sancutuary, mythical space) is essential. *Epibainein*, therefore, is to put oneself in contact with certain forces, notably those that emanate from the earth.[217] In the concentration of *heredium* that is in the tomb of a father, there is the basis for an *epibateusis* that puts one in immediate contact with the gods of the paternal lineage.[218]

The Proclamation of the Avenger

Obviously, the forces that are utilized in acts such as the one we have just illustrated do not play an arbitrary role in the prejuridical order; they carry an implicit appeal to society. He who performs the efficacious gestures is assisted by his own relatives, that is, by a group that represents the forerunners of witnesses in the *diamarturia*. The group can also consist of neighbors, like those who participate in the house search for a stolen object. Moreover, the appeal to society can be brought about by the very act that unleashes religious forces. A curse against an opponent is a similar act insofar as it is public.[219] Now, an entire series of examples in prelaw is in the realm of the curse, amid very diverse forms. First of all, some curses are direct antecedents of legal action.

The prosecution of homicide begins with a traditional ritual that is called the *prorrhēsis*: the accuser, who has the role of the avenger, pronounces an "interdiction" against the murderer. That is, he forbids the murderer from participating in religious acts and from appearing in sanctuaries or public places. Even in the classical period, although it was a purely private or even a one-sided act, the interdiction theoretically preserved all of its force. In procedure, however, the eventual destiny of interdiction has been quite characteristic. Law, which inherited it, gives it—on its own—the same import as a summons.[220] Law integrates interdiction, as it were, into the judiciary system; but it does it badly. One senses that interdiction, through its immediate and unconditional effect, is an aberrant element. Starting from the fifth century B.C., interdiction is practically replaced by a genuine complaint; it has to come into line with a secular procedure whereby it is sometimes suspended; it is intoned by city magistrates.[221] Interdiction continues to survive, but on another plane, through religious conservatism. At the start, interdiction was nevertheless essential: one has only to see the role it plays in the Law of Draco. At the moment when the sovereign control of tribunals is instituted, interdiction signifies respect for the vengeance submitted to them. The imperious quality to which interdiction lays claim is maintained, therefore, merely by hypothesis, and we must look at it in the context of its history.

One survival is noteworthy: interdiction continues to be uttered against the unknown. This is because it acts independently of the possibilities for human action. With regard to the presumed or designated murderer, interdiction is the equivalent of placing someone outside the law, that is, it is a *sacratio*. Pronounced by an individual, it has the effect of excommunication. On the other hand, it is a prelude to the vengeance that will be put into effect once interdiction acquires a religious efficacy. Between interdicton and the imprecations that the murder sets into action, there is a perceptible kinship: the purpose of the latter is to revive the powers of the dead;[222] the former is connected with these same powers in a rite whose primitive form can be discerned. The *prorrhēsis*, which from the time of Draco is intoned in the agora, was first declaimed on the tomb of the victim. Myth, which supplied well-known and powerful precedents for criminal law, preserved the relic of alleged trials for murder that had begun this way.[223] In fact, in its most ancient meaning, "interdiction" was a complex act. The oral ritual was not separated from a practice whose tradition could still be exhumed by religious casuistry in the fourth century B.C.,[224] and which consists of carrying a spear in the funeral procession, planting it on the tomb, and keeping a vigil over the tomb for three days. The dead man, who "fights with his own," and against whom the murderer protects himself by mutilations with a magical effect, thus finds himself substantially involved with vengeance through this ritual, just as he is involved with a hereditary transmission in the *embateusis*. And through the ritual, the avenger finds a force that assures the fulfillment of vengeance. But this is a force that deals at once with the present. The spear that one "carries against"[225] the enemy not only represents the material instrument of a compensatory murder but is also a religious object comparable to the javelin that the Roman *fetialis* throws into the enemy's territory at the start of a war.[226] The spear is also comparable to the distinctive attribute of Zeus Areios,[227] whose epithet is connected with the name of the famous tribunal for crimes of bloodshed,[228] and who is equally associated with the mythical ordeal at Olympia whereby Oinomaos, the bearer of the spear, perished by the spear of Pelops.[229]

This ensemble of a ritual, for which the *carmen* of the *prorrhēsis* is the oral expression, is not a signal for hostilities in the sense of a single signification; it is active in its own right and in a magicoreligious vein. As such, interdiction enters into the realm of law and imposes itself, but because its function is no longer the same, its original nature disappears.

The Siege of the Debtor

In areas other than homicide it is possible that imprecation gave legal action its first form; at least this is what some linguistic testimonia seem to indicate.[230] Unhappily, however, this is as far as we can go. What we have to consider is the existence of rituals that are also, in their peculiar way, antecedents to law, even if they are less directly related to the legal entreaty. Moreover, it seems that rituals furnish us with an important counterpart for the knowledge of the origins of law itself.

The prejuridical "executions" of sentence (of which we have just seen some particularly clear illustrations) do not constitute a self-sufficient system. There are individual responses that the collective sentiment can authorize because it is in sympathy with them. But these responses cannot benefit from the social power that a family group, for example, puts to use in the case of blood vengeance.[231] Sooner or later certain "executions" will be sanctioned within law (that is, in criminal law, family law, and even contractual law, to the extent that each does not have at its disposal the customary constraints). But let us note as well that they first used magicoreligious procedures, whose efficacy preceded that of law and which were sometimes disallowed (in a contradictory yet instructive fashion) by law, but at other times were essential to the establishment of law.

A well-known practice can supply us with a theme, traces of which are found in Greece. It was absorbed into several Indo-European legal systems, where it testifies, perhaps, to a common tradition. In order to show how it is situated within a social formation, it will be convenient to refer to one of these laws. In ancient Ireland, every legal action begins with a seizure, a fact that should not distract us. But the seizure can be carried out only on a social equal or an inferior. Confronted by a social superior, he whom we would call the creditor is nevertheless not helpless; he will go to the door of his debtor and fast until he has obtained satisfaction. The same institution exists in India, where the interplay is a bit different but still comparable, and where it is designated by the name (which has become classic) *dhārṇa*. When law makes use of this system, it is under the form of a quasi-procedure, one that can have legal effects; and it is in this way that we know it. Still, one may presume from the start that this institution had a past of another sort.

In Greece we do not know of this practice in this state, nor do we have direct evidence for it in a more ancient one. As often happens in the study of ancient Greece, we have mythical derivations, as Glotz was perspicacious enough to note.[232] The particular myth is not "in the air" but is an explanatory story (*aition*) of a Delphic ceremony whose great antiquity is certain.[233] At a time when famine raged, the king's subjects crowded around his door begging a pittance; he, in turn, handed out some food, at least to the most noble, since he did not have enough for everyone; a small orphan girl, Kharila, appears; the king dismisses her, slapping her with his slippers. Kharila goes off and hangs herself; the famine is now twice as bad, and a plague sets in as well; Kharila must be satisfied, and she comes to receive honor in a ritual in which her story is re-created. Until Glotz's observation, the analogy was misunderstood, since it is presented to us in a ritual and in a mixture of ideas and images of great richness that naturally goes beyond the status of a relic of prelaw.[234] On the other hand, the mythical/ritualistic datum has the advantage of suggesting diverse associations and implications that the "legalized" ritual of the *dhārṇa* would not suggest. For in the former an essential element is revealed: a person fasting can doubtless die from hunger at the door of his debtor. Law codes anticipate this situation and view it as all the worse for the debtor. But for the law codes it is a matter of juridical constraint. In the legend of Kharila, however, one that is set "at the door" of the king, the refusal of an obligatory yet gratuitous gift of nourishment provokes a widespread disaster through the actions of the ghost of the dead. The efficacy of the primitive practice resides in the threat of posthumous vengeance. In this case the threat is made real. Death by starvation might suit this purpose— that is, a mode of suicide often mentioned among Greeks. This legend adopts another mode of death, which in story and practice is a feminine one.

Now, this threat of suicide is implied by the very ritual of supplication in general; and the Suppliant Women give expression to it in Aeschylus' play, where it is the tragic element *par excellence*.[235] Supplication has a very extensive role in prelaw, where it serves diverse purposes: integration into the group, infeudation, pacification of vengeance. It goes without saying that it also has a purely religious role. What we want to emphasize here is the symbolism by which supplication is related to the siege of the debtor, an act that has supplied to archaic law one of its most expressive forms, and through which supplication is linked to usages that are deeply rooted in social life. Not only does supplication employ materials with religious power such as an olive branch entwined with a fillet of wool, but it is performed in definite locales and demands a particular posture: namely being seated,[236] a posture that has great symbolic value[237] because it represents, in turn, the state of mourning, the dead in the underworld, the condemned person, and the candidate for initiation or purification.[238] The drama of supplication has links with an entire series of legendary and cult examples[239] in which a magical power of kingship is evoked, a series to which the story of Kharila belongs. In practice one can see supplication functioning with regard to collectivity, and it is characteristic that even the city leaves a place for it:[240] the Athenians preserve a permanent image of Supplication at the altar of Pity by the gates of the old city,[241] where the sons of Herakles—or so the legend goes— begged for and obtained the protection of the city against their persecutor. It is striking that the institution of a ritual at the Pyanepsia, one where we see the *eiresiōnē*, is sometimes linked to this episode.[242] The *eiresiōnē* is itself an olive branch; but it is one with which a person gathers and makes a kind of *eranos*. This collection, which itself has the quality of a blessing (if one responds to it, obviously), is made at the door of each home.[243] In sum, we ascertain a lively analogy within a system of widely varied practices where there is always the question of obtaining assistance or a pledge by means of the efficacious symbol that works as a religious constraint.

Malediction can be conditional or implicit, but it can also be immediate and effective. One goes to the door of the person against whom one has a grievance in order to utter a protest that has magic force. In tragedy, the lyric plaint that the hero or heroine makes at the door of the paternal palace (from which he/she has been driven) has the quality of a *carmen*.[244] It is noteworthy that in the age of law, certain practices, which are the antecedents or descendants of procedures, but whose prehistoric significance remains perceptible, are accomplished at the door of an adversary. It is at Rome that we have the best attestation of these practices: the *vagulatio* is defined by Festus as *quaestio cum convicio*; and the Twelve Tables allow recourse to it for three days with regard to the witness who has failed in his duty.[245] The origin of the word *vagulatio* indicates a ritual complaint;[246] and it is practiced at doors. The law, which elsewhere prohibits the use of the *carmen*,[247] here makes a quasi-procedure out of one of its derivatives. Apropos of the witness also, Greece preserves a trace of ancient constraints,[248] but we shall see them function on another level.

The Malediction of Althaia

There is a word, obviously very old, that remains specialized in a sentimental usage having to do with blood vengeance: *episkēptein*. Properly, it is applied to the injunctions of a dying man who names his assailant to his family and urges them to pursue him.[249] If this ultimate recommendation has a raison d'être in the classical period only in situations where the responsibility that it makes it possible to fix is otherwise uncertain, still it is evident that a much wider meaning persists here, one that is attuned to the notion of the power of the dead in matters of private vengeance.[250] This notion is only a survival, but it is a survival that remains active in the domain of morality and religion. Moreover, *episkēptein* can be used as the expression of final wishes in the disposal of a patrimony.[251] But it does not appear to be a term in law: the accomplishment of final wishes is assured there by a special form called the "testament," *diathēkē*. The latter is distinct from the *episkēpsis*, which has no more juridical status than did the *fidei-commissum* in early Roman law.

Nevertheless, it is instructive that *episkēpsis* has supplied a name for some specific procedures that have a link with its religious use. From the start, *episkēptesthai* was part of the legal terminology in matters of homicide: it designated the action of murder itself.[252] In the family *episkēpsis*, which requires, in the name of the dead person, the punishment of the murderer, the connection with the original meaning is apparent. It is less so in other procedures, but one can still find it. The verb *episkēptesthai* technically designates the summoning of a witness, one that must occur at the precise moment of the trial and one that is the required preliminary in actions concerning false testimony.[253] Such actions, fairly recent as we know them in Athenian law, seem to have been used especially in a more ancient phase against witnesses involved in a capital process leading to execution.[254] At the outset, therefore, it will be the avengers of a juridical murder who, in an urgent entreaty, appeal to the city in the name of the victim. The same measure is put into effect, though only for monetary reimbursement and theoretically as a last resort, when the debt owed to a widow as her dowry is produced as evidence to prevent the threatened confiscation of a patrimony. And from this another legal term[255] is derived, *enepiskēmma*.

Once again, we have technical meanings as well as transformations. But there is also a kind of underlying continuity. Moreover, semantic deviations are always revealing. But the reflection to which the fundamental notion beneath *episkēpsis* gives rise has an equal bearing on very ancient realities, ones that come to deal with law in another fashion.

※

The notion of the rights of the dead is variable and complex. In a prejuridical state, we see it at once as imperious and very limited. A testament of vengeance is not at issue. Likewise, the dead man takes his own belongings to his tomb, or the belongings are cremated along with him (as another way of satisfying him). These belongings, which are, in fact, appurtenances (his arms and the like), constitute the "portion of the dead" as it is described in a Germanic custom. They are also subject to a free disposition that can be devised *in extremis*[256] and can assume the form of a "donation for the dead."[257] But this share is very strict. What we would call the "ability to make a will" is the right that sanctions it in a novel social situation. Inversely, the "share of the dead" disappears with the coming of the city (and law prohibits the equally prehistoric practice of the sacrifice of the dead). But the notion of the testament itself is flexible. In Greece, as in Rome, the testament is at first an operation between the living; in Greece alone it is expressly linked to its social function by means of the form of its adoption. In the course of the classical period, we see the testament evolve. Together with a greater freedom for maneuvering, there also appears a novel idea, one to which the historian may not pay enough attention: it is the idea of an operation that by hypothesis can have an effect only after death, an idea which attributes a power that is peculiar to the person who no longer exists. The use of "testament tablets" —and these have been found in Greece— is imposed on Athenian jurisprudence in the middle of the fifth century B.C. This evolution is remarkable in that it happens spontaneously, without the law having anything to do with it.

What the law consecrates from that moment on as a strictly juridical/institutional power of society is a power that might have functioned before the testament, but only in an oblique way and by means of another order of power. The efficacy of the imprecation—to which recourse is had even very late in order to guarantee the protection of a tomb—was also at play before the testament, properly speaking, so as to ensure the execution of final wishes. What assures us that this efficacy functioned beforehand is the fact that it functioned even later as a supplementary guarantee, one suggested by tradition and one that was difficult to do without. In the fourth century B.C., an Athenian bourgeois reenforces, by means of maledictions that are specified as being "written by his own hand," the articles of a testament whose execution will be pursued independently in court.[258]

🌿

It is a particular type of *episkēpsis* that we see operating in the above case. We find an analogy to it in a usage that can be described as related: the curse of a parent.

Like supplication, which has affinities with it, the curse of a parent is uttered in order that it act directly on certain elements of society with which it is assured cooperation, even if the society in question consists only of blood relatives. Moreover, in the very sphere of familial relationships, the curse can be addressed—with a view toward satisfaction and sanction—to the entire group. We have, therefore, the antecedent to a characteristic part of the law of the city, one that had to assure the respect of familial morality through special procedures when internal discipline was no longer adequate. This is the case when there is a lack of avengers for murder, and especially when there is "poor treatment" with respect to a given category of relations. Such a situation reminds us of the "royal laws" of Rome, among which many—and surely the one about to be cited —are the authentic survivals of an ancient custom. By virtue of a *ploratio* of the father or mother who was struck by the son, the latter's life was involuntarily dedicated to the "gods of the parents" through a vow that went under the heading of *sacer*.[259] This is a disposition that is not at all juridical, since even the social sanction with which it is paired is of an expressly religious nature. But what is the *ploratio*?

A Greek legend—the legend of Meleager—could at least help us to understand it, if not to be thoroughly familiar with it.[260] The hero perishes suddenly following a curse by his mother Althaia; the maternal Erinys is the most redoubtable of all, as we see in this legend. It is quite curious that Homer has not kept the most popular version, perhaps on the grounds that it was of "magical inspiration." According to this version, a firebrand, in which dwelt the "external soul" of Meleager, is thrown into the fire by his mother.[261] Homer's version, however, is no less archaic, and the occasion lends itself to the archaic effect. The curse is justified by an interesting crime: Meleager had killed the brothers of Althaia. Thus, Homer's version preserves the memory not only of the special powers of a mother's curse but also of a special solidarity between brother and sister, between the maternal uncle and the uterine nephew. Althaia, therefore curses her son, kneeling—or rather curled up—on the earth (this is her precise posture), and striking the soil with great blows she arouses the avenging Erinys.[262] Now, a similar practice is attested in a persistent but archaic rite. At the time of the mysteries that are celebrated in an Arcadian village, the priest, who wears the mask of the goddess, "hits with a stick the underworld gods."[263] This can only be explained as an evocation that works in about the same way and perhaps employs the same posture as does the Althaia story.[264]

Whenever possible, it is a good thing to restore to words their full significance. In regard to "curse," the legend indicates not only the *carmen* but another rite as well, one defined as a rite by its religious affinities—a rite that may explain the etymology of *episkēptein* (which started us off).[265] Moreover, the material is flexible; other forms lend themselves to imprecation. There is at least one other that we should look at: a brother, Thyestes, curses the progeny of his brother Atreus while kicking over a table.[266] It is notable that the same gesture occurs not only in another area of legend[267] but in a Delphic cult as well.[268] In any case, it is a magicoreligious efficacy that is at the service of a parent's curse, one that is more than a verbal outlet for anger. Even if we hardly see it any more in Greek legend (which is no longer just legend), we at least see it in the Roman practice from which the *lex regia* is derived, for similar practices can result in the "consecration" of the guilty one, which is tantamount to making him an outlaw. In other words, the accomplishment of a *ploratio* —that is, a magical act—can have an effect analogous to the one that will be produced by prosecution before law.[269]

Transitions

These primitive affirmations of the rule of law that we recognize at various levels have this in common: they lay claim to an unimpeded sovereignty. In general, of course, they are directed at a society that more or less accepts them, and outside of which they would not have the prejuridical quality we have observed in them. But in principle they depend only on their own efficacy, because the forces that they put into play are superhuman. In these primitive forms, there exists a mode of thought of a different sort than the one that is presupposed and supported by a social organization of judgment. However, we have seen that the latter itself depended on them at first. The complement to our inquiry would thus be to examine how—by what procedures, by what evolution—law integrated, at the dawn of history, this primitive mode of thought, which continues to affirm the absolute quality of its prerogatives, but which is created in a framework where it is placed under control. Hence, there is this particular but major consequence: the magical notion of "proof" will yield to another conception of truth. However, this can be seen only in legend and in poetry.

A Homeric Dispute

During the games in honor of Patroklos,[270] a contest develops between Antilochus, who just took second prize in the chariot race, and Menelaus, who claims that his rival came in second only by cheating. The gesture of Antilochus is the act of taking possession, which is valid in it-self,[271] but which the situation makes comparable to the ritual of making a claim *manu tenens*. The protestation of Menelaus is a solemn one, of a type almost juridical.[272] But at the moment he is about to utter it in the as-sembly, the herald places in his hand a scepter and commands the Argives to be silent. It is a minor and isolated detail, but it is suggestive.

The symbolic meanings of the staff are many: we all know that at Rome the *festuca* is used in the most ancient procedure of making a claim, where the sense of a property affirmation is attributed to it; and there is something similar in Germanic law. We also remember, however, that Roman law gives the staff different, even contradictory, significations, since the same *vindicta* imposed on a slave marks a claim on the part of a plaintiff who claims the slave and a renunciation from the master who frees him—all this without mentioning that the freeing is then consum-mated by the imposition of the lictor's rod.[273] In order to function, this formalism of archaic law needs to be observed, and its qualities defined; thus, the imperious symbol of a *dominium*, which occurs in filing a claim and in which the Romans saw the sign of conquest in war,[274] would by it-self imply a kind of concession by society whereby the latter accepts its temporary nature.

Greece has more to offer. The testimony of Homer is all the more precious because the formalism of Hellenic procedure appears only here and there, in vestigial form. But there are, also in Homer, parallels that clarify the significance of the vestigial formalism. In the scene from the *Shield of Achilles* the judges sit with scepters in hand, that is, with the scepters that belong to the heralds.[275] At the moment that Telemachus is about to speak in the assembly at Ithaca, he also receives a scepter from the hand of a herald.[276] For his speech in the assembly of the Achaeans at the start of the *Iliad*, Achilles holds a scepter. This same kind of scepter serves for the improvised and very curious ritual of the solemn oath;[277] and it is precisely the same sort of scepter that is carried by the judges who "uphold the law in the name of Zeus." The latter expression is the one that is regularly applied to the king as he carries the scepter. This object, which is thought always to be the same, circulates from hand to hand; in truth, it appears in this whole series of examples as something that sym-bolizes the impersonal sovereignty of the group rather than the expression of royal virtue. Moreover, the scepter is proper for judges; likewise for the orator, whose social function will remain consecrated, even in the Athe-nian people's assembly, by the religious sign of the crown; and also for Menelaus, who seeks in the assembly personal goals involving the demand for satisfaction. The character of the herald, a necessary intermediary, af-firms the nature of those scenes in which he figures not as the king's vassal —which he so often is—but as a minister of "collectivity."[278]

Thus, in this fleetingly perceived form of archaic judgment, social control is rendered with unusual clarity. The same object that in a parallel law manifests a claim to sovereignty is the sign of authority formally delegated. The claimant appears with a symbol of religious power that commands respect, but the force that commands is borrowed: carrying the staff signifies the plaintiff's right by an act of social deputization.

꽃

But the episode has two sides. Immediately afterward, the contest takes on another aspect, and the Homeric scene announces a moment of transition. We see how, at the threshold of the rule of law, a mode of thought persists which predated it and which will inspire a prejuridical type of regulation.

Menelaus first solicits the judgment of the assembly, and then he changes his mind. He himself indicates the means for settling the dispute: he proposes, or rather he imposes, on his competitor the probative oath. He has the right to set the terms of the oath; they are borrowed from *themis*, a rule that—given the modalities that characterize the ritual it dictates—is precisely the one to be observed in similar cases, and also the one that regulates the practice of games. Standing in front of his horses and chariot, with one hand bearing the whip and the other touching the horses, Antilochus must swear by Poseidon that he did not obstruct Menelaus' chariot. This oath is quite another thing from taking a divinity as witness. It obligates, in the sense that we have seen for the most ancient oath, the person who takes the oath. It obligates by means of the chariot, on which everything is centered—the chariot that is the precious object for the epic warrior, that retains the mythical memory of proofs of kingship, and that had once given rise to a magical strain that lent the purgative oath part of its primitive significance.[279] The chariot is an attribute of nobility and the symbol of its owner's strength; it can be abandoned to religious powers by virtue of the gesture that consecrated it.[280] In an assembly such as the one evoked for the games, in the "reunion" that gave its name to the contest (*agōn*) before giving it to the trial, an oath such as this one, authorized by tradition, has absolute value.

What is the import of all this? If Antilochus refuses to take the oath, then Menelaus wins; if he takes the oath, then the chariot stays in his possession.[281] This does not appear to be the equivalent of proof from which law could emanate. Following an archaic concept, what we would call the "administration of proof" is addressed not to a judge who has to essay it, but to an adversary whom the proof is designed to "conquer."[282] Negatively, what defines prelaw in particular is that there is no possibility of an objective truth that would support a verdict. In this case, there is no place for a verdict, and the adversaries simply decide between themselves. Their testimony constitutes the verdict.

Proof can be various. In prelaw, one can say that it is always of the "ordeal" variety—that is, of a sort that allows settlement or ratification by sending one or both parties to another world, where their destinies are played out. In Greece in general there is abundant evidence of this practice in mythology. We do *not* see it as often as Glotz would have liked for the purpose of resolving conflict before the rule of law. But the mode of thought that governs it is the same one that requires the oath as a self-styled means of proof,[283] and it is the same one that survives later, outside the law, in the ritual oaths that are, in fact, trials by ordeal.[284] In law itself, which here bespeaks a remarkable accommodation, tradition will maintain, more or less on a large scale, the use of the oath as decisive proof[285]— an equivocal notion, since on the one hand it implies the idea of a truth that preconditions judgment, while on the other hand the authority and efficacy of the oath come from what it was originally.

What it was is again something we see in the episode dealing with the race. In this scene, there is a method for extrajudiciary regulation within the framework of an otherwise defined custom, and only between the parties: it resolves the dispute not by making possible the discovery of a fact but through religious means. It would be anachronistic to say that this method of resolution takes the place of judgment; in its original nature, resolution excludes the notion of judgment.[286] But a line of development will be indicated.

The Oath of Rhadamanthys

Concerning the question of who, in the Homeric world, exercises the judiciary function, Homer himself is at first rather disconcerting. The king is often exalted as a judge; in fact, the judgments that we see rendered are rendered by others, and we do not even see the king presiding over them.[287] But what is the substance of the notion of king-judge? An expressive translation of this is supplied by a consecrated formula: the king holds the scepter and the *themistes*. On occasion, these *themistes* can be something like the decrees of justice, but they are really quite another thing: the *themis* is on the order of the oracle; indeed, it is the oracle itself.[288] The Homeric poems perpetuate the concept of a divine quality attached to the person of the king and residing in a symbol such as the scepter. (This concept, it would seem, is almost a conscious throwback.) The "sentences" that such a personage renders on questions about which he is "interrogated"[289] have the character of revelations. How these sentences are obtained we know only indirectly: from relics, allusions, symbols that are made specific (but that are all too few in number), and from the understanding we can glean concerning the consultation of a divinity or divining procedures.[290] It is a kind of memory that persists in Homer, but in reality, as it is presented by poets, the practice of judgment is well established. There is no longer a common denominator between the ancient state of affairs and the new one: the same words have different meanings, as though some kind of gap existed.

In this area, historical inquiry is quite meager; and it is meager just at the point that might be called critical. How does one imagine the establishment of justice in the sense in which the historical Greeks recognized it? With the Homeric data in mind, one could point to at least a condition for change: the separation of *ius* from *iudicium* (which in Rome is something as ancient as history, but not much older) must have taken place in Greece at an early period in certain areas of law. And in Greece, as well as in Rome, this separation must have been of major importance for the institution of a juridical type of procedure.

We have a lively testimonium from a poet: Aeschylus' *Eumenides* celebrates the founding of the Areopagus, a tribunal for murder cases. Athenians found one of their most authentic claims to glory in this legendary event.

Orestes, the murderer of his own mother, is pursued by the avenging Furies. He seeks refuge at Athens, where his enemies rejoin him. The goddess of the region, Athena, intervenes and interrogates the accusing party.[291] The import of their response is that there cannot be a trial, since Orestes is not qualified to receive an oath and is in no condition to take one. The goddess replies that it is not oaths that will decide the matter. As for Orestes, he invokes the patronage of Apollo, who ordered the crime originally. What can Athena do? She muses: "If the legal case is found to be too serious for mortals to decide, then it is no more permitted for me to pronounce sentence." Then she selects judges, who will have to make use of witnesses and clues.

In this scene there is an extraordinary condensation of juridical thought and history. First of all, what is striking in Athena's discourse is a contradiction too conspicuous to leave unresolved: mortals are not able to render a decision, and thus Athena establishes a tribunal that will judge. But she had added that even she, a goddess, could not render a decision. The gods cannot—they can no longer—"judge." Historically, the king also stopped issuing decrees: the word *dikazein*, "to judge," kept designating the high magistrate (who in Athens was still called the king). That is to say, in matters of murder, this high magistrate organized the trial and presided over the tribunal. (This use of *dikazein*, frequent in this domain and isolated elsewhere, is a survival.) But this magistrate no longer "decides." Those who do decide are members of the tribunal that the goddess institutes in the legend. It is at this very moment that modes of proof in the modern sense, however archaic the forms for their use, make their appearance. What preceded them in the ancient system—when the king judged, together with the divinity—were procedures that depended on ordeal. More precisely, or at least in a relatively recent phase, which history almost touches, what preceded them was the oath, whose true nature as a probatory means we have already seen. The memory and, in archaic cities, even the attestation of a custom that accorded decisive force to the oath of the accusing party, is presented under a special form—namely, the *coniuratio*.[292] Several members of the victim's family swear together, the custom being limited to fixing a minimum number of coswearers.[293] This procedure, well known in ancient legal systems, indicates a kind of turning point, since it reveals, rather naïvely, the need for proof, but it also partakes of a primitive concept of justice: neither "witnesses to the truth" nor "witnesses to credibility," the coswearers, by their collective willingness, are not affirming a fact but are rendering a decision concerning the "law." That is, if they are numerous enough, they assure the "victory" of the familial party they represent. Conjuration has left behind its traces in the Law of Draco, which bans precisely its spirit.[294]

Perhaps there is also a relic of this in the *Eumenides*,[295] where the worth of an oath as such is at issue.[296] Athena denies its value: she announces that the oath will no longer make a case succeed if it does not have justice on its side;[297] and justice is what the tribunal renders. Two mentalities confront each other in a short dialogue, and a revolution takes place. Meanwhile, Aeschylus knew quite well that the pre-Areopagus procedure demanded an oath by the parties, an oath (under the name *diōmosia*) that was of special gravity and involved a particular ritual. But this is an oath that no longer decides: it merely introduces a case.

Now, in all the cases heard at Athens, an oath of this sort is a necessary preliminary. Outside of the trial for homicide, the oath takes on more and more the aspect of an inconsequential formality, but tradition preserves it. In effect, the oath survives because only its function is retained. The oath also seems enormously important in terms of logic and religious reflection. Though the average user was reconciled to this contradiction (as is always the case in similar situations), Plato was offended; he did not want this oath for the city in his *Laws*.[298] Indeed, one could not understand it if it were not a legacy or testimony of evolution. It is an oath that is formally distinguished from that which conserves—by exception, or in a custom of arbitration where an archaic condition is prolonged—a decisive quality. Curiously, Plato calls it the oath of Rhadamanthys, which in tradition was instituted by Minos' brother in order precisely to "decide trials."[299] The oath of Rhadamanthys no longer works.

It seems that there was something similar in Rome at that beginning of civil procedure with which we are familiar. We will perhaps never know what was the most ancient *sacramentum*. This "consecrated object," or rather, this "consecrating object," might have been quite different from the oath, but it also might have had some affinities with it, as is shown by the ultimate use of the word *sacramentum*. Anyhow, it must have supplied the means for deciding a case, given our understanding of a "sacral law." (We agree that before it was the deposit of an amount of money, the *sacramentum* could have entailed the remittance of sacrificial animals.) As it passes into civil law, the *sacramentum* changes in function and significance. In the ancient state, the proof to which it gave rise could be offered immediately and in the presence of the king-priest.[300] In the new situation, it is a preliminary element that the trial process confines to a phase *in iure*, which is necessarily followed by a phase *in iudicio*.

What, in prelaw, was the equivalent of judgment was concentrated in the "proof," whose religious quality rendered decisions immediately. This decisive quality no longer existed; but the act that made it a reality became the symbol of the beginning of a temporal series, a seemingly new idea revealed most clearly by the procedure followed in trials for murder.[301] A process is a form that exists in and over time, with a beginning and an end.[302] It is a form that, once devised, imposes itself on minds as an independent reality. It is a creation and it is fundamental. Still, one can see the past behind it.

III
EX IURE QUIRITIUM

Given the beginnings of the organization of procedure in ancient societies, we stand at the threshold of law. And insofar as exigencies and situations ought to be justifiable before law, it is indeed law as such that offers itself for analysis. If there is a change, then we must perceive its direction. Our immediate objective is to locate certain forms of prelaw and to define the thought behind them; but in the end the question of relationships arises.

We can gather a preliminary view at once: symbols of prelaw are essentially efficacious. The hand that gives or receives; the staff that asserts power, or relinquishes or confers it; the ritual of the *tomia*; the blood of the victim or the wine of libation—all of these operate immediately and by virtue of their respective *dunameis*. The forms of law are also efficacious, but their inherent quality functions differently. In law, a symbolism that is recognized and accepted as such is reflective. The juridical mind keeps its distance: instead of the efficacious prejuridical form there is a form that is effective with regard to society, one that affirms an intentional and conventional character. To use the Greek word, the characteristic of *nomos* is affirmed. (Note that the classical Greek antithesis of convention and nature can be linked with the establishment of law.)

We have already seen this characteristic in the formalism of certain archaic laws. In a sense, formalism is a sequel, a prolongation: the symbols that it uses contain those of prelaw, or they are of the same type; but their significance is multiple and is above all the object of a kind of decree or an implicit delegation on the part of society. Even in their imaginative nature these symbols change conditions: in the language of law—in all language—their very expressiveness is subject to a more or less agreed upon convention. If the mentality of the efficacious rite is at the root of formalism, then the formalism itself appears to be a stylization of rite.[303] But in view of the conditions in which the experience presents itself, we will not dwell on this. If ancient Roman law is a type of formalist law, antecedents of which elude us,[304] then, inversely, Greece (although it supplies us with some information on prehistory) supplies us with very little on the formalism that it seems to have gone beyond rather quickly. On the other hand, other data are offered to us by both civilizations.

First, this observation: a certain continuity exists between prelaw and law.

In addition to being special, the Roman case is all the more suggestive on this point. We know that Latin is one of the Indo-European languages that has preserved—with a unique faithfulness that is attributable to a tradition of "colleges"—its early vocabulary pertaining above all to religion, but also to law, insofar as law is associated with religion. Semantic evidence occasionally permits us to recognize or to catch a glimpse of a mixed domain, beginning with the word *ius* itself. But we should not be satisfied simply with this very general truth. It merely helps us to understand that Romans, by reason of their conservatism or the mental discipline that characterized them, evidence—within a series of examples pertaining to a specialized law—both the persistence of words and the transformation of mentalities.

Auctoritas is a juridical word. It is applied to the notions of legal technique: for example, to the legal incapacity of children, or to the guarantee of the seller. Now, it is already noteworthy that these circumscribed usages do not exhaust the content of *auctoritas* and that the word preserves, even in the middle of the historical period, a certain aura of a sentimental and ill-defined mentality.[305] But on the other hand it is clear that the word has its role in religion and that its usage there preceded and determined the legal one. A long-lived tradition links up *auctoritas* and *augurium* (they are, in effect, related):[306] *auctoritas* is the force that confers on a being or an act the consecration that comes from the flights of birds. In the rites of the Fetiales, the *verbenarius*, the bearer of a bunch of sacred herbs with which he has touched the *pater patratus*, plays the role of *auctor*[307] opposite the *pater patratus*. That is to say, the *verbenarius* is the one who protects and sanctifies by virtue of the *sagmina*. *Auctoritas* also denotes the necessary confirmation of an act or situation that it, properly speaking, "authorizes." It concerns the possession or the exercise of a power in law.[308]

An analogous observation can be made concerning the word *addicere*, which was consecrated for a particular type of jurisdiction held by the praetor. It ended up being applied to a transfer or to an attribution stemming from a magistrate; but originally it signified a ratification pronounced by the magistrate for the benefit of a party. *Addicere* is also a term used to designate the favorable signs that are given by birds, especially the indispensable confirmation that such signs supply for the investiture of a military leader.[309] The evidence of words like *damnare*,[310] *obligare*,[311] and perhaps *nexum* could be equally instructive. But we have room to dwell a bit longer on the word that seems on the surface to be the most neutral, a word that bears on what we have said about the beginnings of procedure: *agere*.

It signifies action in justice, especially in the initial phase of law—that is, the phase of "actions concerning law," the oldest of which are marked with a ritualistic character. But the chronological priority of the religious sense is directly attested: certain words from the same family (*ago*, *agonium*, *agonales*) are entirely archaic and deal with archaic forms of religion. There must have been, therefore, a kind of transposition in law. How are we to understand this? The sense of *agere* is of duration in time;[312] it is applied to a process that takes place over time and that consists primarily of the fulfillment of the rituals of sacrifice or, more generally, of a religious act.[313] In the same way, judiciary action implies a temporal dimension in which a series of expected events is set in motion by the filing of a suit. In both cases, a socially valid "form" is inscribed between two terms: the value attached to these acts is different, but the use of the same word no less implies the function of relationship.

Greece does not offer similar examples of continuity. And if the Roman experience is convincing on this point, it is so precisely because of its ethnic peculiarity. But the evidence from Latin leads us to consider a certain number of facts, both institutional and linguistic, that are common to both cultures, and that illustrate the general fact of a passing from prelaw to law. (The same facts can be gleaned from this very passage.) Under the same name and with homologous functions, institutions that are specifically juridical prolong ancient forms that had another content and another mode of dynamism: in short, these forms are identical or are related to the forms that we have seen as examples of prelaw.

It should not be surprising that this observation can be made about acts that, in regard to the law of the person, have as their theoretical purpose a change of status. Adoption and liberation are known to us directly only as juridical acts and at a point where they affect the city. But we do know something about them from an earlier time, when they functioned in a family-oriented society. And we know that this function was exercised by completely other means. Neither Greece[314] nor Rome[315] forgot adoption *in cubiculo*, simulated childbirth by the mother in a family. But this formalism practically disappeared, for it presupposes a concept of affiliation other than the one of the historical epoch, and it actuates, through an efficacious imitation, a physical birth. Similarly, we can at least guess at traditional rites that took place at the time of liberation: among the Romans, the master gives a slap to his slave and makes him twirl around.[316] Among the Greeks, there must have been some rituals that were connected with the hearth; and the drinking of a "water of freedom" that came from a special spring is often attested.[317] In all of this, however, nothing has juridical effect: enfranchisement has other formal preconditions or it has none at all. Still, we can see the legacy of a past that did not include the juridical form, but included instead effective symbols whose efficacy is of the sort we have discussed. The efficacy of absorbed liquid is quite telling, as is that of the hand, which must have left its trace in the very word *manumissio*.[318] It is the same name in fact, and in a sense it is the same act, but the mechanism is entirely different.

A correlative datum is supplied to us by the word *sponsio*. In Roman law it is the name of an otherwise very simple, formal contract, but it is one that requires the intonement of the words *spondesne? spondeo*. As their etymology tells us, the terms are clearly applied to libations. We know, therefore, in what aggregate of practices and in what circle of notions *sponsio* is originally found. What of the common supposition that *sponsio* is linked to the primitive oath? We have seen that this primitive oath is quite different from a more or less solemn verbal engagement. The old meaning is lost, and the change is radical; the original meaning of the word and its use in the historical period have nothing in common. But the word is the same. By means of a transition that we can no longer retrace, an operation of law was substituted for an operation of prelaw. The Greek *enguē* presents a parallel case, but a word of caution is due: the symbolic act that *enguē* must first have signified is of a different sort.[319] As we have noted, the *enguē* deals with an act like the slap. This primitive meaning was in turn forgotten, and it is the etymology alone that informs us. In an intermediate state, we see that the *enguē* evolved into a verbal contract.[320] Finally, following an evolution that is indicated for the Romans, and a change that is achieved early on by the Greeks, the *enguē* becomes a contract without form in the classical era. The comparison is all the more convincing because the similarity between Greek and Roman law does not stop here. We shall see that according to the strict use of the terms the areas of application for the *enguē* and the *sponsio* are the same.

We are beginning to see a line of development that takes us to the point where formalism is attenuated or disappears altogether. There is a decisive turning point in the use of words when one goes from the oath-libation to obligation *verbis*, and, in a general way, from a religiously efficacious act to one that is juridically valid. The latter, in its own way, has a form of its own; it is a form that is as good as any. How does it work?

※

Through the data of archaic law it is possible to recognize this new action. Indeed, it is hard to miss it.

The new given is the affirmation of the juridical act as such. What is a juridical act, and how does it become effective? The Roman experience must be examined first, since the characteristics we are looking for are particularly in evidence there. For an entire group of the most ancient examples of law, scholars have underlined an essential element, "ratification by the social group."[321] Whether manifested by a vote, by an agreement of *comitia*, by the concurrence of a magistrate, or by the attendance of witnesses of a fixed number and quality, the ratification corresponds to a kind of participation by society, one that might be said to establish the social significance of the act. This is a major bit of information.

But here is another that is puzzling. When we come to its provisions, we have to admit that it does not fit in our category, since it does not require the real presence of society. It is not enough to recall that the *sponsio* comes from the oath, for it is no longer an oath and it no longer works through the libation, whose name it took on. The true response consists in invoking another element that this author has highlighted within juridical acts of the most ancient sort: the efficacy of the formal declaration. But we are just deferring the question, Where does this efficacy come from? We all know that it is derived from prelaw, as is the efficacy of formalism in general. The power of words is fundamentally magicoreligious, as we recalled in passing when considering certain forms of oath that are related to the oracular affirmation.[322] But the juridical quality of the oath is another matter: when the law says of one who makes a contract or a will *uti lingua nuncupassit*, it keeps the memory—but only the memory—of a word that creates an act.[323] Law operates as a secularization of the spoken word (the same thing that philosophy had to accomplish at another level). What must be understood is how form, imposed on a "declaration of the will," can represent in its own way and by itself alone "control over a collectivity."[324] Therein lies the problem.

Let us pass on to Greece. Greece offers us more restricted documentation but comparable data. A certain social involvement appears to be the basis of validation for a series of acts.[325] But that element, too, does not furnish a complete explanation. The "declaration of will" can function both in its own way and occasionally by itself alone. There is even reason to suppose that this declaration took on forms that were analogous to those of Roman law. The formalism of procedure, so marked in the Gortynian Code concerning other points, had to be imposed, within the same code, on the formation of contracts whose designations—clearly concrete in their etymologies—leave us otherwise in the dark.[326] In any case, there are at least two positive facts to add to the dossier. The first, a general one, is the intent that is affirmed in the use of words: a kind of *homologia* or "oral convention" (which would supply an entirely appropriate translation for *stipulatio* during the Roman period). In such a *homologia*, the character of a personal promise, *expressis verbis*, is stressed with a view not to proof but to validity.[327] The second fact, more isolated, is decisive in my view. In the romanticized history of the marriage of Megacles, Herodotus talks explicitly about the exchange of *certa verba*, an almost exact equivalent of the Roman *sponsio*, through which—according to the historian—the contract is rendered positively accepted and has thenceforth its full effect (*ekekurōto*). The father-in-law intones "*enguō*," and the son-in-law replies "*enguōmai*." Both grammatical voices of the verb are in force and survive in everyday parlance. In sum, there is the same desire, the same insistence, in the archaic law of Greece as there is in ancient Roman law. And in this particular case there is even the same juridical creation. There are reasons for this convergence.

The group of words to which *spondeo* belongs had an ancient usage that was perpetuated into the classical period, but that then lost its importance: betrothal contracts. And yet the same group of words has supplied the vocabulary for the routine of bail: the *sponsor* is the guarantor, and the term *sponsio* is applied mostly to the obligation *verbis* and the bail.[328] These are precisely the two applications of *enguē*: it is the constitutive act in marriage (and we have reason to believe that the *enguē* was the ancient betrothal contract); and without any direct reference to the other usage, it is also the contract for bail. These are the only two applications for *enguē*, and the parallelism is, to say the least, curious. In truth, *sponsio* has another specialized usage in Latin, one that perhaps explains everything. In the international sphere, *sponsio* designates a kind of treaty that is, in its nature or bearing, inferior to the *foedus*. Still, however one interprets a well-known episode in Roman legend,[329] this treaty puts into play collective responsibilities. Now, in theory, the betrothal contract brought about the intervention of family groups; and bail (an area where the similarity of vocabulary in Rome is perhaps the relic of a primitive indifferentiation between the guarantor and the "principal debtor") presupposes, in any case, certain traditional solidarities, familial or other. When all is said and done, these contractual forms could thus have emanated from a system of accords between groups. These forms possessed a social guarantee somewhat hypothetically when they entered into law. The element of obligation, *expressis verbis*, was self-sufficient from that point on. In certain cases this element responded by itself to that need for a social guarantee which was otherwise satisfied by the more or less direct intention of the collectivity.

※

Even when law gathers the heritage of ancient solidarities, it surpasses them. In a new milieu there appears a new type of relationship, precisely in which the contract can be individualized. The phenomena of prelaw that we have shown—at the mercy of the documentation and therefore at different levels—had at least this in common: they depended on social organizations that were suppressed or absorbed by the polis. It seems that we have the transition here: there is a relationship between the beginnings of law, strictly speaking, and the creation of a form of society. The striking fact is the establishment of the polis, where the notion of the sovereignty of a group in which judicial efficacy is integrated imposes itself. In this ancient world we are examining, the appearance of a mode of thought is evidence of a revolution.

※

What human meaning are we to attribute to this revolution? This is the question to which a study of prehistory like the one outlined above leads, and this is the question that perhaps justifies it.

On the most obvious level, the opposition between law and prelaw is absolute. For purposes of general comparison we could say that juridical thought is abstract and positive in its bearing on things, persons, or relationships. In a situation where law undertakes to regulate religious matters, however, it will declare that the obligation for burial falls on those who have taken over *ta khrēmata*, with succession being thought of as "possessions."[330] The expression *ta khrēmata* is traditional and is used already in Solon's Law Code and the Gortynian Code. The notion of *khrēma* is a typically economic one:[331] no mention is made of religious qualification or specific efficacy. In certain cases, the acquisition of inheritability is even called *embateusis*; merely a word, it no longer represents the power of investiture of land or the tomb. The singular value of objects such as arms, clothing, and livestock disappears (at most, the notion of *res mancipi* could figure as the memory of value or as its transformation). The idea that animates the *traditio per glebam*, as it is authentically presented in Greek legend, has been so completely forgotten by the Greeks that not even the derivative of this mentality can be detected within a state of formalism.[332] What we see of the trace of a similar mentality in the *sacramentum in rem* of the Romans is nothing more than symbolism of pure form.[333] Similarly, the religious power of a *parens*, such as is manifested in a malediction with a view toward *sacratio*, no longer functions. The power of a dead man to take to his grave objects that were his "belongings" disappears by way of its very nature. The power to dispose of his property in a will—which will be accorded to the dead only after being distinguished from transactions among the living—is of an entirely different nature from the power of the curse that accompanies the final wishes and that appears only in an isolated way and in survivals that are clearly identifiable as such. By way of contrast, the juridical capacity, active or passive, is abstractly defined: when law recognizes a distinction in status like the one consecrated by the Gortynian Code, it resolves the distinction by means of quantitative differences. It is precisely in law that an abstract idea of the person is affirmed.[334] Finally, the notion of a juridical bond is opposed to the notion of the creations of state[335] or the notion of changes of state such as those brought into being by a magicoreligious practice. The notion of a juridical link is opposed to the magicoreligious conception of changes of state by means of a fixed idealism. Even in forms that survive into the epoch of formalism, it is human representations and human expressions of will that appear as the true conditions of power or obligation. Even the Roman *sponsio*, without mentioning the Greek *homologia*, is evidence of this thought. If an equivocal practice such as the *nexum*, for which the Greeks have an equivalent, was eliminated rather early among both peoples, the reason is doubtless that because of the quasi-enslavement that supported it, it was no longer compatible with the social structure of the polis. But we can also say that it was condemned in advance by its aberrant nature, since by virtue of the ritual of obligation, it instantly brought into being a "real servitude," one quite different from the bond of the contract.[336]

This is the first aspect of the meaning of all that has gone before, and the reader has doubtless already seen the interpretation that it suggests. Having reached the age of law, our mentality is on a level with the monuments it has left behind: witness the singular prestige of Roman law through the centuries; it is as if the juridical mentality were the product of a human reason that was only waiting to be liberated from the control of mystical preconceptions in order to manifest itself. There is also the inverse possibility: however little one is open to historical considerations, surely it is on social change that the accent should be placed; the juridical mentality merely "reflects" the new given, namely, a society organized on the model of the polis or the state. In truth, both schemes are deficient.

We do not have to dwell on the first scheme. Law does not come about as a result of revelation. Even in its archaic forms, we see at once dissimilarities that are clearly due to differences in structure. Moreover, the theme of the relativity of law is not something recently discovered; the Greeks were already convinced of it. It is necessary to add that the idea of law can be perceived in a history that was not fashioned all by itself. It is under the signs of *kratos* and *bia* that Aeschylus placed the rule of Zeus in the beginning. But inversely, what it is impossible not to see is the fact that legal thought is constructive: it substitutes for the world of the magico-religious representation another world, a world that is both antithetical and homologous. Thus the ancient *fides* that is traditionally symbolized by mythical examples of the oath or by the institutions of King Numa[337] is replaced by another *fides*, a "good faith" that bears the same name but that differs from the first[338] and is not immediately incorporated into law.[339] Nothing is more revealing, in fact, than what we might call the weaknesses or the gropings of nascent law. Law had to construct its notions; it had to organize a new system, one with its own categories and one in which causality and time take on new meanings.[340] Moreover, the solutions differ from one law to another: the notion of subjective law, the administration of proof, and the formation of the contractual bond are not the same in Greece and in Rome. But the modalities of truth that law attained were reached inside that world whose representation in procedure was imposed by its establishment.[341] It is an astonishing world—no more or less so than the world that preceded it—where a creation of thought appears as an objective reality, and where law, whether it is called *ius* or *dikaion*,[342] continues to affirm, by means of that irreducible element—that is, by the need for genuine sanctions—the idea of a new kind of force.

✺

Huvelin has been faulted for "not distinguishing religious from judicial magic."[343] The formulation matters little, but this remark contains the entire question that is of interest to us.

The most ancient Roman law illustrates the notion of a force that depends not on physical constraint but on the inherent quality of the ritual. This, however, is already law; its efficacy is subject to conditions and rules that were instituted by the city and that therefore define it. The force that animates it at every phase is specific; it is no longer the force that is immanent in the religious rite as such. Between the two types of forces there is not merely opposition but also continuity: without the first, the second could not have been produced by the minds of the interested parties. The import of the Roman experience, in fact, seems to have been expanded by an experience that was furnished by neighboring societies developing along parallel lines. In truth, the two experiences are different, but they also complement each other. The transition itself is attested for Rome; it is less so for Greece, where we have practically no evidence of archaic law. On the other hand, Greece has preserved, especially in its mythology, a certain memory of an ancient state, one for which the Roman data may allow speculation, but only speculation. It is a state in which religious forces function for ends that law will realize at a later date on its own.

Does this statement have only historical interest? It is a fact that the notion of juridical force cannot be reduced to positive elements; it is equally a fact that law cannot do without it. We think we have seen the sources from which law inherits this force. Law constitutes a major victory: it allows the formulation in terms of reason of a multitude of still-unspoken relationships. But if it is true—and this was the reading of Lévy—that thought is not only a formulation of law but an anticipation as well, it is because law in its most recent phases preserves something of the "mysticism" that is observable at its very origins.

NOTES

1.   See, in particular, P. Noailles, *Fas et jus* (1948), and along the same lines the works of A. Hägerström, F. de Visscher, and A. Magdelain.

2.   *Année sociol.*, 3d ser., 1949, p. 601.

3.   G. Wissowa, *Religion und Kultus der Römer*[2], p. 382.

4.   See M. Mauss, "Essai sur le don," *Année sociol.*, n.s., I (1925), pp. 135 ff.

5.   G. Davy, *La Foi jurée. Etude sociolog. du probl. du contrat. La Formation du lien contractuel* (1922).

6.   P. Huvelin, "Magie et droit individuel," *Année sociol.*, X (1907), pp. 1–47.

7.   See H. Hubert and M. Mauss, *Mél. d'hist. des rel.*, pp. xxiii ff.

8.   In this sense, the repeated assertions of M. Mauss, in particular in *Année sociol.*, n.s., II (1927), pp. 104 ff.

9.   The Near Eastern world, especially that of the Sumerians and Babylonians, offers us a totally different experience: its astonishingly early development of the law of obligations puts it at odds with the Mediterranean world. This raises a serious question: to what degree is this a localized, or parallel, development? A distinctive quality of the civilization of

"classical antiquity" seems to be the generality of a legal thought relatively recent, and rapidly expanded.

10.   On this distinction, which goes back to A. von Brinz (1874), see G. Cornil, in *Mél. Girard*, 1912.

11.   Pl., *Prt.*, 320C–322D.

12.   For the most ancient uses, see G. Glotz, *La Solidarité de la famille dans le droit criminel en Grèce*, pp. 96 ff.

13.   Hdt., III.139–40.

14.   Hdt., I.61.

15.   The expression *proopheilomenē ekhthrē* (Hdt., V.82)—specifically, a "debt of emnity" (see Dem., XXI.77)—appears in an episode in which acts of revenge are bound together in the same fashion as are obligations; it is also used in reference to a (sacred) object that circulates. In legal terminology, the word *opheilein* refers to debt; and it is this partially juridical terminology that Herodotus uses in his account.

16.   Hdt., VI.62.

17.   Hdt., I.69–70.

18.   See Mauss, "Essai sur le don," p. 139, n. 2. The investigation of Aristotle's ethic could be expanded.

19.   There is already something of this in a Homeric episode (*Il.*, VI.230 ff.). In order to make peace, two heroes, a Greek and a Lycian, exchange armor. The Greek initiates the proposal, and Homer emphasizes that he was quite delighted with the affair.

20.   For the evidence, see G. Glotz, *Hist. grecque*, I, p. 165.

21.   Hdt., V.62.

22.   There is no need here to confuse things by undertaking a general discussion of myth; in the context in which we are referring to it, we admit, without further ado, that myth has a direct connection with what is social.

23.   Isoc., VII.32–33.

24.   Arist., *Eth. Nic.*, II.1107B.11 ff. For the ideas found here, see n. 18 above.

25.   The symbolism of disappearing food and drink is rather telling. Other forms of symbolism are more obscure and need interpretation.

26.   The epic *The Return of the Sons of Atreus*, in Ath., VIII.281B–C.

27.   We at least have evidence of the social practice from a nearby culture; Thucydides tells us that among the Thracians "it was more shameful not to give when asked than to ask without receiving" (II.97). See the commentary of M. Mauss, "Une forme anc. du contrat chez les Thraces," *REG*, XXXIV (1921), p. 395.

28.   For the evidence, see W. H. Roscher, *Lex.*, s.v. Pelops, p. 2282.

29.   F. M. Cornford, "The Origin of the Olympic Games," in J. E. Harrison, *Themis*, pp. 248 ff.

30.   Cornford, op. cit., pp. 251–53; H. Jeanmaire, *Couroi et Courètes*, pp. 417 ff.

31.   We are not looking for a comparison, but it is impossible to deny that one suggests itself. For the same connections, but of course with an array of details that are informative in another way, see Davy, op. cit., pp. 215 ff.

32.   Diod., Sic., IV.24.4.

33.   See M. P. Nilsson, *Griech. Feste*, pp. 449 ff.

34.   The same lack of certitude or the same alternative appears sometimes in the Tantalus legend; it also appears in the practice of Attic phratries.

35.   See S. Eitrem, *Opferritus und Voropfer*, p. 363.

36.   Cornford, op. cit., pp. 246 ff.

37.   Cf. C. Picard, *Ephèse et Claros*, pp. 277 ff.

38.   Strab., XIV.639.

39.   See S. Luria, *Philologus*, LXXXIII (1928), pp. 131 ff.

40.   See Jeanmaire, op. cit., pp. 379 ff.

41.   Ath., X.425B.

42.   For texts and commentary, see J. Toepffer, *Attische Genealogie*, p. 106.

43.   Strab., X.483C.

44.   The ox serves as a sacrifice offered by a young boy. The cup, an instrument of libation and "a precious object" in stories and in works of art, sometimes appears in connection with the rite of initiation.

45.   See E. Bethe, "Die dorische Knabenliebe," *RhM*, LXII (1907), pp. 438 ff.

46.   In connection with Cretan customs, the ancients remembered Ganymede, the boy stolen by Zeus to be his "cup-bearer." It is surprising that Ganymede's name comes to Pindar's mind when he is dealing with the legend of Tantalus; better yet, the carrying-off of the boy is sometimes attributed to Tantalus himself.

47.   Pind., *Ol.*, I.39: *amoibaia deipna*.

48.   See C. Robert, *Die griech. Heldensage*, pp. 232 ff.

49.   We should recall that on occasion its equivalent can be found within the confines of Greece; see the story of the feast of Seuthes (n. 27 above).

50.   A work as short as the *Characters* of Theophrastus mentions it no less than five times. On the *eranos* as loan, which deserves a special study, see at least L. Beauchet, *Hist. du droit privé de la républ. athén.*, IV, pp. 258 ff.

51.   See F. Poland, *Gesch. des griech. Vereinswesens*, pp. 28 f., 519 ff.

52.   See M. San Nicolo, *Aegypt. Vereinswesen*, pp. 212 ff.

53.   *Od.*, I.226.

54.   Artist., *Eth. Nic.*, IV.1123a.22.

55.   Employing a kind of parody, Hesiod (*Op.*, 722) applies the noble term *dais* to the notion of "paying for your own meal."

56.   A good example in Aristotle (*Pol.*, VIII.1322b.40) illustrates the idea of "indirect reciprocity" between generations.

57.   Thuc., II.43: *kalliston...eranon...proïemenoi*. For the verb, see p. 151 above.

58.   In "Ancient Festivals" [= "Frairies antiques," *REG*, XLI (1928), pp. 313–59; see pp. 13–47 above]; we tried to show that in a prehistoric tradition of peasant celebrations a strong link existed between counterpayment and the "expectation" of rewards such as those the very cycles of nature produce. We mention this in passing here, for our present concern lies elsewhere.

59.   From another perspective we can see how deep this idea goes: certain forms of conduct are called *eranoi* in cases where an active and emotional element predominates, or where the idea is "played with"; thus we have the curious Olympian practice of "showering" the victor with "various gifts" as well as crowns, leaves, flowers, and pieces of clothing (Eratosth., *ap.* schol. Eur., *Hec.*, 573); according to another practice, but one that occurs on the same occasion, the victor makes a "collection" of gifts in the manner of an *eranos* that is "assembled." Note that the rite of the *phullobolia*—the throwing of leafy branches—is also attested at weddings and funerals and can be equally associated with an *eranos* (see Eur., *Hec.*,615).

60.   See Jeanmaire, op. cit., p. 590.

61.   Gai., *Dig.*, XLVII.22.

62.   Certain types of precontract in the world of the Kabyles quite naturally call to mind the memory of the *eranos*; see R. Maunier, *Annales sociol.*, ser. D, II (1937), pp. 42 ff.

63.   Gorg., *Pal.*, 8.

64.   *Il.*, VII.303 ff.

65.   *Il.*, VI.230 ff.

66.   *Od.*, XXI.31 ff.

67.   Soph., *Aj.*, 658 ff., 817 ff., 1026 ff. This repetition illustrates how dramatic technique can make use of a theme's haunting power.

68.   See *Journal de psychol.*, XLI (1948), pp. 429 ff.

69.   *Il.*, V.1026 ff.

70.   *Il.*, V.819.

71.   Gortynian Code, XI.11. ff.

72.   Eur., *Med.*, 947 f., 1157 ff., 1188 ff.

73.   It is still necessary to emphasize that in Deianeira's gift the blood (and also the semen) of the Centaur is the active agent with which the tunic has been poisoned.

74.   Petron., fr. 1, *ap.* Serv., *ad Aen.*, III.57.

75.   See G. Dumézil, *Le Crime des Lemniennes*, pp. 42 ff.

76.   Plut., *Dio.*, 56; Corn. Nep., *Dio.*, 8.

77.   Ap. Rhod., *Argon.*, II.30 ff., III.1205 ff., IV.423 f.

78.   See *Mél. Boisacq*, I, p. 396 f.

79.   Ap. Rhod., *Argon.*, IV.1189 f.

80.   Isoc., *Ad Nic.*, 1.

81.   Ibid.; Thuc., II.97.

82.   Plut., *Eum.*, 8.

83.   A transformation on the model of the epic; see *Il.*, VI.286 f.

84.   See L. Deubner, *Att. Feste*, p. 100.

85.   Paus., V.16.2.

86.   Paus., III.16.2.

87.   The cult of Artemis Orthia at Sparta also; and the *Endusia* of Argos (see Deubner, *Att. Feste*), where the designation of the officiating priestesses makes one think of an Athenian cult and one at Ilium mentioned by Homer. The same term brings to mind the ceremonies in which the idol's vestments are changed. Thus it is quite a continuous series.

88.   In the case of Olympia and Athens, the period of ritualistic weaving could suggest a taboo that seems to be attested in Italic and Germanic folklore: the reciprocal exclusion of weaving and agriculture. In any case, it is a very old element that should be recognized in the symbolism—Hellenic and Oriental—of the woman and the spindle.

89.   See Gortynian Code, III.24 f. (the right of the woman to the product of her work).

90.   Schol. Pind., *Ol.*, VII.156.

91.   Pind., *Pyth.*, IV.253.

92.   *Hubristika* of Argos (Plut., *De mul. vir.*, 245E); the practice at Cos (Plut., *Quaest. Graec.*, 304E); the Spartan custom (Plut., *Lyc.*, 15).

93.   Ant. Lib., *Met.*, 17; in an Arcadian legend a namesake of this Leukippos is disguised as a girl (Paus., VIII.20.3).

94.   See Jeanmaire, op. cit., pp. 320 ff.

95.   Apollod., *Bibl.*, III.174.

96.   See *REG*, XLI (1928), pp. 324 ff.

97.   We have only some of the facts. It would also be good to consider the clothing used after death (for example, the shroud), as well as the cloth woven for the infant, the designs of which are sometimes in tragedy a means of recognition (see G. W. Thomson, *Aeschylus and Athens*, pp. 48 ff.).

98.   Festus, *Gloss. Lat.*, *s.v. Sertor*; see H. Lévy-Bruhl, *Quelques Problèmes du très ancien droit romain*, p. 64, n.2.

99.   See K. Sittl, *Die Gebärden d. Gr. u. Röm.*, pp. 130 f.

100.   Ar., *Av.*, 518.

101.   Ar., *Av.*, 975; on the religious rule of Chios, see J. de Prott and L. Ziehen, *Leges Sacrae*, no. 113.

102.   Ar., *Eccl.*, 779 ff.

103.   See P. Huvelin, *Etudes d'histoire du droit commercial romain*, pp. 280 ff.

104.   See *Il.*, VI.302 ff. (the peplos *on the knees* of the goddess). In a "theological" conception such as Homer's, the god is not bound immediately; cf. the expression "to be on the knees of the gods," to indicate what depended on their arbitrary judgment.

105.   *Il.*, XI.192, 753; XIV.491; XVII.206; XX.182.

106.   *Il.*, IX.98.

107.   See L. Deubner, *ArchRW*, XXX (1933), pp. 83 ff.

108.   *Il.*, VII.148 f.

109.   Plut., *Quaest. Graec.*, 45: a legend that is perhaps late, but that is made up of traditional elements.

110.   Eur., *Heracl.*, 462 f.

111.   For the force of this particular act, see *Il.*, XVIII.204.

112.   Pind., *Pyth.*, IV.28 ff.; Ap. Rhod., *Argon.*, IV.1547 ff.; Plut., *Quaest. Graec.*, 13; schol. Pind., *Nem.*, VII.155A; Plut., *Quaest. Graec.*, 22; Conon, *Narr.*, 25. Cf. M. P. Nilsson, *ArchRW*, XX (1920), pp. 232 ff.; W. R. Halliday, *The Greek Questions of Plutarch*, pp. 76, 151.

113.   Schol. Pind., *Nem.*, VII.155A; Conon, *Narr.*, 25; cf. Plut., *Quaest. Graec.*, 13.

114.   Designated by a concrete term, "bird": Pind., *Pyth.*, IV.19.

115.   Pind., *Pyth.*, IV.43 ff. With reference to the motif of clods of earth being thrown into the water, cf., for a procedure of drawing lots, Paus., IV.3, 5; Apollod., *Bibl.*, II.177. For the idea of efficacious prophecy, see J. Bayet, in *Mél. Cumont*, I, pp. 27 ff.

116.   Plut., *Quaest. Graec.*, 13; Ap. Rhod., *Argon.*, IV.1734. For a similar rite in a tale of the same kind, see Hdt., VIII.137.

117.   *Il.*, VI.230 ff.

118.   Pind., *Pyth.*, IV.37.

119.   *Il.*, VIII.289; XXIII.565, 596, 624, 797; *Od.*, VIII.319.

120.   *Hymn. Hom. Merc.*, 497, 509.

121.   Ibid., 516.

122.   The *huposkhesis* of Zeus is introduced in the tale of Tantalus; in Herodotus' Spartan tale there is a double oath of partners.

123.   It would be futile to pretend that we are dealing with this question in its entirety. The question has been raised again in a recent article by E. Benveniste (*RHR*, CLXXXIV [1948], pp. 81 ff.). A classification of the external evidence (above all from the perspective of the classical era) can be found in G. Glotz, *Etudes sociales et jurid. sur l'antiq. gr.*, pp. 99 ff. There is a good amassing of facts, but nothing more, in R. Hirzel, *Der Eid*; cf. P. Huvelin, *Année sociol.*, VII (1902–3), pp. 505 ff.

124.   Basically it is the sacramental *promise* that interests us at present. But the mechanics that lie at the roots of the notion—without which we doubtless could not understand the unified concept of "oath"—do not differ according to type. Furthermore, the classification of oaths into those of promise and those of affirmation does not really take into account all the facts.

125.   Pl., *Criti.*, 119D ff. We refer to the excellent translation by M. Rivaud; nevertheless, we will adopt a different interpretation on several points.

126.   Hyper., *ap.* Ath., X.423.E.

127.   *Il.*, III.269 ff.

128.   Hdt., III.11.

129.   Aesch., *Sept.*, 42 ff.

130.   Xen., *An.*, II.2.9.

131.   Orph., *A.*, 310 ff.

132.   See Jeanmaire, op. cit., pp. 347 ff.

133.   J. G. Frazer, *GB*, I, pp. 359 f.; K. Kircher, *Die sakrale Bedeut. des Weines im Altert.*, pp. 79 ff.

134.   Wissowa, op. cit., pp. 410 ff.

135.   Eur., *Supp.*, 1196 ff.

136.   A tripod, elsewhere an item used for the investiture of vassals, is, in Libya, buried in the ground as a pledge for the land's security; it was received from the Argonauts, and mysterious signs were engraved on it (Timae., *ap.* Diod. Sic., IV.56.6).

137.   In Greece this generally remained a religious custom, as it is in Homer; and what is worthy of note is that it was on the international level that the *spondai* continued to be used.

138.   Ap. Rhod., *Argon.*, II.717; for another, no less striking, expression, see Ap. Rhod., *Argon.*, II.291.

139.   *Od.*, XIV.331.

140.   Eur., *Hel.*, 1235.

141.   See the expression *enoinon kai enorkon*, in *CIG*, 2554 ff.: one enters into the bonds of an oath through wine.

142.   So it is in the regulations of the Andanian Mysteries (Prott and Ziehen, *Leges Sacrae*, II, no. 58, ll. 2 ff.); and in the treaty between Delphi and Pellene (B. Haussoullier, *Milet* [1902], pp. 12, 49).

143.   Thus, in *Il.*, II.296, *enkheō* has this kind of "verbal aspect."

144.   P. Stengel, *Die griech. Kultusalter*,[3] p. 123.

145.   The oath *dia tou puros* (Dem., LIV.40); the formula was pronounced the moment the victim's flesh was consumed by the flames ([Dem.], XLIII.14).

146.   Hes., *Th.*, 775 ff.

147.   It is a concept that could have some connection with the practice of oaths at the sanctuary of the *Palikoi*; see Glotz, *Etudes*, p. 73. A story in Herodotus (III.25) mentions the absorption of bull's blood at the ordeal's end.

148.   See *Journal de psychol.*, XLI (1948), pp. 437 ff.

149.   It "drips down," to be exact, or *kataleibesthai*; we note that the verb *leibō* is one that designates the *libation*.

150.   C. Picard, *Rev. phil.*, VII (1933), pp. 341 ff.

151.   See E. Benveniste, *Rev. phil.*, VI (1932), pp. 118 ff.

152.   *Il.*, III.292; the effect of the knife is added to that of the libation (l. 300).

153.   The judgment takes place when the fire has finished its work (Pl., *Criti.*, 120B). For the active force of fire, we recall the practice of the libation; see [Dem.], LIV.40.

154.   *Il.*, III.310, and schol. ad loc.

155.   Tomb of the horse, Paus., III.20.9; tomb of the boar, Paus., IV.15.7 ff.

156.   Eur., *Supp.*, 1204 ff.

157.   *Il.*, XIX.267 ff.

158.   We have had the opportunity of pointing out the importance of this mythical idea of objects of value (see p. 87 above). But to be more pertinent at this point, we ought to mention an insightful comparison made by Glotz (*Solidarité*, p. 156): piles of red-hot iron are thrown into the waves as a pledge to an eternal union.

159.   See Orph., *A.*, 314 ff. (weapons are thrust into the flesh and entrails of the victims); *Il.*, III.273 ff. Cf. *Il.*, XIX.254 (the victim's hair is held in the hand during the sacrifice).

160.   Hdt., VI.68; Lyc., 20; Isae., VII.16.

161.   Dem., XXIII.68; Paus., III.20.9.

162.   See J. G. Frazer's commentary on Pausanias, III.20.9, in *Le Folklore dans l'Anc. Test.* (French trans.), pp. 138 ff.; and S. Eitrem, *Symb. Oslo.*, XXV (1947), pp. 36 ff.

163.   Plut., *Quaest. Rom.*, III. Cf. Apollod., *Bibl.*, III.173; Hdt., VII.37 ff.; O. Masson, *RHR*, CLXXXVII (1950), pp. 17 ff.

164.   Pl., *Leg.*, VI.753D (*dia tomiōn poreuomenos*); see Eitrem, loc. cit.

165.   In some forms of oaths, one can catch a glimpse of the fact that each party touches *one* of *ta tomia*.

166.   In a passage that contains a possible reminder of a rite analogous to that of Cyrene, a hero questions the effectiveness of the rites (*Il.*, II.339 ff.); but *Zeus* is watching (*Il.*, IV.158 ff.). Elsewhere the poet's offhand manner is almost derisive: the victims thrown into the sea become "food for the fish" (*Il.*, XIX.267 ff.).

167.   Paus., VIII.15.2: *omnuntas . . . tōi petrōmati* (instrumental dative).

168.   See Benveniste, op. cit., pp. 87 ff.

169.   This is especially true for the Styx—water and power—which is many times called *horkos*. In Archilochus, 95 (Diehl), *horkos* means "bread and salt" in the sense of *horkōmotein*, "to touch the *horkos*." Cf. Aesch., *Supp.*, 46; Eur., *Supp.*, 1190; Soph., *Ant.*, 265.

170.   On the flexibility of the idea of an oath, see Hirzel, *Eid*, p. 15. For a culture both archaic and nearby, see the remarkable observations of Lucian's *Toxaris*, 48 (the act of putting one's foot on the victim's hide is a *horkos*).

171.   In *Il.*, I.234 ff., Achilles makes a "great oath" that is neither a promise nor a call for witness. It is directed toward the future, and determines it by the power of the scepter and the gesture as much as by the power of the word. This is comparable to the word of divination that sets the oracle in motion and without which the oracle's effect would be incomplete (Soph., *Ant.*, 1064 ff.).

172.   It is through this that a *technique* predating law defines itself. It is difficult to resist citing the marvelous Assyrian oath of fidelity found in Frazer, *Folklore* (French trans.), pp. 142 ff. (cf. E. Dhorme, *Les Relig. de Babyl. et d'Assyrie*, p. 230): the victim is dismembered in stages and in a symbolic way; and it is specified that the goat is not to be sacrificed to a god (in an ordinary sacrifice), nor is it to be beaten (as though impure)—"it is to be brought forth so that Mati-Ilu may swear fidelity over it to Ashur-Nisari."

173.   *Il.*, XVIII.497 ff., XXIII.566 ff.

174.   See Lévy-Bruhl, *Quelques Problèmes*, pp. 95 ff.

175.   They sometimes survive in a remarkable form that consists in the signing and sealing of a contract by obtaining a judgment at the conclusion of a feigned process. This institution, known in Greco-Egyptian law, seems to have had antecedents in the Greek law of the classical period (W. Kunkel, *Zeitschr. d. Sav.-Stift.*, R.A., LIII [1933], pp. 512 ff.).

176.   See Lévy-Bruhl, *Quelques Problèmes*, p. 112.

177.   The rites of *acquisition* are faithfully preserved in Pl., *Leg.*, XI.914C ff.

178.   See A. Hägerström, *Der röm. Obligationsbegr.*, pp. 37 ff.

179.   See *Rev. hist. du droit fr. et étr.*, ser. 4, XXVI (1948), pp. 179 ff. [= L. Gernet, *Droit et société dans la Grèce ancienne*, pp. 12 ff.].

180.   To which Wundt reduced the essential raison d'être of formalism itself.

181.   In particular, R. J. Bonner and G. Smith, *The Administration of Justice from Homer to Aristotle*, I, pp. 27 ff., 43 ff.; A. Steinwenter, *Die Streitbeendigung durch Urteil, Schiedsspruch und Vergleich nach griech. Recht*, pp. 29 ff.

182.   This is also possible in some forms of "judgment" found in Homer (*Od.*, XII.440).

183.   Between Homer and Hesiod according to some; or only after Hesiod. For criticism of this concept of evolution, see H. J. Wolff, "The Origin of Judicial Litigation among the Greeks," *Traditio*, IV (1946), pp. 31 ff.

184.   *Il.*, XVIII.497–508. For the interpretation adopted, we return to Wolff, loc. cit.

185.   One must add that not only the presence of heralds points to the public nature of the trial. Following the attractive conjecture by Wolff, we also observe here the participation of the people; we rarely see anything beyond their acclamation (see *Il.*, XXIII.534 ff.: *epainein*, 610), which could determine which sentence was better.

186.   On its religious character, see Glotz, *Solidarité*, pp. 94 ff.

187.   On another aspect of primitive "justice" (especially the feudal justice of Boeotia in Hesiod's time), see Wolff, op. cit., pp. 57 ff., who demonstrates that judgment does not
have its origins in this kind of regulative administration. Admittedly his is a negative idea,
and we want only to point it out; but it does help to make our discussion of arbitration complete.

188.   See *Arch. d'hist. du droit or.*, I (1937), pp. 129 ff. [= Gernet, *Droit et société*,
pp. 29 ff.].

189.   See E. Rabel, "*Dikē exoulēs* u. Verwandtes," *Zeitschr. d. Sav.-Stift., R.A.*, XXXVI
(1915), pp. 340 ff.; XXXVII(1916), pp. 1 ff.; XXXVIII (1917), pp. 296 ff.

190.   This is what the trial of Orestes symbolizes in Aeschylus; on the part of the accused, the theme of supplication is highlighted, and we will soon see precisely how this theme
is articulated in other forms of prelaw.

191.   *Hymn. Hom. Merc.*, 371, 372, 373.

192.   Noailles, op. cit., pp. 167 ff.

193.   Huvelin, "Magie et droit," pp. 30 ff. For the ceremony of the Greek *phōra*, a
parallel to the *quaestio lance licioque* of Roman law as well as to procedures in a number of
other law systems, see Glotz, *Solidarité*, pp. 203 ff. Since Glotz, many have stressed the
strange quality of this procedure, for which no "rational" explanation really suffices; but the
Roman details, still unfortunately obscure, are especially suggestive (see F. de Visscher,
Etudes de droit romain, pp. 257 ff.).

194.   Beauchet, op. cit., III, pp. 594 ff., 262 ff., 117 ff.

195.   See *Rev. hist. du droit fr. et étr.*, ser. 4, VI (1927), pp. 5 ff. [= Gernet, *Droit et
société*, pp. 83–102].

196.   Isae., III.22; cf. III.62.

197.   Aesch., *Cho.*, 172 ff.; cf. Soph., *El.*, 909 ff.

198.   The scene of Orestes at his father's tomb probably dates back at least to Stesi-
chorus, a seventh-century poet.

199.   Eur., *El.*, 899 ff.

200.   See Aesch., *Cho.*, 205 ff., for the distinction between these two actions;
the second rite cannot be performed by an intermediary. For the meaning of the first (mount-
ing the tomb), see Soph., *Aj.*, 1168 ff.; Eitrem, *Opferritus und Voropfer*, pp. 435 ff.

201.   Eur., *El.*, 326 ff. A formula for the proverbial oath in *Il.*, IV.177, attests the
idea of the ritual practice. If one examines it carefully, it resembles an "oath" formula in *Il.*,
II.260.

202.   M. Delcourt, *Ant. Class.*, VII (1938), p. 43.

203.   Hdt., III.63, 67 (someone alleges to be the king's son); IX.95 (someone alleges
to be the son of a prophet).

204.   In particular, Hes., *Theog.*, 392 ff., in a remarkable context (distribution of
lots at the time of succession).

205.   In the perfect tense, the verb denotes an acquired sovereignty (*Il.*, I.37; *Od.*,
IX.198). It is good to bear in mind the legendary rite of the founding of Sardis (Hdt., I.84). In
another quarter, the three cosmic steps of Vishnu (in a ritual of succession) are not without
their analogues in the triple course run by Talos on the island of Crete (Ap. Rhod., *Argon.*,
IV.1644).

206.   Pind., *Pyth.*, IV.70 ff. Another oracle—the same one, but in a more general
form (Robert, *Die griech. Heldensage*, p. 767)—predicted his death at the hands of another
Aeolian, that is, a rival belonging to the same lineage.

207.   See S. Reinach, *RA*, I (1932), p. 93; J. Brunel, ibid., n.s., IV (1934), pp. 41 ff.

208.   Plut., *Thes.*, III.5, XII.2–3.

209.   See J. G. Frazer, *Tabou* (French trans.), pp. 258 f.; T. Wächter,
Reinheitsvorschr. im griech. Kult, pp. 23 ff.; W. Deonna, *RHR*, CXII (1935), pp. 61 ff.

210.   See Picard. *Ephèse et Claros*, p. 303.

211.   C. Picard, *RHist*, CLXVI (1931), p. 33; idem, *REG*, XLVI (1933), pp. 390 ff.

212.   Frazer, *Tabou* (French trans.); idem, *Pausanias' Description of Greece*, III, p. 277; W. Amelung, *Diss. della Pont. Acad. rom. di arch.* (1907), pp. 121 ff.

213.   Artem., IV.63.

214.   A famous instance is that of the two hundred Plataeans, who when their city was being besieged made a desperate attack during the night (Thuc., III.22). The practice is elsewhere referred to as a *custom* (schol. Pind., *Pyth.*, IV.133) among the Aetolians; cf. Verg., *Aen.*, VIII. 689 ff., concerning a troop of Italic warriors.

215.   Diog. Laert., VIII.69, an idea which, though late (see J. Bidez, *Vie d'Empéd.*, pp. 67 ff.), need not be a gratuitous invention.

216.   On the connection with initiation—and this includes philosophical initiation—see U. von Wilamowitz-Moellendorff, *Platon*, II, p. 40.

217.   See J. T. Kakridis, *Hermes*, LXIII (1928), p. 427. We may notice such a practice in the consultation of chthonian deities, namely, in the striking of the earth with the foot (Cic., *Tusc.*, II.60; E. Rohde, *Psyche* (French trans.), p. 99).

218.   The association between these paternal gods and the verb *embateuein* in connection with a retaking (and a return to the throne) is shown in Eur., *Heracl.*, 876 ff.

219.   In this extreme case we can emphasize the social aspect of the acts of prelaw; one cannot find the antecedents to law, as Huvelin did, in an activity that is private, secret, and illicit. This is true even of the part of the law that Huvelin especially singles out.

220.   See R. Dareste, B. Haussoullier, and T. Reinach, *Inscr. jurid. gr.*, II, p. 12.

221.   On the *prorrhēsis* in law, see L. Gernet, *Antiphon* (Coll. des Univ. de Fr.), pp. 140 ff.

222.   See, in its entirety, the lyric scene of the *Khoephoroi*, 315–478, and the scene that follows.

223.   See Harp., s.v., *epenenkein doru*.

224.   In an opinion offered by the "exegetes" on the subject of the violent death of a freedman whose former master wanted to prosecute the perpetrators of the deed, the rite is described precisely, and it is an express reminder of the legendary practice (ibid.); but the idea of judicial prosecution is excluded ([Dem.], XLVII.69 ff.).

225.   The rite that is performed at the same time as the funeral is referred to in this way.

226.   The comparison is made by Glotz, *Solidarité*, p. 70. On the "magical" meaning of the Roman ritual, see J. Bayet, *Mél. de l'Ec. fr. de Rome* (1935), pp. 1 ff.

227.   See A. B. Cook, *Zeus*, II, pp. 705 ff.

228.   The name of the tribunal of the Areopagus has always been associated with Ares, as well as with the names of gods that have epithets containing Ares. At the foot of the Areopagus hill there is a sanctuary of Athena Areia (Paus., I.28.5). ·

229.   So the two adversaries appeared on one of the pediments at Olympia. One of the altars of the sanctuary was thought to be the one on which Oinomaos offered sacrifice to Zeus Areios at the time of the ordeal.

230.   See Glotz, *Solidarité*, pp. 251 ff. It is worth noting that the oath that became a preliminary to a suit is not without its similarities to the curse; an interesting example of *katomnunai*, "to swear against," appears in Hdt., VI.65.

231.   According to legend, if blood vengeance cannot be achieved through the ordinary means, one resorts to a curse affecting an entire people (Paus., V.2.2 ff.).

232.   Glotz, *Solidarité*, pp. ix, 64.

233.   Plut., *Quaest. Graec.*, 12. The ceremony belongs to a very archaic group of festivals that take place every eight years.

234.   We could mention in passing the symbolic meaning of footwear; it even allows us to think of the ceremony that appears in the biblical tale of Ruth.

235.   Aesch., *Supp.*, 455 ff.

236.   The terms (*kathezesthai, kathēsthai, hedra*) are constant reminders of this. It is a matter of a type of prostration; see H. Bolkenstein, *Theophrastros' Charakter der Deisidaimonia* (*RGVV*, XXI.2.).

237.   See *Ant. Class.*, V (1936), 334 f.

238.   H. Diels, *Sibyll. Bl.*, p. 123.

239.   See H. Usener, *Kl. Schr.*, IV, pp. 116 f.. Here we should mention the scene at the beginning of *Oedipus Rex* (see M. Delcourt, *Stérilités mysterieuses et naissances maléfiques* [1938], p. 74).

240.   Arist., *Ath. Pol.*, 43.6.

241.   U. von Wilamowitz-Moellendorff, *Aus Kydathen*, p. 207 (a story in Apollod., *Bibl.*, II.167).

242.   Plut. *Thes.*, 22; see Robert, *Die griech. Heldensage*, p. 656. On the implications, see P. Roussel, *REG*, LV (1942), pp. x ff.

243.   [Hdt.], *Vit. Hom.*, 17, v. 12.

244.   Soph., *El.*, 102 f.; cf. Aesch., *Cho.*, 320 ff.

245.   Festus, *Gloss. Lat.*, 514.6; Twelve Tables, II.3.

246.   *Vagire* refers specifically to the cry of a young animal. In the passage of Sophocles already cited, Electra compares her lament to the cry of the nightingale. There is the recollection of myth here (the story of Procne), but we should also mention that the song accompanying the collection of the *eiresiōnē* is the "song of the nightingale."

247.   Notably the *occentatio*, which is a song with magical powers (Huvelin, *Etudes*, pp. 235 ff.); the word's formation makes us think of the verb *obvagulare* (from the text mentioned earlier).

248.   The summoning of a witness to one's door ([Dem.]), XLIX.19), a formalism, since it is practiced only in cases where absence is confirmed (Michel, no. 34, ll. 41 ff.).

249.   Antiphon, I.1.29; Lys., XIII.4, 41, 42, 92, 94.

250.   For an example from legend, see Apollod., *Bibl.*, II.67; cf. Glotz, *Solidarité*, p. 69.

251.   Lys., XXXII.6.

252.   Lys., III.39, 40.

253.   Arist., *Ath. Pol.*, 68.4.

254.   See E. Leisi, *Der Zeuge im attischen Recht*, p. 128.

255.   See J. H. Lipsius, *Das attische Recht und Rechtsverfahren*, pp. 464, 493.

256.   See Soph., *Aj.*, 571 ff.

257.   On the "portion of the dead" and the prejuridical ideas attached to it, see E. F. Bruck, *Totenteil u. Seelgerät im griechischen Recht*, pp. 1–154.

258.   Dem., XXXVI.52.

259.   *Leges Regiae*, IV.1; cf. I.7 (Girard).

260.   The primitive meaning is firmly fixed, but extant commentaries are rather vague; they emphasize the spoken rite—the cry—but this may not be the only aspect.

261.   On the legend, see Robert, *Die griech. Heldensage*, pp. 88 ff. The Homeric version appears in *Il.*, IX.565–72; this passage could have been added later, but we in no way intend to suggest that it is not as old, or even older, than its context.

262.   The so-called magical effect is still transparent in Homer: the gods Hades and Persephone are invoked by Althaia, but it is the Erinys who "hears" her from the depths of Erebus. The ground is likewise touched with the hand in a ritual oath found in *Il.*, XIV.272. And other effective usages appear in *Hymn. Hom. Ven.*, 331 ff.; Eur., *El.*, 678.

263.   Paus., VIII.15.3.

264.   See Nilsson, *Griech. Feste*, pp. 343 ff.

265.   *Episkēptein* means "to throw oneself down upon." Another symbol could be associated with it: the grasping of hands (Soph., *Aj.*, 751 ff.).

266.   Aesch., *Ag.*, 1601.

267.   Apollod., *Bibl.*, III.99.

268.   Plut., *Quaest. Graec.*, 12.

269.   Strictly speaking, in penal law (which we are leaving aside) the curse is widely used as a primitive means of sanction (see K. Latte, *Heiliges Recht*), and often it unleashes a collective reaction such as stoning. A curious instance of *dikazein* in Aesch., *Ag.*, 1412, reveals that there is some belief in the correspondence between the effect of the curse and the modern forms of punishment.

270.   *Il.*, XXIII.566 f.

271.   See *Rev. hist. de droit fr. et étr.*, ser. 4, XXVI (1948), pp. 179 ff. [= Gernet, *Droit et Société*, pp. 11–12].

272.   We shall see *dikazō*, "to judge," made use of in the scene. In the episode immediately preceding it, the term is used in the same sense; it is applied to Antilochus, whose possession has already been contested: *dikēi ēmeipsato* (1. 542)—"he defends himself in justice."

273.   See Lévy-Bruhl, *Quelques Problèmes*, p. 68.

274.   Gai., *Inst.*, IV.16.

275.   *Il.*, XVIII.505.

276.   *Od.*, II.37 ff.

277.   *Il.*, I.234 ff.; see note 171 above.

278.   It is interesting to observe that the heralds actively preside over the duel between Hector and Ajax (*Il.*, VIII.272 ff.); it is a scene in which we are permitted to see the poetic representation of a "judicial trial" of the most ancient kind (on this see Glotz, *Solidarité*, pp. 272 ff.).

279.   It is related especially to the conquest of royal power.

280.   For the meaning of the gesture of imposing hands, see Hirzel, *Der Eid*, pp. 28 ff.

281.   In addition, the oath will be neither taken nor refused; the code of conduct of the king's court does not allow a debate between heroes to develop in this way.

282.   See Latte, *Heiliges Recht*, pp. 10 ff.

283.   On the relationship between the two ideas, see Glotz, *Etudes*, p. 154; P.-M. Schuhl, *Essai sur la format. de la pensée gr.*, p. 59.

284.   For use of the oath at the Sicilian sanctuary of the twin gods, the Palikoi, see Polemon, *ap.* Macrob., *Sat.*, V.19, 15 ff.; for the "grand oath" at Syracuse, see Plut., *Dio*, 56.

285.   This is also the case for the questions directed to slaves. In addition, it takes us back to the idea of an ordeal; see Glotz, *Etudes*, p. 93.

286.   This, to be sure, is seen in a poet who was familiar with the idea of judgment. *Dikazō* is first used by Menelaus when he solicits the judgment of the Argives; it is then used to designate his personal proposal, not because he intends to be the judge in his own case, but because his "judgment" is the kind found in archaic law. And the plea that it allows, because it was inherited (see the Gortynian Code), is seen in a kind of pure form in the Homeric episode.

287.   L. Bréhier, *De Graecorum iudiciorum origine* (1899).

288.   See R. Hirzel. *Themis, Dike und Verwandtes*, pp. 7 ff.; for an even more pertinent study, see V. Ehrenberg, *Die frühere Rechtsidee bei den Griechen*, pp. 3 ff.

289.   In Homer, Minos, the mythical representative of this function, is "interrogated" in Hades in order to pronounce "sentences" (*Od.*, XI.569 ff.). The Gortynian Code (VIII.55) has preserved in isolation a curious usage of *peuthen* ("to inquire") in describing the action in a lawsuit.

290.   In addition to "survivals," we should refer to some of the details that Glotz (*Etudes*, pp. 47 ff.) mentions under the rubric "the public administration of the gods." But perhaps more to the point, we may recall a symbol such as the *scale* (*Hymn. Hom. Merc.*, 324), which is used for judgments. These *talanta* (*dikēs*) appear to have given rise to misinterpretations from the beginning (see C. Picard, *Les Rel. préhell.*, p. 290) and are also part of

some mythical episodes in which destiny plays itself out. (Furthermore, it is not impossible that the Roman formulation of the *aes* and *libra* may have some links with the scale.) It is also necessary to mention a passage in Theognis (543 ff.) that seems to bear witness to the use of divination in the dispensing of judgments.

291.   Aesch., *Eum.*, 415 ff.

292.   See R. Meister, *RhM*, LXIII (1908), pp. 559 ff.

293.   Arist., *Pol.*, II.1369a (a "law" of Cyme that is classified as archaic and naïve).

294.   See Glotz, *Solidarité*, p. 296.

295.   Aesch., *Eum.*, 576, 609. The idea of the "witness" there is that of the Draconian law according to which witnesses were forced to take the same oath as that taken by the party they were helping.

296.   On the meaning of this scene, see W. Headlam, *JHS*, XXVI (1906), p. 272.

297.   Aesch., *Eum.*, 432; cf. *Eum.*, 621.

298.   Pl., *Leg.*, XIII.948B–E.

299.   Plato points this out from the very beginning.

300.   See R. Monier, *Manuel de droit romain*, I, p. 155.

301.   The plaintiff who has won his case is required to swear over the victim's "dismembered parts" that the verdict is true and just (Aeschin., II.87). The procedure is preceded and followed by symmetrical oaths: the mark of the new thought is archaic; and there is continuity and change at the same time.

302.   For the use of the word *telos* ("end"—"intended goal") in the terminology of the courts, see *Arch. d'hist. du droit or.*, I (1937), pp. 124 ff. [= Gernet, *Droit et société*, pp. 69 ff.].

303.   This word would perhaps have the advantage of preserving the aesthetic element that exists in law, as, no doubt, it does in every social activity.

304.   Different perspectives appear, for example, in Germanic law; see H. Vordemfelde, *Die altgerman. Rel. in den deutschen Volksrechten* (1923). And for the study of an entire series of prelaw forms of behavior, one has only to recall the work of Maurice Cahen on the libation.

305.   See H. Lévy-Bruhl, *Nouv. Etudes*, pp. 20 ff.

306.   Cic., *Har. Resp.*, 18; Val. Max., I.l.

307.   See A. Magdelain, *Essai sur les orig. de la sponsio*, pp. 19 ff.

308.   See Noailles, op. cit., pp. 223 ff. (in particular, p. 274 for the *active* idea of *auctor*, in which one finds a connection with prelaw).

309.   Festus, *Gloss. Lat.*, s.v. *Praetor*.

310.   We know that Huvelin made a great point of this in his theses. But his etymological fancies and his narrow interpretation of evidence from "magic" should not discourage us.

311.   See A. Ernout and A. Meillet, *Dict. étym.*, p. 521.

312.   Ibid., pp. 23 ff.

313.   On *augurium agere*, see Wissowa, op. cit., p. 524.

314.   Diod. Sic., IV.39.2; see Glotz, *Solidarité*, pp. 162 ff.

315.   Pliny, *Pan.*, 8.

316.   See Lévy-Bruhl, *Quelques problèmes*, pp. 62 ff.

317.   See U. von Wilamowitz-Moellendorff, *Hermes*, XIX (1884), pp. 463 ff.

318.   For an opposite view, see Lévy-Bruhl, *Quelques Problèmes*, p. 64, n. 2; but Lévy-Bruhl argues from a historical period of Roman law that is later than the stage when the gesture of the *hand* could make a man free.

319.   Besides, *sponsio* has its etymological correspondent not only in the *spondai* of international law but also in the *epispenden* of the Gortynian Code (the latter being an obligation of private law about which we know hardly anything except its name).

320.   Hdt., VI.130.

321.   Lévy-Bruhl, *Nouv. Etudes*, pp. 6 ff.

322.   See pp. 172–73 above.

323.   The term *nuncupare*, which itself became a legal term, has a past in which one finds traces of a magicoreligious meaning.

324.   This is exactly the way Lévy-Bruhl poses the question in *Nouv. Etudes*, p. 6.

325.   In this context we could mention not only the presumably ancient role of witnesses in the *diamarturia*, but also the function of "witnesses of law" in the Gortynian Code, the forms of adoption in the same code, and the forms of the sale of real estate in Theophrastus; see the use of the term *epainein* as the equivalent of "ratify" in *Il.*, XXIII.534 ff.

326.   Gortynian Code, IX.34 ff; see pp. 172–73 above.

327.   The etymological meaning *(idem dicere)*, often explicit in common usage, is particularly evident in a legislative text of Plato, *Leg.*, XI.920D; cf. XI.953E.

328.   The word *stipulatio*, which is the most common designation for the verbal contract, still contains this relic of an otherwise obscure but positive symbol, one that, remarkably, has been forgotten.

329.   *Sponsio* at the Caudine Forks: see Lévy-Bruhl, *Nouv. Etudes*, pp. 116 ff.

330.   A law in [Dem.], XLIII.58.

331.   It is a concept whose autonomy is fully affirmed through the widespread use of money. See Arist., *Eth. Nic.*, IV.119B.26, for a definition of *khrēmata*; for the connection with speculative thought, see Heraclit., fr. 90 (Diels).

332.   We note a curious ritual in which a clod of earth is seized by the one swearing the oath (*PGrenf.*, I.ll), but it is probably an Egyptian form (see E. Weiss, *Griech. Privatrecht*, I, p. 228).

333.   Gai., *Inst.*, IV.17; cf. Aul. Gell., *NA*, XX.109.

334.   See M. Mauss, "Une catégorie de l'esprit humain," *J. Roy. Anthrop. Inst.*, LXVIII (1938), p. 275, for the Roman facts.

335.   This survives into the historical period in the concept of what one might call virtual rights. A *proxenia*, a hereditary link of "guest friendship," was denounced in vain, since it spontaneously came back to life in the person of a descendant (see G. Daux, in *Mél. Desrousseaux*, pp. 117 f.). The *patria potestas* (created at birth by a religious rite) comes to an end only after the sale of the son three times in succession.

336.   See Noailles, op. cit., p. 113. It is curious to find that the Twelve Tables (VI.1) deliberately impute to the *nexum* the character of a legal act, which continues to be partly foreign to them.

337.   The Greek *pistis* is applied with a predilection that is traditional to the oath; it is exactly parallel to *fides*. For the evolution of this idea, see E. Fraenkel, *RhM*, LXII (1916), pp. 187 ff. On its primitive force as a verbal substantive corresponding to *credo*, see A. Meillet, *Mém. Soc. Ling.*, XXII (1922), p. 218. The subjective element in the Indo-European idea of *credo* is strictly trust in the *efficacy* of the rite; see G. Dumézil, *Mitra-Varuṇa*, pp. 35 ff.

338.   In its ideal form, *pistis* ("trust") is opposed to another kind of faith, that which the ritual of an oath, dare we say, "materializes"; it is remarkable that this double meaning appears simultaneously, even at the risk of a contradiction that is readily pointed out (Eur., *Med.*, 731 ff).

339.   With the tradition of a *pistis-fides* going back to the dawn of time, there is a striking contrast in the fact that in Rome the concept of *fides* in contractual matters took hold slowly (note the even slower recognition of *fidei-commissum*), and that in Greece there were still laws that allowed no legal action to a creditor who relied on the *pistis* of his debtor (Theophr., ap. Stob., *Ecl.*, IV.20; Arist., *Eth. Nic.*, VIII.1164b.13).

340.   On the use of the *future* in the formulas of pledges, see Huvelin, *Etudes*,

p. 291, n. 3; compare the formula of the oath in *Il.*, III.281 ff., with that during the historical period, in which the future appears as a regular element. Here, as in other cases, the development of the linguistic category has some connection with the evolution of institutions.

341.   See Wolff, op. cit., p. 84: "Once a machinery for the supervision of self-help was devised . . . it became possible . . . to build, by limiting the scope of liabilities, a law of obligations."

342.   *Ius* seems entirely a creation of the city and a kind of attribute of a subject (an objective and subjective sense for which one finds a kind of synthesis in the formula *meum esse ex jure Quiritium aio*). In Greek we find the element of "justice" in the concept of *dikaion*— and consequently the element of moral claim, at least on the speculative level.

343.   Hägerström, op. cit., p. 601. Nonetheless, Huvelin ("Magie et Droit," p. 27) still talks about the "juridical force" as something characterizing a period following that of "magic."

CHAPTER 8
The Concept of Time
in the Earliest Forms of Law

We shall examine here certain aspects of the notion of time during some ancient periods of law. Our goal is defined in terms of the problem and the materials considered.

A very broad question within social history concerns the hold man has on time. To what degree does he believe that he can bring back the past so as to utilize it for various purposes? To what degree does man claim to master the future by offering himself the assurance of an event or a situation for similar ends? Clearly the question is posed in many ways in many epochs: we may recall, if need be, that an idea like "planning" is recent. It is also clear that law is particularly suited for this inquiry. In our own time, oddities of a similar sort have appeared—for example, life insurance, the legitimacy of which was in question until not long ago; the drafters of civil codes still found it immoral, in the sense that it did not involve a traditional structure. But there are also particular reasons for the law to be of interest to us. In order to understand any given legal system, it is fundamental to know how and in what sense it is based on the past or aims for control over the future. In addition, law offers a certain advantage to a psychological analysis: intellectual facts have an explicit relationship with social situations and with human activity. We will not be tempted to examine them in the abstract, however; such an approach might well falsify them.

We have in mind an archaic law and the mode of thought behind it. The epithet "archaic" is, by itself, rather vague and must immediately be made precise: it concerns the most ancient stages of law in the Mediterranean world of Greece and Rome. This antiquity can be specified. It is de-

This article originally appeared in *Journal de psychol.*, LIII (July–September 1956), pp. 379–406.

fined by its connection with a major event, one that we locate at the core of our study: the appearance of judgment in the proper sense, judgment perceived as the action of a collective sovereignty. This is an innovation that cannot be dated precisely, but our data allow us to see it as being roughly contemporary with the city itself. For us, "the most ancient stages of law" are those that either appear during this phase or that develop from it; that is, we are positioning ourselves at the crucial moment of the adoption of these forms.

At this point we can talk positively about procedures. In a wider sense, "procedure" is the aggregate of efficacious rites specialized within the technique of law. We are dealing with a period of antiquity when law was essentially action. In a narrower sense, procedure is that part of this aggregate which is connected with due process; the purposes of nascent law can only become clearer there, so we ought to examine it first.

PARADOXES WITHIN THE FORMULA OF VINDICATIO

Through good luck, and according to a unique but incontestably authoritative text (Gai., *Inst.*, IV.16), we know what went on before the Roman magistrate during the most ancient epoch, when the ownership of something was claimed in the context of opposition at law.

It is a question of claiming property that is movable, such as a slave. He who made the claim[1] held a rod in his hand and seized the slave while intoning these words: "I affirm that this man belongs to me according to the law of the Quirites; as I have said, behold, I have imposed a *vindicta* on you."[2] At the same time, the claimant placed the stick on the man. The adversary said the same things and performed the same gestures. When they had stated their claims against each other, the praetor said: "The both of you, let go of the man." They obliged. Then the first claimant said: "I ask if you can say according to what cause you have put forth a claim." The other claimant replied: "I have performed the law, just as I have imposed a *vindicta*." At this point, using similar formulas, the two parties provoke each other for the purposes of trial "for having claimed wrongly."

Only recently has pertinent information been extracted from this apparently bizarre text. Traditionally, the affirmation of a "right of ownership" was seen in the first phrase, a right that could have been founded only on the basis of a previously existing fact or situation. Accordingly, one would have expected the opponent to have been obligated to produce his title. But at the moment that would have been appropriate, he responds disconcertingly by justifying himself through the mere fact that he had performed the rite of *vindicta*. This creates the impression of answering a question with a question. Unless we stipulate that our facts are absurd, we must understand our data as presented; we have here a system that stands on its own. In the affirmation that serves as a starting point, the phrase *meum esse* definitely refers not to a past but to a present.[3] We might add that the "times" or tenses involved are the same throughout the description. There is doubtless movement, with several changes in direction, but it is movement the continuity of which is nevertheless perceptible. The perfect tense, which appears consistently in a substantial portion of the dialogue, should be understood in terms of its linguistic import rather than as a past tense. The Latin *perfectum* indicates something that has just been accomplished and that is presented as though attained in the full sense of the present ("I have said," "I have imposed the *vindicta*"). The very repetition of perfects only reiterates, with an effect that might be called deliberate, the *piétinement*. Hence, this dialogue refers only to the present, and almost to the ideal notion of the instantaneous; but we also see what this notion is related to. Gestures and *verba* are the inverse of one another. There is effective quality in the latter in the same way that there is language in acts. This *vindicatio*, which we know is attained (*cum uterque vindicasset; qua ex causa vindicaveris*), is not the kind of "claiming" that is to be realized in the future; it consists of the act of seizure accompanied by the prescribed formula. There is not only affirmation but also realization or creation.[4] In Latin, *ius feci*.[5]

This observation ought to be pursued. The use of the formula *hunc ego hominem meum esse aio* is not restricted to instances of legal claims;[6] it is similarly intoned in acts that are tantamount to a transfer of ownership, whether they be private (*mancipatio*) or take place in the presence of a magistrate (*in iure cessio*). The formula is used in manumission; it is probably used in some forms of adoption; it may even be used elsewhere. If it has so wide an application, it is because it was not devised precisely for the "court petition" that by itself it seems at first to signify; its inherent quality extends beyond its apparent purpose. In modern language, we might say that the formula is the same for the attainment of rights and for their defense. This is the source of occasional indecision and confusion: what pertains to due process and what pertains to the type of act? The final act in adoption, the one that is operative, appears to be an abridged process: before the magistrate, but without adversary proceedings, one claims (or rather affirms) a right of paternity over the adoptive son, as was the case with the ownership of the slave mentioned earlier. The act of *in iure cessio*, which, operating under the same formula, brings about the acquisition of property during an appearance before a magistrate, was for a long time interpreted by modern writers as a fictitious process in which the opponent would forfeit. This interpretation is incorrect, it would seem; but there is room for doubt, since a good deal of similarity in the situations is involved.

What do all these acts have in common? The case of *mancipatio* might serve as a typical example. In the classical period, *mancipatio* was thought of as a "way of acquisition": a person acquires from another, and the acquisition presupposes alienation. But neither the ritual nor the operational formula indicates as much. In what would seem to us an act of conveyance, the one who conveys does not appear: he is physically present, but this is not even stated. The sole actor on stage (along with the witnesses, to be sure, but they are silent) is the one who acquires. In order for the ownership to pass between hands, the quality of a special rite is needed: the "act involving the brass and the scales." But the entire operation is started by the words and acts of the new owner, who seizes the object (as the claimant) and who intones *hunc ego hominem*...(again as though he were the claimant). It is in acts of this sort that we grasp the reason for the behavior and the very ancient thinking from which it emanates. What we call "prelaw"—a stage that precedes organized law and that actually presupposes the social guarantee of the "witnesses," though not the active control of the city as such—is characterized by the multiplicity of the acts of seizure, interdiction, or execution, acts in which an autonomous force and a ritual quality that were magicoreligious at the beginning[7] are affirmed simultaneously. The idea of creation, or at least of innovation, is in the forefront: the action takes place at once, and it does not refer to the past. Seizures,[8] foreclosures, and the like are all effective in themselves, without reference to a precedent or to a "title," which in any event would be anachronistic here.

Let us return to "procedure" in the proper sense of the word: it should allow us to see the point at which the specific idea of law appeared, and how that idea has affected the formulation of "time."

The prelaw that we mentioned above might be said to be mimicked—obligatorily—in the rites of process. The opposing claims must have an absolute ring.[9] They do, in fact, but only in a singular hypothesis in which the contradiction is too visible not to appear intentional. *Aio* signifies another autonomy; but its temporary efficacy is a quality that we know beforehand has been usurped by at least one of the two parties. It is as if judgment—in order to be rendered—requires the most intense and ritualistic expression of the conflict that has need of it. Moreover, the procedural game makes manifest the parties' subordination to the magistrate as well as their antagonism to each other. At the center of the stage the expression *mittite ambo hominem* becomes a very telling symbol. Obviously we are touching on a fact of history here; we would hardly incur a risk if we suggested that the rites of due process were contemporaneous with its institution. The psychological significations of this fact must be seen precisely in the way they were conditioned by history.

On the one hand, the newness of due process is radical enough to orient the collective way of thinking, for judgment could not have emerged from a continuous "evolution in the course of time" from a benevolent and agreed upon arbitration.[10] Judgment corresponds to a mutation: it signifies a sovereign intervention by the city. Through judgment, and through a system that might roughly be called "self-help," the whole game takes on triangular proportions. A reality of another sort is affirmed; it is a reality in which the notion of "socialized" time will emerge.

But the effect is not immediate; the conditions under which the novelty appeared forbade this. At the very start, legal actions concerning murder, ownership, and so on, were not brought to trial. Concerning this prehistory, which our Roman sources cannot clarify, we have, at least, testimony from Greece, especially Homeric poetry. Judgment is first required in the case where the party who was going to undergo a normally permissible execution alleged a violation of the normal rules governing blood vengeance, for example, or in the case of the private hunting-down of a thief. It is in terms of the ancient system of autonomous executions that judgment comes to intervene in the beginning. The results of this intervention will last, at least in Greek law, where we see in the middle of the classical period that a dialogue dealing "basically" with ownership can perforce be produced under the guise of a criminal action in order to find out whether a seizure is valid. Now, in the typical notion behind ownership law, it is indeed the "past" that justifies and confers "title." But in ancient terms, there is no question of rights: the most ancient Latin term is *mancipium*, which denotes a power to dominate[11] that can exist only as it is actualized. The "abstract" notion of law comes later; it is a notion that requires time—in the sense of the temporal dimension and in the sense of the tense of the verb.

At the historical moment that this abstract notion is revealed to us, the *judicial situation* is thus somewhat ambiguous; the restraint that forces itself on justice at first narrows its vision.

ANCIENT MECHANISMS OF PROOF

One must look for the methods of proof within the very lines that are drawn by procedural conduct. Within the earliest workings of judicial institutions, we recognize a notion of truth that, instead of being demonstrated, forces acceptance. In other words, one cannot reach the past; one cannot go back in time. Let us put aside (although it remains in the limelight) a significant series of notions concerning the crime apprehended during commission (*flagrans delictum*); it is a series that precedes law and plays a considerable role in its birth. In truth, it might seem that this series of notions ought not to interest us, since in these cases the judgment of culpability is dispensed with reference to the past, and since there is a hypothetical coincidence between the crime itself and the certitude of the crime. But it is not that simple.

The flagrancy that characterizes individual crimes like theft and adultery[12] ought not to be regarded as the preferred means of proof. Indeed, in a system where the idea of proof has become central, proof loses its essential virtue. On the other hand, in the most ancient system, between crimes that are characterized by proof and those that are substantially identical but lack proof, there is the difference between night and day, in terms of both the forms of legal action and the degree of repression.[13] Self-evidence pertains to the very notion of the crime, making it objective and, by virtue of its presence, demanding the immediate implementation of the sentence (execution or enslavement). This continuity is essential: one does not pursue or execute after the fact; the drama that flagrancy presupposes offers a concentrated unity. We can see here—particularly as a result of Fauconnet's analysis—an ideal for criminal law: the sanction is absolutely and intimately united with the criminal deed. Everything belongs to the present; one can say everything all at once; the idea of even a recent past in no way relates to this conception of crime and instantaneous present. The telling feature of this notion is not that it gives satisfaction to the need for truth, in the juridical sense of the word,[14] but rather that it makes real the crime[15] within a situation that excludes the "application of proof."

Moreover, the analysis must be completed; society, ignored up to now, must be reintegrated into our analysis. Society was there, and it was necessary: relations, parents, neighbors, assembled witnesses, and the magistrate himself, whose role was no less necessary if solely to verify what had already been decided. For all these elements of society, there is a kind of truth. Normally, they are not present at the commission of the crime. The crime is shown to them! Or is it? The (late) concept of flagrant theft as being that which is apprehended in the commission of the act cannot enter into this context; in fact, self-evident crime occurs when the thief is caught with the stolen object;[16] and it is the stolen object that is properly designated by the word *furtum* (later *furtum* signified "in an abstract way" the theft itself). There is no question of convincing the witnesses—who are, in truth, participants—by reconstructing, even implying, what happened. We are in the realm of the "objective" crime. The *furtum*, or the item held in the hand, is both necessary and sufficient. It is not a clue; it is rather a symbol of the crime. The conventional element is even more marked in one of the types of flagrancy. Archaic law assimilates to flagrant crime, which we might call immediate, the crime that is made "manifest" by the discovery of the stolen object in a house search. This time, there is a kind of break, since it is not "at the very moment of the crime" that the discovery takes place. The identity of the notion is all the more remarkable. The intervening time (between the crime and the search) does not count: the mechanism is set in motion after a delay, one might say. It is enough that responsibility be fixed by flagrancy, which is recognized as such by the society. *Reflection* or retreat into time is not at work here; the *furtum* acts like a screen.

Proof, however archaic its forms, represents a different stage of thought: within judgment, a distance, however small, is introduced between a sign regarded as valid and the decision it authorizes or requires. But the idea of the sign differs according to the period. At the most ancient stage, the objective of proof is not to establish what we might call a historical truth, or the reconstruction of a past as past. On this point, Greece offers us much material to work with (unlike Rome, which—at the moment we become aware of her—seems already to have come to a "modern" theory of proof).

Let us briefly recall a fundamental notion that is best illustrated by the Gortynian Code: the notion of decisive proof.[17] The code limits the cases in which one can have recourse to witnesses or oaths. Either step automatically determines the sentence. The judge is obliged to conform to them; he simply pronounces sentence "according to" one or the other. The verb *dikazein*, "to judge," does not signify anything else. There is a decision of "justice" in the sense that recording by the authority is necessary, and that the decision has constitutive power, but the passivity of the judge is inherent in his position. We can therefore see how the judicial institution functioned at the stage in which we placed ourselves earlier. Due process is a struggle (*agōn*) in which, according to the rules of the game, one of the parties is allowed to utilize a given weapon against the other: proof is such a weapon. To vanquish and to convince are one and the same thing; it is the adversary that one convinces[18] (it is curious, moreover, that the French *convaincre* retains this sense). From this we get an initial glimpse of the function of proof: for the judge there is only the judicial drama which is played out in the present; there is no temporal backdrop.

But the two modes of proof that we have just seen ought to be considered in themselves.

Many currently refer to the oath as a kind of trial by ordeal. We shall have to see in what sense this is so. The oath does not operate like a trial by ordeal; it was not expected that the person taking an oath would be struck down by lightning. The oath functions rather like a proof, like a means that is defined as a social technique. (Moreover, the fact of this definition

determines the future, and in the long term the decline, of the efficacy of
the oath.) But it is in keeping with and because of its religious nature that
the oath found its way into law. We know what it consisted of;[19] the expression "the judgment of God" would not do at all. The oath does not
bring about the intervention of a divinity, conceived of as a preeminent
and specially informed man, in a kind of pledge for the past. First of all,
the word *horkos* does not designate the oath in an abstract sense but refers
to a material, a "sacred substance"—whether always sacred or sacred
only in this instance—with which the man who swears is placed in contact. To swear, therefore, is to enter the realm of religious forces of the
most fearsome sort. It is in this connection that we see the extension of the
most archaic thought; for this act of daring, which is signified by a change
of state or, more precisely, by a displacement of being, is indeed the essence of ordeal in its most authentic notion. Moreover, if the ordeal is not
connected to the positive notion of proof, the reason is that ordeal is an
appeal outside human time and space.[20] The fact that this notion appears
to us already somewhat contaminated should come as no surprise.[21] On
the contrary, what *is* remarkable is that rites, modes of behavior, and language still proclaim this notion to be fundamental. In truth, it is not the
idea as it evolved (the one familiar to us, which presupposes the ministry
of the gods as "witnesses" and informers) that can explain recourse to the
oath, since the period in which this notion earned its largest acceptance is
the period of the decline of the oath. The efficacy of the oath results from
the ambivalent situation in which the oath-taker finds himself. A valuable
source[22] tells us that the oath-taker is *enagēs*, that is, in the *agos*, the "sacred" area reserved for inhuman and frightful terrors. At the same time,
our source indicates the kind of respect (the obverse of the state of being
cursed) that the oath-taker commands from bystanders. If the oath had
authority, it was first of all in this manner: the mode of thought was not
that of investigation.

In an already technical legal system, certain applications of the oath
are quite significant.

There is other evidence for swearing together in Greece that would
confirm the sense of a widely diffused institution, one that must not be
regarded as an excrescence or a contrivance; on the contrary, coswearing
can be considered typical. In matters that are mostly of interest to the
family, conjuration was able to prevail on its own: the family is a single
entity. Coswearers were not even minimally certain guarantors of "truth"
or informants concerning a past deed. Their functions included neither
role; most often they had no knowledge concerning the deed. No intellec-
tualizing interpretation can account for the essential character of this
function, one that was to be collective or, more precisely, "of community." Conjuration is an affirmation of solidarity that is validated in jus-

tice by the religious force that the oath confers on it. Laws specify the situations in which conjuration is to have effect, and its effect is invariably absolute.

Perhaps the most remarkable oath is the one that the judge takes (by this we should understand an oath accompanying a sentence and nullifying it if taken falsely). The judge's oath is a practice whose extensions are apparent in classical Greece but can be directly observed in the Gortynian Code. We have seen that within the code the oath of the party or the testimony that the oath provides has an effect. But if the former is not prescribed or if the latter is not possible, then the verdict—which is required, and even obligatory for the judge—can be obtained only by a kind of physical force. There must be a sanction for the verdict: it is significant that this is the same thing that in civil law is supplied by the party himself. The oath in question cannot be termed promissory or declaratory;[23] it is a consecrating means through which the judge makes his verdict authoritative by obligating his own person. In fact, at times the decision he is obligated to impose seems arbitrary. The oath creates truth by defining it; there is no question of the judge's gaining access to the past (in the sense we would assign to that word today) in a system without modes of proof. In principle, testimony is neither more nor less rational than the oath, and is not necessarily posterior to it according to an imaginary law of evolution. What is true about testimony is that, unlike the oath, which cannot exceed its primitive potentialities and which loses its inherent qualities and its raison d'être when its religious nature is altered, testimony lends itself to a positive application, allowing the judge and society a more or less effective control and a grip on time that might be called "social" precisely by virtue of this link to society.

However, that is not how things started. The transition took a long time. It is instructive that we find within a legal system as advanced as that of classical Athens a stage of indecision, an unresolved conflict between two concepts that one might formulate in the following terms: testimony as a duty of justice, and testimony as an obligation on the part of the party who produces it.[24] Many traits of the institution still reveal the principle of a necessary and intentional partiality; that is, they reveal the persistence of a solidarity (one that might function on a plane other than conjuration) between the litigant and the witness. One can well see that this bears on the notion of truth; let us point out a normal procedure. When a witness is called—this witness can be called upon to swear if the opponent requires it and if the witness agrees to cooperate—there is no way he can refuse to testify other than by giving what is justly called an oath of ignorance.[25] This *exōmosia*, which is a disavowal in the full sense, cannot deal with the historical deed. It is essentially negative; the witness is made to swear that *he does not know* what the party calling him wants to make him say. Most often he "knows" something else, or perhaps the contrary, but it is not within the power of justice to make use of knowledge that is, so to speak, outside the field of vision.

The reason for this is that the fortunes of the testimony process were permanently influenced by the conditions of its early use. We have a suggestive historical datum: namely, witnesses referred to in the Gortynian Code are called "witnesses of the law." We would call them "witnesses to a question of fact," that is, witnesses who had been present at a deed or had observed a fact. Among archaic laws in general, whether a transfer of property or the denunciation of a crime is involved, witnesses are first those whose assistance and attendance confer on the act or the fact its juridical truth. Witnesses can be called on to function as so-called probative witnesses: they will "testify" in court. This is a secondary function, since it presupposes the structure of a trial. How does probative witnessing work, and for what purpose? In reality, the witnesses remain "standers-by." They continue to carry out their task in front of the judge; they bring with them a sort of effective certitude; they are, by their very name, those who "know."[26] But this "knowing" is locked up inside them. The communication of a past can be effected only by discussion of the testimony, but the discussion does not occur.

This notion is affirmed even more clearly in a procedure whose archaism continues to the middle of the fourth century B.C. *Diamarturia*[27] is a type of testimony that has the power to block a legal action, notably for the benefit of one's heir, who opposes the right of legal possession against an inheritance petition. The ability to obstruct may remain theoretical: in fact, since testimony can be assailed, there is a return by detour to a truly juridical dispute. The lawsuit for "false testimony" is in this case basically one over inheritance. But it appears that the need to be reconciled with archaism was felt. This clumsiness of adaptation reveals the coexistence of two notions of the witness. The modern one is that of the legal witness, who can lay claim only to relative authority; he is dependent on sources about which he may be questioned, and testifies as to the facts or a situation—that is, about the past. The other notion of witness is that of the guarantor, whose intercession has its full effect by itself, and whose standing is comparable to that of the Roman *vindex*.[28] This type of witness prohibits rather than attests, and the content of his testimony takes on significance before the magistrate. Contrary to his title of "witness," he does not bring to bear knowledge concerning an "established" situation; he merely states negative fact, and that there is no need for a legal attribution. This amounts to a return to prelaw, of which a nascent law had to accept the basic assumptions.

The virtue of proof does not depend on induction; nor is it based on the hypothesis of a relative or revisable credibility. Proof is institutional;

that is to say, it is derived from a system of conventions in which the signifier tends to absorb the signified. Insofar as the "signified" belongs to the past, proof is not offered in order to put the judge in immediate contact with it. Such is the archaic state from which law emerges, but it does not emerge all at once.

CREDIT AND ANTICIPATION

The question we shall now take up is that of "credit," in the largest sense of the word. It is quite a telling word, for it concerns our knowing what beliefs bear on the future, what "expectations" appear valid. To coin an anachronism, we might say that it is the law of obligations[29] that is at issue. Laws that are statutory are of another order; this is important in archaic legal systems. A family—more precisely a household—transcends duration; it is, properly speaking, eternal, reflecting as it does the double technique of legitimate filiation and adoption of "testamentary" heredity from the oldest stages of law. Time has nothing to do with this "credit": it appears only with the "contract."

To nail down our ideas, let us recall a modern view on the subject, the one that Roman law devised at the end of the Republic: "contract by consent." Inherent in this type of contract is the notion that from the moment it is concluded and by the mere fact of agreement, it carries with it for the future certain executory obligations. Psychologically, the certitude of a sanction (through legal action) and the feeling of being able to determine the future (through the guarantee of a deferred payment) are in a reciprocal relationship. However, the same is not true for other peoples under other historical conditions.

That a payment (in kind or in deed) can be guaranteed in advance is acknowledged in some so-called inferior societies, but naturally they formulate the guarantee in their own way. Those societies are the subject in "Essai sur le don." Let us briefly observe a curious opposition between Mauss and Davy: the latter is preoccupied with knowing how there came to be a union between "the two moments of time," while the former ignores the problem and accepts the notion of credit at once because he finds it among the peoples he has studied.[30] We do not want to get into this discussion, but this is the time to insist anew on a certain peculiarity of functionalist history. Progress is not linear and there can be apparent retrogressions. In fact, there is no doubt that in the prejuridical mentality that has been well attested for Greece[31] a certain notion of credit was widely accepted, a notion that, on the principle of generosity, required compensatory acts of generosity; it is also a concept that survives in a form that is characteristic of "friendship" (Arist., *Eth. Nic.*, VIII.1162b–1164b).

Now, in nascent law, "debt" is not recognized in this sense, and it will not be understood in any other sense until after much mental work; law, or a system of juridical sanctions, does not at first sanction obligation for the future, or it sanctions it only under conditions in which no notions of time as such occur.

On the first point, it is Greece, known to us from a more ancient and more archaic date in any event, that supplies us with data. When Aristotle attributes to the "mercantile" operation itself a "more free" character if it takes place *eis khronon*, he means by this, ultimately, that the mercantile operation is not in the "legal" domain (that is, the juridical domain). Moreover, Aristotle is already thinking of the judicial stage that he will later indicate is perpetuated in certain Greek cities of his own day. The latter testimony, corroborated by Theophrastus (on positive law) and by Plato (on ideal law), is of major interest. It verifies that for quite some time and according to a concept tenacious enough to retain the favor of the philosophers, Greeks did not provide for the legal enforcement of all contracts, "where one of the parties entrusted himself to the other" (*kata pistin* is to be interpreted in the bilateral sense of the good faith of the debtor and the confidence of the creditor). Credence, credit, anticipation: the machinery of law has no grasp of time.

Above all, the case of the sale-transaction in Greece might hold our attention, since more than any other it is a case of pure law; it endured, and is all the more significant because it does not concern a very ancient operation. Moreover, it offers us a kind of differentiating experience through comparisons with Roman law, which is appreciably more "evolved" than Greek law, and in which the sale-transaction has become precisely typical of contract-by-consent. If two parties agreed to defer a transaction, we would say that the seller has the obligation to deliver, the buyer to pay. In Greek law, however, there is no obligation for either party. At least that is the principle. But in a developed state of social life, both parties have to find an accommodation. Besides the obligation that began to be affirmed—in an isolated fashion and only late—in the sphere of commercial law, there are lateral methods to ensure fulfillment, means borrowed from a traditional practice which within a new juridical atmosphere supply the equivalent of a draft on the future. The negative conception is truly present at the start; and it is remarkable that in theory—in law there is always theory, or at least there is always implicit theory—this negative conception lasted through the centuries.[32]

Aristotle is not afraid to extend to the entire contractual sphere (*tōn hekousiōn sumbolaiōn*) what he says about the systematic deficiency of ancient laws. If we understand this contract in the modern sense, as Aristotle doubtless would have, his testimony becomes precious for the very terms he uses (the offering of goods for sale is a good illustration of it).

From very ancient times, however, there are bilateral operations that appear to imply for the parties involved speculation over the future, operations for which nascent law spares neither competition nor vigor: Shylock is an example of this. It is necessary to see under what conditions and within what perspective law intervenes.

The methods by which the situation of the "debtor," or rather the "obliged one," is effected at the prejuridical phase apparently consist of efficacious symbols, as continued to be the case in Roman law. Their own effect, without explicit reference to the future and without connection to the psychological notion of obligation or future satisfaction, is to produce a change in the state of the other party. This change is the operative force of the "contract" because it permits the enforcement sanctioned by a magistrate.

The first form of this change is enslavement. It was more or less done away with more or less quickly in Greece and Rome; but in the ancient periods of both, the condition of debt slaves is well known. Juridically distinct from real enslavement, this debt slavery created a veritable social class whose state of inferiority, as a result of a formal obligation, was perhaps facilitated by an initial difference in status. For our purposes (the numberless discussions concerning it notwithstanding), the Roman *nexum* supplies some pertinent information. It is indeed a juridical operation. But for all that, it cannot be called a contract: first, because its efficacy resides in a ritual (in the usual sense of the word), that is, in the act "by brass and the scales," performed according to a mentality that remains prelegal; and second, because it does not truly anticipate the future. The effect of the *nexum* is immediate: it is defined as a seizure of the labor power of the one who is obligated.[33] The ritual creates a condition of inferiority, which allows for the most ferocious sanctions, ones that are imposed by virtue of an "obligation" (in the most concrete sense) that functions through the act itself.

This form was destined not to last. Another, more flexible form is remarkable precisely because of the transition it reveals; it is the oath. The ancients knew that the oath was in the beginning a very general type of "promise." Whether it is promissory or declaratory, its mode of action is precisely the same in principle; it has the same name, it requires the same rituals, and the same procedure brings about a change of state. Under a system of law, the ideology of the oath was naturally worn away within the contractual function, as it has been in the probatory function. Vestiges of it remain, however: witness the Roman *sponsio*, which retains in its very name the notion of the "libation" as an efficacious element of the sacramental operation. In spite of its extreme simplicity, its reduction of the act to the most brief expression (since it consists of the exchange of very short *verba*), *sponsio* is always perceived as fundamentally different from "formless" acts that are nonetheless very close to it—as a relic of this force of the oath, which is immanent from the beginning and which acts in the present. After all, we begin to see a line of development in the direction of a temporal representation. The most ancient formulation (*spondesne? spondeo*) expresses *for the present* a condition of personal "obligation" on the part of the debtor. Later formulas like *dabisne? dabo*, in the future, suggest that advance, in anticipation of the future, that is essential to the modern contract.[34]

Then there is the matter of what is called the guarantee— the "real" guarantee in the pledge, or the "personal" guarantee with security. At a more or less recent stage of juridical thought, the notion of guarantee is that of an "accessory" means, one that is exterior to the contractual operation and that supplies a supplementary assurance of the discharge of an obligation. The guarantee is by definition oriented toward the future. In an ancient stage, for which we have direct and indirect evidence, the notion of the guarantee is quite different: it is not an accessory; it makes operations possible that would not have any force without it; and "obligation" is genuinely incorporated in it. The creditor will obtain satisfaction from the pledge and he will seize the security; otherwise, he has no recourse. What the creditor acquires at the start is a power, a distraint, and he acquires it in the present; the point of reference cannot be the contract, insofar as the contract signifies anticipation.

The matter of the "personal" guarantee calls for certain remarks. We are confronted with a very expansive notion that has the merit of showing us, in a living unity, the correlation of the institution of the contract, the development of society, and a type of representation that we might almost call a point of view. Within archaic laws there is a multiform character whose various types are distinguished in legal language. This character owes the general nature of his office to a prejuridical and precontractual condition that we must define before proceeding. In an entire series of situations, the bond between two parties cannot be constituted at once and by itself without the ministry of a third party. In the same way, certain situations (for example, when there is distraint over an individual who is unable to defend himself) can be resolved by resorting to force, which itself is a kind of legitimate intervention by a third party.

Security, properly speaking, is a "third party."[35] In the beginning, bail seems to have existed as an act of familial or quasi-familial solidarity in situations where custom allowed the redemption of the guilty party, who is theoretically subject to private vengeance—for example, the adulterer caught *in flagrante delicto*. The position of the guarantor is, for the moment, to free from the distraint of the offended party that person who is going to become a "debtor." This *intercessio* is a very basic act: it places the guarantor under obligation, and we must see in what sense this is so.

The guarantor promises no payment on his own, even in the case of the debtor's insolvency. The guarantor's most ancient obligation is, in the case of default, to return the debtor to the creditor to ensure the discharge of obligations that had been provisionally suspended. During this brief period of reprieve, the role the guarantor assumes is that of a guardian. Until a fairly late period, the guarantor would even physically detain the bonded person. He alone is subject to a discharge of obligation over his own person. If he alone faces this obligation, it is because he creates, at this instant, a situation that constitutes, here and now, a "satisfaction." By means of the authority he has, the third party is a living bond; he embodies the force of the accord.

The idea of a personal guarantee can be presented in another way. The Roman *auctor* is one who "offers the basis for a juridical situation,"[36] thereby (hypothetically) necessitating the "increase" that the etymology of *auctor* signifies. The same is true for the guardian, who can confirm an act with his word. P. Noailles, after having studied the varieties and multiple applications of *auctoritas*, finds that "as with all the forces of archaic law... it was first conceived on the model of pure and simple law, carrying neither obligation nor sanction." What he means is that while *auctoritas* is necessary to give juridical value to an act or a situation, it does not imply any reference to a future during which the *auctor* might assume a responsibility.

Similar situations (still pertaining to prelaw) are those with which organized law at first deals. Two observations are equally instructive. One is that the change that leads toward the modern (and temporal *par excellence*) notion of guarantee is not fully accomplished. This is true at least in Greece, where some forms of security retained their archaism and where the concept of security as an "accessory security" was worked out. The other observation is that in at least one case, but in a particularly telling one, we see another *auctoritas* emerging from the primitive one. This new *auctoritas* is by definition aimed at the future, insofar as it creates a responsibility; and the functioning of the judiciary institution seems to be the decisive reason for this evolution. We are talking about the guarantee against eviction that was demanded (rather soon) of the alienator in cases of the liberation of slaves. The alienator is the person whose mute presence gives "authority" to the act of seizure and mastery on the part of the new owner. But the alienator does not at first assume, with respect to the new owner, the obligation of defending him in court if necessary. The obligation is imposed only subsequently and through the workings of procedure.[37] But from then on *mancipium* ceases to be an action dealing with the present.

Naturally, other evolutions offer themselves for analysis.[38] We have a history that is multiple, changing, and varied according to various interpretations and laws. But if the general pattern reveals in the notion of the future a counterpart to the notion of the past, then the symmetry there is not entirely extrinsic. On occasion we perceive the connection: the role of the "witness to a deed" suggests the role of the *auctor*; and primitive functions are homologous, while respective destinies are comparable—in opposite directions. The interpretations of the past and future are complementary: by comparison with the archaic period, they correspond to another type of truth.

THE SEQUELS OF ARCHAISM

If it is true that at the moment when justice, strictly speaking, is instituted, the judge is qualified neither to enter into the past nor to sanction any engagement of the future, then this negative attitude must not be considered abstractly. On the one hand, the juridical institution is oriented toward "objective" thought concerning time and temporal linkage; on the other hand, the latter presupposes its antithesis. In its beginnings, the technique of law comes face to face with an entire series of human actions that, to coin a phrase, lean on a concept of time that we might call mystical. It is possible, in fact, to discover in the most ancient judiciary dealings evidence or survivals of concepts that correspond to those that H. Hubert defined as "religious formulations of time." Meager though they are, they are more than objects of curiosity; they are doubly interesting because they show us the forms of time that had to be made obsolete and they establish for us the change that those concepts underwent at the moment when law more or less absorbed them almost unwillingly.

In Greece, as elsewhere, the notion of a period as a specific part of time that is heterogeneous to other parts pertains strictly to the religious sphere. This notion also played a role in a prehistoric organization of sovereignty: Spartan traditionalism preserved even into the third century B.C. the custom of consulting the celestial signs every nine years to learn if the king ought to be kept in office. One aspect of this "primitive" mentality appears, at least in an isolated way, in certain practices that pertain to law. The idea that a debt terminates with the expiration of a certain period of time, independent of the debt and yet imposing its own rhythm, is well illustrated by the practice or theory of sabbatical leaves. It could also be found in a curious disposition of Spartan law: "After the death of a king, his successor frees, at the start of his reign, all the Spartans who had a debt to the king or to the State."[39] This testimony is complex: the desire for a joyous enthronement, the personal character of the "actively intransmissible" debt, the pairing of the king with an entity as abstract as the *dēmosion*—all this interferes with the notion that we see precisely in the concept of "debt to the State." To wit, it is the unique type of duration that cannot exceed the duration of a king's life span. Because of a persistent formalism, an analogous concept of rhythmic time is still present in a more developed kind of "political" thought in Athens itself. At the time of his installation the archon "makes a proclamation through heralds that each person remains, until the end of the magistracy, master and owner of goods that he had at the time of the archon's entry into office."[40]

Other points could be of greater significance. Certain juridical categories prolong, in a naturally subconscious continuity, a specific and realistic notion of time. In the bases for these categories we can recognize the idea of a quality of time, a veritable *vis a tergo*, whose efficiency is the same when, coming from the past, it deals with the current, or when, oriented toward the future, it manifests itself as a productive force. I shall limit myself to alluding to custom, because customary law does not seem to be recognized as a category in classical antiquity: it is rather in the religious domain that customary law could hold our attention.[41] The fact remains that custom itself is a juridical reality, and that authority, which is granted to tradition as such,[42] implies the active notion of a time that justifies and consecrates. The same notion, in a slightly different aspect, is doubtless not so very different from an institution that is otherwise very positive: prescription in its various forms might seem like a juridical avatar. Time "consolidates" ownership; it is the basis for property. Time protects by interposing itself; it prohibits legal action, that is, in principle, a prosecution. The motivating idea could well be that of liberation, and if so, the remote antecedents become clear. For the religious mentality, time has a specific power to wear out ("my pollution is spent," says Aeschylus' Orestes), a power that is exercised over a period defined by sacred numbers. Admittedly, the transformation was complete enough to thrust the primitive reasons into oblivion. What is more remarkable is the invalid rationalism that tries to justify after the fact an institution that cannot rationally be justified,[43] as well as a certain freedom for law to use a notion that it cannot ignore but adapts instead for its own ends.[44]

Alongside temporal models (and we may wonder if they did not have to be constituted in another realm before being admitted into juridical thought) there is one for which the above question does not arise and whose evolution is quite remarkable: interest, the "product" of wealth. The model for interest is seen in a process of *nature*—not really in the products of the earth (the tithe on grain products is of a different order), but specifically in the increase from breeding livestock (which marks a date in the religious calendar). The testimony of language is clear: *fenus* in Latin and *tokos* in Greek link interest on money with animal procreation. And interest is certainly quite different from remuneration for services rendered or from a compensation for the temporary loss of property. In an etymological note, all of whose words should be underlined,[45] Varro says most clearly what it is: gestation and reproduction. Still, a problem is posed. So long as we speak of livestock or things similar there is no problem, and the deep structure of thought is easy to discover. It is a philosophy of identity: the *yam* in Leenhardt's story is always the same.[46] We know quite well that the appetite for wealth and the desire for domination always lend themselves to a metaphor. But metaphor, an artificial process of thought, explains nothing. In the transposition, the idea of an effectiveness in time must have been kept.[47] The transposition did not occur without mental reluctance. Aristotle condemns interest, not for moral reasons, or those of humanitarianism or economics, but because interest is "against nature."[48] This is so in two senses: there is not in money a "natural" quality of reproduction; and since the purpose of money is exchange, the function of "multiplication" assigned to it is contrary to its very concept. But Aristotle recalls the analogy the vocabulary itself reveals. One senses that we have here a threshold and hence, hesitations or the refusal to accept interest. All this has not impeded usury as an institution. Law limits it intermittently—and sanctions it in general—but before a mercantile mentality could make interest seem like something "rational," there was need for some intellectual work on the notion of time, starting with the archaic data.

One could point out still another series of very special acts that are characteristic of what we call a turning point. And we could note a series of more or less voluntary, and more or less twisted, procedures that are occasioned by this turning point. It is from a very ancient Roman law that we take them (the Romans are specialists). We are talking about triple actions—that is, actions that must be accomplished three times for them to have their effect.

The *obvagulatio* (ritualistic injuries at the door of the defaulting witness) must be sustained for three days. The creditor, before distraining a debtor, is required to present him on three successive business days. The married woman falls under the *manus* of her husband (that is, she is subject to a particular body of marital rules) at the end of a year unless she has interrupted this prescription by sleeping away from home three nights in a row. The son who has been released three times by *mancipatio* is freed from his father's power. All four provisions pertain to laws of the Twelve Tables.

In spite of the diversity of purpose that we see here, these four provisions have something in common. We know that numbers—especially the number 3—confer an efficacy on human acts. When this religious notion moves into the realm of law, it requires this tripleness, but more is involved: the "three times" must be consecutive. The notion that appears here is one of a concentration of time for purposes of a juridical *operation*;

the duration, more or less vaguely conceived but felt as being necessary for fulfillment, is both symbolized and made real in a brief temporal space by virtue of the triple repetition. A father's power, which could be eroded by the fact of estrangements renewed over the course of time, definitely collapses after three consecutive estrangements.[49] A brief period of three nights, likewise consecutive, has the inverse but analogous effect of breaking in one blow, and sometimes at the last minute, that which a period of prescription was going to bring about.

The operative quality of temporal symbolism is certainly not unprecedented. At quite another level, and in the sphere of the religious technique of agronomy, Maurice Leenhardt notes an admirable example among the Melanesians.[50] What ancient Roman law offers in particular is that in view of a properly juridical effectiveness, it utilizes (as well as transposes) an ancient notion,[51] the significations of which it accentuates almost ostentatiously. But this occurs at the moment when the function of Roman law begins to be affirmed. A concrete notion of time, a value for numerical schemes. . . Roman law's offhandedness is already freed of this type of archaism.

※

The history of ancient laws can be utilized in a positive study of the notion of time. The general direction is clear enough: an abstract notion appears, then imposes itself in almost every domain. Doubtless, it would not be hard to show that the allure of this history is not the same in Rome and in Greece. On the one hand, the innovation is more precocious and more decided. On the other, the mode of thought appears less separated from its antecedents; and whether it deals with proof or the contract, it sometimes gives evidence of a sort of reluctance to break with the past. But the comparison is still valid: there is a vector because there is an orientation from a point of departure, which is the appearance of judgment in the proper sense of the word.

In truth, a strange contradiction confronts us. For the judge, under the initial conditions of legal process, time does not play a role. If anyone can be responsible for it—in a totally different sense from that of objective judgment—the third party (*auctor*, *diamarturōn*, cowswearer, etc.) can, for he is the one whose intervention is theoretically decisive. But justice, and consequently the society that expresses itself through justice, does not at first deal with time. According to the rules of the game this is a temporary refusal, but we sense how time is going to conquer: abstraction and verification will result in a change of perspective.

By chance, a Hellenic institution allows us to observe the arrival, in law, of a social function of memory, that of the *mnēmōn*. The *mnēmōn* is the person who protects the memory of the past with a view to affecting a decision in a court of law. The position that this name literally signifies is the one we find in a frequent designation of the witness.[52] But here the task is public and (hypothetically) neutral, and it indicates a displacement of the notion of witness. In fact, in Greece itself the task of the *mnēmōn* takes on the characteristic of the institutions of a modern legal system such as archives and record-keeping. Moreover, if the appeal is transmitted to magistrates entrusted with the preservation of documents, a rather widespread magistracy in Aristotle's day,[53] there is no doubt that one had originally to rely on the fidelity of an individual's memory. The Gortynian Code, which does not acknowledge written documents, does acknowledge the *mnēmones*, who are adjuncts or living "records" for the magistrates. Concerning the position itself, a twofold lesson is to be drawn. To begin with, there was a transformation—and moreover a complete laicization—of a religious practice. Under the heading *mnēmōn*, legend still remembers (and even finds a story motif for) the "hero's servant," apparently a kind of clerk or a depository for divine advice whose memory is called on at the appropriate time.[54] Thus it is originally in a religious model that there appears, on behalf of the collective memory, an element of obligation that is itself necessary and essential. But at what point does such a transposition take place, and under what circumstances does the registration of the past take on value in the juridical sphere? We have a revealing text. It is not all that old, and it is so much the better since the archaism is manifested by the superimposition of two modes of thought. The text is a law of Halicarnassus from the start of the fifth century B.C.[55] regulating the reclamation of real property following a period of civil turmoil: the victims of confiscations are allowed to exercise their rights against those who dispossessed them. It seems at first that the main point is to know which of the two parties will have preference for the oath: during a certain period (defined by the court), the original owner has preference; when that period expires, the new owner does. One might think that the question is thus settled, but the law adds: "That which is the understanding of the *mnēmones* will decide the award." It is clear that the oath has no practical application other than to introduce admissible material; but the fact that the oath is offered to only one of the parties, that the judiciary action depends on the oath-taking, and that the question of preference is initially at the forefront—all this indicates the persistence of an ancient conception of due process in which the interplay of decisive oaths between the two parties at issue allows and imposes a ruling. The awkwardness of the wording is suggestive: the effective law seems like a redrafting of the wording. The law subordinates the resolution of a lawsuit to testimony concerning a past publicly retained and put on deposit. We are seeing here two stages of juridical truth.

Therefore, the category of time had to be constituted in the law. "Abstract and quantitative time" is, in this instance, the framework in which is affirmed, for purposes of filing and deciding lawsuits, the valid notion of a past as such and a future assured as such. These are the two faces of one and the same thought process, a process that seems "natural" only after it is acquired. Admittedly, progress in the social process we have been studying does not take place in isolation or gratuitously. Law embraces an entire historical ensemble—the ensemble of the city, a new organization of human existence. But it is a central and particularly sensitive segment. The change is not inscribed there smoothly. If the first steps of law show an apparently exclusive worry over the present, this bias and this kind of stiffening indicate the suddenness of the transition. What is perceived in the rites of the most ancient type of due process is the novelty of the judiciary institution—that is, the novelty of an organ of collective sovereignty whose field of authority is at first circumspect. In the beginning, the judge was kept from going beyond the current reality of conflicts; but by taking jurisdiction over them he created the conditions for a control that signified the mastery of time, a control in which certain special techniques (procedure, monetary trade, the use of writing) would permit him a more and more secure functioning. It was a continuing process, one that was not without fumbling and unfair victories; but before the indispensable development there was a change that made it possible.

NOTES

1.   The original text of Gaius, *Institutiones*, IV. 16, reads as follows: Qui vindicabat festucam tenebat; deinde ipsam rem adprehendebat, veluti hominem, et ita dicebat: "hunc ego hominem ex iure Quiritium meum esse aio: secundum suam causam sicut dixi ecce tibi vindictam imposui;" at simul homini festucam imponebat. Adversarius eadem similiter dicebat et faciebat. Cum uterque vindicavisset, praetor dicebat: "mittite ambo hominem." Illi mittebant; qui prior vindicaverat dicebat: "postulo anne dicas qua ex causa vindicaveris;" ille respondebat "ius feci sicut vindictam imposui. . . ." Our translation is as literal as possible so as not to prejudge the import of terms or expressions that in another context could be interpreted in the sense of "subjective law" (e.g., *ex iure Quiritium*) or "title" (e.g., *qua ex causa*, or *secundum suam causam*, a phrase that we left intact, but that we interpret as did P. Noailles in *Fas et jus*, pp. 66 ff.).

2.   In sum, the *vindicta* is the rite (in gesture or words) qua legal instrument. Thus it has a semi-"abstract" sense by comparison with the *festuca* ("rod"), which must not be confused with it (see Noailles, op. cit., pp. 52 ff.). The *festuca* is the necessary instrument of the

vindicta, which is in some way incorporated in it. From this we get the double usage of *imponere*.

3. H. Lévy-Bruhl, *Quelques Problèmes du très ancien droit romain*, pp. 100 ff.; cf. Noailles, op. cit., p. 74.

4. See Noailles, op. cit., pp. 86 ff.

5. It is worth noting that because of its special "aspect," unlike the "durative" aspect of *ago, facio* "exprime l'activité sur le fait dans un certain instant" (A. Ernout and A. Meillet, *Dict. étymol.*, s.v. *ago*).

6. From this comes the expression "formule vindicatoire," one adopted by Lévy-Bruhl, *Quelques Problèmes*, p. 96. It must not be understood in the sense that it was *first* used in process and *then* extended to legal actions; in truth, its efficacy came before the procedure.

7. See *Année sociol.*, 3d ser., 1951, pp. 76 ff.

8. For the notion of the "absolute beginning" in the actualization of "ownership," and for the ideal notion that underlies it (the one involving a possession *res nullius*), see L. Gernet *Droit et société dans la Grèce ancienne*, pp. 12 ff.

9. Hence we have the most ancient form of due process regarding ownership, one in which the two parties are placed at parity; it is a form that persists in Greece during the classical period.

10. For a critique of this concept, and for the specific character of "judgment," see H. J. Wolff, "The Origin of Judicial Litigation among the Greeks," *Traditio*, IV (1946), pp. 31 ff. His thesis is accepted by some Latinists.

11. See F. de Visscher, "Mancipium et res mancipii," *Studia et documenta historiae et iuris*, III (1936), pp. 264 ff.

12. In public penal codes (emotional and coercive at heart), due process preserves here and there the use of flagrancy as proof and the notion of its import. Correlatively, the notion of the objective offense persists in the notion of flagrancy (see Dem., XXV), just as it does in the ensemble we shall be seeing.

13. See F. de Visscher, "Le Fur manifestus," *Etudes de droit romain*, pp. 184 ff. The juridical notion concerning nonflagrant theft develops later than that concerning flagrant theft.

14. As soon as the alleged wrongdoer is allowed to "contest" (see Arist., *Ath. Pol.*, 52.1), one enters an entirely different system and scheme of truth.

15. Concerning flagrancy as an element of the crime, see U. E. Paoli, "Il reato di adulterio in diritto attico," *Studia et documenta*, XVI (1950), pp. 123 ff.

16. De Visscher, "Le Fur manifestus." The essential idea is that of contact: the thief holds the object or he carries it (see *Mél. Boisacq*, pp. 391 ff.).

17. K. Latte, *Heiliges Recht*, pp. 40 f.; cf. Gernet, *Droit et société*, pp. 63 ff.

18. See Aeschin., II.87; Latte, loc. cit.

19. See the fundamental article by E. Benveniste, "L'Expression du serment dans la Grèce ancienne," *RHR*, CXXXIV (1948), pp. 81 ff.

20. E. Cassin, "Daniel dans la fosse aux lions," ibid., CXXXIX (1951), pp. 129 ff. In this extreme case (that of the vindicating ordeal) we are on another plane of truth, one where the actual deed becomes immaterial. The "crime"has been committed, in fact and uncontestably; but there is no longer any question about its commission. Interest in that regard has, in a way, evaporated.

21. The most ancient testimonium is Homeric. It is remarkable for the kind of equivocation between two notions of oath it reveals (see P. Stengel, *Die griech. Kultusalter.*[3], p. 123). On the persistence of the fundamental notion of contact with the sacred object, see idem, *Opferbräuche der Griechen*, pp. 78 ff.

22. Soph., *OT*, 656. See P. Chantraine and O. Masson, "Sur quelques termes du vocabulaire religieux des Grecs," *Festschr. A. Debrunner*, 1954, p. 89.

23.   See Gernet, *Droit et société*, p. 64.

24.   E. Leisi, *Der Zeuge im attischen Recht*, p. 38.

25.   See J. H. Lipsius, *Das attische Recht und Rechtsverfahren*, pp. 878 ff.

26.   For designations of the "witness," see Leisi, op. cit., pp. 3 ff.

27.   See Gernet, *Droit et société*, pp. 83 ff.

28.   On the notion of the *vindex* and his power, see Noailles, op. cit., pp. 54 ff.

29.   International law, and the treaties and commitments it entails, figure in this law of obligations, but we shall not deal with it at present. In addition, there is another area that ought to be of interest, namely, that of "public law." By definition, one could say, law ordains for the future. This is a cardinal notion in the ancient city, one that is sometimes regarded as having established law in its entirety as well as the validity of situations and acts in a given period. Moreover, one might wish to see in what way—and with what kind of occasional hesitation—the most ancient laws direct their attention to the future. But that would bring us into the realm of politics, not the realm of juridical thought.

30.   M. Mauss, *Sociologie et anthropologie*, p. 200; G. Davy, *La Foi jurée*, pp. 109, 207.

31.   See *Année sociol.*, 3d ser., 1951, pp. 27 ff.

32.   F. Pringsheim, *The Greek Law of Sale* (1950).

33.   Noailles, op. cit., pp. 110 ff.

34.   See P. Huvelin, *Etudes d'histoire du droit commercial romain*, p. 291, n. 3.

35.   See J. Partsch, *Griechisches Bürgschaftsrecht* (1909).

36.   Noailles, op. cit., p. 274.

37.   Ibid., pp. 223 ff.

38.   The evolution of the *arrhae*, for example. Its ancient function, of which we perceive certain survivals, is to act as a pledge and as a kind of genuine *obligation*. (The word *arrhabōn* is borrowed from a Semitic language; moreover, it occurs only in Hebrew. But the text where it occurs, Genesis 38, is quite significant: it is the passage dealing with the story of Juda and Thamar.) In contractual commerce, we see the *arrhae* utilized, especially in the sale, in order to create laterally and partially the obligation the sale by itself does not bring with it. This usage is quasi-specific in principle, and it always has its bearings in the present. Still, the very vagueness of this procedure-turned-technique favors that commercial mentality through which a sale made for a time period, whatever the letter of the law, is indeed a transaction that is valid for the future. In addition, there is yet another condition, but only in the Roman sphere. The *arrhae* have merely a probatory value, in contrast to the contract, whose anticipatory quality is assured in and of itself (*argumentum emptionis venditionis contractae*).

39.   Hdt., VI.59.

40.   Arist., *Ath. Pol.*, 56.2.

41.   What does the quality of time consist of? In Sophocles' *Antigone* (450 ff.) the question is not posed; the religious law the play deals with is opposed to *temporal* law. Elsewhere, we might be closer to a specific notion regarding custom were it not for the irony of Euripides in the *Bacchae* (where the novelty of the religion of Dionysus is justified by respect for an immemorial past), which directs us to a possibly very general fact, one that we can only note: namely, that time—some time—is a necessary element; but one does not count it (without falling into a puerile casuistry); and it can, in fact, be quite short.

42.   This authority is especially perceptible in the *patria* of the religious *genē*, which are the depositories of a certain sacred law (provided the assets exceed the liabilities for the city).

43.   See Dem., XXVI.22 ff.; Cic., *Caecin.*, 26.74.

44.   Parallel to what we said concerning "custom" in n. 41 above, it is "time" that is in effect put to use; however, one knows that in archaic laws, time extensions for the prescription of purchase, such as the Roman *usucapio*, are of empirical necessity very brief.

45. *Ling.*, III, *ap.* Aul Gell., *NA*, XVI.12.7: *fenus…a fetu et quasi a fetura quadam pecuniae parientis atque increscentis.*

46. On this story, which we mention as an illustration, see I. Myerson, *Journal de psychol.*, LII (1955), p. 380.

47. The most ancient measure of which was the specific period of the lunar month (see Ar., *Nub.*, 16 ff.). It remained the standard duration for interest.

48. Arist., *Pol.*, I.1258b.2–8.

49. See H. Lévy-Bruhl, *Nouv. Etudes*, pp. 80 ff. It seems that very early on—and perhaps the intent of the lawmaker had already been focused in this direction—the regulation permitted, in an instant of time and in a way that we might term feigned or artificial, the realization of the changes in status that emancipation and the adoption of a son into a family constituted. One could readily believe that at the base of all this there is a standard provision according to which paternal power is attenuated after three *mancipationes* (accomplished in the course of an indefinite period). The moment that interests us is when the three are welded together for the purpose of a fixed juridical operation.

50. M. Leenhardt, *Do Kamo*, p. 105. A chief realizes that the rhythm of the communal farming has slowed down, for the planting cannot take place until his fields are cleared, until the brush is burned. Hence, there is a damaging delay. "This chief then resolves to render this month communal: he inaugurates it with a symbolic fire that prefigures the burning of the brush."

51. One of these provisions has an antecedent in religious law: one of the taboos that surrounds the life of Jupiter's flamen is a prohibition against being away from Rome three nights in a row.

52. Let us recall that the most current Greek word for witness, *martus*, belongs to the root *smer*, which is the root for the Latin *memor*. The specific idea of remembrance still appears to be at an intermediate level, one where the "solemn witness" is elevated to an already public office. In a passage already cited, Theophrastus points out such a provision in the law of Thurii, namely, that the three neighbors closest to land that has been sold are to receive a coin "as a memory and witness" (*mnēmēs heneka kai marturias*).

53. *Pol.*, VI.1321b.34, 1322b.34. The continuity of the word does not signify perfect continuity from a psychological point of view. There emerges from this a rather serious question: in a period of literacy, did not the function of memory undergo some sort of regression in favor of a technique that no longer dealt with a represented past? Correlatively, one might mention the notion of writing as being obligatory by itself and being valid *contra fidem veritatis.*

54. Plut., *Quaest. Graec.*, 28. See Eust., *ad Od.*, 1697, 54; W. R. Halliday, *The Greek Questions of Plutarch*, p. 137.

55. *SIG*[3], no. 44.

CHAPTER 9

Some Connections between Punishment and Religion in Ancient Greece

The observations I present here deal with a general question of manifest interest. Punishment fundamentally entails a certain formalism—we might even say symbolism—one that has survived till very late in our own society and that is naturally more conspicuous in the most ancient societies. It is never idle to ask what is the significance of the rituals that accompany punishment or that are actually involved in executing it. One senses that there is nothing quite so illuminating as a walk through the garden of punishments.

There is little point in warning you that the present contribution is quite modest; all the things I will say are simply marginal notes on a text of Plato. In Book IX of the *Laws* (855C), Plato discusses the forms of punishment that are to be employed in the new city: among them he mentions "the infamous exposure of criminals—seated or standing—near sanctuaries at the country's border."[1] Plato rarely invents legal arrangements, nor has he imagined this form of punishment; he had seen it practiced in his own nation. Here one could point to historical attestations. Even in Athens there was the equivalent of the pillory: certain criminals, especially thieves, were shackled in public view.[2] Outside Athens, exposition is mentioned as a punishment[3] for various kinds of offenders, such as bankrupt and insolvent debtors, adulterers, slanderers, deserters, and so on.[4] The condemned undergoes the punishment either standing (this is most frequent) or seated. The exposition is sometimes preceded by an ignominious procession that Glotz[5] has compared to the parade of the *katharmoi*.

This address to the Sixth Congress of the History of Religions, held in Brussels in September 1935, originally appeared in *Ant. Class.*, V (1936), pp. 325–39. It is presented here with the elaborations the oral version did not allow.

The *katharmoi* were the human scapegoats who in several cities and at certain festivals were led through the streets and chased out of the city. They took with them the cities' impurities. It should be noted that this form of punishment sometimes contains elements that must have originally had religious significance.[6] In Gortyn, the adulterer is exposed wearing a crown of wool—and wool's "cathartic" qualities are well known. According to the laws of Kharondas, the slanderer—who also was exposed—was crowned with the tamarisk, the *infelix arbor*.[7]

Plato's text must thus be placed in a particular historical milieu; but it can shed some light on a method of punishment that was more or less in use in this milieu. Two things suggest themselves immediately, and they are not in conflict with the historical data. First, at least in the background, there is a certain religious idea of punishment. It is quite significant that the offenders are pilloried in the vicinity of sanctuaries, even if this point was a product of Plato's imagination. That they are relegated to the country's frontier is no less significant. This last point is related to the earlier one; their explanation is the same. One of the purposes that appears in forms of punishment as they are religiously understood is the desire to eliminate, and more specifically (for the word "eliminate" should be understood in its true etymology) to expel someone beyond the frontiers. So it was that the remains of persons guilty of sacrilege were banished; and in a well-known religious procedure (and one mentioned in Plato),[8] inanimate objects or the corpse of an animal, if they caused a person's death, were treated in the same way. This practice was termed *huperorizein*; the punishment in Plato is a symbol of *huperorismos*.

Second, Plato emphasizes the condemned criminal's posture; he was forced either to sit or to remain upright. Posture is evidently regarded as something important and significant; and Plato would not have described it in detail had it not been an essential component of the punishment itself as he understood it. It is precisely this notion that we will try to understand: what ideas—albeit obscure—does this form of punishment imply?

※

To find the answer, we must resort to exaggeration. We will begin with a postulate that in itself is quite plausible, but that will obviously have to justified: these temporary and relatively mild forms of punishment can be understood as diluted or symbolic forms of the death penalty. What we will deal with immediately, then, is the most extreme penalty, capital punishment, for clearly we will be in a better position to interpret the characteristic element of punishment in general if we find it in some form of capital punishment.

In this regard there is precisely one form of punishment that must be considered: *apotumpanismos*. In 1923 it was the subject of a study by Keramopoullos,[9] who seemed to give the long-waited explanation. Traditionally and quite arbitrarily, *apotumpanismos* had been viewed as execution by cudgel. Using archaeological as well as linguistic and philological arguments, Keramopoullos claimed that the punishment consisted of fixing the condemned person with iron clamps to a pole set in the ground and leaving him there to die. In sum, it was a procedure analogous to crucifixion.[10] What kind of criminals were punished in this way? This is the question I recently asked precisely in connection with Keramopoullos' research on capital punishment in general,[11] and I have concluded that basically the *apotumpanismos* was a summary punishment for criminals who were termed *kakourgoi*: thieves caught in the act, highway robbers, burglars, and the like. At first it seems a brutal punishment, one that is purely reactive and vindictive. It is opposed to religious forms of punishment, which have as their primary object the elimination of a pollution and which presuppose some idea of *devotio* and the consecration to divine powers of the guilty person whom the community abandons in order to save itself (e.g., "hurling headlong," a punishment that in some ways is a trial by ordeal).

There could be, then, "secular" punishment and religious punishment. But as far as *apotumpanismos* is concerned, such a conclusion would be misleading. The antithesis that I shall point out reveals, above all, that there are different tendencies within the psychology of collective vengeance. And yet this is not to conclude that the religious symbolism is radically absent from secular punishment as such.[12] At least two facts suggest the contrary. First, in another Mediterranean civilization, that of the Romans, the crucifixion of criminals sometimes took on religious significance. In the Twelve Tables it is a punishment prescribed for *fures* who under cover of night harvest others' fields. The tree on which *fures* are crucified is dedicated to Ceres.[13] Second, *apotumpanismos* appears in myth; the punishment of Prometheus is a striking example.[14]

Given the necessary relationships between religious imagination and cult practices, we tend to ask ourselves whether or not there is here an almost direct connection between the representation of the executed criminal and that of a victim. Capital punishment has often been interpreted as human sacrifice. But even in extreme cases the two institutions are not confused. They are distinguished primarily by their different functions; and if it is in the area of criminality that this distinction is sharpest, it is precisely that area we have in mind.[15] Suffice it to say—for the purpose of establishing our hypothesis—that the passion for collective vengeance can satisfy and justify itself in the institution of sacrifice, which appeals to the imagination. Such a type does in fact exist in a ritual that is noted for its unusual character,[16] but that is very old: an animal is fixed to a tree or column in order to be immolated.[17] Our sources for this are restricted to some coins from Ilium,[18] certain expressions in Homer,[19] and a description of a sacrifice in Plato's Atlantis (one that he could not have made up)[20]—in other words, to a very few but still very valuable allusions.

Is it rash to accept the kind of connection we are suggesting? Sophocles' *Ajax* supplies the answer. In a state of madness, the hero of the play fixes a ram to a column. Believing that the ram is Odysseus, Ajax whips the animal and prepares to kill it; by doing this he satisfies his feelings for revenge.[21] Ajax's mad passion expresses itself in the form of an ignominious kind of punishment. The treatment of Melanthios in the *Odyssey* is analogous;[22] and there are other examples from the classical period.[23] At the same time, it is noteworthy that Ajax carries on as if he were preparing a victim for sacrifice. The whole episode contains an intentional ambiguity (and ambiguity is frequent in tragedy) between two equally compelling concepts: sacrifice in which an animal is victim, and punishment where the victim is human. In the quasi-technical description of the punishments the hero imagines he inflicts on his enemies, Stengel has found details and terms that refer to sacrifice, even specific forms of sacrifice.[24]

It seems, therefore, that a specific image of capital punishment could subconsciously lend itself to a religious interpretation. This image is all the more striking because it involves a type of punishment that by its very bent is foreign to the whole notion of *piaculum*. And it is the same image that in an earlier study we claimed contained some of the characteristics of the "infamous" punishment:[25] in the temporary pillorying of someone *standing up*, we find the blueprint of our quasi-crucifixion. Moreover, the ignominious procession,[26] suggested by the Platonic text[27] and involving—in the case of Kinadon of Sparta—elements that remind us of the *apotumpanismos*,[28] could precede capital punishment. Inversely, since it was applied to the *furtum nec manifestum*, punishment at the pillory or stockade for certain crimes of theft seems to be a diluted version of the punishment normally reserved for "open thievery."[29] And although we are not as informed as we would like to be on the specific forms of this exposure, we know from the expression *xulon*, a term also applied to the stake used for the *apotumpanismos*, of a device used for pillorying.[30] The iron collar (*kuphōn*)—even if we admit that it was used by itself—conjures up the memory of one of capital punishment's major components.[31] When Aristophanes mentions these forms of ignominious punishment there is something so spontaneously sinister and equivocal about them that we imagine the horrible fate of someone condemned to the "stake."[32] It would be a misrepresentation, however, to say that in classical Athens, where similar forms survived, they regularly retained this halo of religious thought that could surround the image of *apotumpanismos*. But it is not inaccurate to believe that even in Athens they must have derived their emotional power from ancient patterns of thought and from a kind of obsession with an unknown past. The condemned individual, standing in infamy, and the *Laws* of Plato, with their characteristically penitential tone, give us in an instant a glimpse of ideas that have been dormant.

※

Let us now examine the sitting posture. Plato's testimony is enough to assure us that this posture was employed in certain forms of punishment. Nevertheless it is little attested. We might also ask whether in ancient times it was used for capital punishment. On this subject I would mention several texts that indicate it was. First, there is the myth of Theseus in the underworld (to which we will return). Theseus and Peirithoos remain seated while being punished for their alleged sacrilege (for Peirithoos it was an eternal punishment; for Theseus it was to be until his deliverance). Second, among the possible variations of *apotumpanismos* there is a quite curious one involved in the punishment of Prometheus: he is often depicted in art chained in a crouching position.[33] In this connection one of Aristotle's texts is relevant. After explaining the prerogatives of the *Boulē*, Aristotle mentions the circumstances in which it loses its power to decree the death penalty (*Ath. Pol.*, 45.1). A certain Lysimachus had just been handed over to the executioners—the text indicates that the punishment was to be *apotumpanismos*—when a well-timed appeal forced the case to go to trial by *jury*.[34] The text is explicit: the condemned man was already *seated* (*kathēmenon*) in preparation for his punishment. I do not know if the word *kathēmenon*—it is quite unexpected when one has in mind an execution by cudgel blows—has ever been explained. It is possible to imagine that *kathēmenon* has been substituted for *kathē(lō)menon* (an easy correction), the participle of a verb that suits *apotumpanismos* perfectly; this could be justified by several uses of the closely related verb *prosēloun*.[35] In the case of emendation it is best to be economical, and *kathēmenon* is quite satisfactory. As we have seen, it might refer to a characteristic detail of the execution.

So in this case, as in the case of the upright position, a specific form of this ignominious punishment could be derived from a specific form of capital punishment. At any rate, we have established that in certain types of "exposure" that are analogous to pillorying, the man condemned to punishment must remain seated. We ought then, while relying on the Platonic text, to ask ourselves what the ancient significance of this practice was. In dealing with such a question it is necessary from the beginning to note that the seated position is in many instances a ritual one. We must deal with this fact only insofar as it pertains to our subject, but even so a digression is necessary.

Our first point will be to emphasize the fact that the seated position is one of the rites, and even the essential rite, of supplication. There is no point in belaboring this, even though Latte's examination of the relevant texts[36] could be enlarged. Let me just add—I simply want to focus better on the emotional force of this posture—that it involves a tragic motif[37] whose importance and frequency have perhaps not been adequately recognized.[38] Near the altar or at the tomb, which often appears at the center of the stage, there is often a seated suppliant whose act of supplication lies at the core of the drama. Now, the characteristic function of the ritual in its social dimension is to make the one performing the rite a "man" who belongs to the person in whose honor the rite is performed. One of Cyrene's religious laws applies precisely to this type of situation.[39] Moreover, this kind of ritual is much more widespread than we have been led to believe, for in many cases the suppliant asks for asylum and protection. If the ritual is directed to a god, the suppliant dedicates himself to the god; if it is directed to another human being, the suppliant entrusts himself to the religious powers of his household and dedicates himself to the hearth that he holds onto. In both cases, the rite is substantially the same. It is possible to conclude, then, that at first sight, sitting (which frequently becomes prostration)[40] is a symbol of the *deminutio capitis*. But in the case of the *deminutio capitis*, we are dealing with the negative side of supplication; and everyone is aware that supplication puts a formidable force into play, a force that is really quite inexorable and that acts of its own power. The image of a seated suppliant immediately evokes this constraining force.[41] We can understand just what this force is in those extreme cases where the act of supplication goes as far as the suppliant's suicide. This is exactly what happens in the *dhārṇa* (the suicidal fast of a debtor),[42] an institution that is well known in India and Ireland, and traces of which can be found in Greece.[43] We have a precisely similar situation in Aeschylus' *Suppliant Women*, where the king—and this is the tragedy of his predicament, which we suspect from the play's very beginning and which is then made explicit—is threatened with the suicide of the Danaids as they sit in supplication at the altars of the gods.[44]

Could the *deminutio capitis* be a kind of virtual death? If the seated position of suppliants did not play a role in certain rituals of mourning and initiation, we would not be able to attribute this significance to the posture. But here, too, the facts are well known. In the cult of the dead[45] the word *kathedra* is a technical term.[46] Through this posture the living associate with and assimilate themselves to the dead. In the oldest depictions the dead are represented as seated,[47] and we shall see the survival of this motif in the myth of Theseus. Here I pose only one question: is this image the origin of certain funerary practices? What seems to exist here is a necessary connection between the ritual posture and the depiction of the dead.[48] In other words, in a typical instance of mourning where this posture is adopted, the posture of the dead, like a disease, has spread to the living. Another typical case involves the mystery religions: sitting is a position attested in the initiatory rites.[49] And the idea of rebirth lies at the basis of initiation, a rebirth that naturally follows upon a ritual death.

Returning to the rites of supplication, we will see that the connection, or better still the identification, between the symbol of death (represented by the suppliant's posture) and the mythical concept of death itself is revealing. To make the suppliant stand up (*anistanai*) is to grant him the salvation he has sought. To make a dead man rise is to give him life again. The term *anastasis* has quite naturally taken on the meaning of "resurrection": the verb *anistanai* designates Herakles' deed[50] when he raised Theseus from his seated position in the underworld and delivered him from death.[51]

The example of Theseus is instructive for two reasons. Theseus is not only a dead man who is revived but he also plays the role of the condemned;[52] in addition, his posture indicates his punishment. The ideas we have brought together form a complex unit. In the kind of punishment we have been examining, the seated position is obviously symbolic, but of what? We can say that it is a symbol of death: a symbol of the condemned person's annihilation in that he is mythically expelled from the realm of the living at the same time and in the same manner that he is expelled from his society's territory. The two procedures *devotio* and *exorismos* can be considered identical. Plato's text gives us adequate hints about both.

※

How do we account for these ideas? There are some forms of capital punishment for which one might say the symbolism is rather direct. These are the strictly religious forms in which the death penalty tends to be fused with human sacrifice. There are also those for which the symbolic character is secondary and derives from an association of ideas. This is what we believe happens in *apotumpanismos*. Because it is an institution, the death penalty, as different in kind as are its origins, is conceived of as something more or less unified. Even in those forms of capital punishment that one might call "secular," its depiction is colored by religious thought. The death involved is not simply death; it is not a purely physical event. What precedes, accompanies, and clarifies it is a ritual death, a death in the religious sense. This seems to be the case in the Germanic forms of capital punishment, where the symbols, sometimes strangely like those of initiation, represent the condemned person as one who has been committed to the world of the dead.[53]

We might now understand how ignominious forms of punishment can be described as substitutes for, or diluted forms of, the death penalty. In the same passage we have been examining, when Plato takes up the subject of a debtor's imprisonment, he speaks of *propēlakismoi*, cruel types of treatment that could be additional forms of punishment. Ignominious punishment in general consisted of *propēlakismoi*. This word is applied to a whole and particularly instructive series of terms conveying "abuse" and "insult." Though they lose their nuanced meanings by the classical period, terms that deal with actual injury (*aikia*), verbal injury (*kakēgoria*), and outrage itself as it is evoked in words like *lōbē*, *lumainesthai*, etc.—this entire vocabulary reflects the same stamp: acts of insult and outrage had originally a mysterious and efficacious quality. Of such a type was the outrage of *maskhalismos*, performed on an enemy's corpse; it was a typical form of *aikia*.[54] In essence, these were all acts of vengeance. This vital spirit of vengeance recurs in certain forms of punishment. The idea of *infamia*, as Huvelin has adequately demonstrated, is in principle a magical and religious concept. Its purpose is to weaken and—as far as possible—destroy an individual's "mystical" force, the force that gives him his existence and his value: what the Greeks called *timē*.

The ignominious form of punishment, which had its origin in modes of thought similar to these, must have been widespread in ancient times. For the classical period, only a few isolated testimonies exist, almost on the margin of law. Current opinion has it that degrading forms of punishment were for the most part eliminated under the rule of the city.[55] This is true, but some qualification is required. The need for symbols and for their proliferation characterizes societies that existed before the foundation of the polis. This phenomenon can be seen in every area of law, including contractual law. We can never insist too much on the radical and sudden kinds of change that the appearance of a new social form produces. Religious symbolism tends to be eliminated; even in the realm of criminal law, the invention of money allows for the substitution of another type of symbolism, a profane symbolism *par excellence* whereby the principal form of punishment becomes the fine. Forms of punishment that do not involve money also undergo significant changes. Capital punishment is stripped of its primitive purpose and design, and *atimia* becomes a civil form of disgrace. The decline of the ignominious form of punishment is another aspect of the same process. Let us point out that on the whole this removal of ancient symbolism seems to have been more complete and profound in Greece than in Rome. In Rome the relationship between *fas* and *ius* is well known, as is the more lasting subordination of the latter to the former.

NOTES

1.   ...*ē tinas amorphous hedras ē staseis ē parastaseis eis hiera epi ta tēs khōras eskhata.* A literal translation is not at all easy. What is the difference between *staseis* and *parastaseis?* How are the last words connected with the rest of the phrase? I believe that the two questions resolve into one grammatical question. Timaeus' gloss for *parastasis (stasis para tina)* is merely the tautology of a lexicographer and is completely useless. However, since *parastaseis* is followed by a complement that answers the question *quo*, it is reasonable to detect the idea of motion in the prefix. An example from Aristotle (*Pol.*, V.1308b.19) helps confirm this: here the word is used in connection with banishment (cf. *metastasis*). On the other hand, the doublet *staseis-parastaseis* seems to indicate that in both cases the standing posture was imposed on the criminals through the very mode of the penalty, the only difference being that in the first there could have been an initial ignominious parade (of which we shall see some examples) to the place where the convicts were to undergo their punishment. Although the phrase *eis hiera...* can be linked grammatically only with *parastaseis*, it can also be logically joined to *hedras* and *staseis*. There is one last question to pose: are we dealing only with sanctuaries at the fringes of the country? One would have expected at least an article to go with *hiera*, or even a phrase like *ta hiera ta epi* etc. Would it not be more natural to see here, instead of a single, synthetic complement, *two* complements, and to read (in a way that is warranted by Plato's syntax) *eis hiera epi* [*te*] *ta tēs khōras eskhata?* All this is merely a detail that does not affect the overall interpretation.

2.   A law cited and commented upon by Lysias (X.16), and Demosthenes (XXIV. 105). For the iron collar, see Pollux (citing Cratin.), X.177; Patmos Lexicon, *BCH*, I (1877), pp. 143 f; *Suda*, s.v. *kuphōn*; Ar., *Plut.*, 465; Arist., *Pol.*, VII.1306b.3.

3.   See G. Glotz, *Dict. des ant.*, s.v. Poena.

4.   Ael., *VH*, XII.12; Diod. Sic., XII.12.2; Nic. Dam., *FGrH*, 90.103 (Jacoby); Hsch., s.v. *akristios*. The ignominious punishments of this type have recently been studied by K. Latte (*Hermes*, LXVI [1931], pp. 154 ff.). His skepticism concerning the worth of certain testimonia is limited in scope. Even if our sources are less than accurate on certain points, they surely did not invent these forms of punishment. When, for example, Diodorus tells us that in the law of Kharondas the "sycophant" was punished by exposition, one can be incredulous that such an offense was dealt with in an ancient law. Even so, is not a genuinely ancient offense like "evil words" lurking under this newer term?

5.   *La Solidarité de la famille dans le droit criminel en Grèce*, p. 25.

6.   See L. Gernet, *Platon: Lois, Livre IX*, p. 80.

7.   See Latte, *Hermes*, LXVI (1931), pp. 154 ff; Pliny, *NH*, XIII.116, XXIV.68.

8.   *Leg.*, IX.873D–E. This procedure applies both to law (acts of homicide pertaining to the Prytaneion) and to religion (the ritual of the Bouphonia).

9.   A. Keramopoullos, *Ho apotumpanismos: Sumbolē arkhaiologikē eis tēn historian tou poinikou dikaiou kai tēn laographian* (Athens, 1923).

10.   There are differences only in detail between the two modes of punishment. In *apotumpanismos* there is no crossbar and the arms are kept along the sides of the body. Moreover, as we shall see, there are possible variations to this. In general, examples of crucifixion that are cited for Greece (and not those that are of an Eastern sort or that are meted out in the East: see Pl., *Grg.*, 473C; idem, *Resp.*, II.362A) are in fact instances of *apotumpanismos* (as in Hdt., IX.120; Plut., *Per.*, 28; Dem., XXI.105). For the significance of the word *prosēloun* in Dem., XXI.105, see Keramopoullos, op. cit., pp. 25 ff.

11.   It is found in *REG*, XXXVII (1924), pp. 261 ff. [= pp. 252–76 below].

12.   In the article just cited, I omitted this question; see ibid., p. 291.

13.   Pliny, *NH*, XVIII.3.12 (= Twelve Tables, VIII.9, in P. F. Girard, *Textes de droit romain*, p. 18). See P. Huvelin, *Etudes sur le furtum dans le très ancien droit romain*, I, pp. 61 ff. For the meaning of *suspendere*, see Cic., *Rab. Post.*, 13; cf. E. Saglio, *Dict. des Antiq.*, II, p. 1575.

14.   See Keramopoullos, op. cit., pp. 62 ff., where Aesch., *PV*, 52 ff., is examined (cf. Hes., *Theog.*, 521 f.) and where there is a summary of the terms characteristic of *apotumpanismos* in Lucian (*Prom.* and *DDeor.*, 1). We will return to works of art that (since they are free of the invention Aeschylus allowed himself) are at times much closer to actuality. For the significance of the eagle, see Keramopoullos, op. cit., pp. 80, 83.

15.   Clearly, if this kind of crucifixion had been used in matters of religious crime, then the assimilation between the victim and the punished would be immediately evident. However, this is not the case. What interests us here is the spontaneous extension of symbolism.

16.   See M. P. Nilsson, *Griech. Feste*, p. 235; P. Stengel, *Opferbräuche der Griechen*, pp. 124 ff.

17.   See J. E. Harrison, *Themis*, pp. 163 ff.

18.   On the cult of Athena Ilia, see V. Fritze, *Arch. Jahrb.*, XVIII (1903), pp. 58 ff. (Mycenaean gems bear similar depictions); cf. *Dict. des antiq.*, s.v. *Sacrificium* (p. 968, fig. 5999). Concerning the role of the tree and the pillar in primitive forms of *apotumpanismos*, see Keramopoullos, op. cit., p. 66.

19.   *Il.*, XX.403 f. (ritual of Poseidon Helikonios); see Stengel, loc. cit.

20.   Pl., *Criti.*, 119E. Concerning a possible source for the whole passage in which the description is found, see C. Picard, *Acrop.* (1933), pp. 3 ff.

21.   Soph., *Aj.*, 106 f.: *thanein gar auton ou ti pō thelō prin an detheis pros kion' herkeiou stegēs....* See Keramopoullos, op. cit., p. 30. As is known, scourging is an added punishment in the Roman crucifixion. Moreover, there is a religious sense to scourging (to which we shall return). I do not mean to say that it involves an element of sacrifice; it is administered to devotees (cult of Artemis Orthia at Sparta, the rite of Skiereia at Alea, a rite at Delos), and to the god himself (Pan, in Arcadia). I am not sure if it was administered in the case of sacrificial victims.

22.   Od., XXII.173 ff.: *...kion' an' hupsēlēn erusai...hōs ken dētha zōos eōn khalep' algea paskhēï.*

23.   It is a traditional procedure for vengeance which we can still find in Lysias, fr. XVII.2 (Coll. des Univ. de Fr., II, p. 264), and in Aeschines, I.59; scourging also is mentioned in both sources. Other testimonia are cited in R. C. Jebb's edition of *Ajax* in the note for line 108. One should note the constant factor of the pillar (*pros ton kiona* in Lysias and Aeschines); for the term used by Sophocles, see Jebb, loc. cit.

24.   Stengel, op. cit., pp. 95, 120 (especially in lines 298 f., where the most frequent types of sacrifice are mentioned).

25.   *REG*, XXXVII (1924), p. 286 [= pp. 264–65 below].

26.   With the Romans it is a prelude to crucifixion.

27.   See p. 240–41 above.

28.   Xen., *Hell.*, III.3.11: *dedemenos kai tō kheire kai ton trakhēlon en kloiōi* [precisely the characteristics of *apotumpanismos*] *mastigoumenos* [see nn. 22 and 23 above] *kai kentoumenos autos te kai hoi met' autou kata tēn polin periēgonto.*

29.   Lys., X.16; Dem., XXIV.105. The victims are thieves, against whom one has recourse to *dikē* and not to *apagōgē*. The latter is applicable in cases of *flagrans delictum* and results in execution by *apotumpanismos*.

30.   The *tetrēmenon xulon* in Ar., *Lys.*, 680, which is traditionally understood as an "iron collar," should be compared to the *pentesuringon xulon* in Ar., *Eq.*, 1049, a not too explicit designation for capital punishment.

31.   See Keramopoullos, op. cit., pp. 30 and 108 (fig. 16).

32.   See n. 2 above; Ar., *Plut.*, 476.

33.   This posture, known to us from vase paintings and an archaic relief sculpture (*Dict. des antiq.*, IV, p. 682, figs. 5802, 5803), seems to be the most ancient. It is important to observe that this iconography has pre-Hellenic precedents (ibid., fig. 5801). In addition to proving the antiquity of punishment in general and of this type of punishment in particular, this fact suggests once again that works of art from the Aegean period could have provided a foundation for the mythical imagination of later periods. Among our literary sources, the most ancient description of the punishment is found in Hesiod, *Theog.*, 521 ff.; in its specifics, it is a difficult passage to interpret (see Keramopoullos, op. cit., pp. 62–63). I wonder if the word *meson* in l. 522 ought not be connected with Prometheus, not in order to make it refer to the punishment at the stake, but to have it serve as an allusion to the crouched position.

34.   *Kai lusimakhon autēs agagousēs hōs ton dēmion, kathēmenon ēdē mellonta apothnēskein Eumelidēs ho Alōpekēthen apheileto.* It would be of considerable interest to know the date of this event; unfortunately, our evidence is meager. Quite probably it was late (from a period after the archonship of Euclid); see P. Cloché, *REG*, XXXIII (1920), p. 3.

35.   Dem., XXI.105; Lucian, *DDeor.*, I.1, and *Prom.*, 1.

36.   K. Latte, *Heiliges Recht*, p. 106 and n. 17.

37.   In this case the symbol of death, followed by a symbol of resurrection, should have some link with the schema of the *ludus sacer* (see G. Murray, in Harrison's *Themis*, pp. 341 ff.).

38.   In fact, we find this essential element in a large number of extant tragedies. In certain cases misunderstandings arise from faulty translations (currently in vogue) of significant words, like *hedra* and *prosesthai* at the beginning of *Oedipus Tyrannus*. Concerning Electra at the tomb of Agamemnon, see C. Robert, *Bild and Lied*, p. 169; for the significance of the ritual in a similar situation, see S. Eitrem, *Opferritus und Voropfer*, pp. 414 ff. Concerning the supplication of Telephos and its link with a concrete ritual (Thuc., I.136.3), see L. Séchan, *Etudes sur la trag. gr. dans ses rapports avec la céramique*, p. 163.

39.   The law concerning the *epaktos ikesios* (F. Solmsen and E. Fränkel, *Inscr. gr. ad illustr. dial. sel.*, p. 60, par. 5); see Wilamowitz-Moellendorff, *Sitz. Preuss. Akad.*, 1927, p. 157 (in par. 7, a seated posture is indicated for another type of supplication). Cf. Eur., *Hec.*, 249: *doulos ōn emos*.

40.   H. Bolkenstein (*Theophrastos' Charakter der Deisidaimonia* [*RGVV*, XXI.2]) has carefully studied the terms (*prospiptein*, [*kath*]*ezesthai*, [*kath*]*ēsthai*, etc.) that often deal with the posture of the suppliant. He has been able to show that in a certain number of cases these verbs indicate a kind of kneeling. Still, the essential image, the one stressed by all the words (including the substantive *hedra*), is obviously that of the seated posture, which in typical rites at the tomb or the hearth seems to suffice in itself.

41.   See Aesch., *Supp.*, 365 ff.: *outoi kathēsthe dōmatōn ephestioi emōn· to koinon d' ei miainetai polis*. . . .

42.   See P. Huvelin, "Magie et droit individuel," *Année sociol.*, X (1907), p. 22.

43.   The legend of Kharila (Plut., *Quaest. Graec.*, 12.293D f.), one that has usually been dealt with only from the point of view of the ritual for which it is the *aition* (see W. R. Halliday, *The Greek Questions of Plutarch*, p. 72), has fortunately been reexamined by Glotz, *Solidarité*, pp. ix and 64. We point out that one of the details that survived the changes wrought by myth is the *sitting* at the door of the person being solicited (*pros tas thuras*. . . *hiketeuon*). This sitting, more or less attenuated, is a persistent element in certain rites, usages, or expressions (*Vit. Hom.*, 475–76; [Hom.], *Eir.*, 12 ff.; Soph., *El.*, 109; Ar., *Nub.*, 466; etc.).

44.   Aesch., *Supp.*, 345, 462 f.; note the expression *miainesthai*, which evokes—in a characteristic form—the notion of the constraining force of ritual.

45.   See K. Sittl, *Die Gebärden d. Gr. u. Röm.*, p. 65; Eitrem, op. cit., p. 400.

46.   T. Klauser, *Die Cathedra im Totenkult der heidn. u. christl. Antike*, pp. 13 ff.

47.   It is known that the most ancient representations of the "banquet of heroes" have the heroes seated. Of course, there may be in this image something quite different from the mythical relic and the ritual. Still, the notion of an association with the dead in the ritual of the *kathedra* is suggested by the fact that at the funeral banquets it is the dead who are thought to receive the living (L. Malten, *Mitteil. d. arch. Inst.*, *R.A.*, XXXVIII [1923], p. 301).

48.   In the *Nēsteia* of the Thesmophoria (cf. L. Deubner, *Att. Feste*, p. 55), the ceremony whereby young girls *khamai kathēmenai* (Plut., *De Is. et Os.*, 69), which in itself has another meaning (see Eitrem, op. cit., pp. 47 ff.), has been interpreted (through an association of ideas) as a kind of participation in the *mourning* of Demeter, who is invariably imagined in myth and in art as being seated (see J. E. Harrison, *Prolegomena to the Study of Greek Religion*, pp. 127 ff.).

49.   E. Rohde, *Psyche* (French trans.), p. 108; A. Dieterich, *Kl. Schr.*, pp. 118 f. Cf. idem, *Eine Mithrasliturgie*, pp. 157 ff.; H. Diels, *Sibyll. Bl.*, p. 48, no. 1.

50.   An efficacious gesture both in the realm of magic and in the greeting of a suppliant (*labomenos tēs kheiros*: Apollod., *Bibl.*, II.124).

51.   Ibid.: *theasamenoi de Hēruklea tas kheiras ōregon hōs anastēsomenoi dia tēs ekeinou bias· ho de Thēsea men... ēgeire, Peirithoun de anastēsai boulomenos.* ...For the use of *anistanai* in the sense of "resuscitate," see *Il.*, XXIV.151; Aesch., *Ag.*, 1361; Soph., *El.*, 130–39. For another, but equally ancient, use of the same verb, see Aesch., *Eum.*, 648. For the use of *anistanai* in regard to suppliants, see Thuc., I.126.11, I.128.1, I.137.1, III.27.2, III.75.4, etc.

52.   Concerning this fundamental concept and its mythical and mystical developments, see A. Dieterich, *Nekyia*[2], pp. 91 f. On the notion of eternal suffering, see E. Norden, *P. Vergilius Maro Aeneis Buch VI*, p. 260. Works of art affirm the idea of condemnation (see *Dict. des antiq.*, V, p. 233).

53.   L. Weiser-Aall, *ArchRW*, XXX (1933), p. 217.

54.   The verb *aikizesthai* is used in regard to the deed of Ajax (Soph., *Aj.*, 111). In particular, it implies scourging or flagellation, characteristic cruelties that accompany certain forms of capital punishment (see Keramopoullos, op. cit., pp. 30 f.) and that are used also in rituals (see Eitrem, op. cit., p. 378).

55   Glotz, *Dict. des antiq.*, s.v. *Poena*; Latte, *Hermes*, LXVI (1931), p. 154.

CHAPTER 10
Capital Punishment

...Und auch an der Strafe ist so viel Festliches!

F. Nietzsche, *Zur Geneal. d. Mor.*, II.6.

A certain number of allusions attest to the existence in ancient Greece of a form of capital punishment called *apotumpanismos*. Recently, Keramopoullos has produced a study on this form of punishment that is more than just another monograph.[1] Not only does his study break new ground, but it reexamines this topic as a whole and is, accordingly, a contribution to the history of penal law and ethnography. This book deserves more than mere mention; it should be studied carefully.

I

Until recently, scholars thought they knew what *apotumpanismos* was.[2] In fact, texts contemporary with the practice are not very explicit and provide us with little more than the term itself. In Lysias (XIII.56, 67, 68), Demosthenes (VIII.61, IX.61, XIX.137), and Aristotle (*Ath. Pol.* 45.1; *Rh.*, II.5.1382b, II.6.1385a),[3] we merely find that *apotumpanismos* is a contemporary method of executing criminals. One of the references in the *Rhetorica*[4] could have furnished us with more precise information, since it presupposes a lengthy form of punishment, but no one took time to examine the text. For lack of anything better, scholars resorted to the witness of the lexicographers, and with this we often have to be satisfied. According to them, the word *tumpanon* (which, if it is connected to *tuptō*, has an active force) refers to a kind of club used to execute the condemned man; this would then be the origin of the term in question.[5] But in fact the lexicographers date from a period that affords only a reconstruction based

This review originally appeared in *REG*, XXXVII (July–September 1924), pp. 261–93.

on conjecture, whereas the earliest texts are not very explicit, since they have no need to be for their contemporaries. Some vague survivals may have found their way into the works of lexicographers, who in general were quite diligent in copying one another. But in general they did what we would have to do: they rationalized about these terms—for better or worse.[6] In any case, modern writers were in general agreement with the view that the *apotumpanismos* was an execution carried out by blows with a club.

Following an archaeological discovery, however, Keramopoullos proposed a different interpretation of the practice. Excavations undertaken at the site of ancient Phaleron had twice (in 1911 and in 1915) unearthed a cemetery.[7] In the group of tombs discovered in 1915—tombs that from the pottery found in them can be dated as belonging to the pre-Solonian era (probably the seventh century B.C.)—there was one that was most remarkable. It was a common grave in which excavators found seventeen cadavers without any accompanying objects. Each was wearing an iron collar around the neck and clamps on the hands and feet. Certain observations led to the conclusion that the skeletons belonged to executed criminals: before their death, they had been placed on planks (some pieces of wood remain on the clamps). These were not slaves who were tortured. Their death was the intended result of the treatment given to all seventeen of them. Nor were they innocent victims of the ingenious cruelty of some brigands similar to modern-day terrorists. Such an interpretation would be false; it is not only improbable but impossible as well. There can be no question but that Keramopoullos was dealing with a form of capital punishment. Moreover, by process of elimination, he could determine that of all the known types of execution, the only one that fit this situation was the *apotumpanismos*.

Such a hypothesis needs justifying, and in his study Keramopoullos applies himself to the task with good results. He notes that the word *tumpanon* never has the meaning scholars usually attribute to it, and that by virtue of its very formation the word has a passive, not an active, force. Keramopoullos also examines the uses of the Latin term *tympanum*,[8] which allow the possibility of *tumpanon* and *sanis* being synonymous. He finds the word *sanis* in a very characteristic form of torture mentioned by Herodotus,[9] Plutarch,[10] and especially Aristophanes, where the torture is described in great detail.[11] In Aristophanes' play, we find condemned prisoners being restrained for an indefinite period of time; they are fastened to a board or pole with clamps similar to those found at Phaleron. This helps clarify an allusion in Aristophanes' *Equites* (1037–49), which in turn helps us understand our problem. Reference is made to a *pentesuringon xulon*, or a "wooden device with five holes," for which Cleon is destined according to the prophecy of the "sausage seller."[12] It is in fact the instrument of execution of *apotumpanismos*. A careful reading of pages 21–36 of Keramopoullos' study gives some indication of the compelling nature of his investigation of this whole subject.[13]

There emerges from the archaeological and literary evidence a rather neat picture of the *apotumpanismos*. First of all, it is a cruel punishment. The condemned man is stripped and fixed with five clamps to a pole that is set up in the ground.[14] No one is allowed to approach and bring the man help or relief of any kind *whatsoever*.[15] It is only a matter of waiting until he dies. The procedure in some way resembles crucifixion, except that in the latter the hands and feet are nailed, and the consequent loss of blood tends to cut short the punishment. What is more, one of the essential elements of the *tumpanon* is the iron collar, which because of the body's weight puts pressure on the lower jaw and thus adds significantly to the suffering. It is possible to imagine that the agony of the victim could last for several days.[16] That such a form of capital punishment was practiced in Athens should somewhat modify our ideas concerning the Athenian penal code. Inherited from a remote past, and probably introduced by Draco (pp. 106 f.), whose criminal laws earned him his sinister reputation,[17] it was practiced throughout the classical period. Indeed, we can trace this form of capital punishment to the end of the fourth century B.C.

Understandably this practice had a powerful impact on the collective imagination. Keramopoullos shows this in a curious detail. He demonstrates that in depicting the punishment of Prometheus in a fashion that is quite different from Hesiod's, Aeschylus is actually conforming in the essentials to the traditional national image of *apotumpanismos*.[18] He also examines some formulas and certain gestures of imprecation, where he finds an allusion to this punishment; and he looks at practices of magic, such as the chaining of statues,[19] whose object is to cause such punishment. It is not our purpose to follow the author through his entire exposition, in which he sometimes goes too far. We limit our interest to (1) his confirmation of the importance of *apotumpanismos* as a punishment; and (2) his demonstration once again (through a specific example) that the penal code is one of the sources from which magical and religious representational forms spontaneously draw nourishment. What should be emphasized here is Keramopoullos' contribution to the history of a penal code as such. His study suggests certain points that could lead to one's not always being in total agreement with him.

II

Our interest is not in the punishment itself; as we have already noted, Keramopoullos gives a quite satisfactory account of this. It is appropriate to note, however—and there are certain indications of this in his work—that *apotumpanismos* as it has been described does not constitute a rigorously isolated type of punishment, nor is it one that is without some variations. In early times at least, the condemned man could be fixed to a pole with ropes.[20] In some cases there was flagellation,[21] and there were local variations in the positioning of the victim.[22] Finally, as we have noted in agreement with the author, there is probably a relationship between *apotumpanismos* and crucifixion. Later we will see the importance of this preliminary observation.

Apotumpanismos nevertheless remains a well-defined punishment at least in Athens (as a rule, Keramopoullos wants to associate it with Athens alone) from the seventh to the fourth century B.C. One could ask what its position was in the whole complex of Athenian law. If there were other kinds of capital punishment, what system determined which was to be used? Or *were* there any other forms of capital punishment? At the end of his review Keramopoullos denies any such variety. We know, however, that poisoning by hemlock was practiced in Athens during the classical period.[23] And we seem to have evidence that victims were hurled into the *barathron*. Still, the former practice appears only late in the classical period—at the end of the fifth century B.C.—so that we can for the moment put it aside. We can be even more radical than the author, since we have only to recall that poisoning did not constitute a type of execution in the proper sense; it must be seen as permitted but controlled suicide.[24] As for the *barathron*, Keramopoullos' view is strongly negative. He believes that this is not an independent form of execution, and admits only that after execution the *corpses* of the victims were thrown unburied into a place that could be located outside the city, between the gate of the Piraeus and the Long Walls (pp. 36 f.).[25] There really would remain, then, only one proper form of capital punishment, *apotumpanismos*.

The problem we just posed, then, would be eliminated; and at the same time, *apotumpanismos* would take on a significance greater than it seemed to have at first. Even where it is not explicitly mentioned, Keramopoullos says that *apotumpanismos* is certainly what is meant. For example, he argues that in the trial of the generals of the Battle of Arginusae, when Euryptolemus proposes to the people a choice between the law affecting traitors and those guilty of sacrilege and the decree of Kannonos (Xen., *Hell.*, I.7, 20–22), the penalty that is prescribed, though not mentioned explicitly in the legislation, would in both cases be the fixing of the condemned to a pole (pp. 97 ff.).[26]

We disagree with the author and think that there were different forms of capital punishment; and such diverse forms make sense. But let us first consider two points. First—on the question of the *barathron*—it appears that Keramopoullos' thesis leads directly to criticism. Second—on the question of the burial permitted or denied to the condemned—the difficulty that Keramopoullos experiences in one respect could provide us with an argument.

One might say, with a brevity that is almost flippant, that the author "does not believe" in the *barathron*. He is not the first unbeliever: Thonissen[27] has already indulged in the luxury of a radical skepticism. But Thonissen is not exactly an authority and is hardly cited anymore. The question of the *barathron* is undertaken anew; it is currently acknowledged that in Athens some of the condemned were thrown off the Tarpeian Rock, and it was precisely this act that was their *supplicium*. There may be some uncertainty as to whether this procedure survived after the fifth century B.C., and there may be some topographical obscurities;[28] but these, for the moment, are not of primary importance. What is important is the existence of the practice. Is it traditional opinion—traditional, at least, from the period of the ancient scholiasts (not in itself a reason to reject it)—that Keramopoullos opposes? He opposes it with an argument that is sufficiently dispersive and very indirect. He begins by dismissing the question of the existence of the *barathron*, content to justify himself later, but having in mind a negative thesis (p. 20). First, because we find several sources that testify to a *barathron*, Keramopoullos represents it as the place where corpses of executed criminals were thrown (pp. 36 f.). He then believes he has grounds[29] for saying that *apotumpanismos* was the only method of execution employed before the practice of taking hemlock. And he argues this by presupposing the thesis, to be demonstrated later, that hurling someone into the *barathron* was not a way of putting a person to death (p. 47). But his anticipated demonstration fails to materialize. By fixing his attention solely on *apotumpanismos*, and by seeing its importance gradually increase at the expense of everything else, Keramopoullos is led unwittingly but with the best of intentions to a *petitio principii*. When considering expressions like *eis korakas* or *eis Kunosarges*,[30] he connects them with *apotumpanismos*. The corpses of the *apotetumpanismenoi* were, as he admits, discarded without burial; they therefore became the prey of beasts (the condemned were already such prey during their agony). It is precisely this *ataphia* that he recognizes in the "hurling into the *barathron*." This additional penalty, then, was added to that of *apotumpanismos*, and was practiced in conjunction with it (p. 83). This is what he should have proved.

One would perhaps like something else—the more so as the employment of a type of execution such as is admitted up to now is almost expected. There is not only the Roman analogue, but we know for a fact that in Sparta, Delphi, Corinth, and perhaps Elis and Thessaly,[31] the condemned were hurled to their deaths from a high rock. There would have to be some compelling reasons to doubt that the *barathron* had the same function as the Keadas or the Hyampeian Rock. Now even if it is correct that the lexicographers have embroidered the historical facts, that we do not have to believe some of their horrifying tales,[32] and that contemporary texts are not always open to a single interpretation,[33] the hurling of the condemned into the *barathron* still remains a fact that is formally attested. It is certainly true in the case of enemies.[34] Will we say that in this instance it is a matter of vengeance and not internal law? This does not seem to be the answer.[35] In any case, how are we to understand the repeated references to it in Aristophanes?[36] What interpretation—other than the obvious one—do we give to Plato's *Gorgias*, 516D? "It was determined by vote that Miltiades be thrown into the *barathron*; and had it not been for the prytanis, he would have been." Whatever importance deprival of burial might have (which, whenever it has to be mentioned, is done so in explicit terms), it is simply incredible that one would have described only an accessory punishment while understanding the essential one. Finally, how are we to interpret the well-known passage in Xenophon, *Hellenica*, I.7.20, where the very terms of the decree of Kannonos are cited: "if someone is found to be guilty, he is to die by being thrown into the *barathron*"? Here equivocation is possible only if we allow Keramopoullos' emendation (p. 97) *apothanonta eis to barathron emblēthēnai*, that is, "after his death he is to be thrown into the *barathron*." But there is nothing to justify this arbitrary emendation,[37] and it produces a phrase that is less than satisfying.

The second question is closely connected with the first. Keramopoullos had to be impressed with something that the discovery at Phaleron made immediately clear. After being executed by *apotumpanismos* the condemned were buried. True, there were no offerings, no honors; but the dead *were* buried. It is a well-known fact that deprival of burial in Attic soil was a penalty added to that of death in a good many cases. And Keramopoullos is forced to admit that in these instances this prohibition of burial is added to *apotumpanismos* regularly, since it is, according to the author, the only mode of execution used until the end of the fifth century B.C. He also admits that corpses of those condemned to die by hemlock were as a rule returned to their families.[38] And herein lies a twofold difficulty. Keramopoullos must establish the direct relationship between *apotumpanismos* and the denial of burial; he must also recognize the exceptional character of the case of Phaleron and then justify the exception. It seems to us that the author does neither. No doubt he is forced to establish—and here, he is for the most part successful—that the prohibition *mē taphēnai en tēi Attikēi* does not necessarily mean the removal of corpses beyond the boundaries. He shows that in addition to a *huperorismos* in the strict sense, there exist other methods with the same function and effect, and that the annihilation of the criminal as well as the purification of the group can be achieved through water, fire, or air. Practically speaking, then, the abandonment of the corpse and the scattering of the bones (a result of its abandonment) can satisfy the religious need that the rule in question conveys. Let us—and quite correctly—concede this point to the author. What use will he make of it? We can guess. He wants to see, in the examples of "hurling," evidence for the kind of treatment inflicted on the corpse of the *apotetumpanismenos*. With these examples, he wants to link those instances in which there is an explicit prohibition against burial. Here his logic is quite arbitrary, and once again he begs the question. He does not cite a single text in which there is a question of actual *apotumpanismos*; and there is only one instance—and it is a very special one[39]—where the denial of burial is actually linked with the punishment. It is simply gratuitous to say that outside of this singular case, denial of burial is "understood" in the others. As far as we are concerned it would be no less arbitrary to claim—and this would already contradict one text—that the two elements are always separate. We can understand why they could be lumped together; but Keramopoullos wants to see an essential association between the two. It is easy to see why. According to him, *apotumpanismos* is normally and by definition applied to crimes against the gods or the state, crimes specifically punished by "hurling," or—and this could amount to the same thing—crimes punished by the denial of burial. We would say that the questions are connected.

Whatever the case, there still remains the matter of those executed at Phaleron.[40] The explanations offered by the author (pp. 99 and 102) are rather embarrassing. For him it is a question of date, locale, or type of punishment. But if this is a question of "type," then we are engaged in a new approach, and it seems quite likely that there is a contradiction here, since in the same period, but elsewhere, a separation of the two punishments is explicitly acknowledged as a general principle. If it is simply a question of locale, one will say that in a period when the law was not yet systematized, the condemned who underwent *apotumpanismos* were buried in Phaleron but not in Athens. This is not a very satisfying hypothesis, for it involves an additional punishment that is so characteristic of a religious outlook. If Phaleron is simply a matter of a date, as the author is inclined to believe, the same objection can be raised with even greater force. It is precisely the antiquity of this supposed exception which provides us with the strongest argument. How can we say that it was only at a relatively recent date that corpses of the condemned were denied burial?[41] How, then, can we understand that a short time before—or in any event, before the period in which *huperorismos* responded to a need that in some instances was so pressing that it was applied to the ancient dead of a *genos*, and even necessitated their exhumation (the story of the Alcmaeonids is well known)—seventeen individuals whose bodies were found in a common grave would be spared *huperorismos*? There exist here—and we say it immediately—two systems of practice and representation that are in principle incompatible. Keramopoullos has reason to recall the general obligation of burial, the purpose of which was the elimination of religious pollution from the community. Should one say that the deprival of burial is best understood as a weakening of a religious scruple? Apparently not. If, for reasons that remain to be seen, the community violates the obligation in the case of certain criminals, surely the situation must be such that the criminals in whose case it respects the obligation would be of a different order. Such a conclusion is made more necessary if we admit with Keramopoullos (whose deductions seem acceptable [pp. 47 ff.]) that the criminals punished at Phaleron were buried by authority of the state.

III

We end up finding in the types of capital punishment a diversity, and more especially a dualism, that must be accounted for, but we have to admit that the problem is a subtle one, and perhaps even insoluble.

Does this diversity correspond to an ethnic one? Such a hypothesis can hardly be held in the case of Athens. It is impossible to see how one could prove it; thus it remains nebulous. In addition, earlier observations take us in another direction; they suggest that the different treatments meted out to the condemned correspond to different kinds of punishment. But this view at first appears deceptive; and it may be that Keramopoullos is conscious of this. He underlines the multiplicity of instances in which *apotumpanismos* seems to be attested. There is the question of quite different crimes: treachery, impiety, extortion, aggravated theft. On the other hand, we admittedly have the impression that this penalty would be applied principally to offenses against the state and crimes against religion. And these are the types of crimes where one finds mention of the penalty of being hurled into the *barathron*. We are, so it seems, caught in a dilemma. We must either admit with Keramopoullos that these two punishments are added to each other so as to be really equivalent to one, or we must be resigned to not understanding this duality.

But a closer study is less discouraging. Let us make one obvious observation: *apotumpanismos* is certainly a very ancient practice. If we want to define its proper domain and original function, we must not forget that from the moment when the state was endowed with a complete penal code, certain close associations and contaminations must have occurred. It is even the nature of this organization and centralization of law to create a syncretism between elements that were originally distinct. In the interpretation of events there is a principle that one could employ.

Naturally it should not be abused. It is used correctly if one can recognize in the very attestations of the classical age the persistent mark of the specifically primitive.

As for death by hurling the condemned from a precipice, this seems to have been reserved for crimes against religion and the state.[42] The denial of burial also applies to these offenses (whether or not it is necessarily connected with death by hurling).[43] We should add that when it began to be used, death by poisoning was the penalty for crimes of the same category.[44] In connection with the links between these, certain questions may arise, but what we wish to emphasize here is the fact that there were specific penalties for impiety, treason, and other related crimes.

As far as *apotumpanismos* is concerned, analysis of the historical testimony about it offers us evidence that can correct our first impressions. Among the sources dealing with crimes against the state, three references in Demosthenes must be set aside. Demosthenes does not say that the criminals about whom he is talking were executed by *apotumpanismos*; he says that they *should* have been executed in such a fashion. An orator's passion—and an Athenian's at that—is not restrained. He proposes for his enemies the most terrifying and ignominious punishments. It would certainly be incorrect to see here a valid testimony about the actual law or its normal practice. In fact, it would contradict what we know from other sources. In the fourth century B.C., criminals of this sort were executed by the administration of hemlock.[45] Again, this makes us see that as a rule, *apotumpanismos* is applied in the case of other kinds of crimes. This is exactly the impression one gets from reading Lysias, and a number of particulars justify it. To begin with, although it is usual practice merely to mention the condemnation to death, there is an insistence on giving a detailed account of the method of execution. These details are for the benefit of the orator's enemies. He evidently takes delight in recalling how they have been treated: they endured the lot of vile criminals. For one of them the situation is at once clear; he was a *lōpodutēs*, a "highway robber" (Lys., XIII.68). Another case (Lys., XIII.67) involves a traitor who was arrested while corresponding with the enemy. But the fact that the execution took place within the army, as well as the character of the criminal— he was a brother of the highway robber and was probably a slave[46]—must be taken into account. The individual himself belongs to the category of petty criminals.[47] The case of Cleon in the *Equites* and that of Mnesilokhos in the *Thesmophoriazousai* are somewhat different. Cleon is depicted as having robbed the public treasury.[48] This kind of *klopē* is easily associated with the image of a common thief.[49] Mnesilokhos, guilty of impiety, is the object of an *ephēgēsis*,[50] a procedure that during the classical period could replace the *apagōgē* (the "arrest"), to the degree that it was considered a kind of *apagōgē*[51] and was equally suitable for the flagrant offense. Here, then, are two cases, both imaginary, that have some link to what seems to us to be the decidedly typical case: Lysias' *lōpodutēs*, who was himself the object of an *apagōgē*. And we could emphasize (if we agreed with Keramopoullos' suggestion) the myth of Prometheus, who is punished as a *kleptēs* and is subjected to *apotumpanismos*. In addition, we cannot overlook the fact that for the condemned figures of myth, the depiction of their punishment came before that of their crime.[52] It would not be at all surprising to learn that it was precisely the image of a characteristic punishment which gave rise to the idea of a corresponding crime.[53]

Finally, there is the case of the punishments in Phaleron.[54] On this subject Keramopoullos develops a hypothesis that he supports with arguments that are believable and that seem highly probable. He believes that the corpses in Phaleron may be those of pirates captured in battle. Pirates qualify precisely as *kakourgoi*,[55] and they belong to that category of "criminals" which includes thieves of all sorts. We can well believe that pirates would have to undergo the kind of execution reserved for this category of criminals.

We now have several clues. On the one hand, *apotumpanismos* seems to have been employed for the punishment of "criminals." But it is also connected with *apagōgē*.[56] We still must define its real domain. We already have some idea that it has a domain or sphere; or to put it another way, we ought to be able to extrapolate from the Athenian penal system a design that would be more satisfactory and more coherent than the one we have in a theory that makes *apotumpanismos* the only method of execution. It is already clear that this horrid punishment was used in Athens; but its use must have been rather specialized, since it is so seldom mentioned and it remained a puzzlement for so long a time. We need to answer two questions: (1) Is there a class of criminals which is both definite and comprehensive, and which originally constituted the proper domain of *apotumpanismos*? (2) Are the procedure that characterizes *apotumpanismos* and the ideas attached to it capable of an extension that justifies the less well defined use of the method in the classical period? The answer to the first question is beyond doubt. The very concept of the *kakourgoi*, the subjects *par excellence* of *apotumpanismos*, remains strictly and technically defined even in Aristotle's period. We should recall the list in the *Ath. Pol.* (52.1), a list that is confirmed in other sources:[57] *kleptai* (thieves), *andrapodistai* (kidnappers), *lōpodutai* (highway robbers); we could add to these *toikhōrukhoi* ("wall piercers") and *balantiotomoi* ("purse-snatchers"). All these individuals can be arrested if they are caught in *flagrante delicto* (*ep' autophōrōi*). Without any other process—that is, without a summons (*proklēsis*)—one drags them off to the competent authority, which at least since Solon's time[58] is the Committee of the Eleven. If the criminals plead guilty, they are immediately executed.

What we must keep in mind in all of this is the process of *apagōgē* or *manus iniectio*; there is no need to insist on the importance of the procedure within the law, especially in terms of its origins. The procedure is a principle of unity for the specific cases and a principle of organization for juridical theory. We define *apagōgē* as an improvised and hasty process, the aim of which is immediate execution. It applies to a category of criminals which is determined each time by the type of crime committed and the flagrancy of the offense. A primitive nucleus can be observed all the more readily in this instance since evolution has for the most part respected it. It is enough to abstract from what is more properly "judicial" and has been imposed on the process of *apagōgē*. Thus there is the possibility that a lawsuit (in the modern sense) could be grafted onto the *manus iniectio*.[59] This is indicated by the need for this legal action in a number of cases where it is certainly the result of later developments,[60] as well as by the option of resorting to other legal means, means that are regarded as complementary to *apagōgē*, but that could lead us into error regarding its fundamental nature since they signify essentially a direct and immediate recourse to public authority.[61] Finally, there is the intervention of a city magistrate, which however early it may have been instituted would not as such have any connection with the most primitive form of *apagōgē*. *Apagōgē*, then, appears to be a private process that can function only at the hands of a victim and for the sake of vengeance. The specific use of the verb *agein/apagein* leaves no room for doubt; it is connected with the private seizure of a person.[62] The aggrieved party seizes his thief for the purpose of summarily executing him.

Are we, then, strictly in the realm of private vengeance? No. Instead we are in a complex domain, or in any event a different one. To begin with, the use of *apagōgē* must be distinguished from what we might call "self-defense"; a victim can kill the nighttime thief or the daytime thief who puts up resistance. But one can also use *apagōgē* against these criminal types,[63] and as such it appears to be a social institution, a device that seems above all to put the solidarity of a territorial group into operation.[64] It is very different from the blood feud, or repression of crimes like homicide or adultery.[65] *Apagōgē* is a private affair in terms of its effect. The word itself is not unimportant in this regard; the make-up of the verb *apagein* seems to exclude the idea of a vengeance exercised solely by the victim, who "would drag along" the guilty person to the victim's place.[66] On the contrary, the verb seems to indicate an act directed to the outside, toward the public. It could be that it evokes that ignominious promenade inflicted on some criminals.[67] In any case, it suggests that the individual's vengeance is reinforced by the community's collaboration and assistance. This is surely what appears in a striking way in the very operation of *apagōgē*. Given the development of the procedure, public collaboration is already apparent in situations where the tradition has been established for such a long time that the execution, which is the very raison d'être of *apagōgē*—actually its first act—must from the very beginning have had a public character. It is possible to concede that from an early period local authorities could have presided over it; but such a hypothesis is not essential, for the social group can serve in a retributive capacity and at least endorse the vengeance. In addition, not only does the private repression of *kakourgēmata* presuppose the cooperation of the "group," since in a rural milieu the primitive varieties of theft provoke a strong sympathy for vengeance,[68] and not only has the thief been regarded as the most ancient criminal in the precise sense of the term,[69] but *apagōgē* of necessity requires publicity, for such publicity suits the glaring quality of the crime. In a developed legal system, flagrancy no longer has much significance except that it provides more proof.[70] However, in a primitive stage of legal development it seems that the flagrant quality of the crime must be regarded as relevant to its very definition, at least in the category we have been discussing.[71] In most cases, if not in all, a flagrant criminal act will result in an investigation under public control; this is therefore the necessary antecedent to the execution the traditional act of *apagōgē* initiates. In this typical case the punishment of the criminal and the very affirmation of the offense are subject to society's rules; that is to say, they are subject to certain rites in which the offended party is no doubt the principal actor. But all this is done with the obligatory assistance of a "chorus":[72] the participation of "neighbors"[73] who both oversee the procedure and guarantee its regularity. We all know about the *phōra*, that is, the *quaestio lance licioque*, which is designed to prove the defendant guilty of flagrant crime.[74]

Apagōgē, then, involves popular justice. Even for an occasional and ephemeral society, one of the first needs is to mark the place where the *kakourgoi*, objects of the *apagōgē*, have to be executed.[75] By definition and origin, *apagōgē* has two aspects. First, it originates from private vengeance. Second, it is connected with societal discipline. In this second aspect, *apagōgē* in the classical period is related to the suppression of public crimes. Thus we can explain the evident extension of the *apagōgē*, but we need not make this an issue at present. Let us limit ourselves to emphasizing the two facts that interest us.

To begin with, the instances of *apagōgē* that are foreign to the domain we have come to recognize depend on a more recent body of law and, if we can call it that, a second layer. These cases may involve an *apagōgē* used against *atimoi* who are caught in forbidden areas or acts;[76] or they may be directed against certain crimes that do not fit into the primitive category of *kakourgoi*.[77] Or it could be a question of the *manus iniectio*, which in certain circumstances can legitimately be deployed against specific public enemies.[78]

Second, there are still visible points of agreement between the primitive *apagōgē* and its later applications. The latter are explained by the necessity of giving arms for private vengeance;[79] or by the legitimacy of summary procedures against a foreigner;[80] or by the concept of *actio popularis* exercised in situations that amount to *kakourgēma*.[81]

The extension of *apagōgē* is an indication of the artificial state of penal law. It is created out of regard for the polis, where there has been so much equalization between various types of crime that the religious dimensions—and certain conspicuous ones at that—have already begun to disappear.[82] The result of this process is a softening of the penalty (e.g., permission to commit suicide by hemlock). However, as the idea of *kakourgia* tends to exceed its provenance,[83] something else can occur as well: the application of a special punishment such as *apotumpanismos* for crimes that in primitive times did not incur this punishment.[84]

Therefore, what in primitive times called for *apotumpanismos* was, in our view, a *kakourgēma* in the strict sense of the term. This hypothesis seems to be confirmed by the treatment of certain thieves in the classical era. Legislation regarding the thief gives the impression of incoherence, as happens whenever layers of law of different ages find themselves in chance contact with one another. After being subjected to the *apagōgē*, the perpetrators of qualified theft—and flagrancy remains a necessary element[85]—are executed by *apotumpanismos*. But what of other thieves, against whom there has been no resort to *apagōgē* or in whose cases it would not be allowed—for want of the act being *flagrans delictum*? Those unaffected by primitive law have to be the concern of legislation; they are dealt with in a different way and their penalty is generally milder.[86] Still, some relic of the ancient penalty survives even in their case; when the penalty is monetary the tribunal can, in addition to imposing the fine, order that the condemned man be kept in chains for five days and nights.[87] How should this *prostimion* be understood? The law cited by Demosthenes and Lysias—the law of Solon—says of the guilty party: *dedesthai d'en tēi podokakēi*.[88] But Lysias informs us that even in his time the term *podokakē* had fallen into disuse, and that in a parallel case one ordinarily used the term *xulon*. *Xulon*, however, is a possible equivalent of *tumpanon*;[89] yet it is also used as a synonym for *kuphōn*, "iron collar."[90] We cannot determine the precise nature of the thief's punishment—whether several parts of his body were chained by turns—or affirm that the *podokakē* had to be a *kuphōn* as well. But it is still possible to say that these terms evoke a weakened image of *apotumpanismos*. We should picture a wooden instrument on which the victim was restrained with iron clamps.[91] There is something else: the use of the *kuphōn*. Even though it is independent of the *podokakē*, it evidently resembles it and is especially well attested in the case of certain criminals like the *kleptai*;[92] it also shows that the guilty man was *exposed*.[93] In admitting that the *prostimion* in question consists of this form of ignominious exposure, one can better understand the raison d'être of a punishment whose methods and succinct quality attract our attention immediately. For thieves who do not undergo *apotumpanismos*, *prostimion* appears as its mitigated form.

Finally, let us note that among legal systems that were at first more or less isolated or independent but were eventually integrated into the penal code of the polis, there exists—in this group—one system in which *apotumpanismos* was a specific form of execution. It is characterized by all these specific ideas, which suggest one another: *kakourgos, ep' autophōrōi, apagein*. It is the system that concerns itself with the primitive varieties of theft. And since this system deals with a very ancient punishment, whose origins could go back to the earliest Mediterranean civilizations, it is our opinion that the punishment itself is the equivalent of the crucifixion inflicted according to the Twelve Tables. This was prescribed for the category of *fures*,[94] who by night either harvested the farmland of others or grazed their own livestock there.[95] Since it confirms our hypothesis, this fact should be taken into account.

Even so, the link between *apotumpanismos* and its proper area of application could still seem only extrinsic. Is there a more profound nexus, and one that is more intelligible?

IV

We have already alluded to the diversity of origins in the development of penal law. It is a point we cannot overemphasize. *Sacratio* (or "a placing outside the law"), blood vengeance, *manus iniectio*, summary execution in the case of a thief (not to mention the disciplinary law and a kind of collective policing in the religious assemblies)[96]—there are at least three types of penal law here, the individuality of which tends to disappear under the unifying regimen of the state. But given their distinct origins, they still put into play specific sentiments and reactions. This diversity manifests itself even in the execution of criminals. If the act of putting a criminal to death were only a practical solution to the problem of legal responsibility, and nothing more than the brutal manifestation of a quasi-instinctive passion, then our tour through the garden of punishments would hardly merit any interest, even the interest of the curious. But such is not the case; and now it is quite legitimate for us to emphasize a contrast between two types of capital punishment.

One of these might be best represented by typical procedures, two of which are especially well known to us from Greece:[97] stoning[98] and hurling. Here the death penalty is a means employed to eliminate a

miasma, a "pollution." In essence, this type of execution belongs to domestic law and in itself has a religious character. This is because it is applied
specifically to crimes that are religious in nature, an area of criminality
that from early on was a vast one. The most significant term for a crime of
this kind is *agos*.[99] No doubt an act of passion, capital punishment in this
case is still far from being an act of pure passion. It is precisely because a
religious concept regulates it that we miss its true significance when we
define it as the psychological tendency whose object is simply the elimination of the guilty party. First, capital punishment seeks to remove an element that exists on the religious level; and it manifests itself primarily as
an *aphosiōsis*,[100] or as a purificatory "freeing" of the group among whom
the responsibility for shedding new blood is at times diluted or even disappears.[101] Second, the violent expulsion by death of a worthless and accursed
member of a society goes hand in hand with the concept of *devotio*.[102] In
effect, the putting of the accursed to death appears to be an act of piety,
especially when we recall those dispositions of ancient law in which it
is made quite specific that the murder of an outlaw does not incur im-
purity;[103] or when we recall that prescription of Germanic law which
makes a similar type of murder an obligation[104]—a striking antithesis
to the sentiments elicited by the executioner, who is forever an object of
horror.[105]

But there is also a genuine religious function that the victim himself
fulfills in such a case; and it is not without some analogy to the function of
the priest-kings who were similarly executed.[106] This is testified to sufficiently by such designations of criminals as *homo sacer* in Rome[107] and
pharmakos in Greece.[108] It is the same idea of *devotio* that explains
how—through a paradox that is at first disconcerting—in some extreme
cases (which were nonetheless foreseen) the act of execution might not
result in death;[109] and how in particular the condemned who had not died
after being thrown from the Tarpeian Rock was spared.[110] If the divine
powers release the person who has been delivered up to them, no one has
the right to recapture what was theirs. The same thing applies to the
corpse: there is still life in it, some evil or "sacred" power. It is then a possible object of *devotio*. By expelling the corpse beyond the city's borders
and by destroying it completely (through exposure to the elements of
wind, water, and fire), one strives to bring about its annihilation. This is
not the product of rage, nor does it have anything to do with a precaution
taken out of fear that the dead man's ghost will return;[111] it is done as a
piaculum.[112] Thus it is possible to explain the prohibition of burial, which
within a religious concept of crime and the criminal is not unusual. The
ordinary attitude toward the corpse, which would necessitate the ritual
measures of enshroudment, does not apply in this instance, for this religious view is in some way blocked out by the other.

The case of the *kakourgos* is another matter altogether. Here we are dealing with a penal response that of itself and at least in the beginning[113] does not involve religious elements: it involves them no more than does the criminal notion to which it corresponds.[114] In a rural society such as the one we must depict here, the thief and those of his ilk—and among the Romans, the individuals who harvest the crops of others—provoke an angry response. But it is in no way the same reaction that we find in instances of impiety or incest. We catch a glimpse of how this reaction takes place in Greece: it has as its prototype the form of a strictly private vengeance, memories of which come alive again in some well-known scenes from Homer and Sophocles.[115] *Apotumpanismos* has retained some element of this penal reaction.

We are not saying that this penal reaction had no organization or that it did not conform to an obligatory schema; the demands relating to a flagrant offense and the necessity for judicial rites amply demonstrate that it did. But if the penal reaction leads to the death of the guilty party, it is a death that is different from that of the *homo sacer*; it is a death that, though equally predetermined, has a different significance. In this case the need to make someone suffer is fulfilled because the need is a pure one; legitimate acts of cruelty are given free rein. It is thus possible to understand that the method of execution, since it is, properly speaking, social and defined in advance, implies a particular kind of thinking that goes beyond individual reaction to the exasperated wrath of the victim. But this is a *profane* way of thinking. The victim of *apotumpanismos* is *exposed* as an object of public indignation and cruel laughter. The victim is also an *exemplum*,[116] since agony is more telling than a dead body. But the agony is eventually ended; what will be done with the corpse? We will not exactly say that the victim has a right to burial; the victim's enemies may not have been satisfied. Their anger may well go beyond the death of the criminal. But here the ordinary attitude interposes itself, for we are not in the area of *sacratio*; the minimal rites for the dead are required. So strange at first glance, the burial of the condemned in Phaleron merely conforms to the normal mechanics regarding the dead body.

The feeling of social vindictiveness is in principle complex: it confounds a superficial psychology that treats it as a brutal and base response. There is in it something institutional; and following the direction in which this sentiment of society leads us, we find that it corresponds to some associations of ideas which are essential but also diverse.

NOTES

1.   A. Keramopoullos, *Ho apotumpanismos: Sumbolē arkhaiologikē eis tēn historian tou poinikou dikaiou kai tēn laographian* (Athens, 1923).

2.   J. H. Lipsius (*Das attische Recht und Rechtsverfahren*, p. 77, n. 101) restates the traditional opinion in translating it: "Tötung mit der Keule." Thalheim (s.v. *Apotumpanismos*, in *RE*; K. F. Hermann's *Griech. Rechtsaltert.*[4], p. 141, n. 5) wants to correct it. He thinks that the *tumpanon* is a "*Maschine*" on which the condemned man is bound in order to be executed by cudgeling.

3.   There is nothing to be derived, at least on a first attempt, from the exclamation in Aristophanes' *Plutus*, 476: *ō tumpana kai kuphōnes*.

4.   II.5.1382b: *ouk oiontai de pathein an...oute hoi ēdē peponthenai nomizontes ta deina kai apepsugmenoi pros to mellon, hōsper hoi apotumpanizomenoi ēdē....* See Keramopoullos, op. cit., p. 24.

5.   See, in particular, Hsch., s.v. *tumpanizetai*, Anecd. Bekk., I, p. 438, 12. In the *Suda*, one finds *tumpana...xula, en hois etumpanizon*, but it is quite possible that *en hois* simply has an "instrumental" meaning. There are bits and pieces of truth in the rather confused gloss of schol. Ar., *Plut.*, 476.

6.   This is also seen in an entirely imaginary reconstruction of the history of the punishment: see *Anecd. Bekk.*, I, p. 438, 12: *to gar palaion xulois anēiroun tous katakritous, husteron d'edoxe tōi xiphei*.

7.   *Arkhaiol. Ephēm.*, 1911, pp. 246 f. (K. Kourouniotis); *Arkhaiolog. Deltion*, II (1916), pp. 13 f. (E. Pelekidis).

8.   *Tympana ostiorum* (Vitr., *De Arch.*, IV.6.4); *tympana*, in the sense of the solid drum of a wheel (Verg., *G.*, II.444); etc.

9.   Herodotus (VII.33 and IX.120) describes the punishment inflicted on the Persian Artayctes, who was seized by the Athenians and given by them to the inhabitants of Elaeus for purposes of vengeance: *pros sanida diepassaleusan; sanida prospassaleusantes anekremasan*.

10.   Plutarch (*Per.*, 28) relates a story which on his own authority he claims is false and which he attributes to Douris of Samos: after the Samians had been defeated by Pericles, he ordered a certain number of them fixed to planks (*sanisi prosdēsas*), where they remained for ten days; afterward their heads were bashed in. Keramopoullos gives us good reasons not to accept Plutarch's negative opinion.

11.   Aristophanes (*Thesm.*, 930–46, 1001 f.) describes the order of the prytany, which had met to establish Mnesilokhos' flagrant crime of impiety; Mnesilokhos is "fixed to a plank" by a Scythian archer (931–32, *dēson...en tēi sanidi*; 1013, *pantōs d'emoi ta desm' huparkhēi*). From this comes the comparison with Andromeda, which is maintained throughout the scene (1031, *en puknois desmoisin empeplegmenē*; 1054, *laimotmēt' akhē*). Note the word *kremazein* (1028, 1053, 1110). On the object of the punishment itself, cf. 943 (*tois koraxin hestiōn*) and 1028 f. (*koraxi deipnon*); these are elements that Keramopoullos connects partially with the moment of agony (cf. 866–68).

12.   The five holes correspond to the clamps that held the neck, the feet, and the hands. One can also see allusions to *apotumpanismos* in other works, such as Ar., *Eq.*, 367, 705, and Pl., *Resp.*, II.362. See also Dem., XXI.105 (*proselōsthai*), which deals with an Athenian form of punishment.

13.   Let us admit, however, that a difficulty still remains in the composition of the word *apotumpanismos*; this interpretation is perhaps more satisfying than the traditional one, but the prefix is not what one would expect. It would not be too bold to give *apo* the same meaning as *ap-* in *apagein*, especially since there is a relationship between *apotumpanismos* and the *apagōgē*.

14.   As for the necessity of nudity, Keramopoullos makes an ingenious deduction *a contrario* from Ar., *Thesm.*, 940 ff., where the case of Mnesilokhos, who was exposed in full dress, appears to be an exception. As for the position of the condemned being upright, this is fairly well attested in accounts by Herodotus and Plutarch, as well as in Aristophanes' scene [see nn. 9–11 above]. Hesychius must have preserved some vague idea of the *apotumpanismos*, since he used the verb *krematai* when speaking of the condemned in this form of punishment (s.v. *tumpanizetai, Anecd. Bekk.*, I, p. 438, 12).

15.   During the entire punishment scene of the *Thesmophoriazousai*, the archer keeps guard over Mnesilokhos; *phulatte kai prosienai mēdena ea pros auton* is the order enjoined on him by the prytany (932 ff.).

16.   After death, the victim can remain exposed to wild beasts; even before he dies, this is the case. The *tumpanon* of the Samians remained in the upright position for ten days (Plut., *Per.*, 28).

17.   We would accept the author's view in the case of theft, the crime that particularly concerned Draco. Let us understand that he would have adopted a traditional and customary practice as a legal form of execution (see section III of this chapter). Without doing anything really new, he gave his approval to the practice, and this would have been enough to justify his fame for cruelty. As to whether the affirmation by Keramopoullos here appears to be a little arbitrary in terms of determining whether or not the *apotumpanismos* was the punishment anticipated by Draco for intentional murder, that is another question. It is true that a passage in Aeschines (II.181 ff.: *ou gar ho thanatos deinon, all' hē peri tēn teleutēn hubris phobera· pōs de ouk oiktron idein ekhthrou prosōpon epengelōntos, kai tois ōsi tōn oneidōn akousai*) agrees nicely with the punishment in question and could be used if one had to relate it (as did G. Glotz, *La Solidarité de la famille dans le droit criminel en Grèce*, p. 309) to the punishment for murder. For nothing indicates that such a connection should be made (the connection with Dem., XXIII.68, would be insufficient). On the subject of the execution of murderers, we remain totally ignorant.

18.   Keramopoullos, op. cit., pp. 61–66. The author admits that the depiction of the punishment of Prometheus could only have been represented by a mannequin.

19.   See C. Dugas, *BCH* XXXIX, (1915), pp. 416 f.

20.   Keramopoullos, op. cit., p. 68; cf. S. Reinach, *Répert. des vases*, II.48.1.

21.   Keramopoullos, op. cit., pp. 30 ff.; cf. Soph., *Aj.*, 108 f.

22.   In Aristotle's account (*Ath. Pol.*, 45.1) there is one word that attracts our attention: *kathēmenon* (*Lusimakhon...kathēmenon ēdē mellonta apothnēskein*). One thinks of *sedet aeternumque sedebit....* Is there a trace of something that could relate to the punishment itself and to the position of the condemned? Such would hardly be the case if one saw in the "punishment" of Theseus the simple memory of an underworld iconography (see Paus., X.29.9), and in any case, the detail would remain a mystery. But perhaps it is fitting to place a question mark here.

23.   We cannot state with certainty that there were not other methods as well; it is a fact that very often the texts say nothing about the execution. It would be too much to say that execution was always accomplished by one of the methods we have seen in certain cases; we have already said that nothing is known about the execution of the murderer. Elsewhere the *xiphos* is used at least on occasion; it is attested for Sparta (Zen., VI.11) and for Athens (Lys., XIII.78).

24.   G. Glotz, *Dict. des antiq.*, s.v. *Kōneion*; cf. Pl., *Leg.*, IX.873C. We continue to employ the traditional word "hemlock."

25.   According to Pl., *Resp.*, 439E. It is here that one ordinarily situates the *barathron*.

26.   Keramopoullos seems to give too much importance to the decree of Kannonos; he is prepared to place it far back into the past, and sees it as the dominant law even in the fourth century B.C. In fact, it was a legislative action analogous to the decree of Diopeithes.

Like that decree, it was designed to implement in certain instances the procedure of *eisangelia*. It is difficult to see why it would be compared with the *arkhaios nomos* of which Demosthenes speaks in reference to the *apatē tou dēmou* (XX.135).

27.   J. J. Thonissen, *Droit pénal de la républ. athén.*, pp. 94, 98 f. For a criticism, see G. Glotz, *L'Ordalie dans la Grèce primitive* (1904), pp. 91 f.; cf. H. Hager, *JHS*, VIII (1877), pp. 6 ff.

28.   According to *Anecd. Bekk.*, I, p. 219, the *barathron* was located in the deme of Keiriadai; Plutarch (*Them.*, 22) seems to locate it in the deme of Melite; elsewhere, the scholiast of Aristophanes (*Plut.*, 431) mentions an *orugma* that was filled in perhaps in the fifth century B.C. Thalheim (in *RE*, s.v. *barathron*) and W. Judeich (*Topogr. der St. Ath.*, p. 375) extricate themselves from the difficulty, each in his own fashion. If pressed, we would admit that the new *orugma* of the fourth century B.C., as distinct from the older, fifth-century one, served only as a place in which to throw the corpses of the condemned. Throwing people in is no longer mentioned expressly after 406, and a grammatical interpretation of Dinarchus (I.62: *thethnasi...paradothentes tōi epi tōi orugmati*) does not necessarily presuppose this practice (for a contrary view, see Glotz, *L'Ordalie*, p. 92, n. 2); however, see Lycurg., *Leoc.*, 121, which corresponds to the year 410 B.C., but in which the expression *paradounai tōi epi tou orugmatos*, if it is to be intelligible, must mean that the practice of tossing in had persisted into the orator's own age.

29.   An affirmation that relies on the scholiast of Aristophanes, *Ran.*, 541, which clearly is not a very valuable text.

30.   This last expression would be a popular burlesque and a corruption of *eis kunas*.

31.   For Sparta, see Thuc., I.134.4; Paus., IV.18.4. For Delphi, see Paus., X.42, and Plut., *De sera*, XII.557A; cf. Aeschin., II.142. For Corinth, see Steph. Byz., 402 (where we note that the *kōs* has become *desmōtērion*, like the quarries in Syracuse and the Keadas in Sparta; cf. Strab., VIII.7.367). For Elis, see Paus., V.6.7 f., a text that assumes the ancient practice of hurling in. For Thessaly, see Zen., 87 (*en Thessaliai topos esti korakes, hopou tous kakourgous eneballon*).

32.   Schol. Ar., *Plut.*, 431, in which there is a distortion of reality rather than an invention or fantasy (the *onkinoi* are relics of harshness such as is found in the Keadas; see M. O. Rayet, in A. H. Couat, *Poésie alex.*, p. 344, n. 2).

33.   This is the case for some of Aristophanes' texts; for Dinarchus' text, which is mentioned in n. 28 above; and for Thucydides, II.67 (see n. 34).

34.   This seems to be proved by Herodotus, VIII.133: the envoys of Darius are thrown into a pit and a well in Athens and in Sparta (...*esbalontes ekeleuon gēn te kai hudōr ek toutōn* [from the pit and the well] *pherein para basilea*). This act can be understood only if the emissaries were thrown down while alive. On the other hand, Thucydides, II.67.4, on which people readily base arguments, is less clear: he speaks of nonbelligerent enemies of Greece who were killed by the Lacedaemonians and (in reprisal) by the Athenians (*apekteinan...kai es pharangas esebalon...apokteinantes kai es pharangas esbalontes*).

35.   See Thuc., I.134.4: ...*ton Kaiadan houper tous kakourgous emballein*. This can be no other place than the one from which the Persians were thrown (Hdt., VIII.133). As for the *barathron*, in addition to the passages already mentioned, see Plut., *Arist.*, 3, which presents an "apophthegm" of the hero: there is more safety for the Athenians *ei mē kai Themistoklea kai auton es to barathron embaloien*.

36.   The number of these allusions is already contested; and if, in a strict sense, texts like Ar., *Ran.*, 574, and *Plut.*, 431, are subject to misconstruction, there is all the clarity possible in *Eq.*, 1362 (*eis to barathron embalō, ek tou larungos enkremasas Huperbolon*, where the last few words hearken perhaps indirectly to one feature of the execution), *Nub.*, 1450, and *Plut.*, 1109.

37.   On this subject, Keramopoullos refers to Ar., *Eccl.*, 1089, which is an allusion

to the decree of Kannonos; but the word *dialelēmmenon* is connected not with the punishment *apotumpanismos* but, as the scholiast sees it, with the procedure of hurling in.

38.   Lys., XII.18, and Pl., *Phd.*, 115D; cf. Lys., XIX.7.

39.   It is the case of the Samians whom Pericles had executed (Plut., *Per.*, 28: . . . *eita probalein ta sōmata akēdeuta*).

40.   It is true that they were buried apart from the rest of the dead, near a crossroads (Keramopoullos refers to a prescription in Plato's *Laws*, IX.873A); still, burial was permitted.

41.   But this could not be later than the beginning of the sixth century B.C., when because of the *katharmos* ordered by Epimenides the corpses of the Alcmaeonids were disinterred (Keramopoullos, op. cit., p. 104, n. 2). There is even some reason to believe that this exhumation occurred in the seventh century B.C. (see Glotz, *Solidarité*, p. 461, n. 2). Concerning the antiquity of denial of burial, see ibid., pp. 29 f.

42.   Pl., *Grg.*, 516D (cf. Hdt., VI.186); Ar., *Eq.*, 1362, and *Plut.*, 1109; Xen., *Hell.*, I.7.20; schol. Ar., *Plut.*, 431; Lycurg., *Leoc.*, 121. In Delphi the *katakrēmnismos* was the punishment for sacrilege and for religious crimes in general (Paus., X.4.2; Eur., *Ion*, 1102, etc.; Aeschin., II.142).

43.   In Greece, denial of burial was a general rule for tyrants, traitors, and those guilty of sacrilege (Diod. Sic., XVI.25.2). In Athens, it was anticipated by the law concerning traitors and those who committed crimes of sacrilege (Xen., *Hell.*, I.7.22) and by the law concerning *eisangelia* (Hyper., *Eux.*, 18). Cf. Pl., *Leg.*, IX.855A.

44.   The political crimes under the Thirty Tyrants (Lys., XII.17, XVIII.24); the cases of Socrates and Phokion.

45.   In Demosthenes' texts it is a question of popular justice (see especially IX.61); Demosthenes really enjoys bringing this up (cf. Aeschin., III.150; Dem., XXIV.208).

46.   Both are brothers of Agoratos, who was born a slave.

47.   The third case (Lys., XIII.56) does not lend itself to interpretation. Under the Thirty Tyrants, the individual in question had caused a man's death by his denunciations, but he was evidently not convicted as a murderer (see P. Cloché, *Restaurat. démocr.*, pp. 341 ff.), and we do not know what crime set the judicial process in motion. At the most, we could suspect that the process was initiated by means of *apagōgē*.

48.   Ar., *Eq.*, 79, 205, 248, 296, etc.

49.   Pl., *Leg.*, IX.857A f.

50.   Someone goes to find the chief of the prytany, who then comes and catches Mnesilokhos in *flagrante delicto* (Ar., *Thesm.*, 930 f.).

51.   Dem., XXII.26.

52.   See U. von Wilamowitz-Moellendorff, *Homer. Untersuch.* (*Phil. Unters.*, VII [1884]), pp. 200 f.

53.   See S. Reinach, *Cultes, mythes et religions*, II, pp. 159 ff.

54.   We do not know for what crime Lysimachus had to undergo *apotumpanismos*, according to Aristotle's version (*Ath. Pol.*, 45.1). It must have been a public crime, since the accused was handed over before the Council; but this public crime could have been sacrilegious theft or the stealing of city property, the flagrancy of which justified the *apagōgē* (see Libanius; the *hupothesis* of Demosthenes' *Contra Aristogeitonem*). The instances quoted by Herodotus and Plutarch (citing Douris of Samos) have to do with external enemies. The execution of Antiphon the poet (Arist., *Rh.*, II.5) is the act of a tyrant.

55.   This use of the term is fairly well defined: Thuc., I.8.2, II.22; [Dem.], LVIII.53, etc. It is possible to admit with Lipsius (op. cit., p. 79, n. 105) that in the classical era this term did not have a technical meaning. But it can also be said that in an earlier period the *apagōgē* was employed in a similar way, as it happened later, *outside* Athens (Lucian, *Vota*, 14), and even *in* Athens in some instances in the fifth century B.C. (Lys., XIII.78).

56.   On the first point, see Dem., IV.47. On the second, see Sext. Emp., *Math.*, XXX.295: *tinōn men eis to desmōtērion, tinōn d'epi tumpanon apagomenōn.*

57.   Isoc., XV.90; Ant., V.9 f.; Lys., X.10. Cf Dem., XXXV.47; Xen., *Mem.*, I.2.61; Pl., *Resp.*, IX.575B, VIII.552D.

58.   See Arist., *Ath. Pol.*, 7.3.

59.   Here the noun *apagōgē* applies more specifically; see H. Meuss, *De apagoges act. ap. Ath.*, pp. 3, 14, 22.

60.   Cases in which the guilty party denies the crime. It is clear, however, that in principle a denial has little effect if an instance of flagrant action is involved. It was allowed only when flagrancy, which continued to be demanded, ceased to belong to the very definition of the crime. See P. Huvelin, *Etudes sur le furtum dans le très ancien droit romain*, I, p. 148.

61.   It seems that the *dikē* takes place in cases of general or unspecified theft; that is to say, when the crime is not a *flagrans delictum*. The *graphē* doubtless applies to a specific form of thievery (Lipsius, op. cit., p. 438), but it came into being late in the classical era. Two other procedures are closely related to the *apagōgē*: *endeixis* and *ephēgēsis*. But there is some doubt that the first was applied to *kakourgoi* (ibid., p. 331; for another viewpoint, see Huvelin, op. cit., p. 146; but cf. Dem., XXII.26). As for *ephēgēsis*, it appears that its primitive domain was crimes of a public and religious nature (Lys., VII.22), and in any case it seems that it could not coexist with the *apagōgē* at first.

62.   On the essential nature of this procedure, see Huvelin, op. cit., p. 145, n. 4. Even when *apagein* and *agein* are distinguished from each other, the compound form applies to *apagōgē* no less than does the simple form, which is sometimes used in its place. We know the meaning of *agein*; it is enough to recall its use with regard to the *iudicati* and the *nexi* in the law of Gortyn and elsewhere. It applies to a summary and private execution in Ant., V.34.

63.   Dem., XXIV.113.

64.   See Glotz, *Solidarité*, pp. 198 ff.

65.   The *moikhos* does not belong to the category of *kakourgoi*; there is no way to make allowances for the information in Aeschines (I.90), who includes murderers (see Lipsius, op. cit., p. 79, n. 105) when using the verb *kakourgein* in a general sense. This does not imply—for naturally there are links between these two types of penalties—that the *flagrans delictum* was not established according to more or less solemn methods (see Lys., I.23 ff; cf. especially par. 25 and Ar., *Ran.*, 1361 ff.); but the flagrancy resulted in a purely private execution.

66.   Note the opposition set up by Demosthenes (XXIII.32) between *apagein* and *hōs hauton agein*.

67.   See Glotz, *Solidarité*, pp. 26 ff.

68.   According to Plutarch (*Sol.*, 17), this is the origin of the structure of Draconian law. Even much later, the law of revenge with regard to the thief is more widespread in the countryside than in the city; see the text of Harmenopoulos, VI.5.3-4 (fourteenth century), cited by Huvelin, op. cit., p. 39. For solidarity in revenge, see *Od.*, XVI.424 ff. and *Il.*, XXIV.264; see also the texts cited by Glotz, *Solidarité*, pp. 202 ff.

69.   See O. Schrader, *Reallex.*, pp. 137 ff. Notably, theft comes before homicide in the table of crimes.

70.   But it no longer exempts one from judicial action in the classical period (see n. 57 above). Moreover, the solemn investigation of the *phōra*, which was at first intimately connected with the idea of *ep'autophōrōi*, no longer has the power to determine the *flagrans delictum* or its consequent punishments (see Glotz, *Solidarité*, p. 206, following Pl., *Leg.*, XII.954A–B).

71.   See Huvelin, op. cit., pp. 142–43. There is little need to mention the obvious etymology of *ep'autophōrōi*, which allows us to define the primitive domain of the concept of flagrancy.

72.   This is more than a simple metaphor, since the ritual procedures furnished themes for the dance and drama (see Xen., *An.*, VI.1.7 [Sophocles' *Ikhneutai*]; Ar., *Ran.*, 1343 ff.).

73.   For the social importance and function of this category, see L. Radermacher, *Beiträge zur Volkskunde aus dem Gebiet der Antike*, pp. 3 f. (*Sitz. Wien, Philos.-hist. Kl.*, CLXXXVII.3).

74.   On the juridical scope of the *phōra* or *quaestio*, there is now some information in Huvelin, op. cit., pp. 143 ff. and 299 ff. (he is inclined to find in the *phōra* the unique source of flagrancy). On its ritual character, see Glotz, *Solidarité*, pp. 203 ff.

75.   Lys., XIII.78:... *agousin...hōs apoktenountes houper kai tous allous apes-phatton, ei tina lēistēn ē kakourgon sullaboien.*

76.   This is the second main application of the *apagōgē* in the classical period; see Lipsius, op. cit., pp. 327 f. On the priority of the other, see ibid., p. 320. It is evident, more-over, that the former presupposes the mitigation of the primitive concept of *atimia*.

77.   This is especially the case for murderers who are not citizens (Ant., V; Lys., XIII); furthermore, it is quite clear from these two speeches what the opposition of the juridi-cal conscience to this extension could be.

78.   Thus, in a decree proclaimed after the overthrow of the Four Hundred (Lycurg., *Leoc.*, 121), *apagōgē* is used regarding traitors, who are not placed beyond the protection of law, as prescribed in the decree of Demophantos. Indeed, the end result is the assimilation of the two punishments; but the extension of the idea of *apagōgē* in a similar fashion is a recent phenomenon: *agōgimos* becomes the term designating the *atimos*, "one without recourse to law," but not before the fourth century B.C. (P. Usteri, *Aechtung und Verbannung*, p. 57). On the purely private, primitive significance of the word *apagōgē*, see Dem., LIII.11; Arist., *Ath. Pol.*, 2.2. Cf. Diod. Sic., I.79; Dion. Hal., *Ant. Rom.*, V.69, VI.37.

79.   This is so in regard to murderers, but only to murderers who have violated the terms of their exile; that is, the *apagōgē* is subordinated to a social judgment, to an affirma-tion of joint liability. However, it belongs only to the parents of the victim (Dem., XXIII.28 ff.). We are not referring to another kind of *apagōgē*, which has an exceptional character (Glotz, *Solidarité*, pp. 428 ff.) and is merely a special case of the *apagōgē atimōn* (Dem., XXIV.60, XXIII.80).

80.   See n. 71 above. The case is the same for a certain kind of impiety: Plato (*Men.*, 80B) alludes to the *apagōgē* practiced against magicians, but ostensibly against foreigners (who are often the *goetes*: see H. Hubert, *Dict. des antiq.*, s.v. *Magia*); this caution serves to dispel the doubt of Lipsius (op. cit., p. 322, n. 20). Let us note that impiety, which can be handled by way of *apagōgē* (Dem., XXII.27), is applied only in particular cases (Lipsius, op. cit., p. 328; see, in this context, Lys., VII.22).

81.   Understood in the precise sense of the term, the *actio popularis* is sometimes at-tested in the form of the *apagōgē*: E. Ziebarth, *Hermes*, XXXII (1897), 618 ff. One of the two cases mentioned by Ziebarth is instructive; it concerns the procedure carried out according to the rules of the Andanian Mysteries (Michel, no. 694, ll. 78 f.) against the man who *koptei ek tou hierou*. As for the ordinary *apagōgē*, which by means of a late extension of the idea of *kakourgoi* seems to be understood as a method used against the *hierosuloi* (Pl., *Resp.*, I.344B, VIII.552D, IX.575B; Xen., *Mem.*, I.2, and *Ap.*, 25), it really should be interpreted as apply-ing to the flagrant theft of sacred treasures.

82.   In the "natural history of morality" this syncretism is of consequence; we can ask ourselves if the idea of *shame*, so familiar to us, was not at first limited to a special area of crime. We would have to bear in mind certain types of punishment, such as that exemplified precisely by *apotumpanismos*; "the crime produces the shame, and not the scaffold" is not really a historically accurate assessment.

83.   Common usage is sufficient evidence; see especially Ant., V.10.

84.   In this way we can explain the relative extension of this punishment. Besides

the texts of Demosthenes in which *apotumpanismos* is treated, we could cite the allusion we think we have found in Aeschin., II.181 ff., and above all the punishment of Kinadon (Xen., *Hell.*, III.3.11), which bears some relationship to *apotumpanismos*. We know that the latter was inflicted upon the murderers of Philip of Macedon (from an anonymous historian in *POxy.*, XV, no. 1798).

85.   Another condition is added in such a case: it is necessary that the sum total of the theft surpass a specific amount, at least in ordinary circumstances. But it is essentially the old practice that persists. See Dem., XXIV.114.

86.   In such a case the ordinary course is that of the *dikē*, the penalty for which is restitution and a fine double the value of what was stolen (Dem., XXIV.105); that is to say, while the crime, as far as we are concerned, is basically the same, the punishment is very unequal depending on whether or not the crime was a *flagrans delictum*. The *graphē* could have the sanction of death (Dem., XXIV.103); but we have seen that death is probably directed at a specific kind of theft (n. 61), where it is a substitute for the *apagōgē*.

87.   Lys., X.16; Dem., XXIV.105 (cf. XXIV.103).

88.   The text of Demosthenes (differing from that of Lysias) adds *ton poda*, which has the effect of a gloss; whether it is an echo of the classical age or reflects a later period, it confirms what we find in Lysias: the term *podokakē* should, in principle, say more than what the composition of the word tells us at first glance.

89.   Ar., *Eq.*, 1049 (cf. 1040, 367, 705); Alexis, cited by Ath., IV.134.

90.   Ar., *Lys.*, 680.

91.   Aristophanes (*Lys.*, 680 f.) gives us a valuable piece of information: *alla toutōn khrēn hapasōn eis tetrēmenon xulon enkatharmosai labontas toutoni ton aukhena*. The *podokakē*, which Lysias calls *xulon*, cannot be understood as a wooden fetter; it is a plank to which *hēloi* are fastened (the *pedai* also are something different: see Pl., *Phd.*, 59E, 60B).

92.   Poll., VIII.107 (after Kratinos); *Lex. Patmos*, in *BCH*, I (1877), pp. 143 f. (cf. Dem., XVIII.209); Arist. *Pol.*, VIII.6.1306b; Plut., *Nic.*, 11 (cf. Ar., *Plut.*, 476, 606). The punishment of *kuphōn* (Pollux and *Lex. Patmos*) is particularly applied to crimes committed in the marketplace; one automatically thinks of the *apagōgē* in these cases (Alexis, cited by Ath., II.226A–B); and a law of the first century B.C. expressly subjects to the law of *kakourgoi* the individual who is caught *kakourgōn epi ta metra kai ta stathma* (*IG*, II, no. 476, ll. 55 f.).

93.   The punishment is carried out in the agora. (Ar., *Plut.*, 476, 606; cf Poll., VIII.107, and *Lex. Patmos*, in *BCH*, I [1877], pp. 143 f.). Plato (*Leg.*, IX.855C) includes in the category of punishments the *amorphous hedras ē staseis* (cf., a little earlier, *desmois te khroniois kai emphanesi kai tisi propēlakismois*). This is the same kind of thinking that governs the use of the pillory for certain kinds of delinquents.

94.   See Huvelin, op. cit., pp. 61 f.

95.   Pliny, *HN*, XVIII.3–12 (see P. F. Girard, *Textes de droit romain* [Twelve Tables, VIII.9]).

96.   See S. Reinach, *REG*, XIX (1906), pp. 356 ff.

97.   See also Glotz, *L'Ordalie*, pp. 30 ff., on the *katapontismos*.

98.   R. Hirzel, *Die Strafe der Steinigung* (*Abhandl. d. phil.-histor. Kl. d. kön. sächs. Gesellsch. d. Wiss.*, XXVII.7), has established not only that stoning in Greece was a manifestation of "lynch law" but that it also functioned in ancient times as a true penal institution.

99.   See Schrader, *Reallex.*, p. 905, for some characteristic examples, the list of which we could lengthen. *Agos* concerns crimes against a divinity, incest, treachery, attacks on the sacred person of the chief, etc. For the grouping of types, see Tac., *Germ.*, 12, concerning Germanic law. Cf. Livy, *Hist.*, I.51; C. Ferrini, *Diritto pen. rom.*, p. 244.

100.   See Pl., *Leg.*, IX.873B. The drama of the punishment is played out on a religious plane—e.g., Bouphonia, pursuit of *pharmakoi* at the Ionian Thargelia, etc.

101.   This could at least be the case with stoning.

102.   This entire category of punishments has links with the curse (see R. Vallois, *BCH*, XXXVII [1914], pp. 250 f.) and the ordeal (for the *devotio*, see Glotz, *L'Ordalie*, pp. 7, 33, etc.). Hence the designation of the guilty party is *eparatos*, and *hamartōlos*, followed by the god's name in the genitive. Cf. the use of the term *anathema* in modern Greek as explained by Keramopoullos, op. cit., pp. 53 ff. (the connection with stoning). In extreme cases the *devotio* can take place without the active intervention of society—without their being any punishment (e.g., in cases of perjury).

103.   Andoc., I.96; Dem., IX.44; Lycurg., *Leoc.*, 125. The idea is already slightly weakened in Festus's definition of *sacer*.

104.   For the necessity of killing the *friedlos*, see H. Brunner, *Deutsche Rechtsgesch.*, II, p. 472.

105.   The *dēmios* is termed an impure *alitērios*: Ath., X.420B; Eust., ad Od., XVIII. 1.1833.54. The institution of executioner does not go back to very ancient times (see Keramopoullos, op. cit., p. 107). We recall that among the Germans the pagan priests were responsible for this task.

106.   This is suggested by the institution of the *pharmakoi* in Athens (at least in the classical period), Asia Minor, and Marseilles. It is also suggested by the human sacrifices on Rhodes. The subjects of the rituals are selected from among criminals and are sometimes treated with special honor.

107.   For the primitive meaning of the institution, see R. von Jhering, *Esprit du droit romain*, I, p. 282. In the same sense we recall the use of the term *supplicium*. Some doubts have been raised concerning the currently accepted etymology of the word, but they do not seem justified in our opinion; nevertheless, see C. Juret, *Domin. et résist. dans la phon. lat.*, pp. 41 ff.

108.   [Lys.], VI.53 (with the very clear relic of the Thargelian *pharmakos*); Ar., *Eq.*, 1045; [Dem.], XXV.80. See the analogous use of *katharma* in Dem., XXI, etc. On the concept of the *pharmakos* among the Romans, see Dion. Hal., *Ant. Rom.*, II.68.

109.   See Glotz, *L'Ordalie*, pp. 50 f., 90 f. We know the Germanic analogues: in particular, J. Grimm, *Deutsch. Rechtsalt.*, p. 701. For ethnographical comparisons, see A. H. Post, *Grundr. der ethnol. Jurispr.*, II, pp. 268, 269, 273.

110.   For the meaning of the action and character of the punishment itself, see A. Piganiol, *Essai sur les origines de Rome*, p. 149, which has the merit of presenting with clarity the problem of different kinds of execution.

111.   According to Keramopoullos, op. cit., p. 105.

112.   The function of the *huperorismos* is clearly present in the institution of the Prytaneion, where it is applied to animals and inanimate objects. The same psychology is found in the ritual of tearing down a house.

113.   In Rome, a religious element was introduced into the punishment of crucifixion: the tree used for the punishment was consecrated to Ceres. But the primitive idea of execution still appears in the obligation of either abandoning the condemned at night (this can be applied to the corpse [the citation of Gaius in the *Autun Gaius*, 82]) or paying a settlement (see Huvelin, op. cit., p. 63, n. 3). It is true, of course, that practices of an essentially analogous nature could have been used in a completely different spirit in different cultures: the punishment of the *arbor infelix* in Livy, *Hist.*, I.26, is specifically religious, as is hanging for the Germans. For these, see K. von Amira, *Die germ. Todesstr.* (*Abhandl. d. Bay. Ak. d. W., Philos.- Philol. u. Hist. Kl.*, XXXI.3 [1922]), where all the methods of execution are understood as different forms of the *sacratio* (pp. 198–235)—especially that of the thief (pp. 201 ff.; cf. pp. 182 ff.). It is impossible here to engage in a discussion of comparative law. Let us simply say that it is natural for a penal method, at first foreign to any religious representation, eventually to assume a formal religious quality through the participation of society. We do not find this development in Greece, and are thus persuaded that it was only secondary. In the same work by

von Amira, one should note (pp. 170 ff.) his discussion of the torture of the wheel, the way it works and its antiquity; it is not without parallels to *apotumpanismos* (see p. 109). The author, in fact, makes some direct connections between the two punishments.

114.   For the essentially secular quality of the punishment of *kakourgēma*, see the significant reflections of Antiphon, V.10. Within the juridical and religious system of the classical period, the murder of the *kakourgos* required no purification—in contrast to other equally unpunished murders (Pl., *Leg.*, IX.874C, 865A). This does not mean that there could not have been some magical element in the "prosecution of the thief"; but that is another question.

115.   According to *Od.*, XXII.173 ff., 187 ff., Melanthios is fixed to a column of the *thalamos* (note l. 177: *hōs ken dētha zōos eōn khalep' algea paskhēi*). Cf. Soph., *Aj.*, 105 f., which describes the punishment that Ajax believes he inflicts on Odysseus: *detheis pros kion' herkeiou stegēs*.

116.   This kind of penal practice is at the basis of the concept of punishment's "exemplary quality"—a concept often found in Greece; see Keramopoullos, op. cit., p. 41, n. 2.

PART IV

SOCIAL INSTITUTIONS

CHAPTER 11
The Nobility
in Ancient Greece

What is currently called the Greek nobility refers to a class that exercised power in several cities during the archaic period, that is to say, during a time when the state already existed but had underdeveloped functions, which the nobility monopolized. One of these functions was the exercise of justice. A system of arbitration was already a thing of the past and there were obligatory areas of jurisdiction; but it is the nobility—in Hesiod's Boeotia—that controls them, and in Attica it is only under Pisistratus that it finally seems to lose this control. In any case, what concerns us here is not the "political" role of the nobility but its function in society and its very nature as a class.

One cannot avoid pointing out—if only to decry it—the paucity of testimonia on the subject. Moreover, for some regions of Greece more than for others, our information is even more meager. And we cannot argue a priori that the nobility evolved in the same way in every part of Greece. We shall first examine it in Athens, at the time when the revolution of Solon is about to deprive it of much of its power.

❀

Although this revolution is poorly understood, it is not our intention to review the scholarship concerning it. Instead, let us examine one element that is an essential ingredient of the state of society presupposed by the revolution.

During the period preceding Solon's archonship (594 B.C.), the region of Attica was in great turmoil. Strong opposition existed between two

This article originally appeared in *Annales d'histoire économique et sociale*, X (1938), pp. 36–43.

groups: those Aristotle calls "persons of importance" or "the rich," and those who constitute "the people." We can readily identify the dominant class in this struggle as the *eupatridai* (the wellborn, the "sons of noble fathers"). As for "the people," according to Aristotle and other writers they are designated by a number of terms evidently in use during Solon's time: *pelatai, hektēmoroi,* and *thētes.* In Homer and later authors, the term *thētes* refers to farm workers who, though free, live in a wretched condition close to slavery. The word *pelatai* in its strict sense means "those living nearby," that is, those living under the protection of a powerful individual; it translates into the Latin *clientes.* Finally there are the *hektēmoroi,* "one-sixth people." Are we to believe that they paid rents of one-sixth or five-sixths? Scholars now tend to say one-sixth, and it makes sense. But these *hektēmoroi* make up a real class, and although Aristotle does speak of "renting" with regard to them, it is not here an instance of "renting out" in our modern sense. In general, if one asks the wrong historical question, the mistake lies in attempting to think of everything in terms of "law." Scholars speak of "tenancy," proprietorship, and mortgage as if these would have been useful concepts in a society that had not had money for long (and did not yet use it adequately), a society where *commercium* could not be expressed in legal categories that only money makes possible. Indeed, what sort of social structure can we discover in this period of Solon?

Aristotle frequently says that in the oldest period the land was in the hands of a few. We can well believe him, since the wealth of the noble *gentes* is certainly landed, and at present we know of only around fifty. Only part of the land is put to direct use (the slave-labor force was still in the early stages of development). But as far as the rest is concerned, we must explain two pieces of evidence: (1) the land belonged to the *eupatridai*; (2) as a result of Solon's reforms, it was "liberated" and given to the people who cultivated it. A clue to the kind of social relationship that exists here lies in the Roman *precarium*—though this represents a more advanced stage of economic development. In this regard, serfdom has already been mentioned, but the way the term has been used is too specialized for our purposes. Nevertheless, the society before Solon brings with it a genuine kind of personal subordination, of which the debtor's bond is only one striking form. This explains the interdependence of the problems of debt and those of landed status in Solon's reform. It also explains the presence of *horoi* on the lands of tenant farmers. The *horoi* have been the subject of much discussion; in the classical period they were used as mortgage marks. The *seisakhtheia* ("the shaking off of burdens"), an ordinance of Solon, involved a cancellation of "debts" in the broadest sense. Above all, it abolished the system of *hektēmoroi*; and there is no trace of such a system from this time onward.

We will have to return to the circumstances surrounding this revolution, but we think that it is best first to point to an interpretation of the *seisakhtheia* which goes back to Fustel de Coulanges but which in our opinion is as sound as ever. To see in the subordination of the "enslaved" only the result of the payment of debts is to confuse the facts. In other words, beyond the crisis itself it is necessary to see its presupposition, and it presupposes the existence of a basic patron-client relationship, a system that is far from chaotic. One has the feeling that it goes far back in antiquity; the Athenian bourgeoisie (Isocrates) inherited a tradition in which the role of patronage, as practiced by the dominant class during centuries of Athenian history, was held in high esteem. But where did this class get its social prestige?

The nobility was organized into *genē*, but we must once and for all discard the incorrect meanings or associations of this word. In Greek, when the word *genos* refers to a group, it always means a noble group. In the classical period this takes the form of a familial body where the individuals who are part of the *genos* are not all seen as related to one another by common descent; but this does not allow us to deny that the *genos* in the past could have been a noble house. The debate over the primitive nature of the *genos* may well persist.

Whatever the case may be, every *genos*, as far as we know, has its own characteristic religious activity. Not only does it concern itself with family cult, but it has a monopoly on certain liturgies. The monopoly is an ancient one, older than the polis, which certainly did not confer it. And the names of several *genē*—not only "professional" names but some "patronymic" ones as well—testify to a special privilege of ritual or magical character. This is the first element we discover in the nobility, and we consider it fundamental. From the earliest times the historical tradition concerning the eupatrids, a tradition that characterizes them on the basis of religious privilege, confirms the importance of this privilege. Since the privilege is exercised within a more extended group, it is possible to say that the earliest condition for the formation of a nobility was the division of religious tasks into a hierarchical structure (a hierarchy can also be found within the inner workings of the nobility itself). But how is prehistory represented in this case?

In the amalgamation of peoples, a phenomenon obscured by centuries, we have no way of uncovering the social traditions that were capable of surviving, their durable qualities and various uses, or the role that must be attributed to evolution or conquest. Sometimes the divisions of the nobility seem to correspond partially to ethnic differences, as, for example, in Thessaly. In Attica, according to Thucydides, before the Persian Wars the "Ionian" nobility had its own distinctive dress; this could represent a kind of "invasion." Nevertheless, given the symbiotic developments that are bound to occur between autochthonous and immigrant populations, the ancestors of the Greek nobility were themselves indebted to earlier traditions. The point we established at the start leads us to believe that this nobility perpetuated a tradition much older than itself, one that could at least in part be Aegean. (For example, Crete often appears in the legend of the eupatrids; important members of the nobility here and there bear the title of *basileus*, a word that is not Indo-European in origin; and every eupatrid family boasts of its "royal" stock.) In addition, the very phenomenon of the nobility is not the same in all places. (The Thessalians, in contrast to Athenian nobles, have real serfs.) The nobility also developed differently depending on geography and local history. (No doubt there were noble families in Sparta; the few we know of also owed their status to religious privilege. Still, their importance—we prescind from the two royal houses—does not seem comparable to that of the eupatrids.)

It will be clear that there is at least one theory we are not likely to adopt: according to it the nobility is a relatively recent phenomenon, an automatic result of the growing inequality of wealth. We would not dream of denying that a monopolistic process led to the development of the nobility's economic power. For example, there is the private farming of common land, the fixing of boundaries for the benefit of families rich in livestock, and the practice of ancient forms of "mortgage." One must also take into account the continual changes that took place within the class structure; circumstances, as well as new laws, could create nobles, at least in Athens. The fact remains, however, that the new elements blend into a whole complex, and nobles are nobles only because they share a unique quality that is traditional.

❧

It must be admitted, therefore, that there is something very ancient at the core of the concept of a nobility. This is precisely why the complex of social features in which the nobility recognized itself points to something other than economic domination by a propertied class. The existence of a separate and specific nobility is an essential element of the social structure. This separation is itself required by the nobility's own discipline: according to Herodotus, the Bacchiads of Corinth were as a rule required to intermarry; at a later date, Theognis bitterly protests the alliances of nobles with the lower classes.

The first characteristic that defines a noble class is naturally the name it bears or sometimes is granted. As with the *eupatridai*, the name naturally alludes to birth. Family trees continue to be part of the tradition of the *genē*. Some names, more ancient and revealing, designate wealth (in several poleis the nobles are the "fat"), especially in terms of land (*geōmoroi*). Still, in a number of places nobles are called "knights." Aristotle emphasized the importance of this designation for an understanding of social history. The nobility is a military order, and a minimum prerequisite for noble status is ownership of a horse (with a view to going to war). Here there is a traditional feature that from the start has links with certain military tactics, namely, those involving chariot warfare. But it is important to note that the title "knight" outlasted this kind of warfare. In the period we are considering, the horse was of little importance in war. There was no longer chariot warfare, and one did not fight with cavalry. The horse was essentially a symbol.

The ownership of horses (a feature that determined the class's inner hierarchy: there were "households capable of maintaining a four-horsed chariot") presupposes a form of wealth in Greece that was land-based. Indeed, this does seem to be the economic base of the nobility and is attested already by the designation *geōmoroi*. One must add to farming the possession of livestock; wealth in this form, the kind that characterized the nobility of Sicyon during a period of revolution, deserves special mention. This is not to say that the nobility lived only off the land. But in terms of its economic activities, there is a good deal of fantasy. Some have recognized in certain locales a commercial class of nobility. If by this they mean a genuine mercantile class, their view must be rejected. Hasebroeck, in his research on the economic and social history of Greece before the Persian Wars, gives the required response. First, the era of the nobility predates by a long time the time when money was introduced. Such was the case in the period of the Bacchiads in Corinth, who according to the works of modern historians sometimes were in the business of armaments and merchandising. Why, it is difficult to understand. What is true is that the governing class of Corinth—Thucydides and Strabo are precise about this—received tribute from merchants passing through the Isthmus. On the other hand, privateering, which is connected with war and pillaging, developed into a more peaceful activity in which the nobility found the means for a very productive enterprise. But to the best of our knowledge we are dealing with occasional or isolated instances. There is no reason to believe that the Homeric scorn for the professional tradesman had disappeared. It is with good reason that the vase painters always depict nobles as "knights." Even in Corinth, Asia Minor, and the colonies, the nobility is essentially a land-based class, but one that supplements its resources, sometimes to a considerable degree, by maritime commerce—but only by maritime commerce and never to such an extent that a noble would qualify as a commoner. Elsewhere, this distinction is clear; not only does the Thessalian nobility reveal an opposition to any mercantile occupation (even those involving the city), but the nobility of Sicilian Megara, as Theognis tells us, inveighed against the wealthy lower classes. The reason for this was simple; the life of the merchant was not compatible with that of a nobleman.

The boundaries of the nobleman's life are multiple; groups will interfere, but their encroachment produces a cohesion in the nobility. The *genos* itself manifests its religious unity with resolute force. What is termed family cult is in fact something quite complex and deserves more precise analysis than it usually receives. There is the cult of the eponymous hero; there are also local cults of divinities fostered by families, cults that are sometimes associated with one another in a kind of system. There are divinities of the "hearths" of the *genē*, and there are some stereotypical cult forms that by definition appear in each *genos*: the cults of Zeus *Herkeios*, Apollo *Patrōos*, even of Dionysus. But the society of nobles does not consist of partitioned *genē*; existing among those with different patronymics are associations of a more or less stable quality which are in some ways free and yet equally products of custom. We can see from the laws of Draco that the group involved in a blood feud does not coincide with the *genos*. Nor does being buried in the same tomb have anything to do with it, even though possessing a tomb is one criterion of nobility. Traditional groupings, or guilds, also exist, and these *hetaireiai* eventually take the form of political societies, but remain quite distinct from parties.

The family occupies an important place in the preoccupations of nobles. Perhaps personal kinship has succeeded in establishing itself in the nobility. There is a glimpse of an opposition between the nobility and large unified peasant families, who according to Thucydides (II.16) could survive with tenacity. From the beginning it was in the eupatrid households that *succession* had great importance. Succession was guaranteed and preserved by legal processes that sometimes became general practice (adoption); sometimes were simply tolerated (common pupillary substitutions of wards); or sometimes were excluded (the *fidei-commissum* or trust). Filiation had to be guaranteed; this was achieved through a solemn form of marriage, the *enguē*, which from the juridical point of view is a verbal contract. Beginning with Solon, the *enguē* itself is made general practice by the laws of the poleis. In theory it is a condition for marriage; but remarkably the *enguē* continues to be applied to a legitimate union while losing its specific and obligatory character. As a matrimonial form, the *enguē* seems to be an institution of the nobility.

Even more than laws and structure, mode of life defines a class. The nobles are city people, members of the polis. In ancient Athens, the word *astoi* ("city-dwellers") is synonymous with eupatrids. This does not mean that they do not also live on their own land and have tenacious connections with one or another rural district. Nevertheless, because they are established in the city, they are at the center of the "political" life and the common religion. For this reason they are distinguished from the peasant population (and even from workers, the *dēmiourgoi*, inhabiting the outskirts or worse quarters of the city). They are also distinguished by their garb; and here one can point to Thucydides' reference to "Ionian" dress (a linen tunic, and the hair held together in a bun by "golden cicadas"). In contrast, a special peasant costume is mentioned in reference to Athens and Sicyon.

Wealth permits spending. Luxury—it would be possible to identify its various domains—corresponds to a major tendency, but it also involves the ethics of gift-giving, which survives in the milieu of the eupatrids. It is the relic of the nobility's *mores* which helps explain the city's "liturgies" and their twofold quality of obligation and generosity. For the most part, the occasions for expenditure are defined: sacrifices called for by the nobility's religious functions, marriages, funerals, participation in the great games (for which purposes the *quadrigae* were maintained)—all of these are strong and persistent marks of the nobility. It is instructive that the ruling polis, which encourages expenditures on the part of the nobility in certain areas, puts limits on them in others, even by legislation. This is the case with marriages, but is even more so with funerals. We are not dealing here with sumptuary legislation in the usual sense of the term. But by its nature the city opposes any special code of behavior that would contribute to the maintenance of a household's unity, the unity between households, and the prestige of the whole order.

By their very existence, nobles qualify as "the good" or "the best" (*aristoi*): it is these names that they carry. Nobles are the best primarily because they are the warriors. Still, at every stage of their social lives, they reveal a concern "to be first" (*aristeuein*). In war, in the festivals, and in their individual dealings with one another, the agonistic idea is a constant. It is impossible to understand this unless some connection is made with another concept that is central to the nobility's code of ethics, namely, "honor" (*timē*). In Pindar, a good source for our understanding of *timē*, the term still preserves the ancient idea of a religious power characterizing a noble *genos*. It also continues to signify the privilege attached to this power, as well as the obligation entailed in the maintenance and defense of moral wealth (such as the integrity of a family or a chivalrous alliance). The *timōria*, which is actually "preservation of *timē*," is the avenging of another's death; it is also aid given out of obligation. *Timē* must have been recognized by emblems or signs, but for an institution as basic as this, we have scant information to go on. We know that armorial bearings appear on the earliest Attic coins. Perhaps the legends of heroes, when they preserve the relic of coats-of-arms and instruments of investiture, could give us some clues about this subject.

※

In certain locales, especially in Attica, economic domination by the nobility was the occasion for the crisis we have already referred to. It is important to define its nature and origin. We do not want to call it "a war between the classes"; the term is jejune. Solon's contemporary poetry supplies us with a useful vocabulary. True, his poetry is a moralizing kind of verse, but he forcefully denounces a state of lawlessness. The moral dimension of this lawlessness is fundamental. Human behavior has been knocked off its course by the forces of wealth, and is the victim of a dizzying form of madness. *Hubris* rules, Solon says, and it is a form of violence, excess, and fatal blindness. *Koros*, literally "satiety," is connected with *hubris*. Behind this ideology it is possible to catch a glimpse of a social reality: there is a psychological orientation toward gain and profit. With this goes the possibility of an economy of excess, that is, an increase of wealth and power through the unlimited exercise of violence. But only one fact of social and economic history explains the crisis: the introduction of money.

In Attica at least, money proceeds originally from the nobility. The oldest coins are those of the *genē*, and in principle they are signs and instruments of privilege. Coins can serve to stabilize and expand one's clientele. But their economic function takes on its primary importance from the power and prestige they give to the people issuing them (those issuing them also invest them with value): this is the power to acquire interest in productive enterprises and to advance profitable loans. The term "advance" (*proesis* originally meant "an abandoning," even "lavishness") remains an essential one in the vocabulary of *commercium*; and in this regard, even in Isocrates, it is possible to find a tradition with a core of historical truth.

Still it is money that proves fatal to the nobility. For the use of money allows and even legitimates losses of equilibrium in society. *Eunomia*, according to its etymology (*nomos*), means precisely "equilibrium." In the ancient state, one can say only that the *genē*—the recipients of local privileges and the *sacra* associated with the earth—have some connection with "demes" (often of the same name). But at the end of the sixth century B.C. the *genē* are strangely dispersed throughout Attica. The locales are all confused, there is no real plan, and one can aspire to the unlimited role of the *prostatēs*, or "patron"; some put themselves up as "patron of the people." However, the *prostatēs tou dēmou* is the tyrant, and what made the phenomenon of tyranny possible was a new kind of economy that both perpetuated and distorted old values. It is from this point of view that we must interpret the facts Ure presented in a somewhat unhistorical fashion in *The Origin of Tyranny*.

On the other hand, the nobility is of necessity compromised by the progress of an abstract economy that favors no particular individual. "Money makes the man" says a proverb dating from a period of crisis. In the political order this means that constitutions based on a census of landed property had appeared. Modern writers readily suggest that these constitutions coexisted with a genuine dominance by the nobility, even though such constitutions were opposed to the nobility. These scholars carry back quite far the constitution of Athens, which Aristotle attributed to Solon (the internal evidence confirms Aristotle's view). In fact, what we find is the advent of a new principle.

❧

The Greece that develops in this period is a Greece of poleis isolated by their individuality. By virtue of a deep-seated tendency, one confers the rights of citizenship only on those who are born of parents who are citizens. And from the moment when law exists in our modern sense of the term, the legal system creates homogeneity within the narrow circle of the polis. In this regard, the nature of the city and that of the nobility are at odds. The nobility is Hellenic in nature; there exist among its members links from region to region, and a *genos* such as that of the Aegidae has branches in several places at once. There are hereditary contracts of hospitality and *proxenia*; matrimonial alliances also are frequent.

For anyone who wants to understand the historical function of the Greek nobility, the following point is fundamental. At no stage is Greece more united morally than during the archaic period. Even wars, which are characterized by the agonistic spirit, give it unity; but wars are not yet institutions of international law, nor are they the means of domination in service of the state. One could say that it is the noble class that produces a civilized community, one comprising an athletic and musical culture.

Moreover, the nobility never died out completely; quite the contrary. What immediately springs to mind in this regard is not only its vitality in an out-of-the-way region such as Thessaly; not only the isolated survivals of its type in the classical period (Cimon is a good example); not only the fact that even in Athens, noble families gained extended preference because of their prestige, and that perhaps none of the lower classes rose to civic prominence before Cleon at the end of the fifth century B.C.; not only the excessive and vain concern about birth which appeared even in some Athenian circles during the oligarchic revolutions of 411 and 404. The essential is found elsewhere.

The very revolution that ended the nobility's power did not completely suppress the concept of their kind of life. What the revolution did was diffuse such an idea. The citizen has a quality of human pride which is comparable to that of the nobleman, and his enduring contempt for things mercantile reflects the nobility's prejudices. The idea of nobility survives in literature and philosophy through the concept of "those who are better," men distinguished by their behavior and style of life. It also survives in the philosophical speculation concerning an ethical "nature" that is equal to "birth" (the idea of *phusis* is set out in distinctive terms). The type of virtue described in Aristotle's writings on ethics retains much of this ancient ideal, even in the very midst of the egalitarian city. In the formation of classical Greece, the heritage of a noble past certainly had its consequences.

CHAPTER 12
Marriages of Tyrants

Out of respect for a man who did so much to direct historical research toward the study of phases in the development of civilization— and consequently toward the study of the different and unpredictable psychological factors involved—I would like to make some observations about a set of facts concerning what might be called the matrimonial politics of Greek tyrants. The facts are meager, and at first sight might seem only arbitrary and accidental, like bits of unrefined history. Still, they might be significant, and I will attempt to show why.

As a Greek phenomenon, tyranny has two faces so to speak. It represents the notion of the state as a unique source of power, and there can be little doubt that it firmly fixed this idea of power in the realities of history and politics. Tyranny inaugurated a long-lived Western tradition of positivism amd amorality. However, although a late phenomenon, the tyrant was a natural product of the past, if only in his quest for the privileges that characterized him and were familiar to his own nation. His excesses had their models in legends that reflected conditions older than the polis. Thus he had his own mythology, which brought him into harmony with certain heritages of thought. The tyrant at times upset the game of balance between "feudal" powers, and always had the last word, but he treated it with respect. It is within this framework of conduct that one must situate matrimonial alliances. In themselves they constituted a political tool and have remained so, since they were until quite recently one of the elegant aspects of diplomatic history. But in the tyrant's case there are recognizable motives or suggestions that cannot be explained in abstract terms of a purely political nature. Every act of the tyrant could well be wonderfully offhanded; but his actions also reveal a form of archaism that is not of his own making.

This essay is an excerpt from *Hommage à Lucien Febvre* (1954), pp. 41–53.

※

We are not afraid to begin with a relatively late example; the evidence it offers will be all the more striking. The tyranny of Dionysius the Elder was established in Syracuse in the final years of the fifth century B.C. Incidentally, this is not the place to deal separately with Sicilian tyrannies, a project P. N. Ure once recommended. In [*The Origin of Tyranny*], an otherwise stimulating book, Ure distinguishes two forms of tyranny: the Sicilian one, which was a specifically military affair; and those of the seventh and sixth centuries B.C., which were more economic in nature. It is our intention to deal with tyranny as a "total" phenomenon, one that reveals more than the military and economic dimensions. The tyrants of Syracuse are authentic examples of tyranny. The marriages of Dionysius and his kin interest us because they were deliberate and unique affairs. Their uniqueness was a source of scandal at the time, but it was in no way arbitrary.

Dionysius' first marriage, one that was understandable but not especially noteworthy, was to the daughter of the well-known "demagogue" Hermocrates. After losing his position as tyrant, and after his wife's death, he regained power and suddenly remarried. He took two wives, a Locrian and a Syracusan, both daughters of persons of high rank. It is said that he married them on the same day.[1] Plutarch adds that no one knew which marriage was consummated first. His reference presupposes that this detail could have had some significance. For Dionysius—who used to "divide up" his days and nights equally—there is no doubt that a real problem existed: Dionysius the Younger, son of his Locrian wife, was destined to succeed him, and at first his rights to succession were viewed as contrary to the expressed wishes of his future subjects. On the other side were the two daughters of Dionysius' Syracusan wife, whose names were Temperance and Virtue (edifying names with political overtones quite suitable for the daughters of a tyrant). Dionysius married one daughter to the younger Dionysius, his son by the Locrian wife; the second daughter was married to the tyrant's own brother. When Dionysius' brother died, the widow was married to Dion, Dionysius' mother's brother.

In this whole affair two subjects capture our interest: Dionysius' own marriages; and the intrafamilial marriages he presided over, or rather ordered.

Polygamy was never a serious matter in Greece. Still, there is nothing in the organization of the polis to suggest that it was possible to have two legitimate wives at once. In contrast, a form of concubinage parallel to marriage was long recognized by law, and it never seems to have ceased having real legal effects. But this is not really relevant to our present concern. There are more ancient realities that gave rise to the legal status of polygamy, and we have every reason to see various forms of their survivals in it. As it happens, the heroes of legend enter into several marriages simultaneously, and quite a few descendants qualify as legitimate. Naturally, history represents the heroes as having only one legitimate wife. But which one was it? Curiously, several versions of a hero's life often disagree about the identity of his wife. And there are instances in which someone is tempted, or could be tempted, to enter into two marriages: Alcmaeon was certainly bigamous.

All of this falls under the category of information. But it does happen that different levels of history shed light on one another, and so we turn to the story of another tyrant, not only because it offers us at least a probable example, but also because it provides us a glimpse of a form of double marriage and the conditions that dictated its regular practice. The matrimonial career of Pisistratus has always been perplexing for historians.[2] He was married at least three times: to an Athenian whose name we do not know; to an Argive named Timonassa; and to the daughter of Megacles, one of his enemies. Although the sources, often contradictory, sometimes label Pisistratus' children by Timonassa illegitimate, it is impossible to believe that his marriage to a woman of such high rank was not a "regular" one. Some propose the unwarranted hypothesis that after contracting his third marriage Pisistratus broke off the second one; according to this theory, he had been able to contract his second marriage only because his first wife had either died or had been repudiated. But there *were* children, and by force of arithmetic one has to struggle to conclude that the sons of the Athenian and Argive wives were not the contemporaries they appear to be. Would it not be easier simply to admit that Pisistratus was bigamous, as was another tyrant one hundred fifty years later? Here we find another example of the games princes play. It is true that our explanation could seem unwarranted, since the two historians of the following century, Herodotus and Thucydides, tell us no such thing. They would have mentioned it only if Pisistratus had married two Athenians simultaneously; apparently this would have been a shocking affair.

It is quite revealing to find Herodotus and Aristotle regarding children of legitimate unions as bastards; they help us recognize in the case of Pisistratus the custom of entering two, possibly simultaneous, marriages that (I will not say they are unequal in rank) are of different weights.[3] As in the case of Dionysius' wives, one of Pisistratus' is "indigenous," the other foreign. Dionysius manifested a brashness due more to his personality than to his profession as tyrant, and installed his two wives together in his own household. Pisistratus, on the other hand, must have been a bigamist of the more conformist sort. I would like to say here that he undertook with one of his wives a kind of marriage for which legend gives ample testimony. Aside from the great number of heroes who marry the king's daughter and inherit his kingdom, there are many tales of itinerant heroes who make alliances in countries where they are not themselves established, but where their offspring are brought up. (Theseus was raised in Troezen, the home of his maternal grandfather; he would only have had to stay there to succeed to the throne. The case of Theseus is a famous instance of foster parenthood and seems to have some connection with the matrimonial practice we are discussing.) The sons of Pisistratus and Timonassa, it is true, remained in their mother's country. It is more than likely that they were not considered Athenians; but they were considered Argives, and not just recent arrivals. One of the two led an army of a thousand which fought for Pisistratus at Pallene. The "Argive Thousand" are well known; they formed a society of young warriors who in a quasi-Homeric sense were "companions."[4] In a country that had not yet fully ceased being "chivalrous," marriage was a form of alliance. Of necessity, a marriage contracted with a foreigner was packed with military significance, even when the wife stayed in her own country and the children remained with their maternal grandfather. This is an isolated case of a survival in the sixth century B.C., but it is nevertheless a real survival. There are precedents in myth for this type of marriage, and they might explain the probable bigamy of Pisistratus.

Let us return to Dionysius' family. One of his sons married his own half sister; one of his brothers married his own niece, and she in turn married an uncle on her mother's side. This third marriage could well have special significance, especially since it seems to have been of a very rare type, to say the least. Still, let us direct our attention to the other two, which, though they do not occur with the same frequency, are both equally licit. In Athens, and no doubt in much of Greece, a man was permitted to marry his father's, but not his mother's, sister. Examples of this practice exist.[5] A man was also permitted to marry his niece; marriage to a brother's daughter in particular not only was allowed but was regarded with favor even in the classical period; and it is significant that this kind of marriage appears frequently in myth. In the law governing the family, it had the value of an institution. If a man died and left only one daughter, under the title of heiress she would normally be married to her father's nearest male relative. Her father's brother would be the first in line. Here we have a set of well-known facts that are of obvious interest to the historian of familial institutions. What is unique to Greece, as compared to Rome for example, is the fact that the concept of incest was restricted to a very small circle. This could not be a very old situation, for in the world of legend—that is to say, in the poetic tradition just antedating the polis—the state of *epiklēros* does not seem to have been a regular sort of thing. In Homer, Alcinous' marriage to the daughter of his brother, who died without any male heirs, is a benevolent act, and the poet celebrates its happy results—perhaps intentionally. The truth is, however, that from the beginning the Greeks must have avoided endogamous marriages. Aeschylus' *Suppliant Women* may be a distant witness to this moral aversion.[6] But the tendency accompanying these unions of important legendary figures can be found in a number of different societies.[7] In the case of the nobility, matrimonial exchanges can no longer take place normally because the daughters risk disestablishment (except in cases where the wife married below her station, "exportation," or *svayamvara*—and Greek legend attests to all of these). The tendency, then, is to "protect the daughters" and have them marry relatives. As an individual case, and at a date too late for the custom to find conditions that would favor its diffusion, the tale of Dionysius' family almost has the mark of an experiment. What makes Dionysius' case special is not the fact that marriages of this sort were deviant—in themselves they are not exceptional (anyway, one could ask why they continued to be regular practice)—but the fact that they became a systematic practice in his family politics. But if we examine the situation of a tyrant like Dionysius, living as he did in a world where he could recognize neither superiors nor equals, we discover that there was hardly a partner left with whom he could play a game of alliances. And so the daughters were simply reserved for kith and kin. His case reproduces historically a form of matrimonial practice dating from "legendary times."

We can enlarge on these points. In general, the tyrants' methods can be understood in terms of a past in which we recognize the elements that tyranny helped overthrow and the processes it adapted for its own purposes.

It is curious that the legendary history of the origin of tyranny in Corinth[8] reveals a nexus between political innovation and the breakdown of a marriage system. The ancient aristocracy of the Bacchiads observed some sort of caste endogamy among the two hundred families that made up the group. But one daughter could not be married, because she was lame; that is, she could not marry another Bacchiad. So she married a Lapith, which was not a bad thing in itself (one might ask if the connection between this marriage and the alleged limp, which accounts for the name Labda, was not reversed: having married "outside," the girl came to be called "the lame one"). This Labda was the mother of Cypselus, who established the tyranny. The Bacchiads' regime, which guaranteed the rotation of political privilege and the regularity of matrimonial exchanges within a closed system, something already abnormal, was doubly antithetical to tyranny. From the perspective of the legend, tyranny could only be the result of a disruptive marriage.

Still, within their own ranks, the tyrants must have found solutions to the same kinds of problems the oligarchies faced. There are other solutions besides endogamy. We have only one example of it, and the circumstances are special, as we have seen. The tyrants belonging to the generations preceding Dionysius' age had different opportunities. Although their world was of a smaller scale than his, they were no less capable of taking advantage of it. Very often, and almost as a rule, they would marry each other's daughters. The very idea behind such a practice might suggest a form of alliance between families and tyrants which was both political and matrimonial. Although our sources are meager, we know of one instance of this practice which is very instructive.[9] At the beginning of the fifth century B.C., the most powerful tyranny in western Greece was that of Gelon and his family in Syracuse. Second to Gelon's (but surpassing all the others) was the tyranny of Theron of Agrigentum. Gelon married one of Theron's daughters, and after Gelon's death, his brother Polyzalos married the same woman. Hieron, another of Gelon's brothers, married Theron's niece (his brother's daughter). And Theron for his part married Polyzalos' daughter. All the evidence points to a continuous spirit of cooperation among the parties involved, which, though it could not always guarantee peace, assured some form of equilibrium. The systematic character of the practice is accentuated by certain peculiarities that, taken individually, are not scandalously abnormal, and that, taken as a whole system—operating for the sake of alliances that were energetically pursued—supported and reinforced the freedom of intellect and life style that prevailed in that period. The men always married women of the next generation; the same woman was successively the wife of two brothers; and two persons found themselves at one and the same time each other's son-in-law and father-in-law.

Undoubtedly these kinds of efforts—surely there were others—could not have been institutionalized. Tyranny's range was precarious; moreover, tyrannies did not have long lives, and their innate state of rivalry and anarchy made the formation of any stable system difficult. Thus, it is all the more remarkable to observe that the organizational features that appeared in the marriage relations between the dynasties of Syracuse and Agrigentum were not of their own making. They were, whether these dynasties knew it or not, suggestions from the past. The tendency that finally prevailed was in the direction of exclusive and reciprocal exchange between the two dynasties. It is really too bad that we are so poorly informed about the chronology in this area, for it could be that the bilateral element appeared only at the end, and that from the beginning the bias was in one direction. In any case, two things are certain. First, the role of the one who gives the women in marriage tends to be well established in

Theron's group (we should note in passing that the relationship of powers could point to a kind of "vassal" situation). Second, at least on one occasion we detect the need for reciprocity. This tentative but nevertheless significant practice corresponds to two "formulas" we find in a prehistoric era that is itself in a state of instability.

In legend there exists in relatively clear form a relic of the system of alliances between two lines, one of which takes in women without giving any of its own to others, and the other of which only gives its women in marriage. The witness value of the different allusions we can gather is confirmed by the fact that we can establish the persistence of a familiar concept that presupposes precisely the system in question. Moreover, it is a concept that occasionally takes on a special linguistic expression: that of the maternal line ("relations from distaff side"), *mētrōes* in contrast to *patrōes*. One senses, especially from a reading of Pindar, that the Greeks did not give up this idea easily. Still, it is a fact that in the "legendary age," it could no longer function within the institution of matrimony. Because of the tendency that resulted in endogamy, and in precisely the same context, we find the practice of "simple exchange"—or at the most a custom involving three parties, all of whom are associated with one another and represent in similar fashion a system of intermarriage and "kingship" under one name. This was the case in Argos and elsewhere.

In some ways the matrimonial relations of tyrants resemble this legendary past; the design of both is, *mutatis mutandis*, the same. There is in both the relic of the preference for a system that differentiates family lines, and there is a solution to the problem of reciprocal dealings between two dynasties that are more or less isolated from each other. The resemblance might appear superficial, but it is not so when one looks beneath the surface into the minds of the tyrants. The practices of certain "houses" and the mythology they construct for themselves reveal some rather curious obsessions. On the occasion of a famous marriage between two houses (to which we shall return), the line of Pisistratus and the Alcmaeonids (the latter are enemies of tyranny but nevertheless play its game), the two genealogies are harmonized by making both families descendants of the two sons of Nestor.[10] This is a regular pattern in the mythologies of dynasties joined by marriage. Some matrimonial relationships between the Cypselids of Corinth and the Philaidai of Athens (the *genos* of Miltiades, who was himself a tyrant, or at least a tyrant "for export") pass for traditional, and were legitimized by precedent from legend.[11]

✻

However much tyrants have deviated from arrangements found in the "history" of ancient kingships, it still remains true that their behavior is neither as gratuitous nor as novel as one might think. The big difference is that while tyrants by definition represent a kind of thinking that is agnatic in terms of succession, and a type of dynasty that owes nothing to any person, the arrangements in question do presuppose a dualistic form of thinking. The difference is perceived at once in the extreme case of the legendary kings of Thebes: the two lines benefit each other by alternating power through a systematic process of intermarriage.

But the world of tyrants was no stranger to the archaic preoccupation with two naturally related subjects: the role of the female line of succession and, willy nilly, the importance of women. We have already seen how Dionysius made use of the ideas in connection with the line of his Syracusan wife. The sons did not count, but one gets the impression that he needed to neutralize the female line in some way: the daughters are married off to Dionysius' son and brother. In the next phase, when Dionysius is about to marry his second wife, a different but related idea comes into play: the daughter marries her uncle (not, as was customary, her paternal uncle, but her maternal one). By this means Dionysius reinforces the alliance he had originally contracted for his own benefit. By means of a reverse *epiklēros*, his action also affirms the special worth of the maternal line. And this could be the appeal of subsequent unions if the issue of this line, all of whom were designated to provide wives for the "males," allowed the family of Dionysius to continue to be self-sufficient. From one end to the other, the lineage of Dionysius' Syracusan wife (its purpose was not to produce princes) appears to have been an effective means of providing princesses.

Everything happens as if Dionysius were adapting a latent and repressed concept for his own calculated purposes; it is a concept he has come to terms with for the sake of a dynastic egoism. We might even say he has manifested his respect for the concept by eliminating it: it is the concept of maternal descent. Suddenly this becomes highly significant in the history of tyrants, but elsewhere its significance goes back even further.[12] The Corinthian tyrant Periander (his period stretches from the end of the seventh century to the beginning of the sixth century B.C.) has his wife killed for no express purpose. When they are adolescents, his two sons are taken in and entertained royally by their grandfather Procles of Epidaurus, who also is a tyrant (the significance of this episode is clear; it is symbolic of foster parentage). Procles incites his grandsons to revenge. One of them, Lycophron, cuts off relations with his father, who in turn uses every possible means to bring the boy back. Eventually Periander sends his daughter (the boy's own sister) to the son to try to convince him to return; if one can believe Herodotus, she employs a whole litany of maxims (she had a good source, since Periander was one of the Seven Sages). One of the maxims, and probably the most relevant one, was, "There are many who, because they were attached to their *metrōa*, lost their *patrōa*." No mention is made of the alternate possibility, that Lycophron might have wanted to be his maternal grandfather's heir. The essential point is the opposition between the father's "side" and the mother's. And from this opposition there occasionally arise certain legal consequences, such as the possibility of succession within either of the two lines. All this is intelligible only in light of a past in which the link with the maternal grandfather is of special importance and succession to him is sometimes the dominant principle.

Here we are touching upon a group of prehistoric facts that not long ago were used—with some pleasure—as evidence about maternal lineage. But in fact they are related to matrimonial systems, not to structures of kinship, for one can see that maternal lineage has no place in this complex; it is the *males* who carry on from their grandfather (and, in legend, generally establish a family through agnate descendants). We are also dealing with a more general fact, and one that far predates the legal concept of succession. It is certainly only an accident to conceive of Lycophron as having a choice between the two branches, but it is nevertheless revealing. In the world of tyrants, only *dramatic* events could allow primacy on the side of "maternal relations" to develop, even if it did so fleetingly. At least, then, we have evidence that even in the world of tyrants an old idea either survived or could be revived. And what gives the evidence its force and stature is the fact that we find the notion expressed in a proverb.

In connection with this subject, it would be quite futile to call attention once more to the powerful religious force of the mother if one did not find evidence of it in the legend of a tyrant who happens to be Periander. In Periander's case there is a new edition of a motif from myth (and dreams): incest with the mother.[13] But this mother calls herself *Krateia*. The name is not just any name; what it really means is "sovereignty," and one recognizes that in this instance the mother "signifies" the earth. There is a nostalgia for a power that comes from the one and emanates from the other.

✻

Still, from the deep recesses of history—which also happen to be those of psychoanalysis—we come back to that very concrete political reality which in effect has its origin in the *combinazione*, but whose movements and maneuvers sometimes reveal very special concerns.

In connection with the thoughts we have evoked, we ought to emphasize the value of the woman in her role as wife. In Greece itself this finds concrete expression in some very "primitive" forms; but even as late as an era that is already "historical" (the archaic period), the power of woman as wife continues to play an effective role. In fact there is a kind of postulate without which it is impossible to understand these practices of endogamy (and we have had occasion to refer to them). The crisis of the matrimonial institution, this "blockage" of exchange which sometimes takes place, is only one aspect of the phenomenon. If daughters are protected, it is because they are valuable possessions. In the classical period this idea survives in the *epiklēros*, where the woman, though her status has diminished, is nevertheless an object of respect.

In the history of the Sicilian tyranny, one could point to a transition that, though episodic, is suggestive: it is the appearance of a certain style of marriage. One of Gelon's brothers married Gelon's widow; actually Gelon bequeathed his wife Damareta and his military command to the brother[14] (it is curious that legend offers this association as an analogue to justify the succession of a son-in-law). But this is really a special case. In the classical period there are several attestations of a husband bequeathing his wife to someone; but here the context is quite different. It may well be that this practice was archaic in origin, and that the story of Gelon is only a chance example of it. Still, Gelon's tale should be put back in its proper context, that of the aristocracy, where people think in terms of dynasties. Long ago Wilamowitz observed that tyrannical powers sometimes belong to familial groups, and that in dealing with the family that interests us, it is a question of the Deinomenidai—sons of Deinomenes—as much as it is a question of individuals.[15] There is more, for these Deinomenidai offer an anachronistic but irrefutable example of an institution that appears elsewhere and that we may well believe was forgotten by the time of Gelon: the custom of succession from brother to brother.[16] According to a theme that is strongly rooted in legend, we know that marrying the wife of one's predecessor (or, if necessary, the wife of one's father) is a complement or title to succession. In a system of succession such as that practiced by the Deinomenidai, a parallel kind of thinking leads directly to the levirate system. It is not easy to tell whether we have here an institution that has survived or a practice that may in some way have been rediscovered. Save for this explicit reference, the levirate system in Greece is known to us only from a number of obscure allusions.[17] It is a well-known fact that no trace of levirate survived in the historical memory, for the method of inheritance favoring it had been largely eliminated; on the other hand, there were profound reasons why marriage in that period excluded it.

We should note that Damareta, whom Gelon bequeathed to his brother, was a woman who lived in the public eye. She was the daughter of one famous tyrant and the wife of another. She was a person of some historical importance and had a place in the annals of history. It is quite possible that in this milieu of princes some elements of the ancient dignity of the woman either already existed or were reborn, a dignity from which Greece, in Periclean fashion, remarkably had strayed. What sheds some light on our example of levirate is the dynastic interest it could have for keeping under the title of wife a woman of high rank, despite the fact that it would have been possible to maintain an alliance by other means.

But a woman's value functions in a unique way in the very formulation of marriage. In that moment people play a subtle game in which desires for power confront one another, and in a strange way a tradition of prehistoric thought survives.

We have been able to discover that on one level there was a paradox in the business of matrimony; it has to do quite simply with the logic of the word "gift." It is possible to "give" away a woman (and she is a precious object) as a token of one's subjugation; but the giving of the gift could also be a sign of superiority and a means of exercising dominance. This ambivalence appears in some of our stories. Herodotus, with his inexhaustible curiosity, is an excellent witness.

He tells us the romantic story of the wedding feast of Agariste, daughter of Cleisthenes; it is a splendid and humorous tale.[18] Cleisthenes was the tyrant of Sicyon; he set up a veritable competition as a means of giving away his daughter (a nuptial theme that is found in myth and epic). In the list of suitors—properly drawn up—almost all the regions of Greece were represented. All of them were "tested" by the master of the house (in gymnastics, music, "good manners," and table etiquette—where even the game of riddles is indicated). For a year Cleisthenes dazzled the suitors with his wealth and generosity. Finally, he settled on Megacles of Athens, an Alcmaeonid. According to Herodotus, *this* was how the Alcmaeonids became famous. Here the formula of giving in marriage is remarkable; the daughter is given away "according to the laws of Athens." In fact, Solon's legislation on this matter was already in existence; but perhaps more is involved than a strictly legal reference. The wife is also accepted according to a set of special rules. But can we say more? We have already seen the way in which Pisistratus' wife, Timonassa, was married, and we have also seen her sons' situation. But Cleisthenes was a grand prince, and it was enough for him to give an ostentatious show to all the suitors, especially to the one who would eventually be selected, for *this* would prove his prestige beyond question.

Different attitudes appear in other places. In another story the deep-seated idea of an alliance appears with all the clarity one could ask for. In some ways it is a more modern bit of history, but it is still so archaic that it is perforce clothed in legend. We left Pisistratus on the threshold of his third wedding; this marriage with the daughter of Megacles did not turn out well (another reason why it is of interest to us).[19] However, the marriage was transacted in proper fashion. Because he was an Alcmaeonid,

Megacles was necessarily at odds with the apprentice tyrant whose exile he had contributed to. But having fallen out of favor with his own "party," he became reconciled with his old enemy. There were two articles in their compact: (1) Pisistratus would marry Megacles' daughter; and (2) Pisistratus would be returned to power. A long tradition suggested to the interested parties that a reconciliation between leaders could be achieved through a matrimonial alliance, or more precisely, that a marriage alliance itself could be an instrument of *peace*. It was in this way that Agamemnon hoped to end his quarrel with Achilles;[20] and the Greek world never lost the memory of the practice of "marriage for the sake of settling affairs."[21] But there are even more lessons to be learned from Pisistratus' third marriage agreement. The two articles in the compact were not parallel; they were reciprocal. Herodotus says that Megacles made some solemn promises to the effect that Pisistratus would marry his daughter "for the sake of the tyranny," *epi tēi turannidi. Epi* is an equivocal word: it could mean "in view of" or "on the condition of." Still, both meanings converge (here Aristotle follows Herodotus literally but in precisely the reverse order, "on the condition that he would marry the daughter"): the marriage is payment for the assistance that will allow the reestablishment of the tyranny for the son-in-law's benefit. What does this mean? We note that up to the very end Megacles appears to be quite in charge of the game.[22] He had devised a ceremony of "reentry" and restoration for Pisistratus. Herodotus is astonished that the Athenians, "the most intelligent people in the world," failed to grasp what was happening. But in fact it was quite marvelous. We can just see it: dressed as Athena, a country girl of beautiful stature arrives in a chariot, and her heralds proclaim that she is bringing Pisistratus back to her own city. A daughter of an Alcmaeonid is of too high a rank to play a role in a situation that turns into a carnival; but the symbolism is transparent. In myth the chariot is a chariot of triumph and marriage; Pelops figures in such a situation as charioteer at the side of Hippodameia. Pisistratus, who cannot risk committing himself too greatly, is at least present in the cries of the heralds. He is the king who is pleasing to the country's goddess, and his kingship is proclaimed on the occasion of his marriage and by virtue of it. In mythical thought the two are connected; the woman a man marries confers the kingship on him.

The stage manager is impartial, but he must get something out of the performance. Would Megacles not have gained something by having an advantage over his son-in-law in reaffirming a suzerainty and perhaps even rights over the succession? We are certain that Pisistratus did not want such a succession in this case. Herodotus, an expert in many things, knew that Pisistratus refused to have normal relations with his wife; this was the origin of their breakup. According to him, Pisistratus did not want his children tainted by the "miasma" of the Alcmaeonids (they had inherited a curse because of a sacrilegious murder committed some time before). But this bit of ancient lore, occasionally revived for political purposes, seemed not to have hindered the alliance with the Alcmaeonids. And Pisistratus could have thought of the curse earlier, since he was the one most immediately affected by it. It is Herodotus who reminds us more opportunely that Pisistratus already had sons who were adolescents, and that he risked having them turned out for the benefit of a succession as much his as it was Megacles'.[23] In fact, an analogous (but reverse) situation developed later in the history of Pisistratus' family. His son Hippias gave his daughter to the son of the tyrant of Lampsacus. Thucydides' tone is contemptuous when he mentions the event, and it is obvious that the daughter was married to a man of lower station. However, for a time things went well for Hippias; he gained a profitable alliance from the marriage and had the distinction of being introduced to the Great King. But his grandsons were still considered Pisistratids, and the olive branch of Athena, the same unambiguous symbol that their great-grandfather had printed on his own coins, appeared on theirs and remained the emblem of their lineage.

Pisistratus, a man for whom the game of politics was important, had to be suspicious. He had always shown himself to be a prudent man, and since he had one more trick in his bag, he chose the road of exile. It is nonetheless curious that we find in this episode the survival of an idea that is attested in a much earlier period: the ambivalent quality of the woman as security in the matrimonial contract.

✺

There is something anachronistic in all our stories. For the sake of a game that in the end is almost without reward, tyranny reintroduced or kept alive concepts and practices that within the complex of the city had lost their meaning. For the city, which made abstract thought the rule, had instituted a communal and egalitarian system in which women were exchanged freely between the households of its participants. It is possible that in the city, marriage had lost some of its aesthetic qualities. Tyrants reintroduced a certain style to it. But one is never really the innovator one seems to be.

NOTES

1.   Plut., *Dion.*, 3.2. Here as elsewhere, it is obvious that the "legend" is at least as important to us as the "history." Often what matters is what is believed: the idea one has of the behavior of tyrants and certain forms of marriage. There is another author who presents these events; see Diod. Sic., XIV.44.3.

2.   Among others, F. Cornelius, *Die Tyrannis in Athen*, pp. 41, 45, 78 ff.; and especially F. Schachermeyer, in *RE*, s.v. *Peisistratiden*, cols. 151 ff.

3.   Hdt., I.61, V.94; Thuc., VI.55.1; Arist., *Ath. Pol.*, 17.3.

4.   Thuc., V.67, 81; Plut., *Alc.*, 15; and especially Diod. Sic., XII.75.

5.   See G. Glotz, *Dict. des antiq.*, s.v. *Incestus*, pp. 450 ff.

6.   E. Benveniste, *RHR*, CXXXVI (1949), pp. 129 ff.

7.   See C. Lévi-Strauss, *Les Structures élémentaires de la parenté*, pp. 567 ff.

8.   Hdt., V.92.

9.   Timae., *FGrH*, 84, 125 (Jacoby); Diod. Sic., XI.48.5; schol. Pind., *Isthm.*, II, inscr.

10.   See O. Gruppe, *Griech. Mythol. u. Religionsgesch.*, p. 24, n. 6.

11.   See H. Berve, *Miltiades* (*Hermes, Einzelschr.*, II [1937]), p. 3.

12.   Hdt., III.50–53.

13.   Diog. Laert., I.96; see M. Delcourt, *Oedipe ou la lég. du conquér.*, pp. 195 ff.

14.   Timae., *ap.* schol. Pind., *Ol.*, II.29. For the connection between Polyzalos and Gelon regarding the Charioteer of Delphi, see C. Picard, *Manuel d'archéol. gr.*, II, pp. 133 ff.

15.   U. von Wilamowitz-Moellendorff, "Hieron u. Pindaros," *Sitz. Berliner Akad.*, July–December 1901, pp. 1277 ff.

16.   After Gelon the relationships are not clear to us; there were, in fact, difficulties between Hieron and Polyzalos. A fourth brother succeeded Hieron. The personal tyranny of Polycrates at Samos was preceded by a joint exercise of collective power by his two brothers and himself (Hdt., III.39).

17.   It appears once in the legend of Lycurgus the lawmaker. (Along the same lines, we should note that in the succession to the Spartan throne it is a supplementary qualification for a brother to have married the daughter of his predecessor.) The sororate, a curious phenomenon, is better attested, but reveals a specific ethnic ("Thracian") element.

18.   Hdt., VI.126–30.

19.   Hdt., I.60; Arist., *Ath. Pol.*, 14.4 For the psychological meaning, it is impossible to ignore Ar., *Nub.*, 46 ff.

20.   One notes that if Achilles eventually accepted other gifts, there would no longer be any question of the gift of the young girl.

21.   G. Glotz, *La Solidarité de la famille dans le droit criminel en Grèce*, pp. 130 ff.

22.   See Ar., *Nub.*, 46 ff.

23.   See G. Glotz, *Hist. grecque*, I, p. 447.

CHAPTER 13
Mortgage *Horoi*

It is to the Italian scholar [Ugo Enrico Paoli], to whom we are indebted for penetrating studies on the Greek mortgage system, that the present article is dedicated. The question we raise is not new, but it has been reappraised in recent works.[1] It concerns the possible relationship between the pre-Solonian *horoi* and the *horoi* of the classical period.

We must remind ourselves that the term *horos*, a word that normally refers to a boundary line, also designates—beginning in the fourth century B.C.—a "boundary"[2] that, while also fixed in the ground, attests by inscription that an estate is mortgaged. On the other hand, from the actual testimony of Solon we know that before his reforms *horoi* were planted in many regions of Attica, and that by uprooting them he liberated the land that until that time had been "enslaved."[3] The significance of the *horoi* from the classical period onward is quite clear; it is the meaning of the *horoi* preceding that period which needs to be clarified.

It is not easy to form a coherent idea of the Solonian reform.[4] In general the ancients tell us that it consisted of the overall abolition of debts; and Solon himself speaks in poignant terms of the liberation of debtors who had been sold abroad as slaves, or who had been reduced to a servile state at home. This liberation had implications for the future as well, since it thenceforth forbade slavery for reasons of debt. This is the fundamental understanding—and the twofold object[5]—of the reform that has prevailed in modern interpretations. In this context, one can ask the following question: What did the liberation of the land, which Solon proclaimed it was his honor to have accomplished, actually entail? It is admitted explictly or implicitly that since the land was involved in some way as the guarantee for monetary loans, it benefited from the general abolition of debts. But according to this hypothesis, Solon would have done nothing to

This essay originally appeared under the title "Horoi" in *Studi in onore di Ugo Enrico Paoli* (1955), pp. 345–53.

prevent the return of a state of affairs that he had earlier put an end to by the "uprooting of boundaries." For in legislating for the future by suppressing the enslavement of persons for reasons of debt, he would have indirectly favored the use of property as surety. Thus the revolution would have had no future. This is the initial problem, but it is not the most serious one.

Let us agree that bringing together the most ancient and most recent *horoi* was tempting and almost unavoidable—the words are the same and the analogy is obvious. But it is definitely from this identification that all the difficulties come: if the land could serve as a surety—however one wants to represent it—this means that one could dispose of it. But is this conceivable in the Attica of the seventh century B.C.? When Swoboda proposed as a principle that "individual property" had been a phenomenon in Greece from time immemorial, he attached little value to the long persistence of family property and what we recognize as the oldest system of succession. Nor did he hestitate to describe the functioning of an entire system of sureties, which included varieties of mortgage, *stricto sensu*, and the sale with an option to repurchase. Given his postulate, the thesis was logical. The postulate, however, seems untenable. But if we reject it, how can we understand the mortgaging of land before Solon? For Glotz, an essential element in Solon's achievement was the "enfranchisement of property," which was tantamount to a conversion into the goods of the land. Therefore, before Solon there could have been no question of a free disposition or consequently of "mortgage." Scholars, especially Glotz,[6] nevertheless continue to think in terms of mortgage: the suggestion of mortgage is that strong. Fine is even more radical; he allows for the "enfranchisement" only well after Solon, and he is precisely the one who has the liveliest understanding of the contradiction; but he persists in preserving the idea of a conventional pledge of land as a guarantee for a debt. From this Fine proposes a juridical structure somewhat along these lines:[7] the land is inalienable, and the execution of a mortgage applies not to it but, as our sources tell us, to the person. Still, when the debtor is on the verge of being reduced to slavery, a deal can be struck: he will give up his land without *really* giving it up; that is, he will transfer the land (but not in a definitive way) to his creditor, who will from then on receive a share of its produce. The transfer will take place under the most effective form, a sale, but the sale occurs with an implicit condition, the option to repurchase. The debtor remains in possession, in contradiction to the most ancient notion of "a sale with option for redemption" (*prasis epi lusei*). Except this is not a case of *prasis epi lusei* in the sense of a true mortgage; it is an instance of a "fiction" whose purpose is to "get around" the principle of inalienability.[8]

It seems quite difficult to accept such a complicated and conjectural interpretation, one that postulates the concept of a uniquely refined sale, and employs from start to finish a juridical fiction that is suspect in such an ancient period. And yet one is always reduced to an interpretation of this kind. If the *horoi* attest to an obligation that burdens the land as a result of indebtedness and reduces the debtor to the status of quasi-owner because of an *alienation* he agreed to, nothing is gained by emphasizing the fact that the debtor could not be dispossessed. It is impossible to avoid the dilemma: either the land is inalienable or it is not; if it is, there can be no mortgage (as is admitted), nor can there be something on the same order as a mortgage (and yet this is Fine's presupposition).

I would not hestitate to say that all the ingenuity so far expended on the subject has produced little. Without a doubt, Fustel de Coulanges, who in essence seems to have a clear view of this subject, was wrong to deny debts and their effects; there were debts. But there was something else.[9] From Aristotle and Plutarch we know of the Attic social category the *hektēmoroi*. As their name indicates (it is usually translated as "one-sixthers"), they paid a rent. According to a commonly held opinion, it is this group that agreed to the "mortgages" which the *horoi* attest. In fact, the *horoi* did exist in the lands owned by the *hektēmoroi*; and this fact must not be misrepresented. Between the juridical state of the one and the landed system symbolized by the other there is a reciprocity; both disappeared at the same time. If the *hektēmoroi* are not the mortgaged debtors, they still make up a class that apparently existed before the crisis that Solon resolved.[10] It is evident that they have a kind of status; the very fact of a uniform rent fits poorly with the hypothesis of a more or less anarchic system of individual transactions. This status is connected with a social structure that is sufficiently attested in Greece; and an important part of Greece, "Dorian" or otherwise, preserved this structure. It was characterized by a two-class system: a noble, military class (the "knights"), and the peasant class that supported it.

Admittedly, all this is too schematized, but it will do, for it translates an essential part of social reality and allows us to give some intelligible meaning to the formula in Aristotle which says that Solon "put an end to the enslavement of the people"—insofar as the *dēmos* existed.[11]

The significance of the pre-Solonian *horos* is now apparent: it marks well what Fustel called the "eminent domain of the eupatrids."[12]

Nearly two centuries later, we rediscover the *horoi* as "mortgage boundary marks." To be precise, the *horoi* that have been found do not predate the fourth century B.C. We can well admit—even accept as a presupposition—that the custom began at the end of the fifth century B.C. It is precisely from the last quarter of the fifth century that we find the oldest literary references. The chronological accuracy of the literary material could be rejected with some legitimacy, but that of the *horoi* could not. We now have a good number of them (more than two hundred, a large majority of which come from Attica); our documentation has doubled within the last half century, and the *terminus a quo* is always the same. This is a situation where one can establish a date with some degree of approximation and appreciable probability.

The archaeological evidence is of singular importance. We can hardly say that recourse was made to a kind of crass and ineffective form of publicity only after the event; in other words, we cannot say that the mortgage already had a long history when the practice of the *horoi* was instituted. Quite the contrary; it is reasonable to assume that both began simultaneously. This is a troubling assumption, since the conclusion one draws from it is absolutely contrary to the traditional opinion, according to which mortgages were in use well before the end of the fifth century B.C.

But this traditional view is quasi-intuitive and in a word never justifies itself; and some recent works have allowed us to revise it.[13] Once again the question of mortgage goes along with another one, or rather is only one aspect of another question: namely, the mortgaging of land presupposes the free disposal of land or, more precisely, the disposal of family property.[14] Even in Aristotle's period this property is still inalienable in many places. When does it cease to be such in Athens? Not with Solon, in any case: his alleged testamentary law, which has been interpreted as "enfranchisement of property," signifies something quite different and actually quite opposite.[15] Between the period of Solon and the one we have been talking about, people have looked for *testimonia*, but practically nothing has come up. The oldest texts that mention the sale of land date from the end of the fifth century B.C.; the oldest references to the practice of mortgaging land date back no further than around 425 B.C. Of course, there is no question of having recourse to an *argumentum ex silentio*. In one case, at least, it is not precisely *ex silentio*: in Aristophanes' *Nubes*, Strepsiades, in debt as he is, and knowing about distraint on property and the use of posessions as a pledge, does not even dream of disposing of his land in order to get credit (nor does he seem to fear the seizure of his land as a means of paying his debt).[16]

Strepsiades is a kind of peasant; he represents Old Attica. If his behavior is intelligible, it is so because it constitutes a kind of witnessing to a "custom," as we shall emphasize.[17] It is important that we grasp this: it is not the case that there was at one time an Athenian *law* forbidding the alienation of family property; if such a prohibition did exist, it functioned as a principle of domestic and religious morality,[18] and what we need to know is when this principle could be bent. We have a very remarkable synchronism here: not only are the earliest attestations of mortgage (and we are going to examine their tone and quality) from the same period as the archaeological evidence, but the period of time in question corresponds precisely to a social and consequently moral crisis. This crisis was provoked by the Peloponnesian War and the devastation it produced. Rural populations migrated to the city, and the terrible loss of human lives was increased by the plague of 430/429 B.C. How many "households" were "deserted" in this period?

There is something else to consider: the oldest references to mortgage[19] testify to a rather curious form of popular designation. A fragment from the comic poet Cratinus gives a certain Callias the epithet *stigmatias*.[20] This term usually refers to a branded slave;[21] but the scholiast to Lucian, our source for the fragment, informs us that the term alludes to the fact that the person in question was covered with debts.[22] The remainder of the text speaks of mortgages and inscriptions. Here, then, is an ignominious term applied to a debtor who consented to the erection of *horoi* on his land. If this were an isolated bit of evidence, then the insult might well be considered a product of the comic poet's imagination and carry little weight. But that is not the case. This designation is attested as regular, at least in its negative form, and is applied to the land itself: nonmortgaged land is *astikton khōrion*. The expression continues to be used for some time, for according to the same scholiast it is still frequent in Menander (*eiōthei legein*). According to Harpocration it also occurs in the orators (he mentions the *horoi* in this regard). It is consequently an expression that has become common; but its primitive meaning has survived in the text of Cratinus.

In all this we emphasize two things: first, the earliest fiduciary alienations were so scandalous that the case of a Callias was the occasion for an insulting epithet. This evidence fits in quite well with the historical context. Second, the concrete idea of *nota* is associated with the most ancient form of mortgage *horoi*. The significance of this evidence for social history demands some clarification.

But first a question. The *horoi* from the classical period have a function we have not yet discussed: they serve, one might say, as a means of publicity. Does this mean that they were actually devised for this purpose? In human events, we often find a discrepancy between the historical origin of an "institution" and the purpose one recognizes for it *post factum*. With *horoi* the discrepancy is marked. The function is poorly carried out, and the methods are rather rudimentary. We should not have to recall the observation often made by legal historians on this point. We should insist on one characteristic detail only: in an era in which—according to Aristotle and Theophrastus—other cities knew of a system of land registration, in an era in which the small islands of Tenos and My-konos had inscribed land registers (important fragments of these have come down to us), Athens, the most developed city from an economic standpoint, and the city best equipped administratively and the most advanced in other judicial aspects—this Athens held onto a form of "land credit," the inadequacies of which were notorious. A very general question bears directly on the issue of the publicity of the mortgages. All the evidence points to the fact that in the practice of the *horoi* there is an element of tradition. How could such a tradition originate?

Should we say that it was natural to use *horoi* specifically to signify the limits of a mortgaged field, inasmuch as they were already used for vague designations of boundaries?[23] Historians often resort to common sense in order to dodge a question. In the present matter we cannot avoid taking into account the quasi-emotional force we recognized in the earliest mortgage *horoi*. Some account must also be given of the analogy that is revealed in the *horoi* of Solon's period. And here we find a certain paradox. We are dealing with a custom we might label specifically Athenian; there is little evidence of it in other cities, and we encounter it under such conditions (colonization or very restricted diffusion) that we conclude it is one of the facts of legal geography, facts that are not so rare in Greece. The place of origin, as well as the preferred place, is Attica. It is here, more than anywhere (or perhaps only here), that a more or less pure memorial of a social revolution such as the one carried out at the beginning of the sixth century B.C. has survived. This survival of a revolution that suppressed precisely the state of affairs in which the concept of *horoi* was translated as "enslavement" of the land was not, then, without some connection with the concept of mortgage, which the new *horoi* in a way came to symbolize.

But this rapprochement requires some comment. The question is often asked how other *horoi* could replace the detested ones of the pre-Solonian period. They were not able to do so for a long time; and when the attempt was made, collective memory must have counted for something. "Limits," if this is what we want to call them, or the mortgage stones, must at first have been commonly perceived as disquieting reminders of the past even by those who utilized them. *Horoi* still suggested subjugation, and public opinion spontaneously referred to the practice— still considered immoral—in reproachful terms: the very land on which a *horos* was erected was marked by a "stigma."

✻

There is no doubt that the significance of the symbol was quickly forgotten.[24] Very quickly in fact; once the disassociation occurred, the land truly entered "the realm of commerce." But it is still true that the mortgage *horos* was introduced into law because of the symbolic value of the *horos* itself. We can see the direction our study might take from this point, but we will not go in that direction. We are content to point out certain themes that surface among our data.

The first theme is that of "religious" substrata, which even in the historical period are recognized in a certain idea of the stone. The planting of a stone in the soil is a universal symbol, and the purposes of such an act are obviously many. But in Greece there is one that is quite well defined; it is designated by the word *horos*. The uses of the *horos* are remarkably diverse: for example, it can be a limiting boundary, a mortgage boundary, a sign of ownership, a mark of consecration.[25] The word's unity[26] attests to a certain unity of thought; but this is not a juridical form of thought, since it actually resists the need for analysis which is so characteristic of law. And in at least one instance the idea of a *value* attached to an object remains expressed: I refer to the *terminus*. A text from Plato assures us of the survival in Greece, in the background, of the same "complex" that existed among the Romans.[27]

One of the social meanings, where the relative plasticity of the symbol allows some definition, appears to have been that of the pre-Solonian *horos*. The values of permanence and unbroken order[28] find concrete expression in the affirmation of an "ownership" that is essentially a form of power. But no specifically legal concept really corresponds to this kind of thought as represented in this particular symbolic phase: the word *kratein* (which remains in the legal vocabulary of ownership and mortgage) expresses, at first, a form of power, especially the kind exercised over persons. Finally, we have attempted to see under what historical conditions the symbolism of a "eupatrid ownership"[29] established itself.

One other consideration might have some bearing on the significant meanings that emerge from *horos* in the classical and Hellenistic periods. For the *horos* to endure, it had to change its character. It became a more or less abstract sign, but remained an essential one. In other words, it entered the sphere of formalism. Under this guise it can be analyzed. First, it seems to confirm what one might assume to be the antecedents of legal formalism in general, as well as the antecedents of a transition from an effective symbol to a simple means of publicity. Second, the *horos* seems to represent a somewhat extreme case: we might almost say that it is an example of gratuitous formalism. If we can recognize that it has a function, then it is not enough to say that it performs its function badly. The truth is that the *horos* is neither necessary nor sufficient. Finally, one might even argue that the *horos* was set up for no reason at all.[30] But the problem with this is that the *horos* is regarded as indispensable,[31] and that normally it goes hand in hand—if not under penalty of invalidity—with the legal process. Perhaps this curious state of affairs is due specifically to the very origins of the sign.

NOTES

1.   John V. A. Fine, "Horoi: Studies in Mortgage, Real Security and Land Tenure in Ancient Athens," *Hesperia*, suppl. IX (1951); and Moses I. Finley, *Land and Credit in Ancient Athens, 500–200 B.C.: The Horos-Inscriptions*. The first of these works is of special interest to us at the present time; we owe Fine a great deal, and if we criticize him on an important point, it is only to resolve a contradiction that he seems to present to us.

2.   It is expressed in this way *brevitatis causa*; on a certain variant, see Fine, op. cit., p. 45 (stone embedded in a wall of a house).

3.   Sol., fr. 24.3 f. (Diehl).

4.   It is not our intention to discuss the problem in its entirety here. In order to define the ideas, we will distinguish between the moment of crisis (following the advent of a monetary economy), which was the cause of reform, and the state of society the reform put an end to while at the same time resolving the crisis.

5.   See G. Glotz, *Hist. grecque*, I, pp. 431 ff.

6.   Ibid., p. 411.

7.   Fine, op. cit., pp. 181 ff.

8.   We are sensitive to the difficulties the two forms of distraint (the one over the individual, and the supposed one over the land) allow to exist; see ibid., p. 184, n. 52.

9.   The confusion between the two categories of facts must have been caused from ancient times onward and is easily seen in a text like Arist., *Ath. Pol.*, 6.1: *kai khreōn apokopas epoiēse* [scl. Solon] *kai tōn idiōn kai tōn dēmosiōn*. In any case, Plato, one Athenian who in his time would have the clearest insight into the past, points out two things about Solon's type of revolution: a remission of debts and the surrendering of lands (*Leg.*, V.736D)—the latter being conceived of as a "sharing" (see n. 12 below).

10.   Arist., *Ath. Pol.*, 2.2. Aristotle puts this group in a period markedly earlier than Solon, and *before* he talks about debts.

11.   Arist., *Resp.*, II.1237b.37.

12.   This formula will suffice for our purposes. We do not pretend to reconstruct a historical institution that may have been rather complex; in particular, the relationships of clients (which Fustel de Coulanges makes much of) could have interfered with the general situation of social dependence. Still, we would do well to specify the meaning of the *horos* in connection with an opposition of classes: in the seventh century B.C. it is (or came to be) a distinguishing mark, and alludes to something like "servile tenure," as distinguished from a "reserve," which from then on was of interest to the "nobility," whom the economic revolution had raised from the status of "squire" to that of gentleman-farmer. It is well known that the Eupatrids continued to possess a good deal of property; what they gave up was the land held by the *hektēmoroi* ("one-sixthers") under the sign of the *horoi*.

13.   See Fine, op. cit., pp. 185 ff., who follows in the footsteps of W. J. Woodhouse, *Solon the Liberator: A Study of the Agrarian Problem in Attica in the Seventh Century*. Cf. F. Pringsheim, *Gnomon*, XXIV (1952), pp. 351 ff.

14.   There is, after all, no reason to doubt that there was free disposal of marginal lands that were privately acquired or occupied; it could have been that way in Gortyn (see especially *Inscr. jurid. gr.*, I, p. 402), where it is inconceivable that the *klaros* itself was *in commercio*. In the case of Athens, we know of no such thing; it is true that at the end of two generations such an acquisition would enter the category of *patrōa*.

15.   See *REG*, XXXIII (1920), pp. 123 ff., 249 ff. [= L. Gernet, *Droit et société dans la Grèce ancienne*, pp. 121–49].

16.   It goes without saying that the public distraint over property would be of no

use as an argument; moreover, it remains to be seen whether or not it appears in a form other than that of confiscation, which is a kind of *atimia*—destruction of a familial unity—an exception that in its own way would reinforce the rule.

17.   This evidence is almost contemporary (423 B.C.) with one that allows us to recognize an example of mortgage; but it is a scandalous example (see below). There is no contradiction, or rather the contrast is well explained: this is not the same world.

18.   It is of interest to note that this morality survives, and even after the event is indirectly written into the law. There is a *graphē katedēdokenai ta patrōa*, or at the very least a secondary procedure (J. H. Lipsius, *Das attische Recht und Rechtsverfahren*, p. 341), directed against the person who ruined—specifically "devoured"—the patrimonial inheritance. It is not of the same variety as the *graphai argias* or *paranoias*, which go back to Solon and concern the administration of a father's income. It must be later than these, a fact which puts it—within the framework of legislative history—in the fifth century B.C. at the earliest.

19.   Besides the fragment in question, we have another piece of evidence from the same period, but it is slightly more recent. It is also a comical fragment (Pherecr., 58 [Kock]). In some respects interpretation of this fragment is difficult (see Fine, op. cit., pp. 171 ff.), but it seems to deal with a case of mortgage, and as such the case is given unfavorable treatment.

20.   Cratin., 333 (Kock). The fragment dates from between 430 and 420 B.C.

21.   It is enough to recall briefly the ignominious (and magical or religious) qualities attached to branding and tattooing. In the case of the mortgage debtor it is a metaphor; but one can understand how the "transfer" works in the psychological sense of the term.

22.   Schol. Lucian, *Zeus Trag.*, 48.

23.   See L. Beauchet, *Hist. du droit privé de la républ. athén.*, III, p. 348. Furthermore, we shall recognize a certain affinity between the two types of *horoi*; but as we shall see, this will be true in an entirely different sense.

24.   The civil unrest following the Peloponnesian War accelerated this movement. The oldest evidence from oratory concerning mortgages is found in the age of the Thirty Tyrants; it indicates the need people felt to protect their fortune by converting it into movables (Isoc., XXI.2).

25.   See Fine, op. cit., p. 41. This category is abundantly represented.

26.   See the pertinent observations of F. Pringsheim in *Festschrift H. Lewald*, p. 153.

27.   Pl., *Leg.*, VIII.852E ff.

28.   This basic symbolism, whose different usages were from time to time unified (see ibid., where Plato speaks of *philia enorkos* in reference to the *terminus*, thus evoking the well-known solemn-oath stone, notably the one in the Athenian agora), is surprisingly translated into the same term in the two historical areas that interest us. In Plato's *Laws*, the word *kinein* refers to Solon's type of "agrarian reforms" (III.684D.3, V.736D) *and* to the permanence of the *terminus* (VIII.842.3), but also to the "treasure" placed under the protection of the powers of Earth (XI.913B).

29.   See n. 12 above.

30.   The insightful observations of E. Weiss on the Athenian regulations for publicizing sales, as known from a famous text of Theophrastus, lead to a troubling conclusion: a creditor could be foreclosed in spite of his *horos* if, in the case of alienating security, he did not contest the move in time—and in reaction, he could do nothing with the *horos* if he proceeded with this act (*Griech. Privatrecht*, I, pp. 332 f.).

31.   It is considered indispensable not so much for purposes of publicity as to affirm the right itself. See the interesting passage in Demosthenes, XXV.69–70, where the orator's emphasis poorly disguises the superfluous nature of a document that could be casually disposed of ([Dem.], XLIX.12)—and apparently without any intervening sanction.

CHAPTER 14
Law and Town
in Greek Antiquity

It is possible to say right away that the laws of Greek cities made no distinction between urban and rural elements; differences in dwelling place had no practical significance.[1] Doubtless there was opposition between town and countryside in Ptolemaic Egypt; but it was of secondary importance and it belonged to a political system in which traditional Hellenism was kept in a state of isolation. The situation in Egypt had nothing to do with a law that was specifically Greek, a law that made no distinction among persons according to locale. Only in an exceptional case is it possible to find any "real" significance attached to place of habitation. According to the Gortynian Code,[2] "the town households and their contents" were assigned to the sons who succeeded their fathers, whereas in the case of other holdings (apparently those in the country), there was competition for inheritance between the sons and the daughters. This is a singular situation, but it involves a unique quality of a state that in other ways is archaic. What the exception reveals—as we shall soon see—is something of the prehistory of Greek law[3] rather than anything about Greek law itself, and it is a completely isolated example.

In general the temptation is simply to respond negatively to the question this Congress has raised—at least insofar as it applies to ancient Greece. But it is a question that is connected with a larger problem: the relationship between law and the shape of society. This is an interesting problem for the Hellenist, who might formulate the question as follows: What role did the establishment of an urban center play in the establishment of law? And why did this factor not play a discriminatory role?

This article originally appeared in *Extrait des Recueils de la Soc. J. Bodin*, vol. VIII, *La Ville*, pt. 3 (1957), pp. 45–57. For purposes of the distinction posited by Gernet in this article, *ville* has been translated as "town"; *cité*, as "city."

312

First, we should remind ourselves that many Greek cities—usually the most important ones—did not have to be founded (at least not in European Greece); they were simply continuations of already existing prehistoric towns. In the "Middle Ages," when Greek history began, the life of these towns must have been a very slow affair. From that period onward, the town had a function, and a quasi-economic personality, but they were, of necessity, limited. The town was generally the site of the marketplace, and in addition to a domestic industry and itinerant artisans, produced an urban artisan class. But this was not enough to give an urban economy the autonomy and initiative that in other milieus had given rise to a juridical system.

The next period of history brought with it nothing essentially new. The elements in question—the artisan and mercantile classes—were more or less developed; but it is significant that they were so often denied the right of citizenship. They were consistently held in low esteem. There was nothing that allowed them a separate place within the law, since nothing resembling corporations existed. Economic progress occurs in a city that has already been established as a juridical state; it does not precede this development. Aristotle demonstrates[4] that it was economic progress (in the constitutional order) that made democracy, in its most recent form, possible. In the period to which he refers—and it is Athens that Aristotle must have had in mind—law had already been long established. But above all, we can learn from Aristotle his fundamental theory concerning *the city* from which law arises. In his view, the city does not arise from the urban community or from a system of markets and exchange; the existence of the city is based on something else.[5]

It is not as an economic reality that the town became a creator of law.

Indeed, the "town" did not seem to be a distinct or especially privileged element either in the idea or even in the administration of the city. There was the town and its territory (sometimes very small but always essential), but no special recognition was associated with belonging to one or the other. *Athenaioi* was not the name of the people of Athens, but referred to all the inhabitants of the Athenian city-state, and consequently Attica.[6] Even though it was surrounded by walls—and this was far from always being the case—the town did not symbolize an independent legal entity. It may have had its set of rules and some structures that suited its own interests, for it had to look after a road system, buildings, and the policing of the market.[7] But the magistrates charged with these tasks (*astunomoi* and *agoranomoi*) were, like all other magistrates, chosen from the entire assembly of citizens. There was no specifically urban organization. There was no municipality. Consequently these existed no differentiation on which to base a heterogeneity of law, even one of a very restricted kind.

To put it in the simplest terms, the town was still an essential element of the city-state. But it was not so because it was a town, so to speak, but rather because it was the center and principle of collective unity. In the idea of belonging to the city-state, it was only a point of reference. The word *astos* refers etymologically to a city-dweller; but in the language of Athenian public law,[8] it meant a citizen, even if he lived in the most backward village. This is not to say that citizens were at first only inhabitants of the town, and that the term *astos* was later extended to rural inhabitants. History suggests nothing of the sort. This understanding of *astos* implies that "political" life was concentrated in one and *only one* urban establishment. It is because of this that there emerged a territorial unity of law. Such unity was transmitted not only through concrete events but also through well-defined and systematic formulations.

There is a minimal definition of a "town" which applies to the most humble of cities:[9] it is a place where there exist together—and exclusively—the buildings and establishments that are the characteristic ingredients of a state.[10] These are generally located in the vicinity of the agora, the ancient and persistent term for "assembly."[11] Here are found the courts of the magistrates, the council hall, and the prytany with the communal hearth, which is, in a simultaneously religious and political sense, the heart of the city.[12] It is necessary to add that when the form of government in the city is developed,[13] by definition the judicial function can be exercised only in the town.[14]

On the other hand, the communal spirit that characterizes the city is connected with the social space concentrated around the town, though this phenomenon has no special importance for its occasional inhabitants. In the type of democracy Aristotle considers to be the most stable, there exists a general and old rule—so he tells us—that within a certain radius of the town, the extent of the land one can own is limited.[15] Beyond the complementary idea of marginal territory, this rule reveals rather strikingly that there is a reciprocal relationship between the land of the city and that of the citizen. Such a relationship is in fact a regular feature of political theory. It should always be remembered that in principle, laws governing landownership exist only for citizens, and inversely in some constitutions, it is almost a philosophical principle (as well as a condition in certain constitutions) that ownership of property be a prerequisite for citizenship.[16] One should add that agriculture, valued more highly than other and more directly urban factors,[17] is more closely connected with the nature of citizenship. In sum, the city-dweller as such has no real place in the *politeia*. But if the citizen is connected in an essential way with the communal element of the land,[18] it can truly be said that the town itself is also something communal, for town and land are essentially connected. When a colony is founded—and it reflects the image of the metropolis—steps are simultaneously taken to build a town and distribute land to all the citizen-colonists.[19]

❧

Behind the human reality of the city, there is obviously a history, or rather a prehistory. The standardization of the law cannot be understood save in terms of its connection with the past. Before the ascendancy of the city—and in some backward states, alongside it—we find a pluralistic society that has parallels with the structural distinction between the town and the open countryside.

In the Athenian constitution, the word *dēmos* designates an abstract territorial unity that is both political and administrative. Thus, there are both urban and rural demes. This is a form of quasi-technical terminology that derives from a significant bias, though the word is a very old one. *Dēmos* is first of all a "village," and in its ancient meaning, still in use in the fifth century B.C., "the *dēmoi*" are opposed to "the town."[20] The opposition between the two is not only geographical; it has social implications that date far back in history. Primitive kingships were centered in the *akropolis*, which the term "polis" itself originally designated. Moreover, the emblems of the early kings were "urban": the sacred olive of Athens is the "olive of the town," or the *astē elaia*.[21] In the archaic period, by some prerogative, the town becomes the residence of the well-born.[22] Over against these urban-dwellers are pitted the rustics,[23] who occupy a different world and, indeed, are systematically excluded from the town.[24]

The opposition between the two is complete; but the conclusion we draw from it could well remain superficial. There is perhaps more to say about the social elements of the age antedating the city: enough, at least, to allow us to point out the diversity of the "laws" that separately apply to them. The world of the peasant, by necessity, had its own customs. It was not only involved with the agrarian law pertaining to planting, the use of springs, and so on, which had been transferred into the city's law. It must also have been the "joint family's" place of privilege. In the rural life there are traces of matrimonial organization as well as some specialized forms of collective barter. There are also some quasi-formal but nevertheless revealing survivals that indicate the existence of peasant communities.[25] The peasant's world is a subordinate one; they support and feed the society of warriors (whose importance in an archaic structure has been demonstrated by H. Jeanmaire).[26] The warrior society lives apart from the rural populace; they are organized into *hetaireiai* (groups of "companions"), and live in the town,[27] where there are places for exercise. Even in

Crete in the fifth century B.C., a man who frequents the gymnasium will qualify as a citizen.[28] And though young warriors undergo their training in the countryside, an institution like the Lacedaemonian *krupteia* remains a dramatic symbol of their opposition to the rural populace.[29] Such a situation is not the kind of milieu that favors the maintenance of the extended family or, for that matter, the family in general.[30] Rather, it is suitable ground for the emergence of individual ownership of property gained through pillage and war.[31] Family ownership itself is affected; thus, in the Gortynian Code, if daughters have the right of succession, their right to a whole part of the patrimony is eclipsed by that of the sons, namely, the right to inherit the houses in the *town*.[32]

There is another phenomenon that may not have appeared everywhere and that is almost inaccessible to us; nevertheless, it obviously plays an important role in a country like Attica: the existence of a nobility that sometimes preserves its rural character,[33] but as a governing class is attached to the town.[34] Its particular aim is to establish or maintain "dynasties," for which systems of marriage, marriage forms, and rules of inheritance are of special importance.

The city's distinction lies in the fact that it has transcended these ancient differences. No doubt a city has its different levels. In some states, such as the "Dorian" ones, a dualism survives between the military and peasant classes. Sparta would be an extreme case.[35] There, though the law ignores the peasant class, a unity exists, and a dominant one at that, among those who are considered "equals" or "like" and who, residing for the most part in the town, are no more city-dwellers than inhabitants of the countryside. The situation in Crete seems different, but it is no less instructive. According to the Gortynian Code the serf and peasant classes are part of the legal system; but there are doubtless differences between them which stem from their unequal status, though these differences are not expressed in a corresponding set of heterogeneous laws.[36]

But the city whose system of laws we can observe in its most complete and authentic form is Athens.

The Athenian legal system was formulated essentially in the legislation of Solon, who apparently tended to integrate elements from preexisting legal systems. Thus, family law is standardized in part by a kind of democratization of aristocratic practices: for example, forms of marriage (the *engue* becomes something extended for all) and translative adoption of patrimony. But the individualistic quality of such phenomena is severely restricted by the traditionalism of the great families. The standardization of the procedure and, in general, of the function of the judiciary eliminates a "feudal" practice of justice that was still operating in the world of Hesiod.[37] Consequently, corresponding social differences also are eliminated. Put in its simplest form, the law of obligations, now purged of the

executory rigor it exercised over individuals, becomes a law that is homogeneous and abstract. Because a societal contract is acknowledged, a standardized form of law now encompasses the plurality of groups that have
spontaneously arisen in different milieus.[38]

In a remarkably clear instance, it is possible to see quite well how
the very establishment of the city's legal system did away with all previous
distinctions that could have connections with any preexisting structure.
Still, it also appears that legislation such as that of Solon, inasmuch as it
was an abstract norm, presumed a minimum of circulation and some degree of mobility for persons and things.[39] And here, in the case of a state
that had evolved sufficiently, the role of the town in the establishment of
the law is evident. The town is the setting of a more individualistic kind of
life, namely, one that favors the division of patrimonies; the town is the
milieu for an intense life,[40] and from an early date, money gives transactions an impersonal character. This is a well-known factor, without
which legislative law would not have taken definite shape; but it is a factor of unity just the same, and not one of dualism.

※

To tell the truth, the law, as it can be represented in this perspective,
is not the whole law of the classical city. In the fourth century B.C. a "secondary" but important element is added: commercial law. By "commercial law" we mean the law affecting essentially maritime commerce
(emporia),[41] which is maintained by what one might call "international"
usage; and from the moment the city accepts it, a great many new elements are introduced into the whole domain of obligations.[42] Commercial
law presupposes the existence of places of commerce, and their activities
play an essential role in Hellenic life. Before we conclude, then, we ought
to consider this aspect of the urban reality.

Because from quite an early date the Greeks had a specific view of
maritime commerce (one that is translated into the organization of the
magistracies),[43] it is remarkable that the corresponding law does
not—even at the most advanced level—involve any autonomous or even
distinct administration. There is nothing resembling a "jurisdiction" over
a place of business, nor are there any special agencies and standards that
would characterize it.[44] Consequently, there is nothing about commercial
law which would allow us to identify it as something unique within the
sphere of the city.[45] Judicial organization is the same for all legal procedures, and "commercial actions" depend on regular, common-law juries.
This is a significant fact, and in one way is in accord with the structure of
commercial law. Yet in another way it fits in with the city's attitude toward business. The law in question touches only indirectly on legislation.

Laws that deal with commerce are allowed to perpetuate certain legal principles that result from professional practice. But directly they only make procedures easier in the businessman's interests, and indirectly they serve to enhance the growth of the city and its collective wealth. But commercial life itself is not indispensable, nor is it valued for itself. Commerce in general is viewed with a jaundiced eye; and even in the form of *emporia*, it reveals a deviant character. As a result, it is often the domain of foreigners and metics.

From this develops the concept of a function that is marginal in the fullest sense of the term, and the concept translates itself into a curious form of urbanism. Aristotle,[46] in giving more precision to something Plato desired for his ideal city, says that the "harbor," without being too far from the "town," still should not be too close to it; the two must not occupy the same territory. The town—in this context it is assimilated into the polis and forms its nucleus[47]—must not be contaminated by an activity that is not its own or by a spirit that is foreign to it. The city will engage in commerce "for itself"; there is no question of the city "offering itself as a market" for everyone else. It is not difficult to see that Aristotle's way of thinking may be that of a biased theoretician. Still, his thinking is also based on historical experience.[48] Without a doubt, when he reduces maritime commerce to its extremes, while still recognizing that it is essential, and when he segregates it as much as possible and relegates it to the boundaries of a country, he is following a deep-seated tendency of his own nation, which in a striking contradiction remained faithful to the ideal of *autarkeia*. And in light of the city being mistress of its own law, the *emporion* could not find a way to become the forum for a separate legal system.

From one end of the country to the other, various Greek societies offer the same lesson. Economics could have been a factor of disparity, as it had been in other places and in comparable situations; but in Greece this was not the case. On the level of the city, the territorial unity of the law was complete.

NOTES

1.   No attempt will be made to attribute such a difference to that remarkable provision in the law of Ainos (Theophr., *ap.* Stob., *Flor.*, XLIV.22) whereby the transfer of real property involves an oath that is taken at the altars of different gods, according to whether or not the buyer is a resident of the town.

2.   IV.31 ff.

3.   The same thing can probably be said about the obligation to honor a special law for the purchase of real property in the territory of Attic demes by citizens who did not belong to these demes.

4.   *Pol.*, IV.1292a.

5.   *Pol.*, III.1280b.11 f., II.1260a.35.

6.   There are traces of a more ancient state of affairs: in Homer, there is the distinction between Ilium and Troy; in legend, the distinction between the Cadmeans and the Thebans.

7.   This is a type of organization that is well attested for Athens. Still, Aristotle considers it the normal organization for the Greek city (*Pol.*, VI.1321b.18).

8.   Arist., *Ath. Pol.*, 26.3, 42.1; for a general treatment of public law in Greece, see Arist., *Pol.*, III.1278a.34. The antithesis between *astos* and *xenos* ("citizen"-"foreigner") belongs to the language of that period. On the antiquity of this distinction (in regard to procedural matters involving the cities of Locris), see Michel, no. 3, B.

9.   There are, of course, some very obvious differences. However, except for frontier districts like Aetolia, it must be acknowledged that even the most insignificant polis, once it became a state with magistrates and deliberative bodies, had—of necessity—a center (normally with the same name). A genuine conglomerate of buildings (at least in extreme cases) is quite another matter.

10.   This is true in the political-juridical sphere. We may add that the town is also a religious center, and that the majority of temples belong to it (temples are included in Plato's and Aristotle's schemes for the ideal town).

11.   It should be noted that the sense of "market," which became standard for the word "agora," does not appear in the most ancient texts. Among the Thessalians, there is an agora that is termed "free": it is a place for reunions, not exchanges (Arist., *Pol.*, VII.1331A. 32).

12.   See L. Gernet, "Sur le symbolisme politique en Grèce ancienne: Le Foyer commun," *Cahiers internationaux de sociologie*, XI (1951), pp. 21–43 [= pp. 322–39 below].

13.   Through the agency of "judges of the demes," Pisistratus instituted a system of justice in the countryside. This was probably his way of eliminating the remains of a feudal type of justice (see F. Cornelius, *Die Tyrannis in Athen* (1929), p. 58). The institution did not endure in this form.

14.   In Athens, with a single exception (whose existence was rather symbolic), tribunals for crimes involving bloodshed belonged, as if by definition, to the town (Aesch., *Eum.*, 700 f.). In ancient times, civil justice was rendered by the magistrates in their respective locales. From the time of Solon, it was handled by a tribunal called the *hēliaia*, a word whose Doric equivalent expresses the idea of "assembly" (see R. J. Bonner and G. Smith, *The Administration of Justice from Homer to Aristotle*, I, p. 157). In a state as backward as Locris in the fifth century B.C., it is evident that all legal processes were conducted in urban centers (Michel, no. 3.B; *Inscr. jur. gr.*, no. XI,B, l. 7).

15.   *Pol.*, VI.1319a.6.

16.   We know that in Athens itself, as late as the end of the fifth century B.C., a decree was proposed that would have limited civic rights to those owning land (the decree would have excluded only a minority); see Lys., XXXIV.

17.   On the subject of this dichotomy within the representation of work, see J.-P. Vernant, "Travail et nature dans la Grèce ancienne," *Journal de psychol.*, LII (1955), pp. 23 f.

18.   See Arist., *Pol.*, III.1238a.31: *hē de khōra koinon*.

19.   The mythical transposition of this land division is especially interesting to us; see *Od.*, VI.9–10.

20.   Hdt., I.62 (for the period of Pisistratus); see C. Hignett, *A History of the Athenian Constitution* (1952), p. 135.

21.   Hesych., s.v. *astē elaia*.

22.   *Etym. Magn.*, s.v. *eupatridai*. Such a grouping of houses sometimes continued in subsequent periods; for the most part, the oligarchs of Corcyra lived in the vicinity of the agora (Thuc., III.72).

23.   Theog., 53 ff. As opposed to the *astoi*, this segment of the population had been outside the pale of law.

24.   For the situation in certain cities of the Peloponnesus, see W. R. Halliday, *The Greek Questions of Plutarch*, p. 39 f. The testimonia are ambiguous; or to put it another way, we are dealing with a peasant element that—even in the historical period—is sometimes separated from the polis, but at other times is integrated with it. The ancient state of affairs is attested to, *a contrario*, by feasts like the Saturnalia, which present a world upside down—that is, one where the peasants (slaves) have access to the town (see Ephor., *ap.* Ath., VI.263 f.).

25.   I am briefly summarizing certain points raised in "Frairies antiques," *REG*, XLI (1928), pp. 313 ff. [= pp. 13–47 above]. One clarification: even in the fourth century B.C. ([Dem.], L.8) it was possible to distinguish between members of a deme (*dēmotai*) and those who had acquired land there (*enkektēmenoi*). We know indirectly (*IG*, II.589) that the latter had to pay an *enktētikon*. Although this is meager evidence, it nevertheless suggests a primitive sense of the *enktēsis* (the right to own land), extended as it was under the regime of the polis to the entire territory of Attica.

26.   H. Jeanmaire, *Couroi et Courètes*, pp. 72 ff.

27.   Michel, no. 23, C. 39 (Cretan Dreros): *tais hetaireiaisin...tais em polei* (apparently the normal situation). There is an important indication in Plato's description of the legendary conditions in Attica, where the warriors are said to be positioned in the upper town (*Criti.*, 112).

28.   In Crete the minor, who accordingly does not yet have his full rights, is *apodromos*: that is, he does not yet have access to the public gymnasiums (Gortynian Code, VIII.35; see *Inscr. jurid. gr.*, I, p. 407). On how the gymnasium is a typical feature of the town, see Arist., *Pol.*, VIII.1331a.35.

29.   At certain phases in the training of young warriors, helots could be killed with impunity.

30.   See H. Jeanmaire, "La Cryptie lacédémonienne," *REG*, XXVI (1913), pp. 121–50.

31.   This is dealt with separately in the Gortynian Code (VI.9). On the juridical category involved here, see E. F. Bruck, *Totenteil und Seelgerät im griechischen Recht*, pp. 71 f.

32.   One is struck by a provision that is the inverse of the "liberal" spirit that prevails for the most part in urban law. But in this case the town is the place where the class in question, together with its masculine prerogatives, is most vigorously asserted.

33.   For the rural connections of certain Attic *genē*, see J. Toepffer, *Attische Genealogie*, passim. On the survival of certain very ancient conditions in the society and legal system, cf. the story of Naxos (a curious story indeed!) in Aristotle, fr. 510.4 (Ath., VIII.348b).

34.   After the disappearance of kingships, the town becomes the natural place for competitions between the various noble families.

35.   The possible exception is Thessaly, a rather strange region where an urban mode of life seems to have developed laterally, apart from a nobility that remained rural and a society of serfs (see U. Kahrstedt, *Nachrichten der Götting. Gesellsch.*, 1924, pp. 128 ff.). Additionally, is it even certain that Thessaly ever arrived at the level of the city?

36.   Note that on occasion the serfs could reside in the town itself (Gortynian Code, IV.34).

37.   Concerning this form of justice, see H. J. Wolff, "The Origin of Judicial Litigation among the Greeks," *Traditio*, IV (1946), pp. 98 ff.

38.   Gai., *Dig.*, 47.22.4.

39.   Except for some questionable interpretations, a very sensible view concerning

this historical truth is found in G. Glotz, *La Solidarité de la famille dans le droit criminel en Grèce*, pp. 325 f. On the significance of Solon's work, particularly as it appears in the law concerning the testament, see L. Gernet, *Droit et société dans la Grèce ancienne*, pp. 121–49.

40.   Let us at least note the rental contract; urban life created a modern type of it very early on. The rental contract is to be contrasted to the forms of lease, emphyteutic or otherwise, that were practiced by the sanctuaries.

41.   A similar type is the banking law, which seems to have developed in conjunction with maritime commerce.

42.   Gernet, *Droit et société*, pp. 5 f., 89 ff.

43.   This is in keeping with the distinction between *kapēleia* ("intraurban commerce") and *emporia* ("foreign commerce"): see J. H. Lipsius, *Das attische Recht und Rechtsverfahren*, p. 94.

44.   In Athens (and Miletus), the name of the "port" figures in the designation of a rather late organization, the *epimelētai tou emporiou*. It is a magistracy, however, which performs the duty of the "surveillance" the state had assumed, and which has jurisdiction in matters of criminal accusations brought against merchants who are guilty of having transgressed the rules of public order. See Arist., *Ath. Pol.*, 51.4; and [Dem.], XXXV.51.

45.   The situation in the Greek cities of the Hellenistic period does not seem different. In that era there is merely the very ancient distinction between proceedings, a distinction that is based on whether the litigants are citizens or foreigners (a system that had already become outmoded in Athens). Otherwise, substantial differences are difficult to isolate, E. G. L. Ziebarth notwithstanding (*Beitr. zur. Gesch. des Seeraubs. u. Seehandels im alten Griechenl.*, pp. 118 f.).

46.   *Pol.*, VII.1327a.3–40.

47.   See ll. 3 and 34.

48.   The author speaks here of his own observation. Note that the situation he describes is in particular the one in Athens itself. For a similar view, see E. Barker, *The Politics of Aristotle*, p. 294 (cf. p. xliii).

CHAPTER 15
Political Symbolism: The Public Hearth

There is no need here to insist on the importance the examination of symbols has for our understanding of human society, symbols that have to do with the unity of the group. To study the "signified" in terms of the "signifier" is to study a social mode of thought that is at times actually richer, since it is not expressed in the usual sort of language; but it is, in its own way, no less organized. On encountering it, we discover that it is the means of making contact with some historical values that other modes of thought no longer preserve.

In ancient Greece we find a number of these symbols, which by definition belong to the category of space; they are centers. The tomb of a hero can be a center. Since the hero's world has a special connection with the city, it can appear alone or in the company of other symbols. In fact, the rock of the agora also is a center; it seems to have a long history, and its functions, while quite diverse, have a marked legal dimension. It is used for proclamations of public authority, inaugural oaths of high magistrates, publication of legal acts such as adoptions, ancient forms of punishment such as exposure of the condemned at the pillory, and so on. Here we discover the reflex of an object's special *power*—for example, the agora rock (which nevertheless remains a rock of investiture). Here we also find the feeling of collectivity that consecrates or ratifies this power, as well as the spatial representation of the group, reflected, for example, in the treatment of an adulteress at Aeolian Cyme; as a form of shameful exposure, she is first seated on the rock, then led through the town on the back of an ass, just as the *pharmakoi* are forced to go through the town in their role as scapegoats.

Another symbol that long precedes the city—it survives in the histo-

This article originally appeared in *Cahiers internationaux de sociologie*, XI (1951), pp. 21–43, and is based on a lecture given at the Institut de Sociologie, Paris.

rical period only in a religious tradition in which it becomes specialized and loses much of its force—is the *omphalos*, a bulge in the earth or a conical rock that is more or less a cult object. Its mythical implications are still striking; it is related to the *numen* of the earth itself. The *omphalos* is also the center of the earth, the place where, in Delphi, its most celebrated locale, two eagles met after flying from the two ends of the earth. (The same datum appears, more or less implicitly, at Mount Lycea in Arcadia, where there existed a theater for the celebration of secret and ancient rites that seem to have been tainted with cannibalism.) On the other hand, the *omphalos* has a connection with chthonian powers; here it evokes an image of the tomb (and it had the reputation of being a tomb), and it causes us to think in terms of the Latin *mundus*, which was both the epitome of the cosmos and the reservoir of souls. The *omphalos* is also connected with a form of mantic activity that we know was formerly practiced for legal purposes: Themis, the Delphic variant of Ge (the keeper of the oracle), has a special connection with the *omphalos* "for judgments that are certain"; and Themis is the name of the primitive "justice" that appears to have been administered by the "kings" of the king-magician type. This is a very ancient way of thinking; but at times it still survives behind a much more modern mode of thought. All the same, it is by a quite natural metaphor that the poets designate as the *omphalos* of the city a central point that was the magnet around which were established altars or the seat of civic authority.

But the symbol we will now examine characterizes the city best; it can pass for being as ancient as the city, and it lies at the heart of the political institution. We are referring to the public Hearth. By hypothesis, it has connections with a social creation that contributed to ancient man's beginnings; it is, however, a creation that is not so remote that it is completely beyond the reach of the historian; and it is a creation whose meanings can be illuminated by a kind of projection, which is both institutional and, in the larger sense of the word, mythical.

I

Aristotle tells us of the truly central importance of this Hearth (*Hestia*). He describes it as a religious function that depends on the government, the function "that especially concerns communal sacrifices: that is, all those that the law ascribes not to the priests but to the magistrates, who get their dignity from the communal Hearth, and who are at times called *arkhontes*, at other times kings, and at still other times *prutaneis*."[1]

The word that is translated as "dignity" (*timē*) has come to apply, *inter alia*, to the public function; it means fundamentally an honor, a prerogative or privilege, an attribute that is religious in nature or that refers to things religious. It comes down to admitting that in the concept formulated by Aristotle—an observer who was rather disinterested in the origins of beliefs—the *timē* of the magistrate is his religious qualifications, or even the magistracy itself; the two are apparently closely connected. We might even ask if our text does not preserve a relic of a ritual that consecrated or empowered the magistrate through a direct bond or contact with the Hearth. In any case, we can see a preestablished association between the *Hestia* and the organs of public authority; there was even something like a personal relationship, which could have some historical significance in terms of the origins of the city.

In and of itself, the Aristotelian text could be a guarantee that the Hearth, by definition, has to do with the city. Our data confirm that we are dealing with an institution that is very diffuse, perhaps even universal.[2] The public Hearth is attested for a large number of cities. It is usually kept in a Prytany: the two words [Hearth and Prytany] are in some way reciprocal. The Prytany is a building that by definition belongs to the city; we are told directly that it is the symbol of the city. There is an archaeological discussion of this subject which is not inappropriate for us to pursue here, since the architectural layout of the Prytany indirectly affects the political form of thought, even its formulation. It was thought for quite some time that the Hearth was located in a *tholos*—that is, a rotunda, a very archaic type of building with strong links to chthonian deities.[3] This view is denied nowadays (perhaps too radically because the Tholos of Marmaria in Delphi has been identified as the site of the public Hearth). In fact, in some places (Olympia and Sicyon) the Prytany appears as an aggregate of buildings, of which the Hearth is a part. It is possible—at least in principle—to assign to the Prytany the kind of circular construction that survived in the *aedes Vestae* in Rome. Nevertheless, the Hearth can exist separately from the Prytany, as is the case in Athens. These two facts are equally telling.

One notes that in general the Prytany is situated in the agora—that is, in the lower town as opposed to the acropolis, the seat of a prehistoric and outmoded authority. This implies above all a spatial concept, and such a concept is less compelling (although more free and more abstract) than the symbols already mentioned. An *omphalos*, a hero's tomb, and a sacred rock are fixed on a specific site; they receive their special properties from the earth and at the same time give it value. The same is not true for the Hearth.

To describe better this idea of the Hearth, let us recall that it is not exclusive; it is open to the outside world. In a sense, the Hearths of various cities presuppose one another.[4] The hospitality they provide strangers is one of their most characteristic features. For example, the invitations that are extended to certain religious ambassadors are invitations "to the public Hearth of the city"; they are accompanied by gifts of protocol that attest to the traditional demand for generosity and the need for some kind of "communion at a distance." This institution is not merely a feature of Hellenic civilization; it is consciously felt and affirmed as such. In addition, the pervasive quality and quasi-national use of the symbol are confirmed by a noteworthy extension of it. At certain specified times (whether exceptional or periodic), the "renewal" of the cities' fires takes place for the benefit of a prestigious sanctuary that figures as a Pan-Hellenic symbol: after being defiled by the presence of barbarians in the Second Persian War, the Hearths at Delphi were restored, and each year thereafter an Athenian procession went to fetch a new fire from the Hearth of Delphi.

But correlatively, the Hearth of the city is no less an expression of the city's personal existence. There is a deity, Hestia, who belongs to it and who alone possesses it as her domain. If the social era in which Hestia appears did not, as a rule, favor mythical personification, one finds here a special exception: Naucratis, a Greek colony founded on Egyptian soil, celebrated yearly the birth of its own *Hestia Prutanis*.[5]

These preliminary remarks will do. What remains now is for us to define the meanings that are implicit in the Hearth and—through the behavior of those affected—the articulations of a social mode of thought.

II

Let us first place this kind of thought in its context within a historical (or prehistorical) perspective.

In principle the hearth is a family matter. And it is "the immediate family" that is involved; at least so it seems from our evidence, which cannot go back very far.[6] One might even ask (keeping in mind archaic ceremonies such as the Amphidromia, in which the newborn child is paraded around the hearth) if the limited vitality of the household *numen* does not owe something (by way of reflection) to that Hestia who is, above all, the projection of the public Hearth. It is true that only afterward, and on the model of individual Hearths, could the notion of the city Hearth be established. All the same, it is not a quasi-epitome or composite image of the others. There is more to the city Hearth than to the individual ones. Because of this distinction, we are given Aristotle's imaginative commentary on the notion of the city. The public Hearth is a creation quite separate from the others. It is not superimposed on them; it dominates them. And historically speaking, it is impossible to imagine a social contract between the families the Hearths represent.

In fact, this creation could well presume a social memory; still, the past that it recalls and transforms measures up to it in proportion. The public Hearth emanates from the king's Hearth. This prehistoric reality is attested by archaeology (but only for the Mycenaean period), and the pre-eminent value of the king's Hearth[7] still survives here and there in poetry. But what is also attested is the continuity that links the king's Hearth to the public one. The disposition of certain archaic temples, where in exceptional cases a city Hearth is installed and preserved, reproduces the plan of the *megaron*, the king's residence,[8] the place of a cult attached to the person of the leader, and a place of which the *Hestia* was a central feature. There exists here a past whose meaning has been faithfully preserved by legendary tradition. Witness Erikhthonios of the Athenian acropolis and his association with the goddess's Hearth (*sunestios*). This is a past from which Aeschylus does not feel so far removed; in a scene of supplication in which the connection between the two has dramatic value, he indicates successively a confusion and an antithesis between the royal Hearth and the Hearth of the city.[9]

There is a mythology of the royal *Hestia*. At times it flourishes even in lyric images; and certain elements persist sporadically in legend. It is at his Hearth that Agamemnon, in Clytemnestra's prophetic dream, plants his royal scepter; it sprouted foliage that shaded all the land of Mycenae.[10] In its association with the twofold image of royal power (the scepter and the Hearth), the ancient theme of the blossoming staff here takes on unique significance: it refers to the coming of the son, who is avenger and successor. Life and perpetuity—above all, the Hearth (indeed, the fire of the Hearth) ought to be symbol of these. In some Italian legends with Greek backgrounds, the future king is born from the Hearth itself. In Greece, "the external soul" of Meleager resides in the firebrand on the Hearth which the Parcae designated for the hero at the time of his birth.[11] This is a relic of royal rituals, as the legend of Eleusis itself suggests; and we find the mythical infant in a specific relationship with the Hearth. Such a notion is often injected with a specific meaning for the benefit of legendary kingship. It is very striking that on the basis of these traditional images a ritual designation, one connected with the public Hearth, seems to have been borrowed in the historical period: the "child of the Hearth" represents the city to the Eleusinian divinities.[12] His title signifies literally "he who comes from the Hearth," or "he who emanates from the Hearth" (*aph' hestias*).

In this conception of the public Hearth, which might at first be regarded as theoretical and somewhat artificial, the vigor of a very ancient image has not yet completely died out. Heritages of this kind persist with some stubbornness. The *Hestia* sometimes rejoins the very prehistoric symbol of the *omphalos*. In the same way that the Roman *mundus*, generally distinguished as it is from the altar of Vesta in the story of the origins of the city, nonetheless supplied for Vesta her first geographical site (according to one tradition), so also the *omphalos* of Delphi was accepted as the seat of Hestia (an event preserved in religious language).[13] Thus we see that the royal mythology of the Hearth is itself sustained on a perennial basis, one where the idea of the earth and its dark powers remains ever present. And this idea is maintained in the city itself. If it is not the usual thing for a Hearth to be a hero's tomb, there is at least one example showing that it can be.[14] There is, in addition, the proximity of chthonian divinities and their mysterious rites within the agora.[15]

III

The Hearth of the city is surrounded by an aura of myth; this was apparently necessary in order for a new reality to be understood. The newness, more than anything else, is perceivable; and in comparison with the past, one can already see changes in the way the symbolism functions.

In the most ancient representation, it is the signification of the fire which appears to be primary—the fire and its continuous life in the heart of the human world. Its intended meaning is certainly not lost. The rites of the Hearth's renewal continue to make this meaning tangible; and the image of the Hearth in which the central fire is constantly renewed is naturally associated with the perpetuation of the group over generations. This element appears in the prayers of deprecation or benediction which guarantee such perpetuity. But it seems that the force of this suggestion has worn away.

In reality we are presenting here a history that is not simple. In the beginning the cities may have reclaimed the perpetual fire in a quasi-archaic way; when the first buildings were erected as homes for the gods (and one suspects that this moment was laden with institutional and psychological significance), the plan we have already noted for certain archaic temples (which eventually developed into public Hearths) could have been so general that as a result, poetic tradition quite creditably gives to Hestia (as the power of fire) the privilege of having her place in every temple.[16] But in the public Hearth as such, the concrete and ancestral idea of this power does not allow itself to be blurred. In the historical period there is even a tendency for its importance to reappear;[17] perpetual fires exist which are distinct from the public Hearth. And it is interesting that the kind of thought associated with this phenomenon is a form of archaizing piety, which reveals a rather self-conscious memory of past ages. The "lamp" of the Erechtheum in Athens is a perpetual flame in a residence of mythical royalty. In Argos, a flame "of Phoroneus"[18] is kept burning—Phoroneus, a "First Man," an inventor of fire. In Boeotia, at the sanctuary of a "confederate" Athena, the myth associated with a cult amounts to a quasi-historical narrative:[19] long ago Iodama the priestess had been *petrified*; the fire on her altar was renewed every day, and the formula "Iodama lives and asks for fire" was intoned. This tale contains an image that is a survival of the past, and it is acknowledged as such: maintaining the fire—in general, and perhaps in the royal house—is the office of a female priesthood. The religion of Vesta is evidence of this in Rome, as is the cult of perpetual fires in Greece, some of which might be termed rather specialized and hardly more than local survivals.[20] But the service of the city *Hestia* requires male personnel,[21] which makes it, by definition, even more "political."

For what is stressed in this cultural reality is politics, in all its depth and resonances. This idea of the public Hearth is perceptible, but it is so intentionally. There is no other symbol like it, and in no comparable designation do we find a more domineering and impersonal form of government. In contrast, it is instructive to note a reaction in a milieu that is otherwise quite artificial, a reaction that may be a kind of *ricorso*: Augustus transformed the state cult of the Vestals into the cult of the imperial household.[22]

IV

In essence, what the symbol of the public Hearth expresses is the belief that the polis can have its own identity and presence; the symbol's richness is found above all in its manifestations, which are "implicit." It is best to begin our consideration of this symbol in the area of religion—all the more so because this area possesses its own distinctive mode of thought.

Let us return to Aristotle. His text, which in a way has served as our epigraph, leads us to examine thoroughly the religious meanings of the public Hearth. As we have seen, Aristotle distinguishes between two kinds in the cult. The first is limited to a sacerdotal ministry that is more or less separate and usually hereditary, since it represents the ancient monopolies of *gentes* (the Eumolpids and other sacral *genē* of Eleusis could provide extreme examples). The history and theory of the city within the *Politics* often take note of this. There is here a domain that is recognized by the city, an assignment defined by "law," by *nomos*; and *nomos* is imperative rule derived from a collectivity that represents (etymologically) the principle of distribution. Here we are dealing entirely with social and religious history. In the development of *nomos* it is possible to recognize two successive and antithetical stages. The mythical theme of the *dianomai*, or "distributions" (those among the gods), suggests a principle of classification and "mechanical solidarity" which provides some equilibrium among the *tekhnai*—that is, among those conveyors of magical and religious powers the memory of which is kept alive by the Attic *genē*.[23] Opposed to this principle within the regime of the city is the principle of organization—that is, law that commands and subordinates. But there is more, a second kind of significance in the cult, one that has as its sign and instrument the public Hearth. Aristotle's terse and abstract language provides important testimony. Doubtless, the religion of the city can be regarded from one point of view as a synthesis or federation of cults that are older than the city itself (local, patrimonial, and others). But city religion also has its own significance; it claims a kind of individuality. The "public sacrifices" that have as their center (at least in the ideal sense) the "public Hearth" affirm a collective existence, which in itself is an eminently religious matter. Was the symbolism of lighting the fires of other altars at the central Hearth a general practice? Aristotle's expression could imply it. It is attested several times; and that is enough for it to be the source of a readily identifiable mode of thought.

And it is a very abstract mode, which is to say that it is deliberately expressed. Still, we can see at a quite profound level how it could function.

An Athenian festival that is characterized by striking archaisms (though it is doubtless not one of the oldest festivals) is organically connected with the Prytany: it is the festival of Dipoleia, whose central act was, it seems, the sacrifice of an ox on the Acropolis. This is the origin of the term *Bouphonia* (literally, "murder of the ox"). As far as its alleged origins are concerned, we find several mythical versions, all of which are ingenious; but they still convey the psychology of a religious action, which the myths make explicit.[24] The earliest sacrifice was sacrilegious: when an ox approached the altar of Zeus Polieus (Zeus "of the city" and Zeus "of the acropolis") and ate the offerings of cereal reserved for the god, the angry priest struck it down with an ax. Upset over his impiety, he fled. A famine resulted and the Delphic oracle was consulted; it offered pardon for the past and legislation for the future: thenceforth the sacrifice would have to take place each year and in the same way. In fact, the events in the rite are almost exactly like those in the legend. Conforming to the last part of the story, the rite was concluded in the Prytany, where a make-believe judgment took place (and where, moreover, animals and objects causing death to men continued to undergo judgment well into the classical period). Responsibility was imputed to the ax (or to the sacrificial knife), which was then thrown outside the borders of the town. What is the "semantic force" of these details?

Every sacrifice involves sacrilege: this hypothesis is evident from the fact that the victim is an object of special respect and protection. The victim is an ox, an animal used for labor; and an ancient but still living tradition commands genuine religious reverence. In addition, the theme of the heinous sacrifice with the same victim (but one that is finally accepted) is illustrated in legends that have found their way into the Herakles cycle and that serve to justify certain aberrant rites. In a stage of religion whose origin is alleged to be historical, the theme presupposes some tenacious forms of resistance. We find—at least in its effect (for the actual conditions elude us)—a revolution in ritual and piety; and we see the solution to a crisis, a solution that in terms of ethics and customs stands in opposition to certain elements of a prehistoric society which, up to that time, lacked genuine integration. In this context, one might compare, but in a negative way, the Zoroastrian revolution in Iran and all that it represented. But with this festival we find ourselves in the last month of the Attic year; other festivals that deal with agriculture are close to the Dipoleia and perhaps form with it an aggregate of festivals.[25] In any case, the victim, which is revived in order to be harnessed to a plough (yet another symbol of final pacification), naturally brings the earth's blessings. But the victim's immolation, which is supposed to assure these blessings, at first produces a troubling and disquieting feeling in which the city, through symbols of an agrarian religion, is personally involved. The city assumes this formidable act vis-à-vis the divine world as represented in the person of the god, who by name is in direct contact with the city. In the myth, the first man to perform sacrifice consents to take on his office only if the *responsibility* for the ritual murder is shared by all. This, in effect, is what happens: the guilt is shared. Understandably, it is the conclusion that gives sense to the entire scenario. The last act takes place at the public Hearth; the religious drama is resolved in a legal one where innocence is finally proclaimed as certain, and a consecration is guaranteed which exists from this point on. Finally, the victim's flesh provides food for a communal meal.

It is also to a Zeus Polieus that a festival from Cos is dedicated. Analogies between it and the Athenian festival have been pointed out;[26] once again, the public Hearth, as well as its divinity Hestia, play an important role. We know this from a rather late inscription,[27] but it is a fragment of a religious calendar. The elements in it are obviously traditional. Although the contents and dramatic structure are somewhat different, the symbolic orientation is the same as for the Dipoleia. What is stressed here is the unity of the civic group, the elements of which must be lost momentarily in the "all." (This is a theme of political as well as religious thought: namely, city divisions, however artificial, are sometimes to be represented in their unity, at other times in their rivalry.) Choice of the victim is determined by a procedure involving an ordeal among all the oxen that have been presented. They have to be presented *separately* by each of the divisions of each of the tribes; they are then *mixed together* into a common herd. The ox that is finally selected is immolated only on the following day; but first it is "led before Hestia," where certain rites are performed. Just before, Hestia herself receives homage from an animal sacrifice. Hearth and city divinity are in close connection; they remain so until the moment of sacrifice, when the offerings are placed "on the Hearth." The consecration is concluded; again, it has to occur between periods of purificatory rituals and a night of abstinence.

V

We can see yet another aspect of this moral security that as such had to be acquired. In the representation of the public Hearth, the symbolism of nourishment plays a large role. The Hearth, in general, is naturally associated with food; in the institution of the city, this meaningful aspect is put into rather high relief. We find it in the Roman cult of Vesta,[28] a cult that may well have come from a Hellenic tradition. A fragment of Cratinus[29] makes us think of some of its practices: there is some question in the fragment of the baking of barley grains on the very Hearth of Athena (that is, the question deals with a technique of feeding whose archaism survives in Italic ritual, but which is also attested in Greek legend). In addition, we know that the anxiety about food is translated into a lively expression in Hestia's domain. Plutarch tells us of an annual ceremony that is celebrated even in his day in his native city, Chaeronea.[30] It is the Expulsion of Hunger, celebrated by each *pater familias* at his own expense and in his own home; but the chief magistrate celebrates it at the public Hearth. A slave is struck with the branches of an *agnus castus* (used elsewhere in "apotropaic" rituals); he is then pushed through a gate while these words are intoned: "Outside famine; inside, health and wealth." The concept of *daimon* to be expelled is found in Athens under the same name: next to the Prytany, a sacred terrain is set aside for *Boulimos* (Famine).[31]

Above all, or at least often, the Prytany brings to mind the meals served in its halls. But through a number of practices, wherein a vital and concrete "representation" is diffused, we can trace a mentality that has many different purposes but is possessed of an autonomy that is—despite everything that could be confused with it—worth emphasizing. *Hestia* is synonymous with eating communally. A whole group of terms is connected with the idea, but the central image never disappears. We know what it means to welcome someone to the Hearth: whether it involves a permanent or hereditary right, and whether it concerns an occasional invitation or the obligatory participation of magistrates, the etymology can be seen in related terms. In the derivations, the central idea remains intact. The place where one celebrates a religious festival is a *hestiatorion*; within a special setting it keeps its right to this designation because of the quality of its members and the character of the gathering.[32] But there is also a *hestiatorion* in Olympia; it is intended for the Olympian victors and is located specifically in the Prytany, opposite the *Hestia*.[33]

Let us return, then, to the fundamental idea of the city *Hestia*. Obviously it does not monopolize the symbolism it contains. In ancient Greece, as elsewhere and more so, the common meal appears as an institution at every stage and in fact on every level; but it appears with some social, even historical, meanings that are quite diverse and that, in a way, build gradually, one on another. In the city religion, we still find a very ancient foundation that makes us think of quasi-"primitive" peasant feasts. Here, at least, the memory of ritual and collective consumption of food[34] survives in a practice that is so expressive that a legend is always available to justify it: for example, the Pyanepsia of Athens, a festival in which pulp is made in a communal pot from grain collected during the autumnal harvest; this is the same substance the companions of Theseus used for their improvised meals. But closer to the custom of the *Hestia* is an almost fossilized practice that nonetheless says something about a political state antedating the city. The *parasitoi*, or "assistants at a meal," who perform a cultic office, must in ancient times have been the privileged and obligatory hosts of a royalty that had religious functions and powers.[35] But we are not talking about all those groups or associations whose periodic *agapai* were, so to speak, their necessary expression, and each type of which would have been situated in its own area of social history. There is an institution that attracts our attention even more: the *sussitia*, or "common meals," which characterize a number of Greek cities. The political works of Plato and Aristotle attest to the demand or nostalgia for them. In fact, the social reality of which the *sussitia* provide the most striking expression was thought of as something lying at the heart of the origin of the city.[36] It is something of that archaic organization which has more or less survived in a certain form and by processes of adaptation; it is an organization in which the essential component is a military class whose homogeneous and special quality is reinforced by a whole series of traditions and codes of behavior. Within this group, collective consumption of food is no longer only a symbol but a way of life. The symbolism of the city, as such, does not require this kind of permanent community; rather, it might exclude it (and it might also exclude the type of social exploitation this permanent community implies, since the warriors of the *sussitia* are nourished but they themselves produce nothing). Moreover, the symbolism moves in such varied directions that on occasion the key words contradict one another: the *andreion*, a word that means both the association of warriors and the place where they have their meals, differs precisely in its meaning from *prutaneion*.[37] And one never finds the *sussitia* under the sign of Hestia.

In its tone and meanings, then, the custom of the public Hearth is something different from that of the *sussitia*. By hypothesis, the public Hearth involves only certain beneficiaries. In the privilege accorded them, there is manifest both the unity of the city and the totality of citizens participating (at the Hearth) through representatives. The symbol could first have been one of belonging, and a sign of being integrated into a collective body; one can see this as a possibility even in Athens, where only returning envoys are usually welcomed at the Hearth. For the fourth century B.C., this is above all a mark of honor; but in fact the reception is not a reward, since one does not even know what the envoys did (and on one occasion there was a dispute on precisely this point). The envoys are received at the public Hearth, just as individuals also returning from abroad would be received at their family Hearth, by means of certain rites of desacralization and reintegration.[38] The only thing is that in the city, collectivity as a special power appears to be the dominant idea. We mention a very suggestive myth of the welcoming of heroes under the guise of a legendary *agapē* only in passing, because it is not localized at the public Hearth (in the tale of Orestes, during the Athenian Anthesteria it is set in a nearby building, which is the site for the reunion of the *thesmothetai*). But it goes without saying that participation is a right for representatives of public authority; still, it is more essentially an obligation.

As far as the beneficiaries are concerned—that is, those who receive some recompense or other concession (it seems that at times there was a kind of rotation in the assignment of this right)—the symbolism operates with that "moderation" which is itself the mark of the city. We have the regulations governing the Hearth from Naucratis[39] (where one ate rather well on festival days, but in general the fare was rather meager in the Prytaneis). It is both problematic and instructive, but we have something even better from Athens. The moralizing Plutarch must have been correct when he interpreted a law of Solon[40] in classical terms: to refuse the common meal implies "contempt" for the city, and to profit from the public meal more often than is right amounts to "greediness" (*pleonexia*).

VI

In this deliberately managed symbol, the idea attached to the public Hearth remains communal: what is expressed directly, from the fact that there is a city Hearth as well as individual family ones, is a form of concrete solidarity that makes the well-being of all the well-being of each; it is the very constitutive nature of the city. This nature reveals itself strikingly and fully in theory, in actual events, and even in forms of behavior.[41] At the core there is always the notion of public property: everyone should have access to it, and everyone on occasion exercises his claim to it or participates in it. The system of festivals, the distributions, and indeed the attraction of a windfall to share in—many elements convey this tenacious notion. It is in conjunction with it, and in the sphere of economics, that we must first deal with the institution of the Hearth.

Curiously, in opposition to this kind of thinking there is yet another kind, one that has to do with state organization and, under the state's aegis, with economic individualism. Are they in opposition or complementarity? The fact is that the two antithetical notions have equal links with *Hestia* and represent two extremes between which societies have always found it difficult to strike a balance. And the Greek city, a rather complex reality, attests to precisely the alternative to both of these extremes.

Sometimes there is nothing more instructive than a manual on the interpretation of dreams. One specialist[42] in this area tells us that when Hestia appears in a dream, she signifies the city council and the treasury that contains public revenues. We could perhaps say that a state is born in the ancient city when a state treasury develops. Hestia is directly involved with this basic element. In Cos (in the very calendar to which we have already referred), Hestia's epithet is *Tamia*. It is, to be sure, an ancient word, with significations of "feudal" and religious royalty; but within the structure of the state, it has supplied the somewhat premature designation of "treasurer." With regard to this *Hestia Tamia*, the Cos ritual contains something suggestive: as soon as the victim is selected, it is led into the agora; the owner then announces that he has made a gift of the animal to his fellow citizens, and that they in turn must pay the price to Hestia. Thus we see that in an essentially monetary economy the value of cattle can be put up at compound interest by a Hestia who in the city's service is still independent of the total body of citizens. This increase in value is owed to the generosity of a donor; one immediately recognizes here a *leitourgia*. The "liturgies," or tasks freely assumed by an individual, especially at festivals (one of these *leitourgiai*, the organization of a banquet, is called *hestiasis*), represent an adaptation within the structure of the city and a kind of "nationalization" of the "gift ethic," a practice that predates the city but that is in a way put to use for the city's own purposes. The city is not an abstract entity, and one of its major components is affirmed in its religious life.

In the case of the Greeks, and in the course of this very compromise, the city's structure appears to correspond to that of a "discreet" economy dominated by the principle of *suum cuique*. This same principle sometimes supplies the Greeks' early moral philosophers with a definition of justice. Some features of a religious vocabulary dealing with the Hearth are interesting in this regard. One of the divinities associated with Hestia at her sanctuary in Naucratis is Apollo Komaios (Apollo "of the villages," whose epithet is a form that predates the city; the name sometimes remains tied to topographical subdivisions of the city). Perhaps it is not by chance that we find at Ainos, a colony in Thrace, an Apollo with the same (or practically the same) name who presides over the *sale* of real estate.[43] There is some historical insight to be gained from the name of a divinity in Arcadian Tegea: here, groups of altars are built around a public Hearth on a site dedicated to Zeus Klarios.[44] The career of the word *klaros* is well known: at first it referred to a kind of "fief"; but in the classical period it came to mean true individual property—that is, a patrimony. In any case, one thing is certain (and the archaism preserved through tradition is striking): the first act of the Athenian archon, whose relationship with the Prytany was personal—he resided there from the earliest times—was to proclaim that "each person will remain, until the very end of the archon's magistracy, owner and master of the property he owned before the archon's entry into office."[45]

In studying the Indo-European roots of representations of myth dealing with the functioning of society, G. Dumézil has pointed out the opposition and alternation between "totalitarian" and "distributive" economies.[46] In clearly defined forms he shows that at the dawn of history the symbolism of *Hestia* permits us to recognize the antithesis between two analogous concepts; and within the organism of the city (fragile and restless, as are all human creations), *Hestia* shows us the ideal of a synthesis of these concepts.

VII

We are presented with multiple themes; the preeminent quality of such symbolism is its polyvalence. Moreover, behind the psychological material, whose testimony from an already classical Greece appears to be in a state of almost complete deterioration, one can still find elements of continuity: how, for example, the symbols of nourishment can, within the context of festivals, be associated with sentiments of religious community. One can also see how these symbols convey an idea of the eternal, of social unity, and indeed of discipline or order. One would like to recapture all of this.

To do so is to put it within a context. Mauss observed that if in the study of man and society, we only take into account "collective representations," the "collective psychology" will suffice as a special chapter on psychology only; but there is another dimension—that is, society itself, and consequently its history.[47] In the symbolism of the public Hearth it is already of great interest that economic solidarity especially asserts itself, and it does so as something fundamental. What is more, the different directions in which the symbolism leads allow us to identify a specific stratum: the social age that the foundation of Hearths points to is one in which an individualist economy, the type more or less rejected by the organizations we have identified in the background (peasant communities, "male societies," beneficent kingships, and so on), is integrated into a new form of unity. And this stage is not part of an "abstract chronology." We are fortunate to hit upon something like a historical fact that the convergence of literary, linguistic, and institutional data places around 800 B.C.[48] For the foundation of the Hearth is first the symbol of the creation of the city. Vague as this creation was in the archaic period, it still reveals a "point of maturation."

This is a moment of history of which the public Hearth remains the sole relic precisely because it was the symbol of a sudden change. Because of this, in the classical period there will be a certain ambiguity in the nature of the Hearth. Although it will preserve some of its religious features, it will do so within a network of thought that no longer belongs to its origins. The echoes we detect in the festivals that have an organic relationship to the Hearth; that *Stimmung* which is really stifled within a tradition of *mos maiorum*—these must correspond historically to historical crises. In the founding of the city, we sense a religious eruption; and we sense it too in the semidarkness of legends, in the acts of certain innovators, and in certain associations. These must have been the antecedents to a political "philosophy" whose offshoot might best be exemplified by Pythagoreanism.[49] We also detect an atmosphere in which there emerges, with all its emotive force, an obsessive concept of *homonoia*, or "civic harmony"; and in a way the public Hearth seems to be its immediate and dominant expression.

But perhaps from the beginning, this novelty of the *Hestia* owes its mark of a practical mentality to its more or less spontaneous nature. It is a fact that the symbolism of the Hearth—from all evidence, so weak in mythical development—seems in history to have disengaged itself from ancient contexts. This in contrast to the forms of thought verified in the very symbols from which that of the Hearth emerges. Despite their persistent proximity, chthonian connections no longer appear in the symbolism of the Hearth. The Hearth's symbolism excludes the element of mystery and rule based on a religious secret; but survivals of these elements are not entirely lost in a tangential but otherwise innocuous tradition. The symbolism of the Hearth is synonymous with publicity; the very representation of the social space that is bound up with its symbolism is itself something new. Men arrange as they will the mathematical disposition of

land; it can be almost anything.[50] Where the center is is an arbitrary[51]—
indeed a theoretical—matter.[52] Even in legend, a Hearth can be removed
at will.[53] No doubt colonies remained faithful to the piety that had them
take their fire from the *mētropoleis*; but colonization, above all a manifestation of civic vitality, conditions men to disregard prescribed spaces. Let
us also say that the ancient meanings, which are not really so ancient,
have been obliterated. Within an isolated tradition it is difficult to catch a
glimpse of the primitive notion of a space that is structured in terms of a
center. Here we are referring to the *omphalos*. But the only symbol of a
centrum which had real significance no longer represents anything of the
sort; nor does that idea of time which depends on this mythical space survive. (This is a more adhesive notion in the Italic *mundus*—indeed, in the
Roman Vesta.) And if in the course of free speculation a cosmic significance is restored to the *Hestia*, then the name does nothing more than "exhibit" a geometric concept of the universe.[54]

Let us go back to where we began. The *Hestia* touched a political
reality that from the earliest days the Greeks characterized as rational, almost preordained. Its true destiny was to initiate a mode of thought which
no longer used it except as a deliberate symbol. This means that it was no
longer needed for the functioning of institutions in which Hestia's earliest
qualities were manifest. In a mysterious practice in Delphi, a drawing of
lots (perhaps for magistrates) takes place at the Hearth;[55] but it is an isolated custom, and from early on the religious implication of drawing lots
is diluted. In Athens the name of a tribunal, the name of a formality preceding a court case, and certain aspects of Plato's laws attest to the memory of a substantial link between jurisdiction and the Hearth—but in effect,
only the memory of such.

By supposition a religious symbol, the Hearth is something quite different from a literary metaphor, but it is on the way to becoming one. In a
period of crisis, it had the privilege of conveying what lay at the origin of
the city. But the turning point it signaled put Greece on its own course:
the major innovations of Hellenism asserted themselves very rapidly. We
have outlined some of them here.

NOTES

1.   *Pol.*, VI.1322b.26 ff.
2.   See A. Preuner, *Hestia-Vesta* (1864), pp. 95 ff.; cf. W. Larfeld, *Handb. der
griech. Epigr.*, II, pp. 778 ff.

3.   For this interpretation see F. Robert, *Thymélé: Rech. sur la signif. et la destinat. des monum. circul. dans l'archit. relig. de la Grèce* (1939); cf. M. Eliade, *Traité d'hist. des relig.*, p. 320. On the discussion alluded to, see F. Robert, *op. cit.*, p. 132.

4.   See Pl., *Leg.*, I.612C. Let us also say briefly that the public Hearth itself sometimes appears to be associated with marriage.

5.   Ath., IV.149D.

6.   Hdt., V.72; *Inscr. jurid. gr.*, II.1.16; and with some reservations, ibid., XI.1.7.

7.   On the connection between the *Hestia* and the religious representations from the royal age, see L. R. Farnell, *Cults of the Greek States*, V, pp. 353 ff.

8.   M. Guarducci, "La *eschara* del tempio greco arcaico," *Studi e mater. di storia della relig.*, XIII (1937), pp. 158 ff.

9.   Aesch., *Supp.*, 365 ff., 372.

10.   Soph., *El.*, 417 ff.

11.   Apollod., *Bibl.*, I.65.

12.   See P. Foucart, *Les Grands Mystères d'Eleusis*, p. 279.

13.   P. Roussel, "Hestia à l'omphalos," *RA*, XVIII (1911), pp. 86 ff.

14.   Paus., VIII.9.5; cf. I.43.2.

15.   F. Robert, op. cit., pp. 151 ff.

16.   *Hymn. Hom. Ven.*, 29 ff.

17.   In a Delphic formula of an oath, the "immortal fire" is distinct from the *Hestia*.

18.   Paus., II.19.5.

19.   *Id.*, IX.34.2.

20.   See Plut., *Num.*, 9.

21.   See L. Deroy, *RHR*, I (1950), p. 41, a study that deals with the still-valuable hypothesis of an Etrusco-Greek origin of Vesta.

22.   G. Wissowa, *Religion und Kultus der Römer*[2], pp. 76 ff.

23.   See R. Hirzel, *Themis, Dike und Verwandtes*, pp. 163, 220, 226, 246.

24.   See, among others, P. Stengel, *Opferbräuche der Griechen*, pp. 203 ff.; H. Hubert and M. Mauss, *Mél. d'hist. des rel.*, pp. 36 ff.; A. B. Cook, *Zeus*, III, pp. 577 f.; L. Deubner, *Att. Feste*, pp. 162 ff.

25.   With an implicit theme of "sacred ploughing"?

26.   See M. P. Nilsson, *Griech. Feste*, pp. 17 ff.

27.   J. de Prott and L. Ziehen, *Leges Sacrae*, no. 8.

28.   In particular, G. Dumézil, *Tarpeia*, pp. 100 ff.

29.   Plut., *Sol.*, 25.1.

30.   Plut., *Quaest. conv.*, 693F.

31.   *Anecd. Bekk.*, I.278.4.

32.   Hdt., IV.35; Strab., X.487.

33.   Paus., V.15.12.

34.   See *REG*, XLI (1928), pp. 319 f. [= pp. 15–16 above].

35.   Ath., VI.234D ff.

36.   It is one aspect of the valuable work of H. Jeanmaire, *Couroi et Courètes*.

37.   *CIG*, 2554.49.

38.   See E. Samter, *Familienfeste der Griechen und Römer*, pp. 2 ff.

39.   Ath., IV.149D.

40.   *Sol.*, 24.3

41.   K. Latte, "Kollektivbesitz u. Staatschatz in Griechenl.," *Nachrichten der Götting. Gesellsch.*, 1946–47, pp. 74 ff.

42.   Artem., II.37.

43.   Theophr., *ap.* Stob., *Flor.*, XLIV.22 ff.

44.   Paus., VIII.53.9 (a legend traced back to a primitive division).

45.   Arist., *Ath. Pol.*, 46.2; cf. 3.5.

46.   G. Dumézil, *Mitra-Varuṇa*, pp. 155 ff.

47.   M. Mauss, *Sociologie et anthropologie*, p. 287.

48.   V. Ehrenberg, "When Did the Polis Rise?," *JHS*, LVII (1937), pp. 147 ff.

49.   A typical detail is that Zalmoxis, who belongs to the legendary cycle of Pythagoras, received from the common Hearth the laws he gave to his fellow citizens.

50.   See Pl., *Leg.*, V.745B.

51.   Where is the Prytaneion in Athens? Admittedly, the site changed in the course of time.

52.   On the purification of assemblies by the *Peristia*, a word derived from the "hearth" (*Suda*, s.v. *Istros*), see S. Eitrem, *Opferritus u. Voropfer*, pp. 177 ff.

53.   Paus., VIII.8.4.

54.   This is in the Pythagorean tradition: see Stob., *Ecl.*, I, 468, 488; and Arist., *Cael.*, II.13.

55.   Plut., *De E apud Delphos*, 16 (see R. Flacelière, *REA*, LII [1950], p. 319).

PART V

PHILOSOPHY AND SOCIETY

CHAPTER 16
Things Visible and Things Invisible

Recently in a note, P. Schuhl called attention to an antithesis we often see in Greek thought (philosophy, scientific reflection, religious speculation): the opposition between things "visible" (*phanera*) and things "invisible" (*aphanē, adēla*).[1] Schuhl points out that this antithesis appears elsewhere, namely, in the legal domain, where it signifies a kind of dichotomy between visible and invisible property (*ousia phanera, ousia aphanēs*). The coincidence is, to say the least, a curious one. I would like to say a word about this method of classifying property, since it also functions as a concept in law. It has its own particular forms or "detours," which are not without parallels—perhaps even connections—with those in other areas.

🌿

But first, for purposes of orientation, a few remarks about an area that is not our particular specialty. It is possible to observe a number of quite diverse tendencies in the documentary sources Schuhl has managed to collect. With some thinkers, the opposition between things visible and things invisible very often has a correlative import: the two exist on the same plane, and in the case of the invisible the sense is of something temporary and negative. With others, the two terms correspond to differences of an ontological character: the "hidden" is true reality, as opposed to what one sees. Here it might be good to recall one of the themes of *Essai sur les origines de la pensée grecque*. Even so, one can recognize that the concept of the "invisible" as absolute reality has a certain primacy. It exists in the background even for the most ardent "positivists." And a very

This article originally appeared in *Revue philosophique*, CXLVI (January–March 1956), pp. 79–86.

marked tendency appears in the dualism that continues to haunt Greek thought; in its most extreme form it is found in the provocative agnosticism of the Sophists.

The dualism in question was not an invention of philosophy. It has its antecedents in belief and religious practices. Divination, in all its forms, was based on the possibility of a momentary manifestation of the invisible world; the theme of "hidden things that one later discovered" appears frequently in rituals. A major element of the Mysteries was the notion of "secret things" that one "shows" at the culminating point of *epopteia* (the title "hierophant" is itself significant). But historically speaking, how this tradition survived in the early stages of philosophy is another question. Suffice it to say that philosophy plays a role in this tradition, and that there is reason to hypothesize an archaic period in which *revelation* may have come before *instruction*.

One of the most striking changes in Hellenism was its complete transformation of the mode of thought it had inherited. In particular, Hellenism created a formally philosophical kind of thought out of that inheritance. In Plato, where the philosopher is still aided by images from myth, Hades is interpreted as the world of the invisible and becomes a striking symbol,[2] but a symbol nonetheless. At another stage—in a form of knowledge which alternates between empiricism and theory—the mediation of *logos* is also a guarantor of intelligibility. By permitting an inference from the known to the unknown, the process of analogy guarantees a connection between one world and the other. The antithesis is still necessary, but it has lost its significance. We find ourselves on a level of thought where Bachelard's formula might be appropriate: "There is no knowledge except knowledge of the hidden."

We must not forget that such a complete revolution of thought was a product of a specific human milieu. Other levels of ideology are no less affected, even those belonging to the same movement, and they are not without their points of contact. Let us examine one of these points in particular.

It has often been suggested that legal disputation had already supplied a kind of rough draft for dialectic. There is some basis for this, but it is still a hasty observation. There is one point we should insist upon: In the development of the philosophical and scientific thought to which we have made some reference, the notion of the *tekmērion* is fundamental. *Tekmērion* refers to the "visible" as a "sign," in the sense that it allows one to pass from one domain to another by rational inference.[3] Now the *tekmērion* is quite important in the legal realm; it lies at the core of a rhetoric that is, in judicial and quasi-judicial debate, the "artisan of persuasion."[4] If rhetoric interests us, it is not because it sanctions debate or the quirks of the law, but because it symbolizes, in a way, a turning point and a new civilization of law and the courts. From the time a primitive system of decisive proof gave way to the rule of "free handling of evidence," the inference— termed rational—from the "visible" to the "nonvisible" (basically from fact to law) became the established and obligatory practice. Although this form of reasoning has a completely different object than science, it is an analogous *method*, and is attested on two levels of thought under the same name.

We come now to the distinction that interests us: visible as opposed to invisible property. Two elements are equally striking. The distinction is quite common, and there are constant references to it in court speeches for the defense. But it is an extremely loose distinction, and moderns have long given up trying to pinpoint its meaning.[5] In this regard we find a paradoxical datum that merits reflection.

A note in Harpocration could lead us to believe that the first term refers to immovable property or real estate, and the second to movable property.[6] It appears that, in effect, land holdings are visible property *par excellence*;[7] but ancient sources have no difficulty including in this category movable property, slaves, and so on. On different occasions the same entries are classified in one or the other category. Money is a good example. Sometimes it is possible to find it in the category of "invisible" goods (to convert landed property into money, *exargurizein*, is really to make it disappear). But even a bank deposit that is part of an inheritance can under certain conditions be regarded as "visible" property.[8] This distinction does not correspond even to the one between "corporeal and incorporeal things." A text of Isaeus is proof of this.[9] He lists the elements of a patrimony in haphazard fashion—and they include land, houses, credit, furniture, livestock, commodities, repayment of personal loans—"without mentioning the other items the plaintiffs do not declare (*ouk apophainousin*), and mentioning only of the visible fortune (*ta phanera*) acknowledged by them." This is an extreme example, but there is little doubt that the concept of the two was based above all on the ability (which one did or did not have) to conceal this or that property—a purely circumstantial matter. But in fact it is possible to see the distinction functioning concretely in some clear-cut situations: for example, when there is question of an inheritance about which the beneficiaries can be more or less informed, or from which they could expect certain kinds of subtraction; when it is a question of a tax on capital or a *leitourgia*, in which case the city can tax only the visible fortune; or, again, in the case of confiscations, which can hardly apply to anything but visible property.

In sum, the distinction is left as undefined as possible and is essentially pragmatic. But one gets the impression that it is not so arbitrary in principle as in application, and that it is based on something other than the contingencies of dividing inheritances or of fiscal indiscretions. The very idea of a dichotomy (along with the rigorous terminology) suggests it. We might also point to the traces of certain legal concepts which appear in the data we have only briefly reviewed.[10] The problem is that thought moves in many directions; a technical vocabulary tries to establish itself but does not succeed. We have the history of a flawed category, but it is still an interesting one.

This history is interesting first of all because a mode of classification asserts itself: more precisely, that of binary oppositions, which are fundamental in a number of different forms of thought, but especially in law. Everywhere we can find a distinction (or several distinctions within different perspectives) between two *types* of property. But it is important to note that the two types often correspond to different degrees of value. Moreover, this seems to have been the case at the dawn of Roman law, when it appeared in the terms *familia* and *pecunia,* and even in *res mancipi* and *nec mancipi.*

If we are to understand the deep-seated basis of this dualism in Greece, we must grasp the idea of "goods." The concept has two poles. One of them is formulated by Aristotle: "We call goods (*khrēmata*) all those things whose value is measured by money."[11] This notion is abstract, quantitative, and economic.

There are other words, all of which are more or less concrete, and never abstract. *Ousia* is something substantial and usually individualized; it normally means a patrimony. But what is a patrimony? Some other terms are clear enough: *oikos* also designates this collection of goods, and at the same time denotes the social unity of the *domus* as it is perpetuated ideally in an indefinite series of descendants. This understanding of *oikos* is mentioned explicitly in Plato's *Laws,* but it indicates only that the *oikos,* the "house," is both the family and the family's possessions. In this context the term *klēros* has special application. It was still in use in the fourth century B.C., when technically it meant "the inheritance"; but the term has a long history. In the beginning it referred to a "lot"—in fact, an assignment of lands made under social conditions that later changed. The meaning of *klēros* is fixed in the concept of familial property, the property "that does not leave the family." Even in Aristotle's day such property remained inalienable in part of Greece. In Athens, such a notion was quite out of date, but perhaps not before the end of the fifth century B.C.; and the persistence of the term *klēros* attests to its survival, at least in theory. But what does it entail? The most ancient kind of "ownership" is, to be sure, that of the land, which continues to be mark of, and perhaps even the very condition for, citizenship. In a sense, such ownership remains privileged because it pertains to the family.

This is essentially what is meant by "visible" property. In principle, it is the only kind with which laws governing inheritance are concerned; other types of property are the subjects of "free gifts" and are of an individual character; they are marginal, private, and more or less secret in nature. When an orphan's patrimony is involved, the ideal course is to convert the inheritance, if necessary, into a "visible fortune," for it is a question of the survival of the *oikos*.[12] If confiscations bear directly on visible property, it is because their intent is to destroy the guilty party *and* the social unity he represents. One litigant might argue that his family can no longer "answer" before the state because misfortune has caused it to lose the honorable *phanera ousia* that not long ago it owned.[13] In this example the possibility that the man could be equivocating is not important, nor is the material aspect of the subject; what matters is the emotional effect the litigant's plea evokes. In French, we still call landed property *"biens au soleil."* Surely a sentiment that has not entirely disappeared from our own experience could still be alive for the Greek, indeed for the Athenian of the classical age. Its religious reverberations did not have to die out everywhere—or very quickly.

But the idea has been drastically weakened, for we find significant patrimonies that have almost nothing to do with landed property; we even find some where the largest part consists of credit. However limited economic development has been, the economy has done its work. The norm has been by-passed, and land itself can be alienated. Everything is evaluated in terms of money; and Aristotle, despite his theoretical biases and sentimental preferences, finds himself obliged to define wealth as something neutral and homogeneous. However, at this point it might be possible to conceive of a dichotomy that is, in the strict sense of the term, legal, a dichotomy between personal property and real estate, between one's own objects and those one acquires, between corporeal and incorporeal things, between the law of real estate and the law of person. Sometimes a tendency in this direction does exist; but it is certain that the Greeks never recognized categories of these sorts. They always and instinctively possessed a sense of dualism; but it was a dualism that could not be expressed conceptually, since its two poles might not be of the same order. There was no common denominator between ownership that was strictly "patrimonial" and ownership that was strictly economic. For this reason, the terminology that the Greeks preserve—and they are, in their own fashion, preservers—is inexact and arbitrary; and since they are not jurists, they do not dream of rationalizing it.

Nevertheless, the kind of tension we find here has a positive result; and it is one of great consequence for the *exercise* of abstract thinking. In the relatively varied series of texts we have used, one major antithesis stands out: that between goods that can be physically seized, and financial claims or credit of all types.[14] Opposed to *res corporales*,[15] which are visible, the invisible has become something ideal, conceptual, and imaginary. It has become the *legal right*.[16] This is a very significant kind of dualism, and the Greeks express it in many different but always striking ways: a credit not based on a mortgage (which would give it some substance)—that is, a claim qua claim—is something "in mid-air," *meteōron*.[17] The meaning is not that a claim is ineffectual but that the "invisible" takes on positive significance on a new level—a somewhat disturbing significance, for the term introduces a new world that is not without mystery. The person who symbolizes this new world is the banker, and he is already an energetic participant in it. By vocation and in the strict sense of the word, he is a receiver of the other's goods.[18] Even more, the banker is occasionally a creator of fantasies. An amusing passage in Isocrates shows clearly how the game of bankers can turn "appearance" topsy-turvy and "make you see" only an imaginary debtor in the case of a real creditor.[19]

In conclusion—and does not the transition call for it?—I would like to return briefly to philosophy and pose the following question: What is the significance of the parallel we have seen between speculative thought and law in their modes of classification and in their terminologies? And is there only one point of significance? We must always allow the accidental connections in a vocabulary to play a larger role; and in particular it would be absurd to think that there is a transformation in one direction or the other. But perhaps there are some more subtle links to point out. Sometimes hidden processes of assimilation exist between the meanings of the same word, even though these meanings have become unique within a specialized language.

In both realms—philosophy and law—it is possible to recognize at their core the dynamics of values that are in opposition to each other. Without a doubt, by moving from the visible to the invisible, the dialectic involves an inversion: it is the visible fortune that from the beginning is the "real" one (the term survives in law); but to be invisible amounts to being real. The essential thing is that there is always the value and the opposition. And there is another word that should be kept in mind, namely, *ousia*, which designates precisely the fortune itself.

The term *ousia* also appears, and in a quite independent way, in the language of philosophy. It does not seem to have made a very early appearance—according to Herodotus, it is already well established in the fifth century B.C.—and the legal meaning of the term probably predates its philosophical usage. In any case, in Plato's time *ousia* appears frequently. His dialogue the *Sophistēs* allows us to make a rather interesting observation. *Ousia* appears in it often; it is used alternately with *to on* as the substantive for being. The Sophist himself symbolizes nonbeing; to be precise, he lives by it. And of the six attempts to define such an inaccessible and faint person as the "Sophist," three have some connection with business. In light of this, the Sophist himself represents an extreme transition, for he deals in the merchandise of illusion and nothingness. He is a symbol on both levels.

There is no need to remind ourselves of a social attitude in Plato which never changes and is opposed to modern forms of economics. In passing from the utopia of his *Republic* to the ideal of the *Laws*, his purpose is to establish the familial ownership of land—the *klēros*—as something indivisible, inalienable, and perpetual. This for Plato is true ownership; in contrast, other goods are only accidentals. But *klēros* is *substance* in the strict sense. In the city of the *Laws*, there will be no real money. Commerce, in its widest sense, is banned; for Plato, it is "on the side of" *to apeiron*. In the plan of a society there is a kind of ontological reflection. But can we not also say that within this ontology and "sociology" there exist some needs that are analogous and some oppositions of comparable significance? In fact, the special term "invisible," as it is applied to ownership, has a significance that is essentially religious; other "goods" are profane and therefore sensible. We can recognize a certain parallelism in Platonic philosophy.

From a different perspective, one can find another and very general correlation. Thought itself has worked on the concepts "visible" and "invisible"; they tend to be intellectualized on both levels. On the level of philosophy, we can explain this process while observing our point of departure; we began with a simple intuition, an idea supplied immediately in the realm of the visible but capable of being supplied by means of revelation in the form of something "hidden."[20] With Anaxagoras, Democritus, and Plato a different kind of subtlety is at play. Similarly, in another order of thought the mind's workings had to remain unconscious, and relatively archaic, though their orientation was the same as philosophy's. We discovered something representing the "invisible" in the very concept of legal right as an ideal, distinct from its object, and recognized as a relation-ship. What we find is that an impersonal and abstract idea of relation—one that lies at the very core of legal thought—developed and flourished with the help of a traditional antithesis. And if we have reason to admit that the advent of this form of thought marks one of Hellenism's advances, it is not unimportant to observe the same line of development in two quite different domains, in both of which the distinction of the visible and the invisible is maintained.[21]

NOTES

1.   "Adēla," *Annales publiées par la Faculté des Lettres de Toulouse, Homo: Etudes philosophiques*, I (May 1953), pp. 86–93.

2.   Cf. *Phd.*, 79A and 80D.

3.   It is under this definition that Aristotle takes up *tekmērion* in logic. In the popular language, the term is generally used to signify proof drawn from experience; from the earliest examples onward, this post-Homeric derivative very quickly loses its connection with a fundamental concept, the sign of recognition, or with the signal (and on occasion with an effective symbol through which we make some contact with prejuridical thought: note the use of *tekmōr* in *Iliad*, I.526).

4.   The judiciary sophistic uses the notions of *eikos* (probability), *sēmeion* (evidence), and *tekmērion* (assumption); the last term is the most general. Aristotle distinguishes and analyzes it for purposes of logic (*An. Pr.*, 70a–b); he studies the changes in the word's meaning in law-court pleading (*Rh.*, I, 1357a34 ff.). The rhetoric of the orators did not advance quite so far; with them, these ideas were, as one might say, "laicized." But this did not happen at a very early date; the concept of *sēmeion* appears once in Antiphon within an entirely religious context (V.81 ff., where a man's innocence is proven by showing that he did not cause a shipwreck or produce any trouble in sacrifices).

5.   There is a concise summary of the question in L. Beauchet, *Hist. du droit privé de la répubic. athén.*, III, pp. 13–21; cf. J. H. Lipsius, *Das attische Recht und Rechtsverfahren*, p. 677. See also E. Weiss, *Griech. Privatrecht*, pp. 173, 464, 491.

6.   S.v. *aphanēs ousia*.

7.   Lys., fr. XXIV.2.

8.   [Dem.], XLVIII.22.

9.   XI.43.

10.   It is important to note at least briefly that in an archaic stratum of law ideas operate in relationship to very definite procedures: the same claim is not made about the "manifest"as is made about the "nonmanifest." That this can happen in the case of something that is *not* "manifest" implies a certain amount of progress in abstract thought; and it corresponds exactly to the progress in organized justice.

11.   *Eth. Nic.*, IV.1119b.26.

12.   Lys., XXXII.23; Dem., XXVIII.7.

13.   [Lys.], XX.22 ff.

14.   Isae., VIII.35; Isoc., XVII.7; Dem. XXXVIII.7. Money is conceived of as virtual credit; when deposited with a banker (an "irregular" deposit, since it is not subject to a return in kind), it can be put to work, and as in modern practice, the banker invests it on his own (and often agrees to a fifty-fifty share with his client). An additional distinction was made between "land-based" and "sea-faring" goods: Opposed to the *engeia* (real estate or mortgaged property [Dem., XXXVI.5]), the *nautika* (Lys., fr. 8, *aparas*.; [Dem.], XXXV.12) are goods handled in maritime commerce; the basic means of undertaking this kind of venture is the large loan, the standard example of the *risky* operation.

15.   Parenthetically, apropos of the Roman concept of "corporeal" and "incorporeal" things (Gai., *Inst.*, II.13), we should mention one of those "intrusions" that interest us: the philosophy of the Stoics, which must have had some influence on the formulation of law.

16.   The extreme form of this polarity—it is at least possible to suggest it—would be the dualism recently explained by E. Lévy between the system of possession and that of value. In fact, Lévy includes in the former, together with the typical form of ownership, credit in its most ancient form; but he adds that "there is already something of value in the

law [of credit]" (*Les Fondements du droit*, p. 88). Let us understand this: Something in the order of "expectation" is represented in opposition to what is collected or possessed. This idea was asserted by the Greeks and favored the traditional antithesis between the visible and the invisible.

17.   Law of Ephesus, in *Inscr. jurid. gr.*, no. V, 42.

18.   Isae., fr. VIII.1; Dem., XLV.66.

19.   XVII.7.

20.   It is possible to find something of this sort in Parmenides' ontology, where the major premise is that an almost material connection exists between thought and being. (But there is also an ancient form of juridical thought in which law is indistinguishable from its object; it exists in the case of a real law *par excellence*—the law of "ownership," which is confused with the thing possessed.)

21.   These brief remarks were given in relatively the same form at the Ecole des Hautes Etudes. One is always indebted to his audience; I wish to thank J.-P. Vernant in particular for the suggestions he offered me on the last part of the paper.

CHAPTER 17

The Origins
of Greek Philosophy

The question about the origin of Greek philosophy is only part of a larger question concerning the origin and development of Hellenism itself as one of the major factors enriching our own civilization. Even so, the problem of Greek philosophy's origin is of special interest. First of all, Greek philosophy is the beginning of what we call philosophy as such, or to put it another way, it is the basis of the intellectual activity whereby man, through reason and reflection, attempts to define the meaning of the world and his place in it. The framework of philosophical reflection was first constructed in Greece, and it is almost a commonplace to say that the basic problems set out there have not changed. But even if the speculations of the Greeks had become a dead letter, their extraordinary historical value would still have to be recognized, for these speculations made systematic scientific knowledge, or at least a confident view of it, possible. It is no accident that from very early times Greek philosophy and science were either associated or somewhat confused with each other; the ancient history of one cannot be written without that of the other. And it is quite possible to speculate that the earliest extrapolations of philosophy—the ones that were in our view the most adventuresome and had to be abandoned the earliest—were necessary to give some substance and coherence to the existence of theoretical knowledge. The quest for scientific truth, as it has been understood since the time of the Greeks, needs its own "good conscience," if one can use such a term. Philosophy assured itself of such a conscience when it gave rational explanation the exclusive right to intelligible reality. By such a standard, knowledge could go beyond the pragmatism of technical skill and the subjectivity of dreams or illusions.

What are the conditions in which such a bias in favor of intellectual

This article originally appeared in *Bulletin de l'enseignement public du Maroc*, no. 183 (October-December 1945), pp. 1–12.

comprehension could assert itself? We speak of reason and rational truth; these and similar terms characterize Hellenism as it is most often represented. But it is origins that concern us here; and origins, since they are antecedents, are not of the same order as the phenomena that follow them. Previously, scholars did not look for antecedents, and they hardly even speculated on the matter. For a long time, the idea that Hellenism in general was created *ex nihilo* was implicit, and it was only startling discoveries that forced us to admit that classical Greece had a very long past. Thus, the question about classical Greece's origin can be asked; and philosophy's origin becomes a special part of that question. Brief mention can be made of the book that Nietzsche began about the "birth" of philosophy, a book that was intended to be a counterpart to *The Birth of Tragedy*. From what we have of it, it is clear that his treatment of early philosophies was romantic; he was heavily influenced by a very popular philosopher at that time, Schophenhauer. In reaction to this kind of approach, more systematic studies appeared which tried to identify the mythical concepts, religious practices, and societal forms that were involved in philosophy's beginnings. In all of these considerations, however, we are dealing with concepts that are unique to philosophy and with the quest for their historical explanation. In my own account—*ne sutor ultra crepidam*—I will deal only with one aspect of the "origins" question: I am interested in the nature of the philosopher as a human type, the behavior of some of the first representatives of this type, the idea the philosopher has of himself, and what others on occasion made of him.

❦

From the end of the seventh century B.C. to the middle of the fifth—the period of the pre-Socratics—philosophy, in the modern sense of the word, already existed in many respects, but it manifested itself in forms and expressions that are often rather confusing for us. Yet it is precisely these forms and expressions that from our perspective can be the most instructive.

As a point of departure, I will take the extant prologue of Parmenides' philosophical poem. And Parmenides is not from a really remote period; he may even have conversed with Socrates. In addition, it is remarkable that he wrote in verse, evidence perhaps, as we shall see in another contemporary example, that he did not want his teachings deprived of the benefit that the tradition of a sort of incantation could provide. Moreover, the philosophy of Parmenides, as a philosophy of being as being, is one of the most abstract imaginable. There is a contrast here which could provoke much thought.

But let us turn to the prologue. The poet tells how he is brought by a chariot to the gates where the paths of Night and Day diverge; their keys are in the possession of the goddess Dike (Justice). His guides are the Daughters of the Sun, and the road he traverses is that of the goddess who alone directs the man of understanding. The gates open and the goddess, after receiving him in friendship, shows him the paths of knowledge: the one leading to Truth and the other leading to the illusory opinions of mortals (Parmenides deals with these in a special section of his systematic presentation).

Even a quick glance at such an unusual narrative (the letter of which we have respected) reveals a masterful conception; the perception of philosophical truth is represented in the form of a revelation and is the end product of a mystical journey. Is such a concept simply a product of arbitrary imagination? It is certainly possible to believe that Parmenides has fabricated the entire tale. Are we then simply dealing with a piece of poetry? But a purely literary treatment is hardly the vehicle for the serious thought of a philosopher! It is not a question of believing that Parmenides went through this mystical experience literally, point by point, or—and this would amount to the same thing—that he sincerely believed that it had happened to him. When one is talking about belief, there are many levels between absolute sincerity and mere literature. The problem is to discover the real emotional and practical force of Parmenides' poetic images. In order to answer such a question, it is first necessary to ask if his images have any precedents.

That there are precedents is beyond doubt. We are already familiar with one, namely, the entire body of apocalyptic literature that we know existed in the archaic period. In it, especially within the circles one would call "Orphic," the theme of a "descent to the underworld" appears, a theme that is somewhat analogous to that of Parmenides' prologue. Of more immediate interest is another motif, namely, the "journey to heaven," a very ancient theme that, perhaps under the secondary influence of Eastern thought, has had as long a life as the other. To ask which of the two influenced Parmenides is perhaps useless, for we may be dealing with a synthesis of images. What is essential to keep in mind is that the core of Parmenides' tale was not invented by the philosopher; it preceded him. One must also remember that the Chariot, the Gates, the Daughters of the Sun, and Dike are not just mythical elements in the strict sense. Above all else, what matters is the utilization and development of these images which occurs in certain mystical circles, within whose traditions the philosopher certainly operates. Nothing demonstrates this better than a series of pictures in which it is possible to see depicted the famous Platonic allegory of souls striving to follow the chariots of the gods. In these scenes, engraved on golden Etrurian rings, the equivalent of an Orphic-Pythagorean vision can be recognized. The rings, it could be said, supply the image; Parmenides, the legend. In a series of three very ancient illustrations, whose antecedents must be sought in Minoan Crete, there is depicted the voyage of one of the blessed in a mythical carriage. He is preceded by a Siren, or accompanied by a woman running next to him, or escorted by a winged demon showing him the way.

Is the similarity irrelevant? Surely not. The kindred images reveal something quite profound, something that it is important for us to clarify. The mystical tradition that shapes these images for the purposes of a doctrine of salvation can deviate in the direction of philosophy without ceasing to be mystical. In the prologue of Parmenides, one image is used for two purposes: the image of the "way." It appears elsewhere, where it is no less haunting, and it has to have had a corresponding reality in the Mystery religions. Examined in its total context, the image of the "way" is multifaceted. The "way" leads to happiness and to revelation; it is the "road of life" and the "road of inquiry." Advocates of discursive reasoning would want to distinguish and analyze here. But any analysis would risk being false. The "way," which is an image of mystery *par excellence*, is radically connected with the happiness that can follow earthly death. It is also associated with the initiation guaranteeing this privilege, an initiation that, in the symbolism of the Mystery religions, is presented and felt as a kind of death followed by resurrection. No less spontaneously, this image recalls the rule of life that is a condition and guarantee of salvation in the Orphic and Pythagorean types of associations. Even more, for the individual elect, who is assured that he has the truth, revelation, associated as it is with the image of the "way of inquiry," is becoming knowledge that is already, strictly speaking, philosophical. Such is the case with Parmenides.

We are led to hypothesize, then, that there may have been some transformations from past mystical thought to philosophy, understood in its strict sense. An attempt can be made to identify some of these transformations.

🌿

Parmenides profits from a certain advantage. For him the philosopher is someone entirely set apart and especially chosen. Intimately connected with such a view is the idea of a revelation that precedes what we would term a theory of knowledge. Implicit in a theory of knowledge is what has traditionally been referred to as a psychology, in the metaphysical or, more exactly, mystical sense. All of this can be recognized as the datum of a nascent philosophy—indeed, of an entire philosophical tradition—and there is reason to search for its original significance.

The theme of the philosopher as a unique or even superior person is one that Plato enjoys developing in several ways, especially in the *Phaedo*, in which he connects it with asceticism. The superiority is a reality, or rather a firm belief of those involved, and is confirmed by a society's acceptance or hostility. This deliberate uniqueness endures up to a very late period. The followers of the post-Aristotelian philosophies (the equivalents of private religions) have to be different from everyone else. As for the more ancient philosophers, one has only to think of an Empedocles or a Heraclitus—the haughty bearing of one and the fanatical isolation of the other—and to note the anecdotal literature to conclude that they must have sought out a completely idiosyncratic life style. But in fact, more weighty points can be made. According to current views, even the name "philosophy" was invented by Pythagoras, perhaps to differentiate it from another school of "wisdom." The Pythagoreans themselves were the only historical reality accessible under the heading "Pythagorean," and from its beginnings their association was a mystical one. For them the term "philosophy," in what could be referred to as a consecrated usage, described an asceticism preparatory to death. It is rather curious, but nonetheless characteristic, that the term that would describe purely intellectual speculation originated in a "school" that today we would not tend to categorize as philosophical. Still, it is a fact that among the first Pythagoreans the idea of philosophy was no doubt established in opposition to that of a religious sect, but all the same with a religious sect as its model. The early Pythagoreans—it is true—did not have "mysteries"; yet that is precisely what "philosophy" was for them. And we find in the Pythagorean tradition concepts of clearly known origins associated with the word "philosophy," concepts that would eventually become rather commonplace, almost secularized. However, their original meaning can be understood only in reference to the discipline of the association. A very early *locus communis* of Pythagorean literature recalls the hierarchy, acknowledged by the sect's members, that was established according to degrees of advancement (a phenomenon that obviously corresponds to the different degrees of initiation in the Mystery religions). According to Varro, at the head of this hierarchy is the one who is called *beatus*, in the sense that he is *doctus*, *perfectus*, and *sapiens*. *Sapiens*, a term inspired by religious scruple, is really a euphemism for "philosopher." *Perfectus* is certainly a translation of the Greek word that signifies the highest level of achievement and *initiation*. *Doctus* refers to the "science" that may already be partly one of the Numbers. But it is a "science" of a very special kind, for it is communicated—in secrecy and through an initiation into a mysterious truth—only to the sect's inner group. The term *beatus*, although it seems jejune, is nevertheless interesting. Its Greek equivalent, *eudaimōn*, will have a long history in Greek philosophy: the ethics of the Greeks are "eudaemonistic," since they involve a quest for that *summum bonum* which itself involves the happiness of the individual. Concepts like these, as they appear in more or less intellectual philosophies, seem somewhat impoverished and weak when compared with the ideas they first evoked within a milieu where happiness, "the crowning of knowledge," is none other than the joy of immortality, an assured liberation for the divine *daimōn* within us. And it is no longer disconcerting for us to discover that for the Pythagoreans the sign of the happy man is the gift of divination, the culmination of "science."

Our interest in Pythagoreanism stems from a desire to examine a tradition of mystical sects to which philosophy owes not only a vocabulary and some of its metaphors but also, from the beginning, a direction of thought. Since we attach special importance to the idea of a "grace of state," it is worth noting that in the archaic age this tradition has been taken up by isolated figures who have taken it upon themselves to be missionaries. Very little is known about them, and this only from legend. They seem to have been profoundly engaged in a similar form of religious thought; but in certain respects they are also the authentic predecessors of the philosopher. For if the philosopher, as is usually the case, desires to create a "school"—that is, to establish the equivalent of a confraternity—it is by his singular deeds of boldness that he qualifies as a founder. Here we are speaking of men like Abaris, Aristeas, Epimenides, Hermotimus—and others, to whom one might add Pherecydes, who is already a philosopher of sorts. These men primarily practiced purification and divination; but theological and cosmological teachings also were attributed to them. Moreover, even in the legends, they have some connection with Pythagoras.

What is the nature of this prerogative they proclaim and authorize for themselves? It has two elements, but is still one: these men are in special and direct contact with divinity, and this contact is manifested by the miraculous revelation they are granted.

The first element fits in perfectly with the thinking of mystical sects; or even better, it is at their core. Minimally, it involves "becoming similar to a divinity" through a special asceticism and certain rites. But there is a much higher goal; for the truly elect, the "road of life" is a means of divinization. "From a mortal, you have become a god"—this is the kind of assurance about the world beyond which initiates of one sect received. Pythagoras is presented as a divinity incarnate, and Empedocles declares himself "god and not a mortal." Subsequent philosophy will echo these formulas of mysticism—in a Plato, an Aristotle, and even in much later authors. In Platonism, when applied to the philosopher, expressions such as *theios anēr* retain some of their original force.

Another expression from Platonism highlights the nature of a prerogative that is at once the consequence and the guarantee of eminent dignity: *theia moira*, "divine portion." It designates a kind of divine election of the philosopher. In particular, it connotes the aptitude one has for philosophical understanding, the talent that makes such knowledge possible. When Plato wants to make the concept of this knowledge present and vivid, he has recourse to comparisons from the Mysteries. Truth is perceived in a kind of *epopteia*—that is, in a vision analogous to the one reserved for those initiated into the higher Mysteries. This concept is not an isolated example but plays an integral role in Platonism. It inspires some of the famous allegories or myths in the *Symposium* and *Phaedrus*; and in Aristotle's earliest philosophy, where the idea is inherited, one discovers the outline of a theory that approaches an intuition of initiation and *enthousiasmos*. What we find here is a trend of thought which moves into Neoplatonism in the Christian era, and it can be traced back. It is significant that Plato implies a comparison between philosophical and other types of *enthousiasmos*, especially the *enthousiasmos* associated with the inspired founders of initiatory rites. It is "vision" that induces or promotes *enthousiasmos*, and the gift of vision is the characteristic feature of those inspired ancients whose unmistakable heritage philosophers such as Parmenides were able to preserve and pass on. They did it by creating narratives that verged on the philosophical. Even details were of value, as the persistent images demonstrate. The "cave" allegory in the *Republic* owes something to reminiscences of sacred grottoes where great prophets experienced revelations. Pythagoras began his mission in a cave on Mount Ida, and not unlike him, Epimenides received divine instruction during a miraculously long sleep in another Cretan cave. What lasted up to Plato's time, at least on the mythical level, was the ideal of a vision of "another world."

That a philosophical transition had already taken place in Parmenides has already been noted. But in his case the myth of revelation is not simply poetic. It is essentially the myth of the soul's journey. In what might be described as its materialistic form, the myth has some obvious antecedents in the legendary material about ecstatic visionaries. While he was asleep, Epimenides' soul left his body and was lifted into the sky. It was also said to have the power of leaving his body at its pleasure in order to meet and confer with the gods. And the souls of other inspired figures also wander. In addition, Epimenides claimed to have lived several lives. But in this milieu, this idea no longer seems original. The idea that souls make journeys is expanded and given some definition in the concept of their transmigrations. Here again an idea is seen which appears to us to be an arbitrary and isolated fantasy. But it played a large role in all religious speculation and in the elaboration of one of philosophy's principal ideas. In an age preceding and propaedeutic to philosophy the doctrine known as metempsychosis can be identified as the major and—without doubt—historically necessary basis upon which the idea of the soul, as distinct and independent of the body, developed. Admittedly, before the Pythagoreans and similar groups, this "mystical" notion was not a radically new idea; but in their hands it became a decisive turning point. This calls for a few words of explanation.

There is little doubt that the first Greeks inherited from their precursors a description of the soul similar to the descriptions found in the research of ethnographers. Even Homer perpetuates the idea of a Doppelgänger. (But Homer also attests to the fact that in one part of the Greek world—the one that from the beginning gives Hellenism its tone, and that experiences not only the first blossomings of poetry but the tentative beginnings of science and politics—the usual primitive representation of the soul had long been eclipsed.) The Homeric vocabulary designating mental activity has scarcely any contact except with positivistic thought; and there is no proportionate relationship between a man when he is alive and his "soul" when he is dead, since his soul is a kind of insubstantial phantom with hardly a glimmer of consciousness. Between such a view of the soul and the Platonic concept of the soul's immortality there is an enormous gulf. How was the Platonic view able to develop? In *Psyche*, one of the finest products of nineteenth-century German research, Rohde has tried to answer this question. Actually, in his treatment of the antecedents to Platonic thought, he emphasizes above all the elements derived from the religion of Dionysus. Perhaps it would be better to note instead the interest—to some degree professional—that speculation concerning the soul had among a whole category of "inspired ones." The theory of metempsychosis, an essential part of their teaching and their rites of purification, prolongs and uses a myth of reincarnation which belonged to prehistoric Greece; but the myth has been given a unique shape by the theory. In the archaic age, it must first of all be perceived in terms of a very defined form of asceticism, one closely related to techniques of divinization.

Pythagoras' prerogative, which makes him an intermediary between man and God, surely does not consist in his soul's being reincarnated many times, but rather in his recollections of successive reincarnations. This presupposes a divine gift; although in one sense gratuitous, the privilege is no less a genuine accomplishment, for it is the reward for certain efficacious practices that we can discern or divine.

It is after his journey to the underworld that Pythagoras reveals to those assembled at Croton the chain of his earthly careers. Existence in the underworld is a necessary link in the chain of a soul's destiny. This idea is almost constant and basic to the different varieties of Greek mysticism. It happens that an express concept of psychological continuity combines with this theme, but it is a form of continuity which does not happen automatically; it is granted only to the elect and is the result of their labor. This doctrine appears in a sect to which Pindar alludes. The Isle of the Blessed is the paradise reserved for those having the energy to guard their souls from evil after having made three sojourns in one world and the other. In order to preserve this continuity, a set of procedures exists. Purification is especially significant in the whole scheme of mystical associations, and its history culminates in Plato's *Phaedo*; there, though expressly preserved by him in a defused and intellectualized way, it is philosophically transformed (as has also been the case with the correlative idea of *anamnēsis*). Indeed, all this is part of the same discipline, a discipline where positive practices are the obligatory complement, or the obverse, of negative ones. We are only interested in the discipline's connections with the idea of the soul's salvation, a concept whereby the soul, through purificatory trials and ecstatic adventures, not only preserves itself but in a way achieves its own victory. The rule of silence in the Pythagorean communities and the memory exercises to which Pythagoreans were so devoted form an integral part of the "philosophical" apprenticeship. However, we are more interested in expressions such as "intensity" or "concentration," whose original force is understood only in the context of a very special tradition.

According to an extant Sybilline formula of Alcmaeon, a naturalist and mystic, "Men die because they cannot connect the beginning to the end." However, some of the elect do establish at least some continuity. One of these was Pythagoras; and it is probably to him that Empedocles alludes when he speaks of "that man who had acquired a treasure of knowledge, and, through the intensity of the forces of his spirit, easily saw what one sees in ten or twenty lifetimes." On the other hand, the *Phaedo* recalls an "ancient tradition" in which purification consisted of "reassembling the soul" and "gathering it to itself from every point of the body," all in order to concentrate it in its absolute being and free it from the fate of successive deaths. Such a view can be compared with an Orphic theory, itself derived from very ancient ideas, which claims that the soul is "dispersed" in the body, borne there by the winds. In the thinking of the Orphic sects, this theory was understood in a very concrete way. Another very concrete theory is that of *exercises*, which has its parallel in Orphism and which the etymology of our own word "asceticism" recalls. If, in Pythagorean terms, we translate "asceticism" (for better or worse) as "to stretch the forces of one's spirit," the text will still have the old term *prapides*, which refers specifically to the diaphragm. Incomplete as they are, these bits of information nonetheless converge. The idea of the soul, which Platonism eventually assimilated, had formerly been associated with something similar to a shamanistic discipline.

In the notion of the vocation of philosopher, and in all the thinking that underpins it, we recognize a heritage and catch a glimpse of derivatives that point to a very long history. Is it possible to shed some light on this history, and thereby better understand a certain kind of philosopher?

Among the pre-Socratics it is Empedocles who seems to provoke the most interest. He is one of the better-known pre-Socratics, but he is also one of the strangest. The fact that his period touches an age of "enlightenment" reinforces his strange quality. Through his own teaching he is a kind of symbol, for he is both the thinker preoccupied with rational explanations and the mystic engaged in the most imaginary and, as we would say, most primitive forms of thought. But above all, it is his person—or, to be more exact, the kind of person he was and the ambitions he professed—that holds our attention.

He introduces himself at the beginning of his poem *The Purifications* (Empedocles is even more of a poet than his elder Parmenides). Since he is no longer a mortal, he goes among his "friends" as a god. As soon as he enters the towns, people press in around him and pay him homage. Some ask him for oracles; others seek cures for their illnesses. He promises to teach his disciples remedies against old age, the art of stopping the winds, and the power of bringing rain in time of drought or dispelling it in time of floods. He will even grant his disciples the power to "bring back a dead man from the underworld." In addition, Empedocles' legend—and a legend always merits attention—attributes to him some truly astonishing public labors: a successful attempt at breaking the force of the Etesian winds by using a donkey's hide, the resurrection of a woman, and—his crowning glory—a miraculous death, one that belongs to the category of sacral deaths.

Curiously, when these traits are taken together, they produce a figure that is familiar to us from ethnology. One of the major subjects of the *Golden Bough* is kingship. The king is responsible for the material prosperity of his group because he has power over the elements; because magical power resides in him; and finally, because he is in his own *persona* god himself. The haughtiness and ingenuity of Empedocles are on the same level as those of a king. Moreover, it is possible to see the ancient ideas Empedocles uses more or less unconsciously when, in a kind of catalog of the elect, and according to a tradition found in Pindar and even in Plato, he groups together (as beneficiaries of privileged reincarnations) soothsayers, poets, physicians, and princes. After seeing in the philosopher a successor to the kind of inspired person who reveals not only characteristics of the ecstatic seer but also the ambitions of a prophet and healer, we now recognize in him a more ancient, yet striking, reminiscence: the relic of the "king-magician," one whose unique character and authority derive from his ability to control nature, from his infused science of divination, and from his miraculous feats of prehistoric "medicine."

As for the Greeks, doubtless one does not expect to find this mythical concept in such a context. But in other ways the Greeks have certainly not ignored it. Legend attests to the fact that some cult survivals are derived from it, and relics of it are preserved up to Homer's time. Indeed, in Homer it is the relic of very ancient realities, which by Homer's time had certainly vanished. The tenacity of certain themes from legend and poetry is quite remarkable and therefore merits explanation. Why is it that these images and beliefs, belonging to extremely distant ages, were able to cross over so many centuries? Such a question involves a problem that it is not really our concern to treat extensively: social prehistory. Nevertheless, something should be said about it in an attempt to understand the strange avatar of the "primitive king," which in the person of Empedocles arouses our curiosity.

At the dawn of Hellenism we still catch a glimpse of religious associations that have been inherited by the *genē* of the nobility; and these *genē* last into the historical period. Sometimes they retain in their names, and no doubt in their ritual activities as well, remnants of a magic through which they formerly presided over the growth of vegetation or the beneficial powers of the weather. Since nobility suggests social domination, religious clans ought to be a governing class. Even before noblemen were deprived of their political domination by the establishment of democracies, they seem to have been the objects of a powerful religious counterrevolution, which was associated in some way with disturbances in the Near East, and whose symbol was the god Dionysus. In any case, it is certain that this revolution profoundly changed the conditions and structures of religious life. The *genē* survive, and their professional skill in rituals continues. In fact, their power and prestige will be dissolved within the polis, which itself puts them to use. In the archaic period, their life is not in the polis but in the Mystery religions, in the confraternities, and with those who might be called the magicians of Greece. In this period a number of innovations occur which are more or less interdependent. And it might be observed that the most remote tradition is renewed then rather than broken. The vocations of those who have been inspired had to have some relation with the religious power embodied in certain heroes by the guilds of the Healers, Singers and Dancers, Pacifiers of Winds, Men of the Vine or Fig Tree. That is to say, this religious power was embodied in some king from a distant past. Between a myth of "kingship" and the myth of these heroes there is an analogy that one might term functional. It turns out that their legend is only partially attested; what it indicates is the survival of a *medicine man*. It is a paradox of history that the collective memory is crystallized in an actual person; and it is a philosopher of the fifth century B.C. who resurrects for us the model of the type in its fullest.

We must go back further than the pre-Socratics, further even than the archaic period (where we believed we saw their predecessors) in order to explain the persistence of the haunting theme of the king-magician. It is possible to see in such a theme the mythical projection of human activity, whose importance in ancient societies is obvious. The man armed with magical secrets and endowed with extraordinary powers is entitled to govern his peers. This primitive kind of belief bases authority on privileged knowledge and, inversely, attributes extraordinary powers to the man who exercises the authority. It is also a deeply rooted concept; its survivals are long-lasting; and there are strange recurrences of it. One specific form exists in many societies that are more or less related to prehistoric Greece—that is, the Indo-European groups. Analysis of myths concerning diverse social activities among the Latins, Hindus, Iranians, and others provides evidence of three societal types: the warrior, the magician, and the provider of food. The first two groups collaborate and work in opposition simultaneously. If we are allowed to find in the case of Empedocles the heritage of this very ancient kind of thought and, in fact, beneath all the changes, a certain kind of continuity, perhaps we can better understand an intermittent but nonetheless vital kind of reality that I would like to call "the imperialism of the intellectual"—the intellectual who, under different names and through periodic renewals, has achieved some position and, at times, caused some havoc in human history.

In any case, we understand better certain aspects of philosophy in ancient Greece. Apropos of the philosopher himself, we have taken up the question of the *theios anēr* and its connections with the old idea of the "inspired man" and with the concept of the initiate in higher degrees of "secret societies." And here there is a strange coincidence, for the same expression is used by Xenophon at the end of his *Oeconomicus* in an unexpected context. He applies it no longer to an aptitude for knowledge but rather to the aptitude to exercise authority. Found in such a rich context, this usage of *theios anēr* implies a very precise kind of thinking that Xenophon was incapable of inventing. Such a notion is similar to that of the inspired philosopher and continues the idea of initiation—even the word is there—one involving a kind of power granted by divine election. Plato, after all, does not allow us to forget that *theia moira*, itself the divine privilege that gives a man access to true knowledge, also consecrates him for authentic kingship. No doubt, such considerations are valuable only in the ideal order.

But for someone who throughout his life has been preoccupied with political action (which has been ineffective), is the ideal unattainable? The famous axiom, that cities will not be ordered unless those ruling them become philosophers or philosophers become their rulers, is evidence of a constant ambition that the nobility, in Plato, never doubted, an ambition that is open to suggestions from the unconscious but that in the case of the philosopher is almost atavistic. Here again a philosophical transition has occurred, but it is a sort of testimony. Even if we know little of the political theory of the first philosophers, we know that in general they had one. And on occasion they were regarded as lawmakers. According to them, a political philosophy is the crowning point—*the* "achievement" in the Greek view—of all philosophy. This imperious tradition can be explained by recourse to the origins of philosophy.

In fact, the claim inherited by the philosopher from a prehistoric past is not really codified in the actual polis. Beforehand it was disavowed by the polis. The very conditions that made the philosophical movement possible could not support the quasi-religious assent that domination by sages would have demanded. One can see this almost symbolically in the history (or legends) of the Pythagorean communities. Their ideal of sanctity or sainthood could not have developed exclusively for the individual's sake, any more than it will in Platonism. It seems that in several cities of Magna Graecia they governed for a time. And it might be noted, with mythical precision, that their reign came to a bad end. The Pythagoreans were not only overthrown; they perished almost to the last man. This did not prevent their school of thought from benefiting in a way from such a setback. It is remarkable that we can attribute hardly any scientific thought or quasi-philosophical speculation to the Pythagoreanism of the period before the catastrophe. These are the features of a later form of the school. It is as if one activity, no longer capable of functioning in the political order, is diverted to a priestly class that no longer commits treason because it no longer has the temptation to do so.

It must be said that we have noted antecedents rather than a transition. Admittedly these views are incomplete. With regard to the presumptuous question posed by our title—we needed a title—we have considered only one of its aspects. There are other facets of the subject; this we have also said. There are also other parallel questions of origin which involve the most diverse areas of study, and no doubt these are in some way related. In a society all things are interdependent; the word "Hellenism" represents a complex of new elements that are themselves interrelated.

Must these aspects remain unintelligible to us? The formula "Greek miracle" is a convenient one, but it is only a formula. What is labeled a miracle is really a creation. And perhaps in human history creations are contingent and gratuitous in nature. But they have their antecedents and preconditions. We have seen, in some of the traditions, that they could have had their own prime matter. We will begin to learn about these creations only when we start seeing the "new" as nothing more than alterations of the "old."

Index

❦

※

THE JOHNS HOPKINS UNIVERSITY PRESS

This book was composed in California text and Korinna display type by Britton Composition from a design by Cynthia Hotvedt. It was printed on S. D. Warren's 50-lb. Sebego Eggshell paper and bound in Joanna Arrestox cloth by the Maple Press Company.